The Overcomer's Handbook

Preparing for the Best of Times, the Worst of Times and the End of Times

Jerry Steingard

PRESS

The Overcomer's Handbook
Preparing for the Best of Times, the Worst of Times and the End of Times
by Jerry Steingard

Printed in the United States of America

ISBN 9781624196621

www.xulonpress.com

Endorsements

"*B*ecause Jerry wrote this book it's worth reading. He's a man who has been willing to give up comfortable popular mindsets in the pursuit of Truth. Reading his book will challenge you to rethink what you've taken for granted. You will entertain possibilities that may have never crossed your mind. It just might save your life."
Maria Walsh, Stratford, Canada.

"*Jerry Steingard is my good friend, a diligent scholar and the human being on the earth today with the quickest corny pun. I have greatly enjoyed walking with him and his wonderful wife Pam in this revival and outpouring called the Toronto Blessing.*

Jerry's new book is a stimulating read through the ebbs and flows of discipleship and issues relating to revival in our generation. His grasp of church history and its application to us today is refreshing. I love the mix of theology, revival and personal awakening. As Christian leaders like myself walk through the various questions and options of eschatology I appreciate Jerry's sharing of his perspective in a scholarly and humble way. I highly recommend this book as a great read. Well done Jerry."
Dan Slade, International Coordinator, Partners in Harvest, Toronto, Canada

"*It is not always comfortable to have the paradigms by which we live our lives challenged, but for those who want to walk into*

the pending perils that may be coming in these end times with eyes wide open, this book compels us to look hard at evidence that may cause us to make some radical shifts. Jerry has shown vulnerability in sharing his own journey, as well as doing an excellent job of compiling research done by others. He fearlessly addresses topics that may not be popular, and will probably offend some. There is something to challenge everyone, no matter where you stand on some of these issues. Jerry's heart, though, is to prepare the body of Christ in order to be ready to partner with God in His end time plan, walking in His empowerment to bring the fullness of His kingdom."
Connie Sinnott, Associate pastor/worship leader, International Trainer for Catch the Fire, Toronto, Canada

Acknowledgments

I wish to acknowledge Jonathan, Michael and Joanna, our three amazing children who have been a joy to watch as the Lord has fashioned each of you into the men and woman of God you are today. We are so proud of you and believe in you. We love seeing the creative gifts God has given each of you and how you use them to bless others and touch the heart of God. We want to keep cheering you on in the unique call and destiny Christ has for you. We are your greatest fans! And regarding Jonathan's wife, Jess, and Joanna's husband, Collin Gibson, we couldn't be happier with their choice of mates. You are both such an inspiration to them and to us.

To my dear wife, Pamela, who has been my best friend and companion for almost 35 years. You have been such a support and inspiration to me through thick and thin. There is never a dull moment being around you. Your love for life, adventure, God, our grown up kids and me puts a smile on my face, joy in my heart and a spring in my feet. Watching your many creative gifts blossom and grow over the years, the lives you touch, your passion for the Lord and for life has challenged me to not coast through life or settle for mediocrity.

I wish to honour my parents, Bill and Carol, who are now with the Lord. My mother's steady love for her eight children, her prophetic intercession and her love for learning and reading as well as my dad's big and generous heart for others, his child-like sense of adventure with ultra-light planes and aerial photography, his Scripture plaque and photography businesses and his musical talents have all inspired and impacted me over the years.

I also want to honour and thank the Lord for spiritual leaders who have mentored and inspired me in ministry: the late George Mallone, Lawrence Rae, John and Carol Arnott, Fred and Sharon Wright, and Dan and Gwen Slade.

To the many friends who have given Pam and me prophetic encouragement along the journey and have been a joy to grow and serve the Lord with, we thank the Lord for you. I started a list but it was way too long however I can't resist mentioning my dear friends Zak and Karen-Marie Gariba who have been such a constant blessing.

To the guys from "The Moose", particularly David Brandon, Allen Remley, John Cook, Richard Given and Zak Gariba; what a joy to meet monthly over the years for breakfast, a hike, a book read and to challenge each other to think and dream big.

To friends in the house church movement such as Ken Stade, Rad Zdero and Allen Remley, thank you for your friendship and camaraderie.

Thank you to Gateway Harvest Fellowship in Barrie, Ontario, for allowing me what turned out to be a four month sabbatical to focus on the writing of this book and for the ten years I had the privilege of being your lead pastor.

And let me say thank you to David ("Mo") and Joanna ("Jo") Morrison and the missionary staff, house parents and children of Iris Ministries in Malawi, Africa, for graciously allowing Pam and me to spend three months on the mission base and be a part of this amazing family. This was a real gift from God. It was a long time dream come true for Pam and a wonderful place for me to do some teaching at the Bible school as well as have large chunks of undistracted time to write.

Thank you to our good friend Maria Walsh, for being the first to challenge me prophetically (fifteen years ago) to write a book, for encouraging me throughout the process and for giving an endorsement. Thanks to another old friend, Jeff Duncan, who also prophetically challenged me many years ago and twice gave me twenty bucks as seed money towards it.

I am so grateful to other friends who gave helpful feedback as they read various portions of the manuscript - to Yvonne Sydenham,

Doris Schuster, Sharon Beattie and my son Jonathan early on. Also thanks to Lesley Biehn, Keith and Joan Gerber, and John Bootsma for their input later in the process and finally to Dan Slade and my dear sister, Connie Sinnott, for their constructive feedback as well as their endorsement of the book.

I also wish to express my gratitude to Wendy Reis, my editor and new friend in Stratford, for all her hard work and expertise.

Appreciation also goes to Xulon Press for all their help in getting this book published and available to the public.

For the author's photo taken by Michael Steingard Photography, thanks Michael.

For several of the graphs and diagrams in the book and invaluable help with your computer skills, thank you to my son-in-law, Collin Gibson.

Finally, I wish to say thank you to Susan Card, an awesome artist at Morningstar Ministries, for her inspiring painting of the coming tsunami.

Table of Contents

Introduction

"*T*here's going to be a tsunami, listen to me" she pleaded with her parents.

Ten-year-old Tilly Smith of England was on Christmas vacation with her family in Thailand in 2004. The family was walking the beach near their hotel resort on a Sunday morning when the young girl noticed that the water was acting very strangely. It was frothing, bubbling, and swirling. Just weeks earlier she learned some basic information about tsunamis in school and now she was seeing the precise warning signs of an impending killer tidal wave. Although Tilly's parents initially ignored her frantic outcry, her persistence finally convinced her father, Colin Smith, and they approached a security guard standing on the beach to consider asking the tourists on the beach to head up to the hotel just in case. Ten-year-old Tilly's astute observations and prompt and urgent warnings saved upwards of one hundred lives that day. She and her family barely got to the second floor of the hotel when the wall of water hit. Stunned, they watched the horrendous disaster unfold from the balcony. That beach became one of the very few in the region that did not experience any loss of life on that tragic day which saw at least a quarter of a million casualties. Tilly was declared a hero, "child of the year" in 2005, and even went to the UN and met Bill Clinton, the UN Special Envoy for Tsunami Relief. [1]

Tilly is one of my heroes too. Oh to have many more like her who not only have a little practical and vital knowledge, but the courage to apply it and share it when needed, even at the risk of ridicule, so that they as well as those who do take them seriously can be prepared for what may be coming.

We need people like "the sons of Issachar, who understood the times and knew what to do" (1 Chronicles 12:32), rather than like the simpleton, the mocker or the fool in Proverbs One. They did not listen or heed Wisdom shouting in the streets and were overtaken by calamity and disaster. But "whoever listens to me (Wisdom) will live in safety and be at ease, without fear of harm." (Proverbs 1:33)

With all the sense of urgency I can muster, I write this book with an ever growing conviction that we too need to prepare, spiritually and practically, for not just one but two unprecedented tsunamis that are on the horizon and which will forever change the spiritual landscape of our world and life as we know it.

The first massive wave is that of unprecedented turbulence, trouble and shaking on the earth that will be increasingly felt in the economic, geophysical, political, religious and military realms. We think we have already experienced a once in a lifetime shaking in the global economy (fall of 2008 to March 2009) and in natural disasters over the last number of years but we have only tasted the appetizer. The main course is now ready to be served.

I don't believe, however, that this time of trouble is the end (as some have interpreted the Mayan calendar to convey). Rather, I see it as the days and events leading up to the final events of Matthew 24 and the book of Revelation, which could still be decades away. The present time is described as "the beginning of birth pains" (Matthew 24:8 NIV) and in the King James Version as "the beginning of sorrows".

The other tidal wave bearing down upon us is that of an unprecedented spiritual awakening, of God's Spirit being poured out and His glory covering the earth. This will ultimately result in a promised end time harvest of souls coming into the Kingdom of God, community and societal transformations, and the formation of a beautiful, mature and passionate bride who is ready for the return of Jesus Christ, the Bridegroom King.

Rick Joyner writes that, "We are coming to the most exciting times in history, but this is also a warning. If we are not prepared for what is coming, we will be victims of it. This coming worldwide revival will also be one of the biggest challenges ever. Moves of God are often referred to as waves in history because a wave is an accurate metaphor. For a surfer, there are few things as thrilling as catching 'the big one.' However, if you're casually strolling in the surf and the big one catches you by surprise, you will likely eat a lot of sand and drink a lot of salt water." ²

I don't claim to know how far apart in time these waves will be or whether they will strike simultaneously. I just know they are both on the horizon and moving quickly towards us.

When a tsunami is moving across an ocean, it is barely a ripple in the water, but as it approaches land, it begins to build very quickly into a monster wave (or waves) of gigantic proportions that can take out everything in its path if there hasn't been preparation. But we don't merely want to get out of its destructive path in order to survive, we want to capitalize on the opportunity and be overcomers. As Rick Joyner describes it, surfers can have the thrill of a lifetime if they catch the big one and ride it for all its worth by discerning where it is going to break, be in the right place, positioned in the right direction and then begin moving with the wave when it comes. We want to be "in the zone", the "sweet spot", having the privilege of riding through the pipe of the wave, partnered with our Lord and feeling the surge of His loving power and presence for redemptive purposes.

Whether one depicts what is coming as only one tsunami with two contrasting dimensions to it (as Rick Joyner) or as two separate but virtually simultaneous tsunamis as I am describing, may be mere semantics. We find the Old Testament prophet Isaiah communicating exactly these two dynamics in Chapter 60:1-3, in reference, I believe, to the end times we are now entering:

"Arise, shine, for your light has come, and the glory of the LORD rises upon you. See, darkness covers the earth and thick darkness is over the peoples, but the LORD rises upon you and his glory appears over you. Nations will come to your light and kings to the brightness of your dawn."

And in Daniel chapter 2 as well as Hebrews 12:26-29, we see the Bible speaking of earthly kingdoms collapsing and created things being shaken while the Kingdom of God endures and even thrives.

We are beginning to step into what Charles Dickens writes at the outset of his book Tale of Two Cities: "It was the best of times and the worst of times". [3] We are on the verge of experiencing "the tale of two tsunamis" that will cause everyone to either be in continuous distress at what is happening on the earth or amazement at the stunningly glorious things God is doing in the midst of crisis.

With such a growing conviction, I feel an increasing urgency to compel people in general and believers in the Lord Jesus in particular, **to get prepared spiritually, mentally and practically. Not out of fear and panic but rather out of a faith-filled sense of divine adventure and destiny.**

At this point, you may be far from convinced that such tidal waves are about to hit the shores of your life. I can understand and appreciate that. I simply urge you to read with an open mind and a hungry heart like the Berean Christians of the Apostle Paul's day. (Act 17:11) They were eager to learn and receive, which included doing their homework and examining the Scriptures for themselves to see if what the one teaching was saying was true. Such teachability involves a willingness to make changes and "paradigm shifts" in our perceptions, our thinking, and our living in order to line up more thoroughly with God's Kingdom reality and purposes.

I don't profess to have it all figured out - far from it. I am aware that five or ten years from now, I may look at what I wrote and say, "Wow, some of this is pretty shallow and immature"! Paul tells us in 1 Corinthians 13 that "...we know in part and prophesy in part, but when perfection comes (the return of Christ), the imperfect disappears...Now we see but a poor reflection; then we shall see face to face. Now I know in part; then I shall know fully, even as I am fully known."

Followers of Jesus are on a journey of discovery. We are in the process of seeking truth and of growing and maturing in Christ. This book is a reflection of where I am at in my journey as of the year 2012. If even a good portion of what is conveyed in this book proves to reflect truth and reality fairly accurately and makes a contribution in better preparing folks for their part in the days ahead, I will be grateful. My heart's desire is that we not just survive but thrive as we partner with our awesome God. These are turbulent but glorious days we are now stepping into. We were born for such a time as this.

The following pages will cover many of the mindset changes or paradigm shifts that I believe God has taken me through in recent decades (with lots more changes, I suspect, yet to come). He has done this in order to equip and prepare me to join Him more fully in His Kingdom advancements, which are about to profoundly accelerate. And I've got a hunch many of you need to wrestle with at least some of these issues, if you haven't already, and hear what God may be saying to you. May the words of a simple but dangerous prayer I first heard Dr. Jack Taylor pray, be your prayer as it is mine:

"Lord, change my mind on every issue in which you and I do not see eye to eye."

Obviously a book that seeks to address a wide array of issues will not be able to do each topic justice in terms of thoroughness and detail. I consider this work to simply be a primer or basic manual for the Kingdom-minded believer. I trust you will give serious thought to these issues that are critical to our times. Hopefully the reader will want to pursue some of these matters further. To help with that process, at the end of each chapter I will recommend various resources.

✶✶✶

It may be helpful to you, the reader, to have a little background on the writer - to know who I am and where I have come from.

I was raised in Canada in a wonderful Christian family, the third of eight children (I got the bronze). I grew up faithfully attending several non-charismatic (some even anti-charismatic) evangelical churches with my family. I am grateful to the Lord for my Christian upbringing and grounding in the authoritative written Word of God, the Bible.

I was a late bloomer in terms of physical development into manhood, having a very young face and small frame. I was the cautious and conservative type, rarely taking risks. My decisions in life were often fear-based with little confidence in myself or in God's ability to back me up. I suspect some of this goes back to a traumatic event in my life at the age of five.

One day, in kindergarten, with my bladder ready to explode, I raised my hand to ask of my teacher that I be dismissed to use the bathroom. She said I would need to wait until the story was finished. We were all sitting on the floor together for story time and soon I had a little puddle on the floor beneath me. The teacher promptly (and disapprovingly) told me to get my coat from the cloakroom and go home. After retrieving my jacket, I went out the door and literally crawled passed the large classroom windows so that none of them could see me and so that I would not need to look into their smirking faces.

Taking about two hours to make the ten-minute journey home, so my mother would not suspect anything (though mothers always know), I had plenty of time to assess my situation. I made an inner vow that day that my life's goal would be to avoid shame, embarrassment, and rejection at all costs. And so my heart embraced a philosophy of life where you do your best to avoid taking risks. You make sure you play it safe so you "don't stand out like a sore thumb". For instance, when I finished high school, I had no intentions of further schooling or excelling in any challenging career. I just wanted to work in my father's woodworking shop that was safe and familiar to me and wait until Jesus returned (after all, some popular Christian books in the early 70s gave us the impression that He should be coming back by the end of the decade).

But the Lord wanted to get me out of my little cocoon and teach me to fly and soar in life. While still a teenager, I was impacted by a vibrant Christian group of youth and young adults who were bold, confident, and unapologetic about their relationship with Christ. This group called The Hakamu, held Friday night home Bible studies and traveled throughout Ontario ministering musically in coffeehouses and churches on weekends. This was in the days of the Jesus Movement when you simply sneezed and young people came to faith in Christ! My sister, Connie (who later married Jeremy Sinnott, the lead musician of the band) and I soon started a Tuesday night Bible study in our home to disciple youth. We also organized evangelistic coffeehouses.

Out of this experience of one-on-one discipling and leading small group Bible studies over half a dozen years, I developed an insatiable hunger to learn and discover more truth about God, His Word, His world, and my Christian faith. I even left the safety of my father's woodworking shop to try other job experiences and took a two-year community college course to work with people with special needs. While in college, I got a part-time job, driving city bus before and after classes. I even survived the traumatic maiden voyage when a young girl on her bicycle rode out from a side street and brushed against the side of my bus. What could have had a very tragic outcome became a very minor mishap. I almost quit that day, thinking that if that is what the first day is like, whom might I hurt or possibly kill tomorrow? But I'm glad I stuck with it and it became a fabulous job and experience for me.

Regarding the Bible study group, many started to tell me that I was a natural when it comes to discipling and pastoring believers and that maybe I should consider Bible College to get further training. Soon, I was off to Canadian Nazarene College, a Christian liberal arts college in Winnipeg, Manitoba for my undergraduate studies. After graduation all my friends started pastoring churches, but I felt I needed further schooling (partly out of hunger to learn and partly to stall for time since I felt and looked so young).

After marrying my sweetheart, Pam, whom I had met in our home Bible study group four years earlier, and doing further studies at the University of Toronto, where Pam was a student, we moved to Vancouver B.C. where I went to Regent College. I am thankful for the privilege of studying under such godly and biblically grounded teachers as J.I.Packer, Clark Pinnock, Michael Green, John Stott and John White who stretched and challenged me in my thinking.

When I graduated from seminary, however, the Lord spoke to me and said, "I have helped you to develop your mind so that you can think more biblically. Now I want your heart to catch up with your head". I wasn't sure what that all meant but I had a hunch that it would involve a process of even more stretching and more growing pains, not just in the academic realm, but in matters of the heart and day-to-day living out one's faith in Christ in the dynamic power of the Holy Spirit.

Before looking at specific issues in which God radically stretched me in preparation for what I believe He is about to do on the earth, let's take the first two chapters to step back and reflect on the process and dynamics of learning and seeking truth. Let's possibly increase our ability to see more objectively and accommodate change more readily.

Notes

1. From Fear to Survival: Knowledge is Key, by Jessica Hornig, ABC News, 20/20, By JESSICA HORNIG, Jan. 22, 2009, http://abcnews. go.com/2020/fear-survival-knowledge-key/story?id=6691940#. TwdfomNWr_E (accessed Aug. 2011).

2. Rick Joyner, Prophetic Bulletin (2011) The Great Tsunami, Morningstar website, (accessed Dec. 6, 2011).

3. Dickens, Charles. Tale of Two Cities, Signet Classic, New American Library, division of Penguin Group, New York: 1997, page 13.

"What gets us into trouble is not what we don't know. It's what we know for sure that just ain't so." Mark Twain

"Men occasionally stumble across the truth but most pick themselves up and pretend that nothing happened." Winston Churchill

"It is difficult to get a man to understand something when his salary depends upon his not understanding it." Upton Sinclair

"In times of change learners inherit the earth, while the learned find themselves beautifully equipped to deal with a world that no longer exists." Eric Hoffer

Chapter 1

Learning to Learn -
Seeing with Fresh Eyes

*U*nprecedented, massive, and accelerated changes have been bombarding all of us as we have stepped into the 21st century. Some electronic gadgets barely get out of the box and they are already obsolete, knowledge is doubling at a dizzying pace, weather patterns are getting wackier, and social upheaval is resulting in drastic changeovers in government regimes, leaving many of us in a frazzled state of information overload, feeling powerless and out of touch.

It's quite ironic that I am writing a book on our need to change, particularly in our mindsets and perspectives. I really am quite a conservative and traditional kind of guy. You could just ask my wife. She tries, at times, to get me to upgrade in the clothes I wear to be a little more "hip" and fashionable. I tend to like wearing the same old clothes until they are practically worn out.

And with all the advanced communication and computerized technologies coming out in recent years, I find myself feeling like an old man who just can't keep up. They say that the average young person sends over one hundred text messages a day. I hate to admit it, but I was afraid to step into the texting world until just a couple of years ago and probably only send a dozen texts in a month. I need my very smart and patient wife, kids and son-in-law to hold my hand practically through every step of learning how to use some of this new stuff. I'm proud to say that as of Christmas vacation 2011, they finally got me on my very own Mac laptop, using Facebook (a little more), and wearing some new shirts and jeans that aren't baggy. And in early 2012, I finally did it. I joined the smart phone club! All these changes came just in time for me to become a grand-father for the first time. Who knows, maybe they'll even get me to change the hairstyle I've had for decades.

So I can relate to Christians and churches that are stressed and overwhelmed by all the changes and the pressure to change, whether it be with new technologies, church structures and methods, ways of relating and reaching out to our culture, or biblical and theological ideas and perspectives not part of our western cultural and denomi-national upbringing. I personally know how easy and tempting it is to take on a maintenance or fortress mentality of just hanging on (to the status quo) until Jesus gets here to rescue us.

The Lord, however, is not threatened or intimidated by all the changes. He is behind many of them. The Changeless One, the Creator who does not make two snowflakes or two human beings exactly alike, loves variety and is often doing something fresh and new. And He made mankind in His image, not only capable but also destined to be creative, innovative, and discovering new things for man's benefit and God's pleasure and glory.

Rather than be stressed out victims of change, God encourages us to be teachable, flexible and inspired in the midst of it. Even more, He invites us to become proactive change agents with Him in bringing His Kingdom righteousness, justice and love to precious lives, communities and cultures. Desiring to be the salt and light of the world, we can embrace the saying, "the best defense is a good offence."

The popular term, **paradigm shift**, though probably overused in some circles, can be useful in helping us to understand the nature of change that is all around us as well as the need for change within us. To understand what a paradigm shift is, we must first understand the meaning of a paradigm.

The word, paradigm, is a compound Greek word, "para" meaning "beside" and "deima" meaning "pattern, model, example". In the social sciences, the term paradigm has been used to describe one's worldview, the lens with which people see reality. It is the perceptual grid or mental road map used to view, interpret and make value judgments of the world around us.

Our paradigms are formed through the input of life experiences: parents and family, church, friends, education, media, and culture. Murray Dueck gives us an interesting example. In Canada, chances are your paradigm pertaining to dogs is that they are "man's best friend". In another culture such as in Southeast Asia, a dog may be on the menu. Dueck writes, "...in Canada, you walk a dog. In Vietnam, you "wok" a dog – two completely different perceptions of the same animal." [1] However, regardless of cultural shaping, all it takes is one traumatic life experience such as being bitten or viciously attacked by a dog to cause that unfortunate person to perceive all dogs as neither friend nor food but foe.

Despite the fact that paradigms are necessary and have a positive function in our lives, some of our paradigms can also work against us. We forget that our paradigm, our worldview, is not the only one and possibly not even the best one. Others may see something completely differently and yet we both could be right.

Take a look at this famous but anonymous image (below) used on an 1888 German postcard. How old would you estimate the lady to be?

Do you see an old lady? Do you see a beautiful young lady? If you only can see one woman, make the effort to go beyond what you initially see. Go deeper to see another perspective. The young lady's left ear is the old lady's eye and the young lady's necklace is the old lady's mouth or lips. The young lady's nose is a wart on the old lady's nose.

All of us grow up with a narrow or an incomplete perspective at best. At worst, a distorted or a skewed view of reality.

History abounds with examples of people's limited and even down-right inaccurate worldviews that are both sad and laughable:

For a very long time mankind believed that the earth was flat. The "Flat Earth Society" apparently still has members today.

In a Senate speech in 1848, Daniel Webster declared: "I have never heard of anything, and I cannot conceive of anything more ridiculous, more absurd, and more affrontive to all sober judgment than the cry that we are profiting by the acquisition of New Mexico and California. I hold that they are not worth a dollar"!

Alexander Graham Bell, the inventor of the telephone, could not get financial help from the bank. On one occasion Bell supposedly placed a telephone on the bank manager's desk in an attempt to get a loan. The manager replied "get that toy off my desk."

One of the biggest investors in Ford Motor Company pulled all of his money out in 1906 because he did not think the automobile had much of a future. Today, roughly one in five jobs in North America is auto related.

"The concept is interesting and it's well formed but in order to earn better than a 'C', the idea must be feasible." This was from a Yale University professor in response to Fred Smith's paper proposing reliable overnight delivery service. Smith went on to found Federal Express Corp.

"We don't like their sound. Guitar groups are on the way out. They have no future in show business," claimed Decca Records Company who rejected The Beatles after an audition in 1962.

"There is no reason anyone would want a computer in their home." Ken Olsen, founder of Digital Equipment, in 1977.

We need to be able to laugh at ourselves and our narrow and small thinking. We can often be like the guy who spent the afternoon fishing for trout but ended up only saving the small fish and throwing the large ones back into the river. After awhile, his fishing buddy inquired about the bizarre behaviour. He replied, "It's simple. I've only got an eight inch frying pan at home!"

Many of us expect and even welcome change from time to time so long as it is merely cosmetic or helps to break up our boring routines. It helps that the changes not come at us too hard and fast nor hit our pocket book too deeply. A few individuals, by nature, are what social scientists would identify as early adopters, others are middle or late adopters while some are laggards who refuse to accept virtually any new idea, change or innovation at all. I've heard the cute saying that "some minds are like concrete: thoroughly mixed up and permanently set!"

Unfortunately, the majority of us tend to be quite stubborn, proud, and provincial when it comes to our mindsets that we hold

27

dear. We rarely take the time or have the courage to critically evaluate our assumptions and "think outside the box." When faced with another viewpoint or perspective, we easily get threatened. This confrontation with a contrary worldview creates fear, anxiety and insecurity - what social psychologists call "cognitive dissonance." The most popular defensive mechanism to kick in is denial.

After all, our paradigms are our primary source of identity, order, comfort, and security. They function as our North Star as we navigate through life. And so we don't want our world rocked. As a result, we often become guilty of paradigm paralysis. We shut down like an overloaded computer, unable or unwilling to see beyond our current models of thinking. We refuse to look at any evidence that might force us to surrender our precious worldview. Instead we will seek to ignore, dismiss or even discredit any new and disruptive information, experience, method or technology that appears to challenge our cherished position.

In fact, it has been observed by many that a new idea or revolutionary concept that challenges the status quo goes through a fascinating and often lengthy process of first being ignored, then ridiculed, then militantly opposed and attacked, before it is finally accepted as truth. A tipping point is reached as truth ultimately wins out over time and becomes self-evident to many.

It is Thomas Kuhn who has been credited with coining the term, paradigm shift, in his 1962 book, The Structure of Scientific Revolutions.[2] Kuhn argued that science does not progress via a linear accumulation of new knowledge, but undergoes periodic and dramatic revolutions or transformations, also called paradigm shifts. This shift is a quantum change. You see differently which leads to thinking differently which causes you to feel differently and behave differently.

Dr. John White, in his book, Changing on the Inside, likens a paradigm shift to an earthquake. Tension builds as plate presses against plate deep in the earth, usually undetected at the surface. Finally, the built-up tension reaches a crisis point and something gives. The end result is a major shift, a crisis, an earthquake. After the crisis, the effects of an earthquake do not end. Aftershocks and tremors may continue for some time.[3]

It is no coincidence that Jesus, the Changeless One, commands us to "repent, for the Kingdom of God is at hand." The Greek word for repent is metanoia, which means to radically change your mind and the direction you are going. Dr. John White states "repentance seems to begin with a profound change in the way we see reality. This changed perception is not merely an intellectual change...It is one thing, after all, to 'know' we are going to die some day, and quite another to be confronted with lethal danger. The changed perception of repentance is more like that second experience. It involves the shock of 'seeing' some aspect of reality for the first time."[4]

Bill Johnson breaks down the meaning of repentance this way: "Re" means to go back. 'Pent' is like the penthouse, the top floor of a building. Repent, then, means to go back to God's perspective on reality...Jesus urged us to do an about-face in our approach to reality because His Kingdom is at hand. He brought His world with Him, and it's within our reach. He wants you to see reality from God's perspective, to learn to live from His world toward the visible world."[5]

We see this revolutionary shift in perspective take place in the Parable of the Prodigal Son in Luke 15. Jesus said the prodigal "came to himself" or "came to his senses", meaning he suddenly saw himself and the world differently. He faced objective reality, which is a crisis moment of repentance. It's a call to "wake up and smell the coffee" and align ourselves with the Father's truth and reality and step into the joy of His world.

Of course the greatest example is when a person comes to faith in Christ. You begin to see everything with fresh eyes because God has removed the scales from your spiritual eyes, awakened your spirit, and placed "the Spirit of Truth" within you. In your tender and humble state, you begin to receive revelation of your sinfulness, your need of a saviour, and His stunning love, mercy and grace that He is eager to lavish upon you because of Christ's sacrifice on the cross. No wonder Jesus used the now unpopular term, being born again.

But repentance, that is, changing one's mind and direction, is not limited to the entrance requirement to start this new journey of faith with the Lord. It is critical at every part along the way. The biblical command to "repent" is often in the present continuous imperative form (Matthew 3:2; 4:17; Mark 1:15), meaning it is not a one off thing but to be an ongoing process and lifestyle. We have embarked on a new and adventurous journey of discovery and intimacy with the Lord of the universe. And if we remain humble, teachable and close to His heart, the Holy Spirit promises to unveil further understanding. We will have the joy of seeing more and more things from God's eternal perspective and experience His supernatural Kingdom first hand.

Followers of Jesus are strongly exhorted in Romans 12:2: "Do not conform any longer to the pattern of this world, but be transformed by the renewing of your mind. Then you will be able to test and approve what is God's perfect will."

Those who claim to be Christians are strongly urged to live a life of continual repentance and the renewing of our mind as we submit to the Word of God, embrace the cross of Christ, and seek to keep in step with the Holy Spirit. This will, among other things, involve exposing and discarding patterns or paradigms of seeing and thinking that are "of this world", including our western rationalistic worldview that has been so heavily influenced by The Enlightenment of the eighteenth century. Again, the prayer: "Lord, change my mind on every issue in which You and I do not see eye to eye", says it all.

This process of letting go of our sacred cows is often excruciatingly painful. For starters, it involves eating humble pie and acknowledging that we just might be wrong on some things that we hold dear. But it also takes us through the tunnel of chaos. Like the Hebrew slaves, we have to let go of the familiarity of Egypt and go through the unpredictability and the stripping found in the wilderness to get to the Promised Land of new and greater freedom and life. It is like the rules have changed and we are starting all over. Everything goes back to zero, back to the drawing board. We are no longer the expert but rather the learner. It can be very humbling, but oh so life giving and destiny producing.

It is painful not only due to the internal upheaval it causes but also the external turmoil with those we love and associate with. Social pressures come to bear as family, friends, and colleagues do not easily appreciate or understand the changes and we begin to feel alienated and, at times, ostracized.

Robert F Kennedy, the U.S. Democratic politician said in a 1966 speech:

"Few men are willing to brave the disapproval of their fellows, the censure of their colleagues, the wrath of their society. Moral courage is a rarer commodity than bravery in battle or great intelligence. Yet it is the one essential, vital quality for those who seek to change a world which yields most painfully to change."

A delightful 1954 children's story, written by Theodor Seuss Geisel, called, Dr. Seuss' Horton Hears a Who, which was made into a powerful full-length animation movie in 2008, depicts this dynamic quite vividly. Horton the elephant, while playing and splashing around in the water, faintly hears a sound when a small speck, a clover, flew past his big ear. It seemed as if someone was shouting for help. And so Horton catches the floating speck and guards it protectively like a mother hen. "There's a tiny person on that speck that needs my help" cries Horton.

In response to Horton's claim, the sour kangaroo retorted, "Absurd, there aren't people that small...believing in tiny imaginary people is just not something we do or tolerate here in the jungle of Nool...Our community has standards Horton. If you want to remain a part of it, I recommend you follow them."

The kangaroo seeks to rally support from others in the jungle to have the clover destroyed and Horton locked up.

In the meantime, Horton ends up communicating with the mayor of the town that lives on the speck. Both Horton and the mayor have to put up with a barrage of mockery while seeking to convince their respective peers to think outside the box and thus avoid impending disaster for the town's microscopic-sized inhabitants. Thankfully the story ends happily. Both worlds make the necessary paradigm shifts just in time.[6]

It seems the Lord has taken me through a major shift in mindset every three to five years (which you will hear about in the following chapters). I wrestled with each new perspective not only because it is inconvenient to have to unlearn and reprogram your thinking and walk in a different direction but also because you feel like people with whom you associate look at you as if you were from Mars. It's like I'm a fish swimming up stream while everyone else is swimming down.

Who wants to be classified as a maverick, a rebel, a trouble maker (like Horton)? The progression of being ignored, ridiculed, opposed, but hopefully eventually vindicated is a long and emotionally taxing process. But I've come to see that it is more than worth it. If you are a follower of Jesus, you can sense it bringing you further into your calling and destiny in Him. You want to please your Lord and become more and more like Him. You want to learn to love what He loves, hate what He hates, have His mind and see from His perspective.

Let me give you a couple of historic **examples** of individuals who went through a controversial and costly shift in perspective that ultimately brought revolutionary breakthroughs:

Martin Luther was an intensely pious Augustinian Catholic monk from the 15th and 16th centuries in Germany. After years of misery seeking to earn God's forgiveness and favour, he finally had a powerful revelation of "justification by faith" through his studies of the Book of Romans.

Luther wrote his Ninety-Five Theses, which challenged the status quo of the church and its corruption and abuses of power and posted it on the Wittenberg church door. This created an unprecedented shockwave throughout the religious Western world. The pope referred to Luther as "a wild boar who had invaded the Lord's vineyard". Luther was dragged before the church interrogation council and urged to recant his supposed heretical teachings. After a night's soul searching Luther gave his reply before these livid religious leaders: "Unless I can be instructed and convinced with evidence from the holy Scriptures or with open, clear, and distinct grounds of reasoning...then I cannot and will not recant, because it is neither safe nor wise to act against conscience. Here I stand. I can do no other. God help me! Amen."

With his new found freedom in Christ through faith alone and his teachings on Scripture being the sole and final authority in a believer's life (not the Roman Catholic church, the pope, and tradition), Luther was used by God as a catalyst for a massive spiritual earthquake, a tipping point that would bring much of Christianity out of the dark ages and into what came to be called the Protestant Reformation.

For many years British sailors were suffering and dying of scurvy on their expeditions. Though **Dr. James Lind**, a surgeon in the British Royal Navy, was not the first to recommend citrus fruit for dealing with scurvy (Dr. John Woodall did the previous century but it was not widely implemented), in 1747 he conducted the first ever clinical trial and came to the conclusion that oranges and lemons were effective in addressing scurvy. It took over forty years of ridicule, opposition and the unnecessary loss of tens of thousands of lives before the British Royal Navy finally accepted and implemented his recommendation of using citrus fruit. The British used lemon and lime juice on their voyages and eventually the sailors came to be known as "limeys". It is well established today that scurvy is caused by a Vitamin C complex deficiency.

Let me add a contemporary example. Billy Beane, General Manager of the Oakland Athletics baseball team, challenged and defied conventional wisdom in how you identify players to build your team. Billy Beane, restricted to a very limited budget compared to rival teams, came up with a fresh new approach in the 2002 season that resulted in much opposition from the old guard of talent scouts, media, and fans but ultimately proved stunningly successful. With the help of a young Yale grad in economics who crunched the numbers, Billy used statistical analysis instead of the way it's always been done, using experienced and seasoned scouts and seeking to acquire superstar athletes. Instead they rounded up affordable players that were considered misfits and rejects to build a winning team. This has forever changed how many think in the baseball business and has given other sports something to consider. In 2011 this inspiring story was made into a Hollywood film called Moneyball starring Brat Pitt.[7]

We are living in very exciting days when our God is on the move in unprecedented ways and magnitude. It is no longer business as usual. We are about to see sides of God that we are not familiar with ("Consider therefore the kindness and sternness of God," Rom. 11:22). Jesus is not just the Lamb of God, but also the Lion of Judah. He will be showing all sides of His nature in these last days as He seeks to draw the hearts of men to Himself and accelerate the fulfillment of His Kingdom purposes upon the earth.

To avoid running the risk of getting offended and fighting against God and His unconventional ways, it is paramount that we continuously and critically evaluate the presuppositions and assumptions that we hold dear. We need to give the Lord permission to stretch and challenge our smallness of vision and bring us more in line with His heart and mind.

The Lord wants to move us towards a more comprehensive and multi-dimensional understanding of His truth, His ways, and His supernatural Kingdom reality. As this takes place, we are in a much better position to embrace wholeheartedly and confidently what God is doing and partner with Him in doing great exploits at the end of the age. (Daniel 11:32)

In the next chapter we will look further at this process of developing a biblical and Kingdom worldview and the need to be simultaneously radical, liberal, and conservative.

Recommended Resources:

The Supernatural Power of a Transformed Mind, Bill Johnson, Destiny Image, 2005

The 7 Habits of Highly Effective People, Stephen R. Covery, Simon & Schuster, 1990

If This Were a Dream, What Would It Mean? Murray Dueck, Fresh Wind, 2005

Changing on the Inside, John White, Vine Books, 1991

Christianity with Power: Your Worldview and Your Experience of the Supernatural, Charles H. Kraft, Vine Books, 1989

Notes:

[1] Murray Dueck, If This Were a Dream, What Would It Mean? Fresh Wind Press, Abbotsford, B.C. Canada, 2005, pages 177,178.

[2] Thomas Kuhn, The Structure of Scientific Revolutions, Chicago: U. of Chicago Press, 1962.

[3] John White, Changing On The Inside, Vine Books, published by Servant Pub., Ann Arbor, Michigan, 1991, pp. 19-23.

[4] Ibid, pages 14,15.

[5] Bill Johnson, The Supernatural Power of a Transformed Mind, Destiny Image, 2005, pp. 44, 45.

[6] Theodor Seuss Geisel, Horton Hears a Who! made into a feature-length film in 2008, computer animation from Blue Sky Studios, the animation arm of 20th Century Fox, released March 14, 2008.

[7] Movie, Moneyball, 2011, directed by Bennett Miller, distributed by Columbia Pictures. Film based on Michael Lewis' 2003 book of the same name.

"A truth's initial commotion is directly proportional to how deeply the lie was believed. It wasn't the world being round that agitated people, but that the world wasn't flat. When a well-packaged web of lies has been sold gradually to the masses over generations, the truth will seem utterly preposterous and its speaker a raving lunatic."
Dresden James

"Minds are like parachutes. They only function when they are open."
Sir James Dewar, Scientist (1877-1925)

"It is the glory of God to conceal a matter; to search out a matter is the glory of kings."
Proverbs 25:2

"Do your best to present yourself to God as one approved, a workman who does not need to be ashamed and who correctly handles the word of truth."
The apostle Paul, 2 Timothy 3:15

Ancient Prayer (author unknown)
"From cowardice that shrinks from new truth,
from laziness that is content with half-truth,
from arrogance that thinks it knows all truth,
O God of Truth, deliver us."

Chapter 2

Learning to Learn
A Call to be Radical, Liberal, & Conservative

Primary versus Secondary Biblical Truth:

*T*hankfully Christians are, for the most part, in unity over the fundamentals, the essential truths of the Christian faith. We believe in the Trinity, the Father, Son, and Holy Spirit. We believe in Christ's humanity and divinity, His virgin birth, His teaching, His atoning death, physical resurrection and His personal and glorious return. We declare that God has spoken, has revealed Himself in His Word, the Bible. The Scriptures are the final authority over our lives. We acknowledge the predicament of man's sinful condition, separated from a holy God and deserving of divine judgment and hell. We believe God, in His immeasurable love, took the initiative and sent His Son, Jesus, to be the sacrifice for our sins, providing a divine solution to our dilemma. Salvation comes by grace through faith in Christ alone. We also believe in the convicting and sanctifying work of the Holy Spirit to bring us to Christ and become more Christ-like as well as integrate believers into the body of Christ, the church. God is committed to preparing an eternal bride for His Son and establishing His glorious Kingdom, which will have no end. By the grace of God we stand together on these great biblical truths (though there has been a growing number who are flirting with heretical views in their attempt to be relevant to the post-modern culture). These fundamental truths that are revealed in the Scriptures and illuminated by the Holy Spirit to us are absolutes that we can and must embrace together with joyful confidence and conviction.

But in regards to secondary truths, matters of lesser importance (they do not pertain to one's salvation), Christians have not always been united. God has not provided as clear and plain revelation on these matters. I wonder if it may be partly to keep us humble and challenge us to learn to get along in mutual love and respect.

It is a simple fact that sincere, godly, and intelligent Christians seeking biblical understanding have come to different conclusions. We have disagreed and been divided over such matters as the nature and administration of the Lord's Supper, water and Spirit baptism, worship, gifts of the Spirit, of what constitutes worldliness versus holiness, church government and structure, ministry, leadership, revival, and eschatology (the study of end times). Historically we have dogmatically disagreed, even bitterly battled, persecuted, and killed over these and other secondary issues to the delight of the devil, the grieving of the Holy Spirit, and the tarnishing of the name and cause of Christ and His church.

We need to humbly acknowledge "now we see but a poor reflection; then we shall see face to face. Now I know in part; then I shall know fully, even as I am fully known." (1 Cor. 13:12) We must learn to not press our position about non-essential matters dogmatically on others but give each other grace, freedom, and respect. We would do well to remember the old and famous epigram attributed to Rupert Meldenius and quoted by Richard Baxter:

"In essentials unity, in non-essentials liberty, in all things charity."[1]

Learning to live with Paradox and Mystery

We are very much like the blind men in the famous story about the elephant. Each blind man touched a different part of the elephant and then generalized from his experience that the whole animal was like that part. One blind man touched his tail and concluded the elephant to be like a rope. Another, after handling the elephant's trunk described the elephant to be a hose. A third blind man, after grasping a leg, insisted that the elephant is like the trunk of a tree. A fourth man experienced the tusk and confidently concluded that an elephant is like a spear. Each was correct when he concluded that this part of the elephant is like a rope, a hose, a tree, or a spear. But each was very wrong when he generalized about the whole animal on the basis of his limited experience with but one part of the creature.

The call to radical allegiance to Jesus Christ entails a commitment to becoming biblically balanced, wise, mature, and integrated in our Christian faith and life. We must seek to avoid the mistake of those blind men with provincial and dogmatic thinking. We must be willing to step out of the box and embrace a more comprehensive and integrated understanding of truth and reality. For example, we talk about a person being dependent and needing to mature to a place of independence as if it is only either/or. But there is a third possibility; that of maturing beyond independence to a place of inter-dependence and team work.

We need the Holy Spirit to jackhammer and get rid of this "either/or" thinking, which I call "stinking thinking". Such a mentality tends to cause us to be selective in which Scriptures we will focus upon and emphasize rather than be fully honest and objective and "proclaim the whole counsel of God." (Acts 20:27)

I love how Stacey Campbell expresses this very point: "The sounds of God are often in stereo."[2]

We need to go beyond an "either/or mentality" towards a "both/and mindset". Nobody asks which wing on an airplane is more important or which pedal on a bicycle is needed. Of course you need them both to maintain balance and to maximize forward movement. And yet, as John Stott states, "...we seem to enjoy inhabiting one or the other of the polar regions of truth. If we could straddle both poles simultaneously, we would exhibit a healthy biblical balance."[3]

For instance, some Christians gravitate to the Word to the exclusion of the Spirit (who inspired the Word) while others polarize themselves by emphasizing the Spirit at the expense of the Word. But the truth is:

"The Word without the Spirit, you dry up. The Spirit without the Word, you blow up. And blending both the Word and Spirit together you grow up!"

We need to learn to glean and embrace the truth found in both (or several) extremes, seeing them as complementary rather than competitive and hold them in creative tension.

Ecclesiastes 7:18 states: "It is good to grasp the one and not let go of the other. The man who fears God will avoid all extremes."

Charles Simeon, Vicar of Holy Trinity Church in Cambridge, wrote the following to a friend in 1825: "The truth is not in the middle, and not in one extreme, but in both extremes...Here are two extremes, Calvinism and Arminianism...Sometimes I am a high Calvinist, at other times a low Arminian, so that if extremes will please you, I am your man; only remember, it is not one extreme that we are to go to, but both extremes."[4]

Some would argue, "You can't eat your cake and have it too". In other words, you just can't have it both ways. It is one or the other. Logic tells us something is black or white, true or false. I would argue that the nature of biblical truth is often paradoxical in form. Larry Christensen defines a paradox as: "a statement of truth which comes in two parts which appears to be contradictory. Yet both of them have a ring of truth about them."[5] The Bible is loaded with apparent contradictions or paradoxes. Why? Our little peon brains are incapable of comprehending the unity and majesty of God's massive truth. His thoughts and ways are too high for us. (Isaiah 55:8)

A paradox, an antinomy, is not solved in our finite mind intellectually, but rather we solve it in terms of time, history and experience. Depending on the circumstances we find ourselves in, we will accent now one statement of the truth; again at a different time its contrary.

For instance, with the issue of faith and works, in Galatians 2:16, the apostle Paul declares that no one is justified by works of the law (he was dealing with legalism that was creeping into the Galatian church). But James 2:24 argues that man is justified by works and not by faith alone. James is making the point that works provide evidence that faith is active and alive. Martin Luther however, called the book of James an "epistle of straw" because he lived in a day when the faith alone truth desperately needed to be emphasized to counter the works righteousness error.

We must not rely just on our cold rationality that can lock us into His truth in one dimension but rather walk in continual dependence on the Holy Spirit to guide us to that part of God's Word that is applicable to the specific situation at hand.

Let us glance at a few **examples from Scripture** regarding this matter of holding apparent extremes or opposites in tension and avoiding polarization to one extreme:

Romans 11:22 urges us to "consider the kindness and severity of God." We don't have the luxury of choosing one aspect of God's character over another, and yet many Christians zoom in almost exclusively to either His loving kindness or His justice.

1 Cor. 13:1, 2 states that if we speak in tongues or have the gift of prophecy or faith, but without love, it means nothing. 1 Cor. 14:1 bids us to "follow the way of love AND eagerly desire spiritual gifts, especially the gift of prophecy." It is not an either/or proposition. We are exhorted to embrace both the fruit of the Spirit and the supernatural gifts of the Spirit, not one over against the other.

Of course there is the tension between the sovereignty of God and the responsibility of man. As King, He declares, "My purpose will stand, and I will do all that I please". (Isaiah 46:10) He is in charge. Yet He instructs us to pray for His Kingdom to come and His will to be done on earth as it is in heaven (Matt. 6:10) because His will is not always done on earth at present. This sovereign Lord is also a Judge who holds every man responsible for the choices he makes and the courses of actions he pursues.

The subject of the Kingdom of God is possibly the most profound example in Scripture. In the coming of Christ two thousand years ago, the Kingdom of God invaded this world and this age. Yet we still look forward to the consummation of the Kingdom at Christ's second coming. Believers live in the tension and contradiction of the Kingdom being now but not yet. It has come partially but not fully. The age to come has impinged upon this present evil age.

Some Scriptures speak of the now dimension of the Kingdom: Luke 17:21 declares, "The Kingdom of God is within you." Mark

1:15 announces, "The Kingdom of God is near." This is not merely a theological issue. It has "in your face" repercussions to our lives here and now.

Because the King and His Kingdom are powerful and supernatural, when the Kingdom impinges on our world, we should not be surprised to see manifestations of His supernatural power. The challenge however, is that we, as products of our western culture, unknowingly have a bias against the supernatural realm. The secular worldview of our western culture is steeped in naturalism and rationalism. And so we may theoretically believe that the Kingdom is partially here, but when it actually comes in power (what the Bible calls signs and wonders), we are unnerved, skeptical, and inclined to automatically dismiss it as hype or demonic.

Other Scriptures speak of the not yet future dimension of the Kingdom, such as Matthew 24 & 25:31, 34; Luke 22:29, 30; Rev. 19:11; 16. When Christ returns a second time, we will see this climax and culmination of the coming Kingdom, heaven will begin to declare that "the kingdoms of this world have become the kingdoms of our Lord and of His Christ, and He shall reign forever and ever." (Rev. 11:15)

Dr. Derek Morphew, in his insightful book, Breakthrough, states, "Wherever there are truths in Scripture that are in creative tension with each other, the danger exists that people will try to explain away one side of the tension in favour of the other. This is especially true of the Kingdom."[6]

Related to the matter of the Kingdom of God is the whole subject of the end-times. Over the years I've often been asked, "Jerry, before Jesus comes back, are we going to see things get better and better or worse and worse?" My response has usually been "yes". Scripture seems to speak in stereo on this question as well.

According to the Bible, we should anticipate a great demonstration of God's Kingdom power and glory on the earth before Christ physically returns to consummate the Kingdom, but we should also expect the end times to get very intense and cataclysmic. As depicted in Isaiah 60, we will see the light of the glory of God increase upon His people while darkness and chaos blankets the earth. But man's tendency to either/or thinking causes us to either run to an extremely optimistic or pessimistic eschatology and accusing the other camp of heresy. We will wrestle with this very relevant issue towards the end of the book.

Although there is a valid place to do what is traditionally called "systematic theology", we need to humbly acknowledge that the whole counsel of God's truth within Scripture is simply too large to fall neatly into our nice little systems and categories of theology. Our attempts at systematic theology are useful but limited and cannot do full justice to God's vast and marvelous truth. We need to learn to relax and be at ease with mystery and paradox. We cannot put God in a box. He cannot be domesticated.

Growing in Truth by Being Radical, Liberal and Conservative

It may be helpful at this point to define some terms for clarification.

The word, "radical" literally means to go to the root of a matter, to investigate something thoroughly. In popular usage, the term has come to apply to the conclusions reached which have moved considerably from a traditional view rather than to the methods used. We need to be radical in our thinking and in our investigating of a matter.

Proverbs 25:2 declares, "It is the glory of God to conceal a matter; to search out a matter is the glory of kings." The Lord hides truth for us not from us. He delights in seeing us earnestly search out and seek truth with diligence and integrity, with dependence upon the Spirit of Truth. He loves for us, with child-like curiosity and awe, to explore and discover facets of the wondrous nature of both our Creator and His creation.

In this journey of discovery, being radical entails getting to the root, the core, and the bottom of something in a thorough and honest manner, even if the conclusions turn out to be quite conservative. Someone being radical in this literal sense, would not jump to conclusions and adamantly hold on to them but rather would learn to be patient, disciplined, and secure enough to suspend judgment or at least hold conclusions lightly until one gets further light on the matter.

Tom Sine tells a humourous but true story in his book, The Mustard Seed Conspiracy, of a couple who didn't get all the facts on a matter and jumped to conclusions. After gathering more wild mushrooms than they could consume on their own, they decided to throw a dinner party and invite friends over to devour them in mushroom omelets, soufflés, and crepes. After they ate all they could handle, they scraped the leftover mushrooms into the pet cat's dish. As people were about to leave around midnight, they heard a scream coming from the kitchen. Everyone dashed to the kitchen only to see the cat on the floor thrashing about violently, her sides heaving – having what looked like a full-blown seizure. The doctor was called and he told them to rush to the emergency ward. By one o'clock in the morning, the guests of this wonderful dinner party were stretched out on tables side by side having the wretched experience of having their stomachs pumped. After this humiliating experience, they all went back to the party house to get their personal belongings. As they were about to leave the house the second time, someone remembered the cat. What had happened to the poor thing? The guests went to the kitchen and slowly opened the door. There on the floor was the pet cat, lying peacefully and quietly...with eight brand new kittens![7]

To be radical in one's thinking means you seek to get to the root, do your homework as objectively as possible, getting all the facts, and not prematurely jumping to conclusions.

The term, "liberal" literally means, "free". It implies freedom from bondage to traditional perspectives and free to pursue true scholarship wherever it may lead. One is hungry and eager to seek truth and to be as teachable and objective as possible. Unfortunately the word has come to be associated with a particular group of theological conclusions that are generally based on more humanistic assumptions and that reject miracles and the supernatural.

The term, "conservative" literally refers to the conservation of the past. It implies a more cautious acceptance of new ideas and ways, not an automatic rejection of them. But the popular usage of this term has been associated with an unwillingness to examine and critically evaluate traditional views and ideas.[8]

Kenneth Howkins argues, **"The true scholar should be liberal in his outlook, radical in his thinking and conservative in his conclusions. This means that he examines the issues as deeply as possible, from all points of view, conserves what is good, and accepts new ideas or theories when there is sufficient evidence."**[9]

Although we seek to understand truth more fully, we must humbly acknowledge that we still see only in part and prophesy in part. (1 Cor. 13:9-12) In humility, we recognize that the bigger and fuller picture can only come more into focus as we are inter-dependent on other believers ("iron sharpens iron") and utterly dependent on our heavenly Father for "as the heavens are higher than the earth, so are my ways higher than your ways and my thoughts than your thoughts" declares the Lord. (Isaiah 55:9) He has promised us (those in Christ) the Spirit of truth who will guide us into all truth. (John 16:13) What is required of us as disciples of Jesus is to "do justly, love mercy, and walk humbly before our God" (Micah 6:8), constantly "enquiring of the Lord" to find His opinion and mind on any specific matter.

One of the scandalous things about the ways of the Kingdom of God is that **accessibility to biblical revelation is not dependent on one's IQ but rather on one's hunger for God and His truth**. The Scriptures were not written primarily for the educated elite but for the uneducated peasant, the average Joe. Matthew 11:25, 6 quotes Jesus praying: "I praise you, Father, Lord of heaven and earth, because you have hidden these things from the wise and learned, and revealed them to little children. Yes, Father, for this was your good pleasure."

One of my contemporary heroes, Bill Johnson, says it this way: "What you know can keep you from what you need to know if you don't remain a novice. The moment I become an expert my theology becomes firm and rigid and becomes a wineskin that is not ready for more increase. Childlikeness is what keeps us in a place where we can continuously go from glory to glory. So what we know is wonderful, but it can become the enemy of what we need to know...We level off when we are experts."[10]

In 1577, Sir Francis Drake set off from Portsmouth, England, on a three-year voyage to explore and discover new worlds. This adventure would literally take him around the world. Before he left, he composed a prayer that would serve both as an inspiration for his grand adventure (and ours) and a warning against complacency and mediocrity:

"Disturb us Lord, when we are too well pleased with ourselves, when our dreams have come true because we dreamed too little, when we arrived safely because we sailed too close to the shore. Disturb us Lord, when with the abundance of things we possess we have lost our thirst for the waters of life; having fallen in love with life, we have ceased to dream of eternity. And in our efforts to build a new earth, we have allowed our vision of the new Heaven to dim. Disturb us Lord, to dare more boldly to venture on wider seas where storms will show Your mastery; Where losing sight of land, we shall find the stars. We ask you to push back the horizons of our hopes; and to push us in the future in strength, courage, hope and love".

With the apostle Paul, our prayer is for more of "the Spirit of wisdom and revelation, so that we may know him better". (Ephesians 1:17) Again, the prayer: "Lord, change my mind on every issue in which You and I do not see eye to eye", is so foundational.

After spending the first two chapters focusing on critical factors necessary for our journey in pursuing truth, I would like to take each of the following chapters to focus on a vital issue or topic that I believe is extremely relevant to helping us prepare for the extraordinary times which we are now entering. God may very well want to take you through a paradigm shift as well on some if not all of these issues, if He hasn't already. I don't consider myself an expert on any of these subjects. The more I learn, the more I realize how little I actually know. But what I have learned so far on my journey I trust can be a catalyst for you in yours as we seek to prepare so we can fully partner with God in all that is coming.

Recommended Resources:

Any books by Bill Johnson, pastor of Bethel Church in Redding, California
Balanced Christianity booklet by John R. W. Stott, IVP, 1975

Notes:

[1] John R. W. Stott, Balanced Christianity, InterVarsity Press, Downers Grove, Illinois, 1975, p. 8.
[2] Stacey Campbell, speaking at the Dare to Dream conference, Jubilee Celebration Centre, Orillia, ON, Canada, Aug. 14, 2011.
[3] Stott, Balanced Christianity, p. 9.
[4] Ibid., p.10.
[5] Larry Christensen, Lutheran pastor & author, recorded on a cassette tape which is now lost.
[6] Derek Morphew, Breakthrough:Discovering the Kingdom, Struik Christian Books, Cape Town, 1991, p. 49.
[7] Tom Sine, The Mustard Seed Conspiracy, Word Books Pub., 1981, pp. 15,16.
[8] Kenneth G. Howkins, The Challenge of Religious Studies, InterVarsity Press, Downers Grove, Illinois, 1972, pp 27,28
[9] Ibid., p. 28.
[10] Bill Johnson speaking at a pastors' conference at the Toronto Airport Christian Fellowship, Jan. 19, 2010.

Chapter 3

The Priority of Praise and Worship of our God

"Yet a time is coming and has now come when the true worshipers will worship the Father in spirit and truth, for they are the kind of worshipers the Father seeks." Jesus (John 4:23)

I am so grateful to the Lord for my Christian upbringing and grounding in solid Bible believing evangelical churches. Corporate worship (in song), however, seemed to take a bit of a back seat compared to the rest of the service, that of the teaching or preaching of the Word of God.

When in seminary in the early 1980s, it was required of all students to show up at the one-hour chapel service that was scheduled three times a week. With all the demands upon my time, I felt I could justify why I often slipped into chapel late. I would get there just at the end of the time of worship in song in order to hear one of the professors give what was for me, a very intellectually stimulating message from the Word. I gave very little priority to the need to worship and minister to the Lord but thrived on the teaching of the Word.

But over time, the Lord began to change my perspective on this matter of worship (as He has with many of us in the evangelical church in recent years). As it turned out, this would be the first of many revolutionary paradigm shifts God would take me through. And who knows how many more are yet to come?

It slowly started to dawn on me that Scripturally, worshiping God, both through praise and worship as well as by the way we live, is really meant to be the number one priority of His redeemed.

From Genesis 4:4 to Revelation 22:9, the Word of God is filled with hundreds, if not thousands of commands to bring our praise and worship to the Lord Almighty. It was God's original intention. We were created for worship and relationship with God. But with "the fall", we turned our back on our Creator and began to worship (that is, give attention, love, and devotion to) other gods. Romans 1:25 states that, "they exchanged the truth of God for a lie and worshiped created things rather than the Creator - who is forever praised."

The Bible is predominantly taken up with the historical drama of God taking the initiative to reveal Him self and to reach out in love to win back our love, trust, and loyalty. The Lord urges us that "You shall have no other gods before me" (Ex. 20:3) and to "love the Lord God with all your heart, mind, soul and strength" (the Shema, Deut. 6:4,5). In John 4:23, Jesus declares that the Father is actively seeking worshipers who will worship Him in spirit and truth. And 1 Peter 2:9 testifies: "But you are a chosen people, a royal priesthood, a holy nation, a people belonging to God, that you may declare the praises of him who called you out of darkness into his wonderful light."

Not only is worship God's original intention for His people, but it is ultimately our destiny.

Graham Kendrick writes: "In the book of Revelation, we see that worship is the dominant and all-consuming activity of the redeemed millions and countless angelic beings. Rev. 19:5-7 says: "Then a voice came from the throne, saying "Praise our God, all you his servants, you who fear him, both small and great!" Then I heard what sounded like a great multitude, like the roar of rushing waters and like loud peals of thunder, shouting: "Hallelujah! For our Lord God Almighty reigns. Let us rejoice and be glad and give him glory! For the wedding of the Lamb has come, and his bride has made herself ready.

"Worship is our destination and there is no doubt that praise and worship should be the dominant feature of the journey there, Our praise and worship begins now, not then. They just get perfected somewhat when we arrive!"[1]

A. W. Tozer, a great church statesman of the mid 20th century, complained that the evangelical church had, for the most part, lost sight of its primary task. He argued, "Worship is the church's missing jewel" and wrote a booklet bearing the same title. Tozer criticized the church for taking new converts and making them workers first and worshipers second. It is the issue of Martha vs. Mary, "one thing is needed". (Luke 10:42)

The Lord's instruction to the Levitical priests regarding their primary function was to "come near to minister before me". (Ezekiel 44:15) And we, the New Covenant priesthood of all believers, have this same mandate.

Thankfully many in the body of Christ have been making this shift in priority regarding praise and worship in the last couple of decades as is evidenced by the proliferation of books on the subject and worship CDs in Christian bookstores. Before the 1980s you would do well to find one or two books about worship (in contrast to dozens on Christian counseling and evangelism).

Richard Foster's book, Celebration of Discipline, has greatly impacted me. In his chapter on worship, he argues that: "If the Lord is to be Lord, worship must have priority in our lives...The divine priority is worship first, service second...Service flows out of worship. Service as a substitute for worship is idolatry. Activity may become the enemy of adoration...One grave temptation we all face is to run around answering calls to service without ministering to the Lord himself."[2]

Making this shift led me on a delightful journey of discovery. Let me summarize some insights that revolutionized my relationship with and worship of the Lord:

1. I learned that **service we do for the Lord is more fulfilling and more fruitful when it flows out of a life of worship.** Lovers are much more productive than workers!

2. I also discovered that **the fuel and goal of evangelism and missions is worship**.

One of my favourite authors, John Piper says it best: "Worship is ultimate, not missions, because God is ultimate, not man. When this age is over, and the countless millions of the redeemed fall on their faces before the throne of God, missions will be no more. It is a temporary necessity. But worship abides forever. Worship, therefore, is the fuel and goal of missions. It's the goal of missions because in missions we simply aim to bring the nations into the white-hot enjoyment of God's glory...But worship is also the fuel of missions. Passion for God in worship precedes the offer of God in preaching. You can't commend what you don't cherish...Where passion for God is weak, zeal for missions will be weak...Missions is not the ultimate goal of the church, worship is. Missions exists because worship doesn't."[3]

3. **Worship is my personal response to God's gracious initiative.** We love Him because He first loved us. It's love responding to love in an authentic relationship.

4. Furthermore, **my response is to involve all that I am, have, and do; all of me (mind, emotions, body, possessions) and all the time as a daily lifestyle**. We are to worship the Lord our God with all our heart, mind, soul, and strength. But I grew up worshiping predominately from the neck up. Without swinging to the opposite side of the pendulum of anti-intellectualism, I realized God was beckoning me to go beyond just a cerebral and doctrinally dense dimension of worship. As mentioned earlier, the Lord said to me after finishing seminary, "I want your heart to catch up to your head". I love how William Temple put it: "to worship is to quicken the conscience by the holiness of God, to feed the mind with the truth of God, to purge the imagination by the beauty of God, to open the heart to the love of God, and to devote the will to the purpose of God."[4]

5. Although everything we do should be an act of worship (Eph. 6:7; Col. 3:23), **our response must include frequent times of concentrated and laser focused worship** (a more narrow definition of worship).

6. **Worship is to be an offering up to God of our very best, not the leftovers.** David declared, "I will not sacrifice to the Lord my God burnt offerings that cost me nothing". (2 Sam. 24:24) In Malachi 1:6-14, God is upset with the offerings that are blind, lame, and diseased. In verse 8, He argues: "Try offering them to your governor! Would he be pleased with you? Would he accept you?" Verse 14 declares; "Cursed is the cheat who has an acceptable male in his flock and vows to give it, but then sacrifices a blemished animal to the Lord. For I am a great King and my name is to be feared among the nations." The New Testament declares that Christ's death at the cross was the ultimate and final sacrifice to atone for sin. Therefore, we, as the universal priesthood of believers, are called to continually offer up, not animal sacrifices, but sacrifices of praise, the fruit of our lips and our lives. (Heb. 13:15; 1 Peter 2:9; Romans 12:1-3) Our possessions and money are to be included as well. (Heb. 13:14; 2 Cor. Ch. 8 & 9) God apparently loves a "cheerful giver", which, in the Greek, literally means "hilarious giver"!

7. **Biblical worship will be inspired and ignited by the Holy Spirit.** It is not a man-made technique or formula, nor can it be produced on our own. Worship is to be the enflamed love response of the heart, set on fire by the Spirit of God. (Luke 10:21; John 4:23; Rom. 8:26,27; Eph. 5:18) The Spirit enables us to cry "Abba Father" (Gal 4:6; Rom 8:15) and to confess "Jesus as Lord". (1 Cor. 12:3) The theologian, Tomas Smail states: "By the Spirit, man gives and God receives. He is the Spirit of faith, the Spirit of praise, the Spirit of prayer, who glorifies the Father through the Son...Creation, as it is made responsive to Christ, is the Spirit's gift to the Son. He (the Spirit) is fashioning in us the doxology of the created universe: he is teaching us in a 1000

ways to sing the new song to the Lamb and to confess in a 1000 tongues that Jesus is Lord to the glory of God the Father."[5]

8. Biblical worship is a VERB, not a noun.

The predominant view of the dynamics of corporate worship, at least in many evangelical churches, sees the congregation as the audience, the leaders on stage as the performers, and we are not quite sure where God fits into the equation. It was a radical wake up call for me to realize that the more biblical view of the dynamics of corporate worship entails seeing the congregation, not as a passive audience or as spectators to be entertained, but rather as the performers or active participants. The leaders, rather than the performers, were to be prompters or facilitators and God was the "audience of one" that we are to seek to address and minister to.

If it is worship in song, for instance, then a paradigm shift is needed from just singing about God to actually singing to Him. The penny dropped for me when in 1983, my wife and I fought the crowds one night to get a glimpse of Queen Elizabeth on her ship docked at the Vancouver harbour. The Queen and many Canadian political leaders were on the deck enjoying the party and the pomp and ceremony. Then at one point in the evening, the band began to play "God save the Queen". The whole crowd, including ourselves, automatically joined in singing this song we have song all our lives, only this time, the difference was that we were singing it to her. We were in the presence of her majesty, the Queen, and so we sang with gusto, from our hearts, with tears flowing down our cheeks.

In the context of worshiping our King, in His presence, the pressing question is not "what did I get out of corporate worship today"? But "Lord, were You pleased and blessed by my/our worship today"? It is first and foremost about Him and for His benefit.

9. Something happens to us in the process of worship.

Although the focus must be on blessing and ministering to God, often we are blessed. "You cannot out-give God!" Psalm 22 speaks of the Lord inhabiting the praises of His people. He comes and visits us. Scripture also tells us that God's power is unleashed and the enemy is banished through our worship. (2 Chron. 20; Ps. 8:2; Acts

16:25; 1 Cor. 12, 14) Not only does He continue to do His "mighty works and deeds" in the context of worship but also worship draws others to God (evangelism). In John 12:32, Jesus states, "If I be lifted up, I will draw all men unto me".

When we praise and worship Jehovah God, He promises to be present among us, and when He is, things happen and we are changed. He is the "Great I Am", not the "Great I Was"!

10. Worship also gives us a fresh perspective to life and reality, not an escape from it.

Low self-esteem is lifted, those with an exalted view of self are humbled, our hearts are softened, sin is confessed, our problems shrink down to a manageable size and our faith, love, and awareness of God is enlarged.

I have a super thick book of sermon illustrations in my library. It is so heavy you can use it for weight lifting. Years ago when looking for sermon illustrations for a teaching series on worship I was preparing, I noticed something very interesting. This book, though a massive volume of over a thousand pages, only had one page given to this vital subject of worship. Then I happened to notice that the word that came before the word, worship, in this alphabetically ordered book was the word, worry. The compiler of the book had devoted seven pages of stories and illustrations on that subject. I felt the Lord say to me that when there is little focus on worshiping Him, then you are bound to have a lot of worry and anxiety to deal with.

In these coming days of confusion, chaos and turmoil, keeping our eyes fixed upon the Lord and worshiping and adoring Him will be the key to keeping worry down to a minimum. We will see our problems shrivel down to size while our trust and awareness of God and His greatness is increased to more accurately match reality.

11. Biblical worship is multi-dimensional, involving praise, reverence, intimacy and obedience.

Psalm 95 provides a model and an invitation to this multi-faceted worship:[6]

1.) **Praise** (Ps. 95:1-5):

What is praise? It is to declare truth about, delight in, enjoy, exalt, adore, and compliment. C.S. Lewis argued that "men spontaneously praise whatever they value" and "men spontaneously urge others to join them". An example would be "look at that gorgeous mountain!" Praise begins in the heart but scripturally; praise that God requires and delights in is also observable with the eyes and ears. It actively engages our minds, emotions, and bodies. Three key Hebrew words for praise demonstrate this:

a. **Halal**, which is found over 100 times, means to make a great noise, to be clamourously foolish for God. Its mood is one of extravagant, child-like celebration and festivity. (Ps. 96:4; 146:1) "Hallelujah" literally means "praise the Lord". I was convicted when someone argued that if there is anything we get more excited about than Jesus, it is idolatry. It is interesting that the word "enthusiasm" means "in God" yet enthusiastic people at a sporting event are called "fans" but at church they are labelled "fanatics".

b. **Yada** is used 90 times and means to praise through bodily action, particularly extended hands before the Lord (the universal sign for surrender is the extended hands). We are to "clap our hands" (Ps. 47:1) and "lift our hands" (Ps. 134:2). I remember the first time I ever lifted my hands up to the Lord in a corporate worship setting. It was at a conference with over two thousand people in Vancouver in 1985. As we were praising and worshiping the Lord, I sensed God clearly ask me to lift my hands towards heaven while I sang to Him. It was such a big deal for me to raise my arms and extend my hands to the

Lord. I felt my arms weighed about two hundred pounds. I also felt like every eye in the room was staring at me. But once I got them up and I looked around, I realized not a soul was looking at me or even cared. They were too busy raising their arms and praising the Lord with total abandon. At this point in time I had this tremendous sense of breakthrough into a freedom of expression that I never knew before. It was a landmark moment in my relationship with the Lord. Yada also involves whole body movement and dance. The Hebrew worldview sees man as a whole, a unit, with each part inter-connected. You could not praise God with all your heart without it greatly engaging all other parts. Psalm 149:2, 3 declares "let Israel rejoice in their Maker; let the people of Zion be glad in their King. Let them praise his name with dancing". Unfortunately, the Greek Platonic influence in the church throughout the centuries has been profound, causing us, among other things, to see our bodies (and our imaginations and emotions) as intrinsically evil and suspect. But thankfully many in the church are waking up to the realization that we have been duped and are missing out on so much of what God has for us in our worship of Him.

c. **Zamar** is found about 40 times in the Old Testament and means to celebrate through songs and all sorts of musical instruments (Ps. 98: 1,4,5,6; Ps. 33:1,2; 150) with skill and great shouts of joy.

We are not only given permission to praise our God with abandon, but are commanded to do so, for the Lord takes great delight in the praises of His people. (Ps. 149:1-4) The challenge is to be biblical even if it goes against the grain of our traditions, temperament, and personal tastes.

The first time I had opportunity to preach on this very subject of praise and some of the Hebrew terms in Scripture, I was pastoring in a wonderful but very conservative little country church. After the sermon, tradition dictated that I shake the parishioners' hands at the door as they left the church. I remember the chairman of the board shaking my hand and quietly but firmly whispering into my ear, "Jerry, stay normal". I didn't have a quick response to his advice in the moment but on reflecting later I realized I had already made a non-negotiable commitment to become normal, according to the plumb line of the Scriptures, not my denominational or Canadian cultural traditions and definitions of normalcy.

2. Reverence and Awe (Psalm 95:6-7):

In this passage, three times we are told to come low before our God. It literally means to prostrate oneself and have your arrogance knocked out of you! Kneeling causes us to swallow our pride and acknowledge his greatness and our dependence. We do it now voluntarily but some day "every knee shall bow and every tongue confess..." (Isa. 45:23; Phil. 2:10). In silence, meditation, and godly fear we are able to receive a fresh glimpse of the majesty, all-sufficiency, holiness, and mercy of the Almighty One. Such an encounter brings us to a place of humble and honest confession whereby we cry out, "search me O God and know my heart, see if there be any offensive way in me". (Ps. 139:23,24; Isa 6:1-5)

On January 28th, 1994, I was at the renewal meeting at the Toronto Airport Vineyard Christian Fellowship (now called Catch the Fire, Toronto). I had been prayed for and was on the floor "under the power" and having a vision, which was very rare for me. I saw a sea of humanity on their knees passionately worshiping before the throne, completely unaware of self. Everyone was totally enraptured in the beauty, wonder and splendour of the King and it felt so right, so natural, so normal. Then I heard the words "as there, so here". I was in awe, overwhelmed with the liquid love and glory of the Lord. As I was coming out of this vision, I could hear the worship team and people in the room singing the song "Now unto the King eternal" and could feel the anointing and pres-

57

ence of the Lord very thick and powerful. My prayer became "Lord, as in heaven, let it be here on earth".

Hebrews 12:28,29 states: "Therefore, since we are receiving a kingdom that cannot be shaken, let us be thankful, and so worship God acceptably with reverence and awe, for our God is a consuming fire".

Tragically, godly fear and a sense of awe and wonder seem to be lacking in many of our Western churches. Our services are often characterised by a feeling of boredom, over-familiarity, and predictability. Why would that be? I think our services are predominantly cerebral and content oriented, are very structured and pre-planned, have little use of the creative arts that reach down and grip the imagination and all the senses and the leaders and people have a very low expectation for God to actually show up and do anything unusual. What a contrast to the church in the book of Acts when they saw the living God and His tangible and manifest presence in action with signs and wonders that caused them to be filled with awe. (Acts 2:43; 3:9; 1 Cor. 14:23-25)

What can we do about it?

We need to cultivate structures that promote our capacity to see God at work and to hear His voice, such as: greater interactive body life as the Head directs each member by the power of the Holy Spirit, utilizing the creative arts in worship as well as meditation and other spiritual disciplines and giving permission for free, spontaneous and joyful expression of our worship. We need to break out of our puny theological boxes of what God can and cannot do in our day. We need to confess our fears and our obsessive need to be in control and trust God to be the good yet untamed and unpredictable supernatural God that He is. And we need to eagerly seek His face, long for a return of the glory of the Lord among us and be aggressive and undignified about it. That requires a "holy dissatisfaction" with the way things are and a "holy desperation" for more of God and His kingdom.

3. Intimacy (Psalm 95:6-7):

The verb "to kneel down in reverent worship" also includes the idea of "drawing near to kiss the hand". The New Testament equivalent is "proskyneo", found some fifty-nine times.

You and I are called and invited, not to "be religious", but to an adventurous and authentic relationship of intimacy. The death and resurrection of Christ have paved the way for restored intimacy with our Creator. We are invited to boldly and confidently draw near into the very heart of God, as a child to a father and as a wife to her lover. The life changing joy and ecstasy available in the Father/child and divine romance paradigms deserve attention of their own, which we will turn to in the next chapter.

4. Obedience (Ps 95: 7b-11):

"Today, if you hear his voice, do not harden your hearts..."

Obedience completes the integrity of our worship, otherwise our worship is hypocritical and superficial. (Rom. 12; Heb. 13:16)

In Conclusion

We actually touch the heart of Almighty God with our child-like and expressive praise and delight in Him, in our reverent holy awe of Him, in our intimate love and affections for Him, and our heart's resolve to trust and obey Him. It may not be fully mature or per-fected yet but the Lord looks at the heart. I love how Tommy Tenny puts it:

"God says: "It's not how pretty they worship. It's just that they are my offspring." He would rather hear you stumble through a song with a voice like a cracked foghorn than to hear the six winged seraphim surround Him with chants of "holy" in tones of heavenly perfection."[7]

Thankfully, the Spirit has placed a renewed emphasis on expres-sive, passionate and "pull out all the stops" praise, awe-filled reverence, and intimate heart to heart worship of the Lord upon the body of Christ in recent decades.

He has also brought a renewed emphasis upon contemplative worship, which some have come to call "soaking worship". The outpouring of the Spirit in Toronto in recent years has given a high value in this practice of soaking worship. They have been training thousands of passionate believers from around the world who feel called to establish and facilitate "soaking centres".

The explosion of Spirit-inspired creativity and heart-felt passion for the Lord has brought such a breath of fresh air and new life into many churches and it is so encouraging to see many in the younger generation pick up the baton and run with it beyond what my generation had. Many Houses of Prayer and Worship have been popping up all around the world, some even ministering to the Lord 24/7, with many of the younger generation not only playing a critical role, but being the catalyst behind it.

As a result of this acceleration of emphasis upon passion-packed praise and worship of the Lord in recent decades, many readers may not find this chapter on worship telling you much you have not already heard. I am so encouraged to visit such a wide variety of churches, including traditional and conservative ones, and seeing priority and time given for more passionate and expressive worship of our God. My sense is that this heart engaged worship is a critical gateway (as it was for me) into much more of His manifest presence and the supernatural realm of the kingdom that He desires His people to experience. Many conservative pastors and churches just don't know it yet. It's a divine set up! We have a sneaky God, a dangerous God, but He is good and can be trusted.

In the next chapter we will elaborate on the paradigm of intimacy with God and the invitation to find irresistible pleasure in Him as He does in us. This paradigm is foundational to being ready for what is coming in the days ahead.

Recommended Reading

Worship is a Verb, Robert Webber, Word, 1985
Celebration of Discipline, Richard Foster, Harper & Row, 1978,
chapter 11 Desiring God, John Piper, Multnomah, 1996, Chapter 3,
"Worship: The Feast of Christian Hedonism"
The Hallelujah Factor, Jack R. Taylor, Broadman Press, 1983
Exploring Worship: a Practical Guide to Praise & Worship, Bob
Sorge, Oasis House, 1987
Worship, the Pattern of Things in Heaven, Joseph L. Garlington,
Destiny Image, 1997 The Lost Glory, Dave Markee, Sovereign
World Ltd., England, 1999
Audience of One, Jeremy and Connie Sinnott, Destiny Image, 1999
God's Eye view: Worshiping Your Way to a Higher Perspective,
Tommy Tenny, Nelson, 2002

Notes:

[1.] Graham Kendrick, Learning to Worship as a Way of Life
(Minneapolis: Bethany, 1984) pp. 14-15.
[2.] Richard Foster, Celebration of Discipline, Harper & Row, 1978,
p. 140.
[3.] John Piper, Let the Nations Be Glad! The Supremacy of God in
Missions, Baker Books, Grand Rapids, Michigan, 1993, pp. 1,2.
[4.] Richard Foster, Celebration of Discipline, p. 138.
[5.] Thomas Smail, The Giving Gift, Hodder & Stoughton Ltd.,
London, 1988, p. 86.
[6.] George Mallone, Furnace of Renewal, IVP, 1981, Ch. 3, 4.
[7.] Tommy Tenny, The God Catchers, Thomas Nelson, 2000, p. 27.

Chapter 4

The Call to Find Superior Pleasure in the Trinity

"In light of the mounting pressures at the end of the age,
we can't afford not to drink of the pleasures of His heart."
Mike Bickle

O f all the paradigm shifts necessary to prepare us for the days ahead, perhaps the most critical is our perception of God the Father, God the Son, and God the Holy Spirit coupled with our view of pleasure. All other changes in mindset described in this book will flow out of how we picture our Lord and our relationship with Him. Let's begin by first discussing the matter of pleasure and satisfaction.

Pleasure

Years ago Blaise Pascal made this astute observation, "All men seek happiness. This is without exception. Whatever different means they employ they all tend to this end..."[1]

The yearning for happiness is universal. It is woven into the very fabric of what it is to be human. God placed this inescapable longing of the human heart deep within us so that it would find it's greatest fulfillment in Him.

Many Christians however, view happiness or pleasure with suspicion and disdain. They consider desire and pleasure to be synonymous with sin and worldliness. If it feels good, we may subconsciously think, it must be of the devil. Somehow they have come to the conclusion that the highest virtue in life centers on the negative ideal of unselfishness.

The New Testament speaks often about self-denial, but not as an end in itself. We are instructed to deny ourselves in order that we may follow Christ and so find our greatest joy and satisfaction in Him. And yet, like the elder brother in the Parable of the Prodigal Son, many Christians grit their teeth determined to operate out of a life of dutiful obedience, responsibility and obligation. Taking responsibility and being obedient is a good thing. It's just not the best thing. Sheer obedience to obligations (without a joyful and meaningful relationship to the One you seek to obey), provides little true pleasure and joy to lighten our days.

Over a period of time, lives devoid of joy and pleasure become desperately dry and thirsty, making us dangerously vulnerable to the deceiver who comes along with a tantalizing offer of a refreshing drink that turns out to be polluted water that will poison and kill. So, those who believe pleasure and happiness is itself sinful and to be avoided, end up falling into sin. They spend their time seeking to deny the God-given longings of their hearts and end up fulfilling them in unhealthy, ungodly and even destructive ways.

Gary Thomas, in his book, Pure Pleasure, makes this wise observation: "Jesus' more pleasurable way of life showcases the agony of the way of death. When we unashamedly preach true, holy, and God-honoring pleasure, then the sordidness of sin, the foolishness of spiritual rebellion, and the agony of addictions become shockingly apparent."[2]

We need to come to the revelation that God promises superior happiness, pleasure and satisfaction that is greater than those that seem to be offered by sin. "When you are dazzled by God it is hard to be duped by sin."[3]

Religion, which entails a works righteousness and a joyless spirituality, results in barrenness and death. "Religion kills but Jesus thrills!" is how John Crowder puts it.[4]

Religion has promoted a deadly lie that God is a passionless God who is merely out to get us to dutifully serve and obey Him. One of the world's major religions, Buddhism, for instance, sees all suffering in the world being due to the problem of desire. Therefore, if one can strive to eliminate desire and a seeking after pleasure, one can help create a world with less suffering. A false religious version of Christianity attempts the same thing.

But the answer for struggling against illicit, sinful passions and all the suffering it produces is not by running away from all passion. We don't quarrel with a sinner's pursuit of pleasure. We quarrel with his belief in where real pleasure is to be found. The only kind of pleasure that truly satisfies the human soul and causes us to feel like the eagle who finds pleasure in soaring on the thermal currents in the heights, is finding lasting pleasure and satisfaction in the loving presence of our glorious Creator. He beckons us with this invitation: "Taste and see that the LORD is good"! (Psalm 34:8)

True biblical Christianity paints the very opposite picture of religion. Our problem is not that we have too much desire and a drive for too much pleasure but that we settle for way too little.

In his book, Desiring God, John Piper quotes from C.S. Lewis' insightful sermon called "The Weight of Glory":

"...If there lurks in most modern minds the notion that to desire our own good and earnestly to hope for the enjoyment of it is a bad thing, I submit that this notion has crept in from Kant and the Stoics and is no part of the Christian faith. Indeed, if we consider the unblushing promises of reward and the staggering nature of the rewards promised in the Gospels, it would seem that our Lord finds our desires not too strong, but too weak. We are half-hearted creatures, fooling about with drink and sex and ambition when infinite joy is offered us, like an ignorant child who wants to go on making mud pies in a slum because he cannot imagine what is meant by the offer of a holiday at the sea. We are far too easily pleased."[5]

Here is C. S. Lewis going beyond what Pascal said (that it is simply a fact that all of us seek happiness) and argues that we ought to unapologetically seek our own happiness, knowing that it will only truly be found in our Lord.

In John Piper's words, "this persistent and undeniable yearning for happiness was not to be suppressed but was to be glutted - on God!"[6] We are so easily pleased with cheap substitutes when intoxicatingly deep and lasting pleasures are freely available to us in the passionate heart and presence of the Lord of the universe.

Out of the fiery love and joy of the Trinity came a new creation, mankind, made in the spitting image of God. He created us with the capacity and the rewards of finding our deep and lasting pleasure and satisfaction ultimately in Him who is the very source of all joy and happiness. God went to unimaginable lengths (sending his only Son to win us back) to offer us a mind-blowing adventure into His heart that makes any other love story in history pale in comparison. And our delight and ecstatic pleasure in Him is taken to whole new levels as we receive greater revelation of God's tender and outrageous affections and feelings for us. We can actually bring intense joy and pleasure to God's heart.

Eric Liddel, the Scotsman missionary to China in the 1920s and 30s who ultimately was martyred for his faith, was also an athlete who loved to run. An amazing movie was made of his life called, "Chariots of Fire". Possibly the most powerful line in the movie was when he was talking with his sister. She was concerned he was getting distracted from his calling as a missionary to China. He reassures her that he still plans to go but first he needs to run in the Olympics. "Jenny, God has made me fast, and when I run, I feel His pleasure!" What a contrast with the other main athletic character in the movie. Harold Abrahams is driven by fear and the need to succeed for his own validation. For Eric, his passion for excellence is out of sheer joy he and God get out of it. As Gary Wiens said, "We were never intended to be motivated solely by duty, by the crushing weight of fear or 'oughtness'. Human life is designed to be lived with passionate liberty, running at top speed (within the parameters of the personality God has given each individual) and feeling His pleasure in it - a confident passion, the liberated reality of the sons and daughters of the King of the universe."[7]

The Westminster Confession of centuries ago states "the chief end of man is to glorify God and enjoy him forever." John Piper has fine-tuned that historic doctrinal statement by claiming "the chief end of man is to glorify God by enjoying him forever."[8]

The Psalms and other places in Scripture invite us, even command us to come, praise and delight in the Lord. That implies emotional bliss and joy in the obeying of such commands. We were not created as servant robots that are programmed to obey on command, but as the pinnacle of God's creation made in His image to respond to His overtures of love and instruction with the emotional capacity to feel joy, happiness and pleasure. Even the name of the garden that Adam and Eve were first placed in to live and walk with God was called "Eden", which means, "pleasure". We were made for it. Through Christ's finished work on the cross, He has provided us sinners a way for free access to Himself, which offers bliss forevermore. "True ecstasy is not a street drug but a Person."[9]

God has dazzling and breathtaking realms of pleasure for us. David, the man famous for having "a heart after God", under the inspiration of the Holy Spirit, boldly declared, "You have made known to me the path of life; you will fill me with joy in your presence, with eternal pleasures at your right hand". (Psalm 16:11)

Scripture contrasts this with "enjoying the pleasures of sin for a short time" or what some translations call "the passing pleasures of sin". (Hebrews 11:25) Which sounds like a better deal? A momentary rush of illicit pleasure that ends up jeopardizing one's peace, joy and relationships with others and God, or lasting pleasures of "joy unspeakable and full of glory"? Yep. You are right. There's no comparison.

Through the Psalmist, God gives an invitation and a promise to "Delight yourself in the Lord, and He will give you the desires of your heart". (Ps. 37:4)

Psalm 36:7-9 tells us that God's unfailing love is priceless and we are beckoned to come and feast on the abundance of His house and drink deeply from His river of delights because the fountain of life is found only in Him.

We need to meditate on the truths of such Scriptures until they become a part of what and how we think.

George Mueller, the 19th century Christian who is famous for establishing orphanages in England and for having a joyful and child-like trust in God to provide for all his needs said this about how he started his day everyday for over forty years:

"...the first great and primary business to which I ought to attend every day was, to have my soul happy in the Lord. The first thing to be concerned about was not, how much I might serve the Lord, how I might glorify the Lord; but how I might get my soul into a happy state, and how my inner man might be nourished...Now I saw, that the most important thing I had to do was to give myself to the reading of the Word of God and to meditation on it, that thus my heart might be comforted, encouraged, warned, reproved, instructed; and that thus, whilst meditating, my heart might be brought into experimental, communion with the Lord."

Mueller goes on to say that his mediation of the Word of God was not for the sake of the public ministry of preaching but for feeding his own soul and that by breakfast time, with rare exceptions, he would be in a peaceful and happy state of heart.[10]

Worship and intimacy with our Lord is the gateway into all the pleasures He has for us. And especially in the intensity of battle in the last days, with all it's unprecedented pressures and sacrifices, it will be crucial for followers of Christ to continually live in that secret place of bliss with their Lord in order to endure and overcome.

Let's now turn to the matter of how we view God, more specifically, **how we view the three persons of the Trinity.**

Christians are generally quite familiar with the Great Commission that Jesus gave His disciples before He ascended into heaven. Matthew 28.18-20 declares:

"All authority in heaven and on earth has been given to me. Therefore go and make disciples of all nations, baptizing them in the name of the Father and of the Son and of the Holy Spirit and teaching them to obey everything I have commanded you. And surely I will be with you always, to the very end of the age."

We see that part of the discipling process involves the initiation of water baptism and the use of the Trinitarian formula. This is right and good and an important step of obedience that is like driving a stake in the ground, making a clear and public stand of allegiance to Jesus, our saviour, master and Lord.

But this command to baptize new believers as part of the discipling process is not limited to being literal, but should also be experiential. Baptism means "immersion" so we are to be literally immersed in water but also experientially immersed in all three persons of the Godhead: Father, Son, and Spirit.

The new convert has come to experience the saving and redeeming grace of the finished work of Christ on the cross and now has the Spirit of Christ dwelling within. The greatest miracle of all has taken place turning a hell bent sinner into a forgiven new creature in Christ Jesus. But the Scriptures also urge us to be baptized or immersed and filled (continuously) with the Holy Spirit. (Eph. 5:18) In some Christian circles, this is described as a call to enter into "the full gospel". But there is also the privilege of encountering or being immersed in the love and affirmation of the Father's heart.

Fred Wright, founding coordinator of the Partners in Harvest network of churches, which was birthed out of the Toronto Blessing outpouring, has authored a book called, The World's Greatest Revivals. In it he demonstrates that with each move of God there is a fresh revelational truth that is highlighted by God and recovered by the church.

With Martin Luther and the Protestant Reformation of the 16th century, the church recovered the lost doctrinal gem of "justification by faith in Christ alone". This foundational doctrine was taken further in the "Great Awakening" of the 18th century with John Wesley and others who proclaimed Christ and the need for a personal heart transformation.

Beginning with the Pentecostal revival of the early 1900s and throughout the twentieth century, fresh revelation and experience of the person and work of the Holy Spirit has been released to the church by the Lord.

Then in the 1980s and 90s, through forerunners like Jack Winter, Henri Nowen, Brennan Manning, Ed Pieork, as well as through many others in the "Toronto Blessing" outpouring such as John Arnott, Peter Jackson, and Jack Frost, God has imparted fresh revelational truth and experiential reality to the church regarding the Father heart of God.[11]

Father heart of God

"Jesus answered, "I am the way and the truth and the life. No one comes to the Father except through me". (John 14:6) The Father is our relational destination.

The term, Father - Pater, appears two hundred and forty-five times in the New Testament to refer to Almighty God. That is quite a stretch to begin to adjust one's view of God as a father. But Jesus takes it further by using the term, "Abba", in reference to God the Father. "Abba" is not Hebrew, the language of liturgy, but Aramaic, the language of home and regular life. The word conveys feelings of intimacy and affection. It is a word of endearment, used by Jesus three times in Scripture. This revolutionary term would have been intensely offensive to the Pharisees of the day, a major scandal. But it is a stunning invitation to enter into the paternal affections of the heart and arms of our heavenly Father.

Theologian, Tomas Smail, claims, "If we are in doubt about God's fatherly attitude towards us, we shall be shrinking, groveling and unexpectant in our prayers; and we shall hold back, play safe and refuse to take risks in his service, in fear that at the crucial moment God will not back us up".[12]

Not only does Jesus refer to His heavenly Father as Abba and invites us to do the same, but Jesus goes on record telling the parable of how God feels when His lost son comes home.

Jesus' whole point in telling this story of the "Prodigal Son" is to say, "Hey, this is what my Father is really like". He is not a stoic, emotionally detached father but feels deeply. We can bring Him pain and anguish or bring Him intense joy. He loves us enough to let us leave home and do our own thing. It breaks His heart but He prefers a genuine heart relationship to outward conformity. In Genesis 6:5,6, we see that God was grieved and His heart was full of pain at the evil in man's heart and action. He created us with free will, which meant He took the risk of being rejected and heart-broken.

In this parable, the father loved this son so deeply that he watched every day for him to return home and when he finally did see his son coming, he ran to him (breaking tradition and protocol of that day for an older man), embraced him, and kissed him repeatedly. He then placed upon him the special robe kept for special occasions for dignitaries, conveying the fact that the boy is instantly and totally forgiven and pardoned. He then had the family ring placed on his finger, which declares his unequivocal position of sonship within the family, and given shoes for his feet. Most translations say sandals, but according to Mark Stibbe, sandals were worn by slaves. This son was given expensive leather shoes signifying his freedom in this family of privilege to walk into his destiny. And of course the father's overwhelming joy at his son's return called for a blow out party in his honour.[13]

It is interesting to note that the word "prodigal" means: extravagant, unrestrained, and lavish. This word should actually be applied to the father and call it the "Parable of the Prodigal Father" who pours out his extravagant, unrestrained, lavish love on his son! And this illogical and outrageous love is what God the Father pours out on each of His sons and daughters when they return home.

Deuteronomy 33:12 sparkles with a similar stunning insight: "Let the beloved of the Lord rest secure in him, for he shields him all day long, and the one the Lord loves rests between his shoulders". We get the thrill of riding piggyback on Papa's shoulders!

In Zephaniah 3:16-17, the Father communicates this astounding truth about Himself: "He will take great delight in you, he will quiet you with his love, he will rejoice (twirl, dance) over you with singing".

This truth is even more profound when we realize that the context in which the prophet Zephaniah was speaking in his book was not only about his day but also around the issue of the "day of the Lord" at the end of the age when things will be stressful and turbulent. That is when we really will need this revelation of His intimate pleasure in us and His calming presence and protection.

The Father really does love us, and even likes us! And He enjoys us even in our immaturity and weakness. It's a lie of the enemy that God will only truly love you and be pleased with you once you are mature in the Lord. As earthly parents we delight in each and every stage of development into maturity of our kids and no less does our heavenly Father.

I have a famous picture of President Kennedy clapping for joy while watching his two youngsters, Caroline and John John, dance in the oval office, the most powerful and serious room in the world. We too get to confidently come into the most powerful throne room of both heaven and earth and with childlike abandon, playfully dance and squeal with delight in our Father's presence, pleasure and approval. C.S. Lewis again states it like it is, "Joy is the serious business of heaven!"

We cannot overlook the Father's affirmation of His Son, Jesus, at His water baptism. When Jesus came up out of the water, the heavens opened, the Dove descended and the Father's voice spoke out loud and clear: "You are my Son, whom I love; with you I am well pleased". (Luke 3:21-22) These fatherly words of life rein-0forced Jesus' sense of identity and purpose and assured Him of His Father's approval and pleasure in Him. This comes just before He began His public ministry and mission. Up to this point He has only been hammering nails. Notice Jesus does not launch out and do a public preaching and healing ministry with a need to gain His Father's approval and blessing, but rather it is out of His Father's affirmation that He is able to confidently and authoritatively flow in ministry, doing only what He sees the Father doing, all in the power of the Holy Spirit. And as the King's kids, this is our privilege and birthright as well.

With the Toronto Blessing outpouring that began in 1994, we have seen the Spirit of God create a quantum leap forward of this revelation of the Father's love and heart. The Catch the Fire Toronto church's motto on the back wall of their auditorium says it all,

"Walking in the Father's love and giving it away to Toronto and the world".

I believe the Lord gave me a similar motto to follow,

"Basking in the Father's Blessing, Being about the Father's Business".

Many, including myself, tend to be quick to want to work in the Father's business without first and continually basking in His love, acceptance and affirmation. The result is often a striving to serve the Lord in our own strength that becomes a joyless obligation with little lasting fruit and fulfillment. It can also result in us falling into the trap of comparing ourselves with others so that we end up either feeling really proud and self-righteous or very insecure and unspiritual. But this step of frequently taking the time to soak in the Father's embrace and hear His affirming voice is vital (as is the need to be continually filled with the Spirit, Eph. 5:18). Really knowing our identity and security in Him is critical for God to launch us into our destiny of significance and the devil knows it.

It doesn't take long before the enemy out in the wilderness contests the affirming words of the Father to His Son, Jesus. Three times Satan seeks to question the Father's integrity in hopes of causing doubt to rise up in the heart of Jesus as to His true identity. If you are the Son of God, then do this. If you are the Son of God, then do that. Jesus counters the enemy by utilizing the powerful weapon of the Word of God. He confronts the devil three times by declaring, "it is written".

A student is no greater than his teacher nor a servant greater than his master. If Jesus needed His Father's affirmation to reinforce His identify and sense of mission and destiny prior to His ministry, how much more do we? And likewise, if Jesus needed to employ the Word of God to do spiritual warfare against the enemy, don't you think we do too?

In that safe and secure place in the Father, His opinion of you becomes more your concern than the opinions of others. Rejection and the praise of man don't fizz on us like it used to. The fear of man decreases and the true fear or reverence of the Lord increases.

You and I are no longer cosmic orphans, left on our own. We are loved. We are accepted. We belong. We are His "treasured possession". (Ex. 19:5) We have been given the Spirit of adoption whereby we cry "Abba Father". (Rom. 8:15, 16; Gal 4:5-7) And out of this "coming home" sense of belonging and rich identity as children of the King, we can freely and confidently step out in the world to make a difference, in the power of His strength and love.

We no longer have to believe the lies of the enemy that we are powerless victims, hopeless hypocrites, abandoned orphans and pitiful paupers. We no longer need to walk with a wounded heart and a poverty mindset. We have royal blood coursing through our veins and we have the privilege of being invited into an adventure, a battle, armed with the head and heart knowledge of His personal pleasure and approval and His delegated authority. We are promised that as we get to know our God more intimately (and know who we are in Him), we get to do great exploits together this side of heaven. (Daniel 11:32) We can trust our heavenly Father completely. If He asks us to do something, we can count on Him backing us up.

When my wife, Pam, our two young boys and I left the security of our home province of Ontario many years ago to move three thousand miles to the Canadian west coast to plant a church, we saw our heavenly Father come through for us time and time again in very practical ways that we will never forget. Here are just a few instances.

Even before we arrived in Vancouver, we saw God's fatherly hand at work. Our beat up Oldsmobile station wagon, that was pulling a heavy utility trailer, gave up the ghost within hours of reaching our destination. We were out in the boonies and after trying everything; I was at a total loss as to what was wrong with it and how we were going to get to the finish line of our journey. Finally I put the hood down, laid hands on it and prayed for it's healing. The car started right up and purred like a kitten. We drove it to the nearest garage to have it thoroughly inspected but it was found to have nothing wrong with it.

Three months into our church planting, I still hadn't found employment. It was now Christmas Eve and our savings were pretty much dried up. We had just enough to pay the rent of $495 for our apartment at the end of the month but no money for food, Christmas gifts for our boys, or spending money going into the New Year. The mail came that morning and Pam and I began to open the letters, some junk mail, a small bill or two, but also several personal letters and Christmas cards from friends and family back home. One of the letters had a $20 bill in it. Then a Christmas card had a $100 cheque inside. After a few more letters and cards were opened up, we had a total of $475 in our hands. We looked at each other and at the last letter, wondering, "Is it possible there could be $20 in this last one"?

We opened It up and sure enough, there was a crisp $20 bill, giving us a total of $495, the exact amount of our month's rent!

After we hugged, cried for joy and thanked our heavenly Father for His precise provision, we were able to thoroughly enjoy the Christmas season with our boys stress free and blessed. By the way, the church plant was right on track in terms of seeing God answer our prayer targets and goals for the end of the year.

By mid January, when those funds were just about gone, I received a phone call at eight in the morning. It was a bus company that I had applied to months earlier. They were offering me a part time school bus run driving deaf children out to the deaf school at the other end of the city. I jumped at the offer.

Two hours later there was a mysterious knock on the door. It was a complete stranger who said that he was a carpenter and was wondering if I would like to help him build an addition on a house. I told him I had just accepted a bus-driving job that involved two hours in the early morning and two hours late in the afternoon but that maybe I could help him in the middle of the day. Turns out that the deaf school was just a few blocks away from the house that needed renovating and I was able to go right to the work site with the bus every day. My bus boss was delighted to save on mileage and gas with his bus and I was thrilled to save on two hours of driving daily, while still getting paid for it.

The house was owned by wonderful Christians and during that half a year of renovations they and I got to share our faith with my carpenter boss. And the part-time school bus soon turned into an amazing full-time charter bus driving job with the choicest charter trips on the beautiful west coast that often entailed times of waiting for groups. I would get large chunks of quality time with the Lord, reading, praying, preparing teachings, worshiping the Lord on my guitar and working on my worship song list for Sunday, all while getting paid! This job so complimented my work in church planting. I could not have dreamed of orchestrating things better myself. I could go on for pages giving testimony to the Father's abundant provision in that adventure and the many adventures of faith since.

I think I'll mention one other time when Father opened a door and brought astounding provision for us in such a custom made and personal way. This occasion is not during a time of doing exploits and enjoying victory, but rather a time of going through personal defeat, the "dark night of the soul".

It was the late 1990s. After a series of emotional blows to the stomach that came one after the other, my wife slipped into a dark and deep clinical depression. These rapid fire crises included: our church having a parting of the ways with our denomination, followed by a painful church split among dear friends, the passing away of both our mothers and the threat of a law suit against our church by an unstable woman. Add to that string of events the fact that for years I had been a mild workaholic in pastoral ministry (the church had become my mistress) that often left my wife and children getting the leftovers of my time and emotional energy resulting in my marriage being in serious trouble.

Finally I hit the wall, completely burned out. We had been pastoring this wonderful church in Ontario for almost eight years and we had taken teams out all over the world for several years in the outpouring of the Spirit that we were privileged to be a part of. I was wisely advised to resign, get a job and just pastor my wife and three children for a season. We left the church and that town with our tail between our legs, feeling so defeated and bad that we had let the people down.

At this critical point, the Lord graciously provided outside prophetic encouragement and hope. One word included the promise that "the Lord will make a way where there is no way". Another word, which was so specific to our situation, gave us genuine hope for our marriage and a future in ministry. Our Father then miraculously opened up a Christian retreat center on a beef cattle farm up in the rolling hills of the Niagara Escarpment for us to live and work on. Pam and I have never experienced the tangible kindness of the Father that powerfully before. We felt totally spoiled by Him. This beautiful paradise provided a precious season of God restoring us in mind, body, and spirit as well as our marriage and family. We learned first hand that the Father does not write us off and discard us when we blow it. He really does have a heart to provide, protect and restore His children, not begrudgingly and stingily but with indescribable generosity and lavishness.

Speaking of lavishness of the Father, Graham Cooke recalls the time the Lord dared him, "Graham, you have the resources of heaven at your disposal. Try bankrupting me"! Graham is not only a contemporary prophetic teacher in the body of Christ, but a man with a delightfully child-like faith who actually has fun stepping out and seeing God come through for him again and again. He loves to point out that "the devil works on a limited budget but the Father's resources have no limit whatsoever"! So dare to believe Him. Dare to trust Him. Go ahead. Try to bankrupt heaven.

Before we move on from our discussion of the Father heart of God, let's look at what the prophet Isaiah had to say about the Father, in Isaiah 53:10, "Yet it was the pleasure of the Father to crush him".

Far from being a passionless God, we get a glimpse of the Father who so longs for a bride for His beloved Son that He willed that His Son be killed, crushed (disfigured beyond human recognition, Isa. 52:14). This would provide a way for a sinful, wayward girl to be redeemed and fashioned into a pure and passionate bride to be "equally yoked" to His one and only Son.

Jesus, the Passionate Bridegroom

I was always taught growing up that the parable of the pearl of great price, found in Matthew 13:45-46, is all about us selling everything to gain the Kingdom of God, the pearl of great price. Indeed, that is a very valid application of truth from this parable that challenges us to make gaining the Kingdom of God the top priority in our lives.

But the pearl of great price is actually referring to you and me and the merchant is Jesus who laid it all down to gain us as His reward and inheritance! His suffering and death upon the cross paid it all. Perhaps the most romantic and heroic story line in history is the theme of a king who had somehow had his bride, or soon to be bride, stolen from him and he goes to outrageous lengths to get her back, sailing the farthest seas, fighting costly battles with dragons and armies to see her rescued and returned to him. And when we begin to get a revelation of the passionate longing in our King's heart for us and the great lengths He has gone for us, everything changes.

I first heard the term, "bridal paradigm" through the ministry of Mike Bickle and his associates at the International House of Prayer ministry in Kansas City. This bridal paradigm is not new in our day. It is a biblical theme that has been valued in various times throughout church history within the Catholic and Orthodox expressions of the Christian Church but sadly lacking in the Protestant and Evangelical world. Maybe it is related to the strong Protestant work ethic we have developed over the years, causing us to be quite activity-based, performance-oriented and productivity minded. We have been more like Martha than Mary, concerned with the many necessary things, but at the expense of the one needful thing that Mary chose - sitting at the feet of Jesus in heart to heart communion and devotion. (Luke 10:38-42)[14]

But fresh revelation is increasingly coming to the church in these last days regarding Jesus and His ravaging heart of passion for us. This is the Divine Romance at the very center of creation and the universe. He is the glorious Bridegroom who wholeheartedly delights in us and who intensely longs for deeper and more intimate communion with us now, not just when He returns.

His first coming was as a humble and vulnerable babe born to a nervous teenager. He grew up to be the suffering servant King, the perfect Lamb of God, who rode into Jerusalem on a colt of a donkey, a symbol of peace and humility, and willingly took a beating and a crushing of His life as a ransom for us.

The description of His second coming couldn't be more of a startling contrast however. He will return in spectacular fashion as the mighty Warrior King and Bridegroom riding on a great white horse to do battle with His wicked enemies and, with blood splattered on His robes, He will violently take over the governments of the world, setting wrongs right, establishing His just and glorious Kingdom and collecting His awaiting bride, His treasured possession, throwing a celebration called the wedding supper of the Lamb, and then have His bride rule and reign with Him!

The Third Person of the Trinity

I grew up in church circles that seemed to believe in the Trinity as God the Father, God the Son, and God the Holy Bible. The Holy Spirit was rarely mentioned other than in reference to His limited job description of convicting and sanctifying people. And His King James name apparently was "Holy Ghost", which made young boys like me not want to be within miles of where He or It might be.

But over the years, more modern translations were being used and I started hearing the term, "Holy Spirit" which was more user-friendly. With the Charismatic and Jesus movements in the 1970s, the Holy Spirit was not only talked about more openly and frequently, but as a "He" who has a personality and feelings. He could be grieved and He could release joy, peace and love into people's hearts. He not only wrote God's bestseller, the Bible, our road map for life, but He also offers to be our ever-present personal tour guide in life.

It didn't take long before I was beginning to see intriguing outward signs of His whereabouts from time to time in a Christian gathering of some kind. Sometimes it was hearing someone speaking in tongues and an interpretation, or a prophetic word of love and encouragement or a physical healing or just the sweet sense of His nearness in heartfelt worship of Jesus. His presence mildly caught my imagination and curiosity in those days and I began to make the warm association that wherever the Holy Spirit was moving, there was life, joy and delightfully unpredictable things happening. Church wasn't nearly as boring and routine anymore.

But it wasn't until the 1980s and 90s that the person and work of the Holy Spirit became an extremely positive and precious doctrine and experience in both my head and heart. Now I understand and appreciate why Jesus said in John 16:7:

"I tell you the truth, it is to your advantage that I go away. Unless I go away, the Counselor will not come to you."

Yes, Jesus goes on to say that the Spirit of truth will convict the world, guide us into all truth and glorify the Son. But in John

14:16-18, Jesus says, "And I will ask the Father, and he will give you **another Counselor** to be with you forever...But you know him, for he lives with you and will be in you. I will not leave you as orphans."

The Greek word, "counselor", is "paraclete", one who is called to come along side to help. I find it a powerful revelation to realize that the Holy Spirit comes along side and even lives within us, to encourage and empower. He is "The Encourager, Par Excellence". And it is doubly powerful to hear Jesus say that the Father will send "another" counselor.

In the Greek, there are two words for "another", "heteron" and "allon". "Heteron" means "another of a different kind". It would be like holding a banana in one hand and saying "this is a piece of fruit" and an orange in the other hand and saying "and this is another piece of fruit". "Allon", however, means "another of exactly the same kind" which would be like holding a banana in one hand and saying "this is one piece of fruit" and a banana in the other hand and saying, "here's another (exactly the same kind) piece of fruit".

The word used in John 14:16 is the word "allon", intentionally communicating to us that the Holy Spirit is exactly the same as Jesus. If you like, love, trust and feel safe with Jesus, you will also like, love, trust and feel safe with the Holy Spirit. In fact, the Holy Spirit, at times, is referred to in Scripture as "the Spirit of Christ" (Rom. 8:9), "the Spirit of Jesus Christ" (Phil 1:19), "the Spirit of his Son" (Gal. 4:6) and "Christ in you, the hope of glory" (Col. 1:27).

While Jesus is in heaven interceding for us (Heb. 7:24, 25), the Holy Spirit is inside us interceding on our behalf and assisting us in our intercession. (Rom. 8:26, 27) And the Spirit of adoption enables us to cry out "Abba Father". (Rom 8:15-18; Gal. 4:6 7)

As much as we miss having Jesus here on earth in the flesh, it is true that it really is to our advantage to have an identical Counselor as Jesus who can be everywhere and in every believer all at the same time. To the Holy Spirit who is the down payment guaranteeing our inheritance, who releases the gifts of the Spirit and grows the fruit of the Spirit in our lives, who appropriates all that Christ accomplished on the cross to our side of the relationship, and who is the Spirit of adoption enabling us to cry out "Abba Father" and be part of the family of God, we say: "keep coming Holy Spirit"!

"May the grace of the Lord Jesus Christ, and the love of God, and the fellowship of the Holy Spirit be with you all". (2 Cor. 13:14)

It is in the grace, love and companionship with the three Persons of the Trinity that we truly experience all that God has in mind for us, including the deepest pleasures imaginable. But the enemy of our souls is determined to do everything in his power to undermine and spoil this divine arrangement. In the next chapter we will discuss this very real battle that we all find ourselves engaged in.

Recommended books:

Pleasure and Intimacy with God:

Desiring God, John Piper, Multnomah Press, 1986, 1996
Pleasures Evermore: The Life-Changing Power of Enjoying God, Sam Storms, Navpress, 2000
Pure Pleasure, Why Do Christians Feel so Bad about Feeling Good, Gary Thomas, Zondervan, 2009
The Divine Embrace, Ken Gire, Alive Communications Inc., 2003
The Pleasures of Loving God, Mike Bickle, Creation House, 2000
After God's own Heart, Mike Bickle, Charisma House, 2009
The Seven Longings of the Human Heart, Mike Bickle, Forerunner Books, 2006
Face to Face with God, Bill Johnson, Charisma House, 2007
Strengthen Yourself in the Lord, Bill Johnson, Destiny Image, 2007
The Ecstasy of Loving God, John Crowder, Destiny Image, 2009
The Fire of God's Love, Bob Sorge, Oasis House, 1996

Father Heart of God:

The Father Heart of God, Floyd McClung, Kingsway Pub., 1985
The Father Loves You, Ed Piorek, Vineyard International Pub., 1999
He Loves Me, Wayne Jacobsen, Windblown Media, 2007

From Orphans to Heirs: , Mark Stibbe, The Bible Reading Fell., Oxford, 1999
The Father's Blessing, John Arnott, Creation House, 1996
Experiencing the Father's Embrace, Jack Frost, Charisma H., 2002
The Supernatural Ways of Royalty, Kris Vallotton & Bill Johnson, Destiny Image, 2006
Our Covenant God, Learning to Trust Him, Kay Arthur, Waterbrook Press, 1999

Jesus:

The Jesus I never Knew, Phillip Yancey, Zondervan, 1995
No Wonder They Call Him the Savior, Max Lucado, Multnomah Press, 1986
Passion For Jesus, Mike Bickle, Charisma House, 1993
The Sacred Romance, Brent Curtis & John Eldredge, Thomas Nelson, 1997
Wild at Heart, John Eldredge, Thomas Nelson, 2001
Waking the Dead:The Glory of a Heart Fully Alive, John Eldredge, Thomas Nelson,2003
What's So Amazing About Grace? Philip Yancey, Zondervan, 1997
In the Grip of Grace, Max Lucado, Word Pub., 1996
From Eternity to Here: Rediscovering the Ageless Purpose of God, Frank Viola, 2009, David C. Cook Pub., Colorado Springs, CO.

The Holy Spirit:

I Believe in the Holy Spirit, Michael Green, Eerdmanns, 1985, 2004
The Giving Gift: The Holy Spirit in Person, Thomas Smail, Hodder & Stoughton, 1988
Keep in Step with the Spirit, J.I. Packer, Fleming H. Revell, 1984
Good Morning Holy Spirit, Benny Hinn, Thomas Nelson, 1990
Fire and Blood, Mark Stibbe, Monarch Books, 2001
The Anointing, R. T. Kendall, Thomas Nelson, 1999
The Sensitivity of the Spirit, R. T. Kendall, Charisma House, 2002
Hosting the Holy Spirit, Che Ahn, editor, Renew Books, 2000

Notes:

1. Blaise Pascal, Pascal's Pensees, trans. by W. F. Trotter (N.Y:E. P. Dutton, 1958), p. 113, cited in Desiring God, John Piper, Multnomah Press, 1986, 1996, p. 16.
2. Gary Thomas, Pure Pleasure, Zondervan, 2009, p. 16.
3. Sam Storm, Pleasures Evermore, Navpress, 2000, p. 111.
4. John Crowder, The Ecstasy of Loving God, Destiny Image Pub., 2009, p. 27.
5. John Piper, Desiring God, Multnomah Press, 1986, 1996, p. 17.
6. Ibid., p. 18.
7. Gary Wiens, Bridal Intercession, Oasis Pub., 2001, p. 184.
8. John Piper, Desiring God, p. 15.
9. John Crowder, The Ecstasy of Loving God, p. 19.
10. John Piper, Desiring God, pp. 132, 133, citing the autobiography of George Mueller, compiled by Fred Bergen, London: J. Nisbet Co., 1906, pp. 152-154).
11. Fred Wright, The World's Greatest Revivals, Destiny, 2007.
12. Thomas Smail, The Forgotten Father, Eerdmans, 1980, p. 73.
13. Mark Stibbe, in a sermon given at Jubilee Celebration Centre, Orillia, Ontario, Canada, Jan. 22, 2012.
14. Gary Wiens, Bridal Intercession, pp. 22, 23.

Chapter 5

Spiritual Warfare 101 (micro level)

Part 1

" *T*he thief comes only to steal and kill and destroy; I have
come that they may have life, and have it to the full."
Jesus, John 10:10

"Guard your heart, for it is the wellspring of life." Proverbs 4:23

"You are not what you think you are. There is a glory to your life
that your Enemy fears, and he is hell-bent on destroying that glory
before you act on it." John Eldridge

One of my favourite authors, John Eldridge, in his brilliant book,
Waking the Dead, gives us three crucial truths that provide us clarity
about our situation.

Firstly, **"things are not what they seem**. There is a whole lot
more going on here than meets the eye". There is an unseen world
that is more real and dangerous than the part of reality we can see.

Secondly, **"this is a world at war**. We live in a far more dramatic,
far more dangerous story than we ever imagined." In 1 John 5:19,
the apostle John laments, "the whole world is under the control of
the evil one." One of the reasons we love stories like The Chronicles
of Narnia or the Matrix or The Lord of the Rings is because we

intuitively recognize and relate to the truth communicated that there is a battle going on between good and evil and we long to see the good triumph over evil.

Thirdly, **"we have a crucial role to play."** Whether it is Frodo, "the most unlikely person imaginable", to be flung into the role as the Ring Bearer in Lord of the Rings or a teenager who gets to slay a giant in the Old Testament, or the impetuous Peter who steps up to lead the early church in turning the world upside down in the New Testament, so, too, you and I have been called for such a time as this to step into a bigger story that entails very real danger and adventure. Our days will no longer be ordinary and mundane. These dangerous days are dripping with destiny.

We consider ourselves as pretty ordinary, however. It has not fully dawned on us as to who we really are in Christ. The devil knows who we truly are and shudders at the thought of us waking up to our delegated authority in Him and discovering our calling and mission in life. "The hour is late, and you are needed. So much hangs in the balance. Where is your heart?"[1]

Throughout history, there's been a war going on for the hearts of men. After the fall, God has been seeking to win our hearts with His incredible love and bring us back into the embrace of His blessing, joy, and life. The glory of God is man fully alive. But Satan seeks to rob, kill, and destroy us by neutralizing, dividing, hardening, wounding and offending our hearts and deceiving our minds.

At the close of this present evil age, this cosmic battle will only heat up and come to a grand finale with the very visible and spectacular return of Jesus Christ. In Revelation 12:9, we are informed that, "Satan, who leads the whole world astray. He was hurled to the earth and his angels with him." Verse 12 declares "But woe to the earth and the sea, because the devil has gone down to you! He is filled with fury, because he knows that his time is short."

The devil, knowing his days are numbered, and that Christ decisively defeated him at the cross, lashes out like an injured and threatened animal.

Satan hates what God loves and our hearts our central to God. In fact, your heart is your most precious possession. God promises that if we seek Him with our whole heart, He will be found by us.

(Jeremiah 29:13) His eyes roam the earth searching for those whose hearts are fully committed to Him so He can show His power in and through them. (II Chronicles 16:9) He longs for us to love and trust Him with our whole heart (first commandment) and He laments when His people perform their duties but their hearts are far from Him. (Isaiah 29:13)

With unbelieving, wounded and self-absorbed hearts, we are easy prey of the enemy. Our sin, if not repented of, gives him the legal right to hassle us further. Like flies attracted to a pile of garbage, some measure of demonic harassment, entrapment or demonization becomes a very real possibility.

It was the last night of a great week at teen camp up in the mountains near Hope, British Columbia in the summer of 1982. About eighty young people came from all around the province to our annual youth camp. I was a part time youth pastor in the denomination's flagship church in Vancouver while in seminary. The formal meeting around the campfire was done. Many were chatting among themselves while being delightfully mesmerized by the beauty and dance of the flames. I was quietly strumming my guitar with a few next to me singing along. What a relaxing and satisfying way to wrap up an awesome week with great friends in God's wondrous creation.

Then I heard it. It sounded like a dog growling on the far side of the circle. I ignored it at first because I didn't want to leave the warmth and comfort of the fire. Besides, there were other youth pastors and counselors among the crowd who could deal with whatever it was. But soon my gut, or inside "knower" was telling me that there was something very dark and sinister going on and that I could no longer ignore it.

I set my guitar down, left the light and warmth of the fire and went around the crowd and into the blackness of the night to where all the commotion seemed to be coming from. I was stunned to get there and see, under the dim light of a flashlight or two, a young guy, from my youth group, rolling in the dust and growling like an animal. His friends around him were at a loss as to what to do. I had worked in institutions for the mentally handicapped for a couple of years and had some experience helping people during an epileptic seizure but this was different Soon a counselor or two and some friends were holding him down and frantically yelling as loud as they could (as if volume gives you more authority) for the devil to come out in Jesus' name. I stood there stunned, trying to process what I was seeing and hearing.

Finally the boy stopped writhing about, went quiet and still. We all came close to see how he was doing. In a trance like state, he began to look at each face and very slowly and softly address each one by name and say complimentary things about them, which seemed to wow everybody. I was still agitated in my spirit sensing that this was not the Lord and that whatever evil entity had a hold of him was still there and now trying to con us all with a different tactic. I could sense that he was lapping up all the attention he was getting in this moment from all his friends and it just felt so wrong.

After debriefing with the other leaders the next morning about Friday night's bizarre episode we packed up and headed for home. My good friend, Barry, a worker with a Christian youth organization in Vancouver, who had been there as a camp counselor, told me of a fellow staff worker who had considerable experience in deliverance ministry and offered to contact him and see if he could assist us.

I also raced to Vancouver's biggest evangelical Christian bookstore that Saturday afternoon to see if they had any material on demons and deliverance. All I could come up with was a thick book that was a compilation of academic lectures by some American Christian Psychology group that had one meager chapter on demonization that was totally impractical for my situation. All I knew was that we were way out of our league when it came to this kind of stuff and probably did everything wrong when dealing with the situation. But I tell you; I was one motivated boy who was catapulted into a very steep learning curve.

So come Sunday afternoon, Barry and I and his deliverance friend sat down with this teenage boy at our non-charismatic church to minister to him. Or I should say Barry and I observed while his friend ministered. It was quite an educational experience to say the least to see the process of counseling and praying with him to see him set free. Through it all, the teen admitted that some spiritual entity had come to him some time back when he and his family first moved from Asia to Canada and worked out a deal with him with a promise to give the boy extra physical strength to play sports extremely well and provide him with friends and popularity.

Can a Christian have a demon? I didn't use to think so. In fact, I didn't really think demons were around North America. If any were still around after Bible days, they must be mostly in Africa. I had such a disconnect between the biblical stories about the demonic and our modern day. This truly was a wake up call for me.

For years I had followed the traditional syllogism of logic (which is a theological presupposition, not a biblical certainty based on Scriptural exegesis), which goes like this:

The major premise: Every Christian is in dwelt by the Holy Spirit
The minor premise: The Holy Spirit cannot dwell with demons
The conclusion: Christians cannot have demons.

Yet, I didn't insist on having to follow this syllogism of logic:

The major premise: Every Christian is in dwelt by the Holy Spirit
The minor premise: The Holy Spirit cannot dwell with sin.
The conclusion: Christians cannot sin.[2]

I've come to realize that though a true Christian cannot be fully demon possessed, a believer can be demonized in some measure. Ranging from mild to severe and operating from either outside or inside, demons can directly oppress and harass even Christians. This usually is connected to either habitual sin of the individuals in question or the sin of others against them (ie. sexual sin, control and manipulation). In some cases the demonization may have taken place prior to their conversion to Christ or could be passed down generationally.

Of course the form of demonic harassment most common to mankind is temptation. Even Jesus, the One who knew no sin and on whom the enemy had no hold, experienced temptation. Temptation itself is not a sin. It is only when one gives in to the allurement. Martin Luther said, "You can't stop a bird from flying around your head but you can keep it from building a nest in your hair"!

In the preface to his short but punchy book, Screwtape Letters, C. S. Lewis urges us to avoid the extremes of either ignorance or fascination of the enemy because either extreme seems to serve his purposes well. Lewis states that, "There are two equal and opposite errors in to which our race can fall about the devils. One is to disbelieve in their existence. The other is to believe, and to feel an excessive and unhealthy interest in them. They themselves are equally pleased by both errors..."[3]

According to research done by the Barna Group, only twenty-six percent of the American population believe that Satan is a real spiritual being. And surprisingly only fifty-two percent of born-again Christians actually believe that Satan is real.[4]

And while belief in the reality of the devil and his minions has seriously declined in our western scientifically minded society, ironically a growing fascination with the dark side of the spiritual world and its supernatural dimensions is reaching fever pitch through the arts and entertainment industry, New Age, witchcraft and the occult. So the extremes Lewis warns of are flourishing in this hour.

Now if half of the so-called Christian population is in denial of the devil's existence, no wonder we have a weak and impotent church. John Eldridge argues that, "To live in ignorance of spiritual warfare is the most naive and dangerous thing a person can do. It's like skipping through the worst part of town, late at night, waving your wallet above your head...you don't escape spiritual warfare simply because you choose not to believe it exists or because you refuse to fight it."[5]

Recognizing the Primary Ways Satan Seeks to Neutralize Us and Bring Us Down

Many of us, however, are very aware that there is a crafty and cunning devil and that he intensely desires to keep our hearts far from the Lover of our soul. Scripture is clear that the father of lies continuously seeks to:

Tempt, seduce us (often in the realms of money, sex & power) condemn us

distract us
intimidate us
flatter us
depress us and
divide and conquer us.

This adversary will not play by the rules. Though he is dangerous and clever, he is not equal to God. He is no match for the God of light and love - not even close. Lucifer is a limited created being who cannot create. Using smoke and mirrors, all this con artist can do is mimic, counterfeit, twist and distort the truth and God's beautiful creation. Like a black hole, the devil seeks to suck the light and life out of everything God has created and holds dear.

For instance, in Acts 1:8, we see that God promises his devoted disciples that they will be clothed with power (Greek word is "dunamis", where we get the word, dynamite) when the Holy Spirit comes upon them and they shall be privileged to be His witnesses (Greek word is "martureis", where we get the word, martyr) to bring God's love, life and blessing to the nations of the earth.

But what does the enemy do? He looks at what God does and not only seeks to counter it but mimic it and acquire front-page attention in the process. The terrorizer comes up with a life sucking counterfeit by taking zealous religious fundamentalists with a cause to die and kill for, clothing them with actual dynamite and making literal martyrs out of them, leaving a bloody trail of never ending hatred, carnage and cursing.

What he does on a global scale he also seeks to do on an individual. The serpent is determined to dis-hearten us and get us to believe the lie that God is not good, not all powerful and certainly not worthy of our trust, affection and praise. He instills unbelief, plays on our fears and feeds our pride. He is committed to your undoing and mine.

We need to have a greater awareness of who our enemy is and as to the many ways and realms or arenas in which he operates. According to Ephesians 2:1-3, **the devil** forms an unholy alliance with **the world and the flesh**, creating a trinity of evil, which counterfeits the Holy Trinity. Our uncrucified sinful nature combined with a world system that denies God's goodness and relevance becomes fodder for the god of this age to wreak havoc with God's creation.

The battlegrounds in this war can be found both at the micro (flesh) and macro levels (world), that is, in the hearts and minds of precious human beings as well as in the infrastructures of culture and nations. The enemy is seeking to intensify his stranglehold on both fronts. In this chapter we are focusing more on the warfare to do with our flesh.

In later chapters we will give greater attention to the macro level in which Satan seeks global conquest through a one world government, economy and religion as well as through his dominating the "seven mountains" or sectors of influence in society: religion, business/economy, politics, education, media, arts and entertainment, and the family.

Although the institution of marriage and the family is considered one of the seven mountains of culture at the macro level, let me address this subject here, as it is so foundational and deeply personal at the micro level of our hearts and relationships.

Satan's Assault of Marriage and the Family

God is a covenant making and covenant keeping God. The theme of covenant is found throughout the Bible. In fact, our Bible is made up of two parts: the Old Testament and the New Testament. Testament is Latin for covenant. Paid for by the precious blood of Jesus, we live in a new and improved covenant, which is a superior covenant to the old. (Heb. 7:22; 8:6-13)

Not only do we have the privilege of being in a mind-boggling love covenant with the God of the universe through His Son, Jesus, but He has also created the breathtaking covenant of intimacy in marriage between a man and a woman (which mirrors the covenant of marriage between Christ and His bride).

Satan will do anything in his power to erode and destroy marriage covenants and relationships. Tragically Christian marriages end in divorce at about the same rate as the world (fifty percent). I'm not seeking to judge or condemn anyone. I know it is but by the grace of God that my marriage did not end during a dark valley a decade ago. The challenges and stresses of paying the bills, raising children, and seeking to keep communication lines open and the romance alive in a fallen world, is no small thing. Add to that the fact that the thief works overtime to break in to violate and vandalize this sacred and beautiful thing called marriage and we need all the grace, resources and back up available.

Thankfully the Lord has helped the church to provide an increasing array of practical resources and tools to arm ourselves to fight back and build stronger marriages and families. A countless number of amazing seminars, books, tapes and ministries such as Focus on the Family have arisen in recent decades to help try to turn the tide. Let me recommend a couple of tools that have been very helpful in our marriage: the book, The 5 Languages of Love, by Gary Chapman, as well as the practical and hilarious seminar called Laughing Your Way to a Better Marriage, by Mark Gungor (available in book and DVD format).

Of course, many of the issues that drive spouses apart have to do with our own baggage of emotional wounds, which we came into the marriage with. Often there are buried and unhealed hurts from childhood particularly in relation to either our mother or our father or both that need to be unpacked and addressed.

The need for repentance, forgiveness, renouncing of ungodly beliefs and inner vows, breaking off ungodly soul ties and pronouncing Father God's forgiveness and acceptance are all part of the healing process. Spiritual bondage, dysfunctional behaviours and addictions can all be addressed and defeated as the victory of the cross is appropriated in our lives by the power and leading of the Holy Spirit. We are thankful to the Lord for a plethora of effective materials and prayer counseling ministries that are available to the body of Christ to assist in this vital process of restoration of the heart as well as marriages and relationships of all kinds.

Let me mention as well, that if you or anyone in your family, including past generations have been involved in secret societies such as freemasonry, I would urge you to get informed about the consequences of such idolatrous involvement. Dark secrecy and oaths are not only detrimental to intimacy and transparency within a marriage, but seriously hampers one's spiritual life and places very real curses upon the family.

The booklet, Unmasking Freemasonry, by my New Zealand friend, Dr. Selwyn Stevens of Jubilee Resources, provides excellent information as well as prayers of repentance and renunciation for setting family members free of such curses. It has been quite sobering to me to not only realize how pervasive freemasonry and other secret societies and fraternities have been throughout the centuries and nations, but also in Christian families and churches. Enough is enough. After generations of families being deeply entrenched, often naively, in such dark deception and bondage, God is on the move in recent years to expose it and call people to repent and renounce this evil idolatry and come into greater freedom and wholeness in Christ.

The Family and the Last Generation

There seem to be three pivotal times in history that the enemy has sought to work more furiously to particularly kill the younger generation. It was during a kairos moment in time in which God was orchestrating a major rescue mission of some kind. In the time of Moses, the devil anticipated it and had the Hebrew baby boys killed by the Egyptian Pharaoh. Centuries later we see a jealous King Herod slaughter all the baby boys after the birth of King Jesus, causing Joseph, Mary and the Christ child to become temporary refugees in Africa. And as we approach the end of the age and the emerging of a generation that God plans to use in paradigm jarring ways, we have seen a demonic culture of death being unleashed on the earth under a polished user-friendly veneer called "Pro-Choice" and Planned Parenthood.

America has seen over fifty million babies murdered since the Wade vs. Roe decision to legalize abortion in 1973. With our western culture frowning upon large families and concerned about the environmental footprint, we see the birth rate per woman ranging between 1.1 and 1.6, well below the level of sustainability of a society. Statistics compiled in countries like Russia, China and

India show that they have slaughtered even more children (thirteen million in China and eleven million in India in 2009 alone).[6]

If he can't have them killed before birth, Satan will seek to have this generation of children inflicted with heavy damage through divorce, absent fathers, dysfunctional family woundings, and unbelievably intense peer pressure in a drug induced and sex crazed youth culture. The enemy has also spawned a horrendous human trafficking and sex slave trade of innocent children in Asia and around the world that we are only beginning to wake up to. The demonic forces seek to enslave children and youth and derail them from ever discovering their true identity in the love of God and from ever coming into their God given calling and destiny at this critical hour.[7]

Aside from primary care and protection, we need to recognize the strategic value of verbally blessing, affirming and empowering our children throughout their upbringing as well as providing a formal blessing and celebration as they transition into manhood or womanhood. At the end of the chapter I recommend some books on blessing.

We need to keep communication lines open, love them unconditionally, pray and cheer them on to become all God wants them to be as young, passionate and fearless men and women of God. We want to see and believe for this next generation to stand on our shoulders. We want our ceiling to be their floor in terms of experiences with God and their partnering with Him to do great exploits for the Kingdom of God before the final wrap up and return of the King.

Knowing Your Enemy and How He Assaults Our Hearts and Minds

The apostle Paul expresses concern that we not be ignorant of Satan's schemes or allow him to outwit us. (2 Cor. 2:10, 11) The name, "Satan" is the Hebrew word for **accuser or slanderer**. The Greek equivalent is "diabolos" and in English the word is "devil". Satan constantly accuses us before God. The classic example in the Bible is that of Job. Revelation 12:10 speaks of our enemy being the accuser of the brethren who accuses us before God day and night. In contrast, Jesus is described as one who intercedes on behalf of the brethren 24/7. (Heb. 7:25)

So the question begs to be asked: whom are we aligning ourselves with and agreeing with? Are we partnering with Satan in judging and accusing others or are we seeing their weakness and struggles and choosing to join Jesus in interceding on their behalf?

Taking Offense

Of the many ways the devil seeks to assault our hearts and minds to bring us down, one of the most common and deadly is this thing called taking offense.

John Bevere, in his exceptional book, The Bait of Satan, aptly points out that, "Jesus made it very clear that it is impossible to live in this world and not have the opportunity to become offended. (Luke 17:1) Yet most believers are shocked, bewildered, and amazed when it happens. We believe we are the only ones who have been wronged. This response leaves us vulnerable to a root of bitterness. Therefore we must be prepared and armed for offenses, because our response determines our future."[8]

In the course of everyday life, taking offense at someone is a very serious matter with very destructive consequences. This is even more so as we approach the wrap up of history as we know it. One of many deadly signs that Jesus warned would be prevalent at the end of the age was that:

"At that time **many will turn away from the faith** and betray and hate each other..." (Matt. 24:10)

The Greek word behind the words "turn away" or "fall away" in some translations is the word, "scandalize", meaning, "to take offense". To be scandalized has two ancient picture meanings.

Firstly, it means to be ensnared or entrapped. The skandalon was literally the bait stick or arm in an animal trap where the bait was placed, setting it up for an animal to be lured to its capture or destruction.

Secondly, it means stumbling block or offense, something set in a man's path, usually small, to trip him up.

The consequences of taking offense and holding a grudge against another will include your Christian faith taking a serious hit followed by your heart engaging in betrayal and hatred of another. The next two verses (Mt. 24:11,12), spell out further consequences of being vulnerable to deception, increased wickedness and one's love going icy cold. Verse 13 claims that the person who does not give in to this tactic of the diabolical con artist but "stands firm to the end will be saved."

In Matthew 13:53-58, we see that Jesus could do very few miracles in his hometown, not only because of their lack of faith, but because they took offense at Him and did not give Him honour. So even the release of supernatural healings and miracles can be log jammed by unbelieving, jealous and offended people.

In Matthew 15:12, we see that the religious Pharisees were offended by Jesus because He cut right into their cherished traditions. The religious spirit specializes in setting the bait of offense to ensnare the hearts of Christians and church folk who cling to their religious traditions. And in this day of everything being shaken that can be shaken, including the traditions of man, the hearts of man will be tested and many will end up deeply offended.

Another occasion for people to take offense, according to Jesus' teaching of the parable of the sower, is the one who initially hears the word and receives it with joy but does not grow roots that go down deep. "When trouble or persecution comes because of the word, he quickly falls away." (literally "becomes scandalized" Matt. 13:21,22)

I wonder if this could very well be a major contributing factor to the great falling away from the faith, the great apostasy, at the end of the age that Jesus warns us about. When trouble and persecution confront many Christians, particularly those who hold to a theology that promises them an escape from such things, they may be totally blindsided and ill-equipped to face such pressures, resulting in an offense against Jesus for not coming to their rescue.

So, we see three occasions in which people take offense at God (which will increase in frequency and intensity as we come to the end of the age):

1) His performing supernatural acts such as healings and all kinds of miracles,
2) His upsetting men's precious religious traditions, and
3) Allowing His people to go through trials, tribulations, persecution and even martyrdom for some.

Much of the burden I carry in writing this book is a longing to help as many as possible to prepare for what is coming by making the necessary mid-flight corrections in their mindsets so that such offenses against the Lord can be avoided and greater participation in His kingdom agenda can be realized.

Regardless of how the close of the age plays out in detail, we cannot deny that we are presently in the thick of a war - a battle for our hearts. If the devil can get your heart wounded and offended at God or somebody else and you allow bitterness to fester and grow like a cancer, he's got you neutralized and trapped, without you fully realizing it. A person tends to be oblivious to their heart's condition because they are so focused on the wrong that was done to them. Regardless of whether you have been genuinely mistreated or just think you have, the devil seeks to make us believe we are justified in taking an offense. The devil pushes us to demand justice while the Lord desires mercy to triumph over judgment.

When we do not process our wounds in a Christ-like manner, bitterness and resentment end up growing like poison in the body and those around us get defiled in the process. (Hebrews 12:15) Rather than going to the person or persons who we feel have hurt us and sorting it out as Jesus instructs us to (Matt. 18:15-17), we tend to bury the hurt and feed and pamper it by rehearsing the mistreatment over and over again in our head. We then take every opportunity to verbally vomit on others in hopes of getting them to take our side and share in the offense.

It is often those closest to us that disappoint us or by whom we feel betrayed. Many a friendship, business partnership, marriage, family and church have been torn apart and destroyed by this ugly parasite, leaving people bleeding, the Holy Spirit grieving and the devil grinning.

Judging others

With unforgiveness and offense in our hearts, we easily become critical and judgmental. Scripture warns us however, of the fact that in the same manner and measure that we judge others, so we will be judged. (Matt. 7:1, 2) So if you are going to dish it out, you'd better be prepared to have it come back to bite you.

One particular day when our boys were young and playing in organized baseball one of the kids needed to find a bathroom just as we arrived at their baseball game at the elementary school. We quickly decided that I would take our other two children over to the game while my wife drove a block away to a coffee shop bathroom. Trying to hurry because the game would soon begin, Pam backed the van smack into a basketball pole, smashing the back window and denting the bumper. I don't think I verbally chewed her out but inside I was fit to be tied. I was not a happy camper - women drivers!

Fast forward to a year later, as we arrived at the very same school for another baseball game, one of our kids expressed their urgent need to find a washroom. This time I offered to drive (maybe it's worth mentioning that I consider myself a trained and experienced truck and bus driver) and promptly backed into the very same basketball pole and pushed the original dent on the van's bumper deeper still! Needless to say I ate humble pie and repented to Pam (and to the Lord) for my judgment of her and asked her and the Lord to forgive me. Hopefully I have learned from this costly lesson.

Scripture is very clear that we must not judge others. (James 4:12; 5:9) However, the Bible does instruct us to discern and judge rightly otherwise we may fall into sin and deception.

We are told to stop judging by mere appearance but make a right judgment. (John 7:24)

Regarding prophecy, Paul advises us to, "Test everything. Hold on to the good" (1 Thess. 5:21) and that "two or three prophets should speak, and the others should weigh carefully what is said". (1 Cor. 14:29)

Regarding immorality inside the church, this sin and a litany of others are not to be ignored but addressed with tough love. Paul states that "anyone who calls himself a brother but is sexually immoral or greedy, an idolater or a slanderer, a drunkard or a swindler. With such a man do not even eat". (1 Cor. 5:11) Keep in mind that Jesus gave step-by-step redemptive instructions, found in Matthew 18, on how to graciously but firmly deal with these matters.

He also bids us to examine our hearts and lives as we come to participate in the Lord's Supper. (1 Cor. 11:28)

The apostle John warns us to "test the spirits to see whether they are from God". (1 John 4:1)

So how do we know when we are judging rightly or wrongly?

Let me give you a simple breakdown of the difference between discerning and judging:

Godly Discernment	Ungodly Judgment
To evaluate, examine,	- to pass harsh judgment, react
Seeks truth & the facts	- doesn't wait for facts, pre-judges
Desires truth to help, restore	- enjoys tearing down
Focus is on individual	- lose sight of person, categorizes
Identifies with man's sin	- smug, self-righteous
Not shocked by sin of others	- appalled/despises their sin
Grieves over sin of others	- finds pleasure in fault-finding
Seeks to cover their nakedness	- delights in their sin exposed
Believes best of others	- guilty until proven innocent
Looks beyond appearances	- focuses on externals
Sees past action to situation	- judges their heart
Humble, compassionate spirit	- arrogant/critical spirit
Extends grace to the other	- demands justice
Slow to take offense	- easily offended, petty
Lets go of own rights	- demands own rights
Seeks to defend others	- defensive, justifies self
Quick to own up & repent	- quick to blame, doesn't own up

Security needs met	-feels insecure, insignificant
Seeks to build bridges	- keeps distance, us/them
Intercedes for others	- agrees with accuser of brethren
Flows from love in heart	- recognized by coldness

Ask yourself if you find yourself easily judging in any of these situations:

- People near you succeed easily/get promoted
- People who have not shown warmth towards you
- People who ignore, be thoughtless or rude to you
- People who appear overconfident
- People who talk too much
- People who dress too different for your liking
- People older or younger than yourself
- People of a different ethnic group/have a strong accent
- People of a different denomination or religion
- Leaders who don't meet your expectations
- People with more/less money than you & how they use it
- Left-brain versus right-brain dominant people
- People with different temperaments, tastes in music &art

The Bible is clear that:

- We are not authorized or qualified to judge others
- We will be judged in the same manner if we do so
- We must crucify our instinct to judge, catch ourselves & repent
- We need to grow in true discernment &our passion for Jesus
- We are invited to relax & leave the judging to God.

Someone once observed that, "No Christian is strong enough to carry a cross and a prejudice at the same time."

These assaults of the enemy are very real and very deadly. But we don't have to passively put up with this stuff. In the next chapter we will turn our attention to the issue of fighting back and overcoming with divinely ordained weapons of our warfare.

Notes:

1. John Eldridge, Waking the Dead, Thomas Nelson,2003,pp.26-35
2. Ed Murphy, The Handbook for Spiritual Warfare, Thomas Nelson, 1992. p. 431.
3. C.S. Lewis, The Screwtape Letters, The Macmillan Co., N.Y., first published 1943, p.3.
4. Os Hillman, The Change Agent, Creation House, 2011, p 93.
5. John Eldridge, p. 152.
6. Wikipedia, Abortion in Russia, http://en.wikipedia.org/wiki/Abortion_in_Russia (accessed July 21, 2012).
7. Os Hillman, pp. 114-120.
8. John Bevere, The Bait of Satan, Charisma House, 1994,1997, 2004, 2011, p. 6.

Chapter 6

Spiritual Warfare 101 (micro level) Part 2

Fighting Back with the Weapons of our Warfare

I have heard my spiritual father John Arnott, on more than one occasion speak insightfully regarding our Christian lives involving three journeys:

First is the *inward* journey (the need for healing of the heart through repentance and forgiveness, deliverance, sanctification and holiness of character).

Second is the *upward* journey in Him (praise and worship, prayer and fasting, intimacy with God and the fear of the Lord).

And thirdly, it involves the *outward* journey in mission and making a difference in the world. To avoid burn out and moral failure in this outward journey, we must give continual attention to the other two journeys.

Since we just addressed the issue of taking offense and judging others, let's begin by looking at forgiveness, which is a vital part of the inward journey and the most powerful antidote to these sins of the heart.

Forgiveness

It is impossible to not get hurt by someone at some point. But, by the grace of God, we can determine ahead of time that we will choose to develop a heart that refuses to take offense. We can choose to unilaterally forgive the person and if we find that we are not able to do that, then determine that we will care enough to confront them by going directly to the person in private, sharing with them honestly and humbly how their action has affected us, with the hope of gaining resolution and reconciliation.

The natural inclination of human nature however is to burn bridges and build walls. When another has wronged us, we believe that a debt is now owed to us. We want the other guy to pay up. We want to "get even". Or we at least find ourselves wanting to wallow in self-pity as a poor victim or martyr for a while. Somehow we seem to receive a sick or twisted form of pleasure out of it, at least momentarily.

I remember the time I got offended at another pastor in the city we were church planting. He had asked to borrow our drummer from time to time for a seminar or conference. Although we were a smaller church, the Lord had provided us with one of the best Christian drummers in the area. We were delighted to see him use his drumming gifts in a broader context in the body of Christ but after this particular weekend we caught wind that the pastor had been sending subtle overtures to him in hopes of winning him over to his church and worship team.

Our drummer reassured us that God had called him to be part of our church so it wasn't an issue of fearing we might lose him, but rather a sense of betrayal by a fellow pastor. I didn't have the guts to confront him. I thought I was spiritual enough to process it through and move on. However, over the coming week or two I found I couldn't shake it. I was struggling in my heart with feelings of betrayal and couldn't seem to be able to forgive and let it go.

One afternoon I was replaying the offense in my mind and arguing with God about it while driving down the street I lived on. I had just asked the Lord, "Lord, what should I do?" At that very moment I found my eyes mysteriously drawn to the license plate on the back of a parked car that I was driving past. The license plate said, "4 give". It hit me like a ton of bricks and I responded by saying "OK Lord, I choose to forgive". I felt a huge burden lift off my heart and spirit and I truly believed I had settled it for good.

However, while driving my car a week or two later, I felt this ugly resentment and unforgiveness begin to rise up in my heart again towards this pastor. (Forgiveness is a decision but it can also be a process that takes time.) I was, at that moment, driving through the parking lot at a nearby shopping mall, looking for a parking spot. Guess what my eyes happened to fall upon? Not an empty parking spot but that very same license plate and it was shouting at me, "4 give"! I was so stunned I stopped the car before I might have crashed into something and repented to the Lord right there and then as well I verbalized out loud, by an act of my will, that I choose to forgive so and so and release him into the freedom of my forgiveness. From that point on it was never an issue in my heart again. I continued to have a great relationship with that pastor and I got to enjoy seeing our phenomenal drummer be used in various venues beyond our church to bless so many, including the Lord. I never did see that license plate again.

Forgiveness is a powerful weapon against the enemy. It is about releasing the other person into the freedom of our forgiveness. It involves coming to the place in our heart where we are willing to let it go and let them go, declaring that they owe us nothing. God operates in mercy while the devil, who is a legalist, operates in judgment. By the grace of God we can choose, as an act of our will (feelings can catch up later), to forgive the person, which releases both us and the other party, allowing walls to come down and bridges to go up.

One day a woman came to our downtown storefront office for prayer and counseling from my good friend Zak, who was on our staff at the time, and my self. This woman had a very complicated situation in which the courts had temporarily given the care of the children to the ex-husband. She was naturally very upset and in great turmoil.

She was led through a prayer in which she willingly chose to let go of the anger and bitterness and forgive her ex-husband for many things, including his lack of cooperation in letting her have any contact with the kids. When she came out of the prayer room we saw a woman who looked so much lighter than the woman we saw go In. But none of us were prepared for what happened next. As we were talking with her in the open office area, her cell phone rang. It was her ex-husband calling, whom she hadn't been able to make contact with for sometime, to say in a warm and conciliatory manner, that he just had a change of heart and that he was willing for her to come anytime to see the kids. She and we were all stunned. Forgiveness really does bring freedom to the person holding unforgiveness and can release the Lord to work on both sides of a relationship, in this case within minutes!

The Old Testament tells the amazing story of Joseph who was betrayed by his brothers and sold into slavery in Egypt. Through a long process of passing a series of tests and trials, Joseph was promoted to a powerful place of influence in the land. When the season of famine came, Joseph had the opportunity to bring great blessing to untold multitudes, including his own father and brothers. Joseph eventually settled his family in Goshen, the most fertile land in the nation and provided them food in a desperate time of famine. Rather than rubbing their noses in their sin, Joseph chose to genuinely forgive them and bless them.

Genesis 50 provides interesting details to the story. Verse 15 tells us what the brothers said, "What if Joseph holds a grudge against us and pays us back for all the wrongs we did to him?" Verses 18-20 fill in the story with, "His brothers then came and threw themselves down before him. 'We are your slaves,' they said. But Joseph said to them, 'Don't be afraid. Am I in the place of God? You intended to harm me, but God intended it for good to accomplish what is now being done, the saving of many lives. So then, don't be afraid. I will provide for you and your children.' And he reassured them and spoke kindly to them."

Psalm 105:17-19 tells us, "and he sent a man before them - Joseph, sold as a slave. They bruised his feet with shackles, his neck was put in irons, till what he foretold came to pass, till the word of the LORD proved him true."

These tests purged Joseph's pride and arrogance so that he was then prepared to be used by God to help provide for God's people in the coming famine. If God has given you prophetic promises of promoting you to a place of significance and of being a great blessing to others, be prepared to be tested with such things as betrayal and rejection.

Rick Joyner has provided the body of Christ with many wise and prophetic insights over the years. One such insight states, "You don't fail God's tests, you just keep taking them over until you finally pass!" The Lord longs for us to become like Him. That includes us learning to forgive our brother as freely and as fully as He has forgiven us - no exceptions, no excuses, no loopholes:

"Be kind and compassionate to one another, forgiving each other, *just as* in Christ God forgave you." (Ephesians 4:32, italics mine)

"Bear with each other and forgive whatever grievances you may have against one another. Forgive *as* the Lord forgave you." (Colossians 3:13, italics mine)

Jesus, in fact, tells a parable about an unmerciful servant to convey how ludicrous it would be for us to withhold our forgiveness towards someone in light of the fact that God has forgiven us a humongous debt. In the parable, a servant owes his master several million bucks but he pleads for mercy, which he receives. His massive debt was graciously canceled. But later, when one of his fellow servants owed him a buck or two, he callously showed no mercy, having him thrown in jail. When the master heard about this injustice, he was extremely angry and had the guy turned over to the jailers (literally, tormenters) until he should pay back all he owed. In other words, his cancelled debt was re-instated. The same measure of justice you demand of others and mercy you extend to others will be required of or given to you. (Matthew 18:22-35) Pretty heavy stuff.

The Lord takes this powerful gift of forgiveness so seriously that He warns us many times in the Scriptures that if we do not forgive our brother, He will not forgive us.

"For if you forgive men when they sin against you, your heavenly Father will also forgive you. But if you do not forgive men their sins, your Father will not forgive your sins." (Matt. 6:14-15; see also Luke 6:37-38)

And the Lord expects us to forgive as frequently as necessary. In Matthew 18:21-22, we find, "Then Peter came to Jesus and asked, "Lord, how many times shall I forgive my brother when he sins against me? Up to seven times?" Jesus answered, "I tell you, not seven times, but seventy-seven times." (Alternative reading says "or seventy times seven.")

In other words, don't bother counting. Love doesn't keep score.

With God's help, may we learn our lessons well in this area of cultivating an unoffendable heart that is quick to release forgiveness.

Putting on The Full Armor of God

In Ephesians 6:10-18, we find the apostle Paul offers us further strategic advice on how to defend ourselves as well as advance in this spiritual war in which we find ourselves. Because of its length, I'll let you read it in your own Bible.

Firstly, we are reminded it is all about the Lord's strength and supernatural power.

Secondly, we must remember that our fight is not with each other, but with demonic spiritual beings.

Thirdly, we are called to stand our ground and not wimp out and throw in the towel.

The armour and weapons Paul claims are available to us include: the belt of truth and integrity, the breastplate of righteousness, the boots to prepare us to share the gospel, the shield of faith against enemy darts, the helmet of salvation that protects our hope and our having the mind of Christ, the sword of the Spirit which is the authoritative Word of God and the power of prayer that links us to God's heart and heaven's resources. For a moment, let's look at the crucial weapons of the Word of God and prayer.

The Sword of the Spirit - the Word of God

Someone once wisely said, "Don't put a question mark where God put a period."

A young lady was converted to Christ and was all excited about her new faith. A skeptic came up to her and said, "You don't believe that book, the Bible do you?" "Oh, yes", she replied with great enthusiasm. "All those miracles?" "Yes I do". "Even Jonah and the whale story?" "Yes I do," she replied, "In fact, I plan to ask him about that in heaven!" The skeptic asked, "What if he is not there?" "Then you ask him!"

The Bible isn't just another book. Chuck Colson, in his book, Loving God, argues that, "The Bible - banned, burned, beloved, is more widely read and more frequently attacked than any other book in history...Fragments of it smuggled into solitary prison cells have transformed ruthless killers into gentle saints. Pieced together scraps of Scripture have converted whole villages of pagan Indians...Yearly, the Bible outsells every best seller...Portions have been translated into more than 1800 languages and even carried to the moon! Even those hostile to the Bible sense its inherent power."[1]

Jesus countered Satan's temptations by the Word of God, "it is written". And we need to make use of the sword of the Spirit, the Word of God as well. It is imperative that we get grounded, immersed and gripped with the Word.

We live in a secular/post-modern day where objective truth is considered suspect, authority is questioned, rigorous and disciplined study is frowned upon, spiritual experiences are longed for without regard to their source, and charismatic personalities and celebrities have a wide but shallow following. We need therefore, not only a resurgence of a demonstration of the supernatural power and presence of the Kingdom of God with signs and wonders, but also a revival of devotional reading, disciplined study and expository teaching of the ever relevant and authoritative written Word of God.

Biblical scholars throw around the terms: "exegesis" and "eisegesis" when it comes to interpreting the Bible. "Exegesis" literally means "to lead out of" and is a term used when one gives priority to the biblical text, seeking to find what the original author intended it to mean to the original audience. The more long-winded term is the "historical-grammatical" approach because of taking seriously the historical context and the grammatical structure. This involves seeking the literal, natural, plain meaning of the text and letting the text speak for itself.

The term: "eisegesis", in contrast, speaks of the practice of "reading into the text" or imposing on the text whatever the reader wants it to say. This approach allows one to take his theological beliefs, opinions, and prejudices and use the text as a proof text to back them up - a very self-serving and dishonest way to handle the "word of truth" (and probably practiced by all of us at one time or another, if we would be honest).

To truly understand Scripture however, we must "stand under" Scripture and submit to it as the final authority in our lives. It is to be our compass in life, our reference point, the light unto our path. This approach of exegetical study and the use of biblical tools such as a concordance, Bible dictionary, commentaries, and original language reference tools, combined with the practice of expository teaching, are crucial and foundational.

But, let me add, I do not see this method as fully adequate in itself. It does not do full justice to the dynamic dimension of the God-breathed and preserved Word of God that is living and active and sharper than any two-edged sword. (Heb. 4:12)

First, we need to realize that one could become very skilled in using this historical-grammatical and scientific method but be guilty of worshiping at the altar of our own intellect. We need the heart of an inquisitive child that is both hungry for further truth and revelation and humbled and wowed by it. Isaiah 66:2 declares "This in the one I esteem: he who is humble and contrite in spirit and TREMBLES AT MY WORD".

Secondly, we need to recognize that for centuries Hebrew tradition has embraced at least four methods of biblical interpretation: the p'shat (the literal meaning of the text); the remez (the deeper meaning); the midrash (the allegorical meaning); and the sot (the hidden, mystical meaning). Even New Testament writers such as Matthew, John and Paul dealt with Old Testament passages in some of these Hebraic interpretative ways all under the inspiration of the Holy Spirit.

God is an astoundingly creative God who can inspire Scripture with a variety of layers of meaning. It is those of us who are steeped in Greek thinking that miss out on some of the hidden treasures in Scripture that are available via these Hebraic traditions and the dynamic of the Holy Spirit. The Word tells us that God's wisdom is "manifold" or "many-faceted". (Eph. 3:10) [2]

Thirdly, our study and teaching of the Word that engages both head and heart must be utterly dependent upon the Holy Spirit who wrote the book in the first place. I love the great proverb (already used but bears repeating):

"The Word without the Spirit, you dry up. The Spirit without the Word, you blow up. The Spirit AND the Word, you grow up."

In Matthew 22:29, we find Jesus rebuking the religious leaders, insisting that they were "in error because they did not know the Scripture or the power of God." But that beautiful and dynamic combo of the Word and the Spirit is what the great healing evangelist of the first half of the 20th century, Smith Wigglesworth, prophesied would characterize the great end time revival before the return of Christ.

The Holy Spirit who is our personal tour guide on the journey of faith, not just our rules of interpretation, must be allowed to guide us into all truth. Mark Stibbe, in his book, Times of Refreshing, makes a powerful observation that must be taken seriously:

"If one examines the ways in which the New Testament preachers and authors use the Old Testament, one thing becomes immediately clear: Neither are primarily interested in what the real author meant in his Sitz im Leben (life-setting). In fact, they show very little concern for that. They are far more interested in what God is doing right now, and in finding Scriptures, which illuminate that. In short, they are more concerned with what is called a THIS-IS-THAT approach to interpretation. They start with the THIS that God is doing in the Church, and they then find – under the guidance of the Holy Spirit - the THAT in the Scriptures which explains that work. Thus in Acts 2:16, when Peter stands up just after the Holy Spirit has fallen on the 120 believers in Jerusalem, he explains the work of the Spirit in both himself and in his community by saying, "THIS is THAT which was spoken by the prophet Joel."[3]

Dr. Stibbe goes on to add that this prophetic approach to interpreting Scripture, used by New Testament authors and preachers, is used by Pentecostals today and though it can have its dangers, seems to be a legitimate and biblically valid approach. This method does not neglect asking the necessary questions of historical context but it also sees that "exegesis involves us perceiving what the Father is doing right now amongst us (like Jesus in John 5:19) and then allowing the Holy Spirit to lead us to Bible texts which elucidate that work...'contextualized exegesis'– understanding our own communal story in the light of the overarching story of Scripture (e.g. THIS is THAT in Ezekiel 47:1-12)."

Stibbe wisely points out that the community of faith must test this "prophetic preaching" that has the potential to bear much good fruit, to avoid disastrous results.[4]

Bill Johnson, in his book, Secrets to Imitating God, touches on these very issues with prophetic clarity and fatherly wisdom. Here are a couple of tidbits: "He (Holy Spirit) eagerly reveals His mysteries to all who are hungry - truly hungry...The Word of God is living and active. It contains divine energy, always moving and accomplishing His purposes."[5]

Johnson goes on to state that though rules are useful, they must not be a replacement for getting intimately familiar with the presence and voice of the Holy Spirit. "There is danger, but there is also great treasure. This is the necessary tension...sometimes the rules that keep us from error also keep us from our destiny...The appropriate response to dangerous, and intrinsically important ideas is to stay low, stay hungry, take risks, and keep accountable."[6]

As we excitedly anticipate the last days move of God before the return of Christ, God is going to raise up an unstoppable army of John Wesleys, Charles Finneys, Catherine Booths, Aimee Semple McPhersons, John Wimbers, and Bill Johnsons who are steeped in the Word, filled with the joy and the fear of the Lord, and clothed with power from on high to preach the good news and teach the Word with authenticity, apostolic authority and with Kingdom signs following. And maybe, just maybe you are called to be a part of that army!

Prayer

Scripture speaks volumes to us about this mysterious thing called prayer, urging us to take advantage of this invaluable gift of communication between heaven and earth.

Most of us however, get a little uncomfortable whenever this topic comes up because it stirs up such feelings of guilt, frustration and defeat. The accuser of the brethren is quick to want to point out our weaknesses in this department. He loves to taunt and mock us, heaping layer upon layer of condemnation upon us. "Who do you think you are anyway? You are nothing but a hypocrite. You don't pray enough. Your faith is puny and pathetic. God is very disappointed in you."

We are aware that Jesus made it a priority and a habit to get away from the crowds and spend time with His Father in prayer and that we, as His students are not above our Master. We also know that according to James 5:16, "The prayer of a righteous man is powerful and effective."

We genuinely believe prayer is something we should do, even something we want to do, but something seems to hold us back (besides the devil who shudders at the weakest believer on their knees). Of course we are busy with work and family obligations but it's more than that. For some of us our problem may be that we assume prayer is something to master the way we master mathematics or English. And since we feel so incompetent and foolish (and God often feels so remote and inaccessible), we go to the Lord in prayer simply when desperate as a last resort rather than as our first resource.

True prayer and communication however, comes not from gritting our teeth but from falling in love. Richard Foster paints a warm picture of prayer from God's perspective:

"And he is inviting you - and me - to come home, to come home to where we belong, to come home to that for which we were created. His arms are stretched out wide to receive us. His heart is enlarged to take us in...We do not need to be shy. He invites us into the living room of his heart where we can put on old slippers and share freely.

He invites us into the kitchen of his friendship where chatter and batter mix in good fun. He invites us into the dining room of his strength, where we can feast to our heart's delight. He invites us into the study of his wisdom where we can learn and grow and stretch... and ask all the questions we want. He invites us into the workshop of his creativity, where we can be co-laborers with him, working together to determine the outcomes of events. He invites us into the bedroom of his rest where new peace is found, and where we can be naked and vulnerable and free. It is also the place of deepest intimacy, where we know and are known to the fullest. The key to this home, this heart of God, is prayer."[7]

So why pray?

- To *enjoy* a love relationship with God. (friendship, romance)
- To *give to* God. (worship and thanksgiving)
- To *receive from* God. (petition)
- To *co-operate* with God. (intercession)

We have already discussed the invitations to the pleasure of intimacy and worship in previous chapters. Let's talk for a moment about **petition** then focus particularly on intercession.

God delights in our asking for our daily bread. We are forever dependent upon Abba Father and it pleases Him when we look to Him for provision, guidance and protection. He promises not to give us a stone when we ask for bread. He is not a stingy God but loves to lavish good gifts on His children who ask.

If petition is asking God for something for ourselves; **intercession** is when we are asking on behalf of others. This dimension of prayer is where we co-operate with God in the affairs of men both on the local and global levels. Prayer is not a matter of trying to persuade a reluctant God, but of letting God make the decisions and us working with Him to enforce His will on earth. We are enforcing Christ's victory over Satan and implementing Heaven's decisions upon earth. According to 1 Cor. 3:9, "We are co-labourers with God." (See also Mt. 16:9; 18:18-20; 2 Cor. 10:3)

Mike Bickle puts it this way, "The primary principle of intercession is simply to tell God what He tells us to tell Him as the means of releasing His power. This is profoundly simple. Intercession is God's brilliant strategy for including the saints in ruling with Him in power. Its mystery is in its 'weakness', simplicity, humility and accessibility to all."[8]

In Ezekiel 22:30-31, we find these sobering words, "I looked for a man among them who would build up the wall and stand before me in the gap on behalf of the land so I would not have to destroy it, but I found none."

God is all sufficient in His nature, not needing anyone and yet mysteriously, God orchestrated a game plan in which He has placed limits upon Himself based on our cooperation with Him. John Wesley claimed that, "God does nothing but in answer to prayer."

In his book, Destined for the Throne, Paul E. Billheimer asks,

"Could not He who spoke the worlds into existence and who upholds them by that same word accomplish His purposes without the help of puny man? Then why did He devise the plan of prayer? Why and how did He become "dependent" upon the intercession of men?...

"God's eternal purpose in the creation of the universe and the human race was to obtain an Eternal Companion for His Son...In God's eternal purpose the Church, as Christ's Eternal Companion, is to occupy the highest position in the universe short of the Godhead itself. As the Bride of the Eternal Son she is to share with Him universal sovereignty...

"By practicing in her prayer closet the enforcement of heaven's decisions in mundane affairs, the Church is in "on-the-job" training for co-sovereignty with Christ over His universal empire. She must learn the art of spiritual warfare, of overcoming evil forces in preparation for her assumption of the throne following the Marriage Supper of the Lamb. To enable her to learn the technique of overcoming, God devised the scheme of prayer."[9]

And so, as this spiritual battle moves toward a crescendo at the end of the age, we are seeing God raising up lovesick prophetic worshipers and prayer warriors throughout the earth. Like the widow, Anna, who prayed day and night at the temple before the first coming of Jesus (Luke 2:36-37), so the Holy Spirit is restoring the "Annas" before the second coming of Jesus.

In Revelation 5:10, we see 24 elders falling down before the Lamb in humble adoration, each holding a harp as well as golden bowls full of incense, which are the prayers of the saints. A harp speaks of worshiping God with musical instruments and the bowls speak of the intercessory prayers of the church. Mike Bickle has observed that such a model results in prayer becoming enjoyable and not just hard work.

Throughout the world God is birthing 24/7 houses of worship and prayer that are following this heavenly pattern. Some are connected to or inspired by the prophetically lead forerunners at the Kansas City International House of Prayer that follows the harp and bowl model and is committed to this mandate until Jesus returns. Others have caught the vision through the explosive 24/7 prayer movement out of the UK, which is chronicled in the book, Red Moon Rising.

There are a host of other God breathed prayer initiatives such as the renewed focus on praying the prayers of the Bible, city prayer walks and the prayer and warfare gatherings called, The Call. Many prophetic words have been given as well that the stadiums of the world will soon be used for Spirit-led solemn assemblies, 24//7 worship and revival gatherings with great signs and wonders. An untold number of God's people of every tribe, tongue and nation have been and will be joining the ranks of this unstoppable army of intercessors and worshipers who are destined to be world changers and shakers for the Kingdom of God.

Fasting

Many are realizing too that God has ordained the instrument of fasting to be a very powerful weapon that can take the prayers of the saints to a whole new level. Scripture has much to say about fasting. Here are but a few points:

- Jesus assumes we will do it, "when you fast", not if. (Matthew 6:16)
- Fasting is not just for Bible days but throughout church history, including today, "The time will come when the bridegroom will be taken from them; then they will fast." (Matt. 9:15)
- Often fasting is a personal matter between the individual and God but we see in Scripture public fasts such as the Day of Atonement and times of national crisis and need. (2 Chron. 20:1-4; Ezra 8:21-23)

Fasting helps us to:

- Sharpen our dull spirits as we seek to center upon God (Zech 7:5; Luke 2:37)
- Expose even good things that can master us and take God's place (Ps. 69:10)
- Express our wholeheartedness to the Lord (Joel 2:12)
- Combat the enemy with a further weapon that releases spiritual power. It is not a hunger strike to force God's hand but a weapon of warfare against opposing forces of darkness (Ezra 8:23; Isaiah 49: 24-25; 58:6; Matthew 9:28-29; 11:12)
- Receive needed heavenly wisdom and revelation (Dan. 9:2,3, 21,22)

The revivalist, Arthur Wallis, in his book, God's Chosen Fast, comes to this conclusion:

"Fasting is a God-appointed means for the flowing of His grace and power that we can afford to neglect no longer. The fast of this "church age" is not merely an act of mourning for Christ's absence, but an act of preparation for His return. May those prophetic words "then will they fast", be finally fulfilled in this generation. It will be a fasting and praying church that will hear the thrilling cry: "Behold, the Bridegroom!" Tears shall be wiped away, and the fast be followed by the feast at the marriage supper of the Lamb."[10]

Fear of the Lord

Many Christians avoid this subject of the fear of the Lord, believing it to be an inferior Old Testament concept associated with the Law while we now live in the age of grace and focus only on God's love. But where a healthy sense of awe and fear of the Lord is absent, there tends to be an attitude of casualness, a sloppy agape and a grace that is cheapened and taken for granted. Rather than seeing grace as God's empowering presence in our lives for obedience to His directives, it is seen as an excuse and a cover for our lukewarmness and even blatant sin and lawlessness.

Do you wish to have victory from sin?

The fear of the Lord will help keep us from sinning (Ex. 20:20), as well as help us to hate evil and desire to avoid it like the plague. (Prov. 8:13; 16:6)

Do you long for greater wisdom and knowledge (which will be indispensable in these coming days of turmoil and uncertainty)?

It comes only through walking in the fear of the Lord. (Psalm 111:10; Prov. 1:7)

Do you desire a deep friendship with the Lord in which He shares the secrets of His heart?

It is reserved for those who fear Him. Psalm 25:14 declares that, "The LORD confides in those who fear him". The English Standard Version states that, "The Friendship of the LORD is for those who fear him."

Do you desire to be blessed by God and not be freaking out like everybody else when calamity and disaster strikes in the coming days?

Psalm 112:1 promises us that, "Blessed is the man who fears the LORD"...vs. 6 "Surely he will never be shaken"...vs7 "He will have no fear of bad news; his heart is steadfast, trusting in the LORD."

Do you desire to be like Jesus in every way?

Isaiah 11 tells us that when the prophesied Messiah came, not only would He have the Spirit of the LORD, the Spirit of wisdom and of understanding, the Spirit of counsel and of power, but also the Spirit of knowledge and of the fear of the LORD, resting upon Him. And in fact, He would actually delight in the fear of the LORD!

In case anyone thinks the awe and fear of the Lord concept is strictly an Old Testament thing, take a look at the book of Acts (2:43; 5:1-14) or Hebrews 12:28, 29, which makes this conclusion, "Therefore, since we are receiving a kingdom that cannot be shaken, let us be thankful, and so worship God acceptably with reverence and awe, for our God is a consuming fire."

A childlike sense of wonder and awe mingled with a deep awareness of God's greatness and holiness (and our smallness and sinfulness without Him) can enable us to walk with the God of the universe in a breathtaking friendship and partnership. The fear of the Lord motivates us to be teachable, flexible and eager to see and agree with our Master's perspective and opinion. We find ourselves becoming more sensitive to and caring about what grieves and displeases Him and what brings Him joy. As we grow in the fear of the Lord, we find ourselves becoming less and less man pleasers and more and more God pleasers.[11]

C.S. Lewis claimed that, "if you are taking yourself too seriously, then you are not taking God seriously enough."

Conclusion

If we are going to be successful as overcomers in this very real war, it must be waged according to and with the Scriptures. The Lord has given us the written Word of God as our battle manual with our marching orders, the Holy Spirit as our personal guide for up to the minute instruction and boldness, prayer as our line of communication with our Commander in Chief, a link to heaven's vast resources and a weapon to enforce and decree heaven's objectives, as well as the army of God for support, camaraderie and covering each other's backs.

We have been called to live a daily life of denying ourselves (our carnal flesh), taking up our cross and following Jesus. (Matt.16:24) This entails walking in the fear of the Lord as well as living a grace-based and love filled life of surrender to the Lordship of Jesus Christ. This will be evidenced by a life of prayer, gratitude and worship, keeping short accounts with God and others, being utterly dependent upon our heavenly Father and the power of His Holy Spirit and interdependent upon our fellow comrades in this "salvation army". Such a yielded life will result in us experiencing exquisite joy and sense of purpose as we live in the newness of Christ's resurrection life - a little taste of heaven here on earth.

"Submit yourselves, then, to God. Resist the devil, and he will flee from you. Come near to God and he will come near to you... Humble yourselves before the Lord, and he will lift you up". (James 4:7,8, 10)

In this spiritual war in which we find ourselves one of the areas in which enemy forces have been particularly successful in killing, stealing and destroying pertains to the physical health of mankind. The following chapter we will address the remarkable Kingdom assignment given to Christ followers of praying for the sick in the authority of Jesus to see healing and restoration.

Recommended Resources:

I Believe in Satan's Downfall, Michael Green, Eerdmans, 1981, revised 2001
Arming for Spiritual Warfare, George Mallone, I.V. Press, 1991
The Believer's Guide to Spiritual Warfare, Thomas B. White, Servant Pub., 1990
C.S. Lewis, Screwtape Letters and Screwtape Proposes a Toast, Macmillan Paperbacks Edition, 1959, 1961
Spiritual Warfare for every Christian, Dean Sherman, YWAM Pub., 1990

Victory over Darkness, Neil T Anderson, Regal, 1990
Deliverance from Evil Spirits: A Practical Manual, Francis MacNutt, Chosen Books, 1995
Handbook For Spiritual Warfare, Ed Murphy, Thomas Nelson, 1992
The Three Battlegrounds (of the mind, church, heavenly places), Francis Frangipane, Advancing Church Pub., 1989
Why Some Christians Commit Adultery, John Sandford, Victory House, 1989
Unmasking Freemasonry, Selwyn Stevens, Jubilee Resources
Free From Freemasonry, Ron G. Campbell, Regal, 1999
The Bait of Satan, John Bevere, Charisma House, 1994, 2011
The Fear of the Lord, John Bevere, Creation House, 1997
The Importance of Forgiveness, John Arnott, Sovereign World, 1997
Grace and Forgiveness, John and Carol Arnott, New Wine Press, 2009
Waking the Dead, John Eldredge, Thomas Nelson, 2003
Wild at Heart, John Eldredge, Thomas Nelson, 2001
Dealing with the Rejection and Praise of Man, Bob Sorge, Oasis House, 1999
Envy, Bob Sorge, Oasis House, 2003
Loyalty, Bob Sorge, Oasis House, 2004
The Fire of Delayed Answers, Bob Sorge, Oasis House, 1996
Strengthen Yourself in the Lord, Bill Johnson, Destiny Image, 2007
The Final Quest, The Call, The Torch & the Sword trilogy by Rick Joyner
Epic Battles of the Last Days, Rick Joyner, Morningstar, 1995
Bar Barakah, a Parent's Guide to a Christian Bar Mitzvah, Craig Hill, (Family Foundations Pub., 1998)
The Power of Blessing, Terry & Melissa Bone, self published, 2004
The Blessing Handbook, Terry R. Bone, Crossroads Christian Communication, 2007
Blessing Your Spirit, Sylvia Gunter and Arthur Burk, The Father's Business, 2005
Restoring the Foundations, Chester and Betsy Kylstra, Proclaiming His Word Pub. 2001
Laughing Your Way to a Better Marriage, Mark Gungor, seminars, DVDs, book, 2009

Prayer and Fasting

Destined for the Throne, Paul E. Billheimer, Christian Literature Crusade, 1975
Intercessory Prayer, Dutch Sheets, Regal, 1996
The Lost Art of Intercession, Jim W. Goll, Destiny Image, 1997
Prayer Walking, Steve Hawthorne & Graham Kendrick, Creation House, 1993
Red Moon Rising: Story of 24-7 Prayer, Pete Greig, Dave Roberts, Kingsway Pub., 2003
24-7 Prayer Manual, Pete Greig & David Blackwell, Cook Communications, 2005
Praying the Bible, The Pathway to Spirituality, Wesley and Stacey Campbell, Regal Books, 2003
Adoration Prayer book, Bob Harley, 2010, practical manual that helps us in intimacy and adoration of the Lord, resulting in us possessing unshakeable hope in God
God's Chosen Fast, Arthur Wallis, Christian Literature Crusade, 1968
A Hunger for God, John Piper, Crossway Books, 1997
The Rewards of Fasting, Mike Bickle with Dana Candler, Forerunners Books, 2005

Notes:

[1.] Chuck Colson, Loving God, Zondervan, 1987, 1996, pp. 55,56.
[2.] Johnny Enlow, The Seven Mountain Mantle, Creation House, 2009, pp. 13,14.
[3.] Mark Stibbe, Times of Refreshing, Harper & Collins, 1995, p. 5.
[4.] Ibid., pp. 5, 6.
[5.] Bill Johnson, Secrets to Imitating God, Destiny Image, 2009, pp. 142,143.
[6.] Ibid., pp. 146, 151.
[7.] Richard Foster, Prayer, Hodder & Stoughton, 1992, pp. 1,2.
[8.] Mike Bickle, Forerunner School of Ministry notes, The Revelation of Intercession,p. 1.

[9.] Paul E. Billheimer, Destined for the Throne, Christian Literature Crusade, 1975, pp. 43, 48,49.

[10.] Arthur Wallis, The Chosen Fast, Christian Literature Crusade, 1968, p. 32.

[11.] John Bevere, The Fear of the Lord, Creation House, 1997.

Chapter 7

Divine Healing For Today

"If you live cautiously all your friends will call you wise.
You just won't move many mountains." Bill Johnson

"You know your mind has been renewed when the
impossible seems logical."
Bill Johnson

I remember as a young teen dropping in for a visit several times
to the local Pentecostal healing revival tent meetings held each
summer to watch and be entertained by all the lively and bizarre
activity going on. There was exuberant praise and worship: singing,
clapping, waving hands and hankies and some strange sounds they
called "tongues". There was the fiery preaching and hollering and
then the highlight of the program, watching people get called out and
go forward for prayer for salvation and healing. The salvation part
I could relate to and appreciate but the rest was up for our mockery.

Up front the evangelist and his associates would put their sweaty
hands on them and pray, with the occasional person ending up on
the ground in the sawdust. And after a while many would be up
giving a testimony, claiming to be healed. Man, this beat watching
TV any day! My friend and I would find this very entertaining and
lots of ammunition for ridicule. We thought most of it was a circus
of emotional hype and unreality. Though I loved Jesus and was part

of a Bible believing church, we didn't go for this more demonstrative version of the faith and certainly didn't believe that any of that miracle stuff happens today. Oh, don't get me wrong. Those supernatural things happened in the Bible, for sure. I was no liberal. They just don't happen anymore now that we have the whole Bible. So we snickered and laughed and enjoyed the show from the back. I'm so thankful the Lord didn't strike me dead on the spot!

Then years later, while studying at Vancouver's Regent College for my Master of Divinity degree in the early 1980s, and part of a non-charismatic evangelical church, I heard the pastor preach a Sunday sermon on divine healing. Barry, a good friend and fellow student, and I were both so upset by this message that we made an appointment to go in to the pastor's office during the week and not only challenge him on it, but straighten him out. After all, God stopped healing people, with a few rare exceptions, once his original apostles had died and the canon of Scripture was complete (so we were taught growing up, under the theological name of cessationism).

Pastor Wes, who I grew to appreciate and even work with later as his youth pastor, was very gracious and tolerant of our ranting and raving but did not back down to what he perceived as solid biblical grounds for not only praying for the sick but for actually expecting that God could and, at times, would supernaturally heal people today.

Not long after this experience, a few courses taken at Regent with professors like Michael Green, Clark Pinnock, and George Mallone, began to open my eyes and mind ever so slowly to the possibility that maybe, just maybe, all the gifts of the Holy Spirit, including divine healing and miracles, could be for today. I was thawing out and warming up to the idea, at least in theory.

But then it happened. I attended a Signs and Wonders and Church Growth conference in Vancouver in May of 1985 that really rocked my world and forever changed my life. This pivotal conference was taught by John Wimber, a California pastor, leader of the Vineyard movement as well as co-teacher with Dr. C. Peter Wagner of a course by the same name at Fuller Seminary.

Starting with the fresh and intimate praise and worship at the beginning of each conference session, I was pushed way out of my comfort zone. Then with the very sane and thoroughly biblical teaching on the subject of the Kingdom of God and signs and wonders coupled with real life stories, my comfortable paradigm was shaken to the core. I had taken pride much of my life with the belief that if I saw something clearly taught in Scripture, I would seek to be honest and not try to water it down and explain it away but rather submit myself to the authority of the Word and respond in faith and obedience.

Wimber's breadth of understanding of the Scriptures, his California non-religious laid back style and sense of humour, his down to earth honesty, his obvious passion for Jesus and His Kingdom and his strong compassion for those who suffer all converged to impact me deeply.

After each session of teaching, Wimber would ask us to put down our materials and he would lead us in a very non-hype, non-emotional time of prayer ministry, which he called "clinic time", in which he would invite the Holy Spirit to come. He would patiently wait and seek to only follow the Father's initiative (Jesus only did what he saw the Father doing, John 5:19) in ministering healing to people.

It's one thing to talk about something, it is quite another to actually enter into the experience of what was just taught. Wimber, who is not into being a "one-man show", but rather a team player, would quietly, calmly, and confidently facilitate the "clinic time", utilizing his prayer team to minister to various people. Later in the conference, when most were a little more comfortable with it all, Wimber would invite any of the conference attendees to participate in the laying on of hands and praying for God to come and bring healing to someone in need.

For me, this was a massive paradigm shift that would radically change my life and ministry.

At the end of the conference, John Wimber put out the challenge that we all go out and pray for a thousand people for healing. If no one was healed, then we would have the right to contact him and request a refund for the conference!

A pastor friend of mine and I took up the challenge. My friend actually kept score with his white board in his office, using the

Roman numeral method of adding. After praying for someone and they weren't healed, he put a stroke on the board, then another, then another. When he got to the fifth person and was ready to place the diagonal stroke and move to the next cluster of five, to his surprise, the person was healed. My friend was honest enough to admit that, although happy for the lady healed of a chronic sinus condition, he was quite perturbed because he was actually out to prove that Wimber was wrong regarding God healing today and that God wants all believers to be developing an active lifestyle of praying for the sick.

I went back home to the small country Ontario town where I was pastoring, and began to get past the intimidation/embarrassment barrier by asking people if I could pray for them for God to bring healing to them. I didn't keep precise score but I would say that of the first one hundred people I prayed for, at least three or four saw significant health improvements. I came to realize that there is a learning curve involved and in the principle of being faithful with a little and over time God gives you more. At times when I would get discouraged and almost ready to throw in the towel and quit praying and believing for healing, sure enough, someone would get a healing from the Lord.

When I asked God why most of the people I had prayed for had not been healed, I felt him say that if I hadn't prayed for the one hundred, those three or four would not have been healed. And that if I pray for every one with the love and compassion of Christ in a sensitive and kind way, even if they are not healed at that time, it is still a "win-win" because they feel loved up on and are appreciative of you taking the time to care for them so tenderly. There is mystery to the Kingdom of God. The Kingdom of God is here, but not in its fullness, as it will be when Christ returns. So, we need to humbly live in this tension of the Kingdom being here but not fully and keep praying the Lord's Prayer that includes: "may Your kingdom come on earth as it is in heaven".

A number of years later, when I was an associate pastor and worship leader for John and Carol Arnott at Jubilee Vineyard Christian Fellowship in Stratford, Ontario, I went on my first mission trip. This trip, led by John and Carol, was to Nicaragua in 1992. It was an astounding experience of seeing God save, deliver, and heal so many people. In the evenings we would show the Jesus film in some park or village and then invite people forward for salvation and healing. We saw our "batting average" of miraculous results go sky high, especially the time we did a chapel service in a men's prison. It seemed that those who came forward for prayer for various physical problems were all healed! And, after that, they all wanted to give their lives to Jesus. It was so much fun seeing healings and salvations come so frequently and easily that even in some of our spare time, usually the mornings, we paired up and went door to door to homes and huts telling people that we were Christians from Canada and asking if anyone in the home was sick and in need of healing.

On the flight home from Nicaragua I was wrestling with the Lord about this whole dynamic of seeing the miraculous in a third world country so naturally and readily and wondering why we don't see it nearly as often back in Canada. I sensed the Lord whisper to me that it was the same reason He could do very little of the miraculous in his own hometown of Nazareth. It was the people's unbelief. Our western rationalistic culture is saturated in unbelief, even in the Western church. But the other question I kept firing at God on the trip home was "Lord, when are we going to see you do this kind of stuff more readily in Canada? When Lord? When?"

I got home to Stratford around midnight from this life changing mission trip, barely got to sleep and the telephone rang. It was Paul, the father of one of the families who was part of our church fellowship. His voice was tense and stressed as he relayed to me that his six year old son, Timmy, whom they had just rushed to the Stratford emergency, was diagnosed by three doctors as having spinal meningitis with a prognosis that was life threatening. They were about to transfer the child by ambulance to a larger hospital in London, Ontario but the father asked if I would come immediately to the emergency and pray for Timmy, who was not responsive, in a fetal position, and convulsing.

I quickly got dressed, called an intercessor to get praying, and got to the hospital in a matter of a few minutes. I walked in and saw the family obviously distraught standing by their loved one and at that moment, something happened that I had never experienced before and I can only describe as a rush of faith and peaceful confidence that washed over me and I calmly assured them that everything was going to be OK. I had no more than two minutes to pray for Timmy before they whisked him off in the ambulance to London.

I went back home to bed and woke up at eight in the morning to the phone ringing. It was Paul. He said: "Jerry, you are not going to believe this". I said: "Try me". Paul proceeded to tell me that when they arrived at the hospital in London, a half hour drive away, the medical team standing by for this code four emergency took one look at the child and were completely baffled as to why the Stratford hospital had sent him there and with such a serious report. They said that all Timmy had was a mild headache but because the diagnosis had been so grave, that they would keep him overnight for observation. As it turned out, of the three doctors that came up with the diagnosis, one doctor was the chief pediatrician and had a reputation of never getting her diagnosis wrong. We were on cloud nine to put it mildly!

Since then, we have seen the resurrected Christ perform so many healings and miracles. With the outpouring of the Spirit in Toronto beginning in January 1994, we have had the privilege of seeing God take things to a whole new level. It has been mind blowing to see our God sovereignly accelerate His Kingdom work among us locally as well as give us the privilege of taking teams of ordi nary Christians throughout the world to watch the Lord do what He does so well, supernaturally loving people to life. I've seen blind eyes and deaf ears opened, cancers healed, as well as back pain and simple headaches disappear. We want to celebrate not just the dramatic ones but also rejoice and be thankful over the victories with what we might consider little healings. And we realize that often the healings are progressive and require us to pray more than once for the person. Jesus said: "Keep on asking, keep on seeking, and keep on knocking". (Matt 7:7 The Greek imperatives are present continuous.) And Jesus Himself had to pray a second time for the blind man who first saw men as trees walking. (Mark 8:23-25)

In 2002, Pam and I moved back to our home city of Barrie, Ontario, and with an invitation from Dave Atton, the lead pastor at that time, I came on the pastoral team of Gateway Harvest

Fellowship, a Partners in Harvest church. Thanks to a friend, Steve Stewart, director at the time of the Healing Rooms in Canada, who came to speak at our church, the church caught the vision of setting up a Healing Rooms ministry.

The Healing Rooms were first developed by John G. Lake in Spokane, Washington in the early part of the 20th century and saw over one hundred thousand documented healings in five years resulting in the U.S. government declaring it the healthiest city in America! As of 1999, the Healing Rooms ministry restarted there and in hundreds of cities around the world.

We leased a downtown storefront to use as our church office as well as the Healing Rooms walk-in clinic where folks could come in to a neutral location and receive prayer for healing from a trained team of volunteers. Ana Castonguay was the founding director and Fern and Barb Landry presently give leadership to this citywide outreach ministry. It has been so fulfilling watching with wonder and awe at what God has done when we understand the authority that we have in Christ, the power of unity and team work with other believers from various churches, and pray with confidence and compassion with precious people who need His loving touch and mercy.

Let's look at some of the biblical theology and relevant Scriptures that I had to honestly face and wrestle with in John Wimber's conference teaching in 1985.

One of the arguments I had for dismissing the validity of healings and signs and wonders for today was that the Bible, I believed, promoted the idea that sickness was part of the package needed to sanctify us. So suck it up, accept it, and don't pursue divine healing for it. (Of course, we will do everything possible medically and naturally to try to minimize or avoid it.)

Although in the New Testament suffering is sometimes presented positively, sickness never is. Not only do we see Jesus showing compassion for the sick, but He was consistently fighting aggressively to battle and defeat it. It was an enemy, not a friend.

It is critically important that we see that there is a difference between suffering and sickness. The New Testament clearly distinguishes sickness from suffering. Suffering always refers to the pain of persecution inflicted by persons or demons.

For example, Peter declares: "Since Christ suffered in his body, arm yourselves also with the same attitude...Dear friends, do not be surprised at the painful trial you are suffering, as though something strange were happening to you. But rejoice that you participate in the sufferings of Christ, so that you may be overjoyed when his glory is revealed. If you are insulted because of the name of Christ, you are blessed...if you suffer as a Christian, do not be ashamed, but praise God that you bear that name..." (1 Peter 4:1; 12-14; 16)

The Greek word group in the New Testament for suffering is "pascho". Of the 65 times this word group is used in the New Testament, only once has it anything to do with physical sickness, and in that case the illness (epilepsy) is credited to a demon. (Mt. 17:15)

Ken Blue states: "The New Testament consistently defines suffering as some sort of persecution and not as physical sickness. We are told that persecution has value and merit. We are never told this about sickness...Never do we find New Testament Christians reconciled to sickness, enduring it patiently or rejoicing in it as they sometimes did with persecution...One of the clearest biblical distinctions between suffering and sickness is found in the book of James. James says, "Consider it pure joy...whenever you face trials of many kinds" (James 1:2), but in 5:14-15 we hear James ask, 'Is any one of you sick? He should call the elders of the church to pray...And the prayer offered in faith will make the sick person well.' The New Testament teaches us sometimes to endure suffering but always to pray to heal sickness".[1]

Of course Wimber addressed the possible exception to the New Testament's explicit hostility towards sickness, that of 2 Cor. 12:7, where Paul talks about his "thorn in the flesh" that was given to keep him from being conceited. If the "sanctification through sickness" theory has any biblical grounds, it is here.

But Wimber (and Ken Blue, one of his students) pointed out that the Old Testament concept of a "thorn in the flesh" refers to persecution and harassment, not sickness. In Numbers 33:55; Joshua 23:13 and Ezekiel 28:24 the thorns refer to neighbouring nations harassing and persecuting Israel. Furthermore, the context of Paul's thorn in 2 Cor. 12 needs to be noticed. In the previous two chapters

Paul speaks of his being harassed by false prophets and political and religious leaders, a royal "pain in the neck". So although it is impossible to know with certainty and precision what Paul's thorn in the flesh was, it is more likely to be painful opposition from enemies (driven by THE enemy) than being a physical affliction.

Wimber also made a strong case that aggressive healing and deliverance of the demonic made up a significant part of the ministry and teaching of Jesus. In fact, nearly one fifth of the Gospel accounts is devoted to the healing ministry of Jesus and the discussions that came out of it. Out of 3,779 verses in the four Gospels, 727 relate specifically to the healing of physical, mental, emotional illnesses and the raising of the dead.

Foundational to understanding the compassionate healing ministry and teaching of Jesus, one must understand **the centrality of the Kingdom of God.** The Word of God declares that the planet has been engulfed in a cosmic battle, a raging spiritual war. Because of the Fall, Satan had stolen the authority over the earth that was first given to Adam and Eve. But with the coming of Jesus, the Kingdom of God has broken onto the scene. (Col. 1:13) Jesus came on a mission to defeat the works of Satan and his pseudo-kingdom of darkness.

Christ's works of preaching, healing, casting out demons, and raising the dead were signs of the Kingdom's advance against the dominion of darkness. (Luke 10:9; 11:20) While Satan, the thief, seeks to wreak havoc and destruction of God's creation (steal, kill, and destroy), Jesus claimed He had come to bring the abundant life of the rule of God. (John 10:10) He ultimately accomplished the defeat of Satan through His death on the cross and His victorious resurrection. (Col. 2:15, 1 John 3:8b)

Even though Jesus, "having disarmed the powers and authorities, made a public spectacle of them, triumphing over them by the cross" (Col 2:15), He did not put an end to Satan's power; rather He bound it so that we, the church, may have authority over it to see it continually break up and the reign of God increase. The church, as God's army, is called to continue doing the words and miraculous works of Jesus, in the power of the Holy Spirit. We are to continually bombard the strongholds of Satan and extend the rule of God until Christ comes again and all evil will be finally crushed.

This mission of the church between Christ's first coming and His second entails living with the tension of the Kingdom of God being here, but not fully here. We are invited to partner with Him and pray "may Your kingdom come and Your will be done on earth as it is in heaven". (Matt. 6:10) We are to call "the powers of the age to come" (Hebrews 6:5) into this "present evil age". As His deputized disciples and ambassadors, we are to enforce Christ's victory at the cross, repossessing what the enemy has stolen and restoring what he has destroyed.

Scriptures declaring that Jesus passed on to His disciples (past, present, future) the task of carrying on this supernatural Kingdom mission:

Matthew 10:1 states that Jesus called the twelve disciples to Him and gave them authority to drive out evil spirits and to heal every disease and sickness. In verse 5, these disciples were sent out with the following instructions: "As you go, preach the message that the kingdom of heaven is near. Heal the sick, raise the dead, cleanse those who have leprosy, drive out demons. Freely you have received, freely give".

Luke 9:1 also speaks of the authority Jesus gave to his twelve disciples.

John 20:21, Jesus said to the twelve, "as the Father has sent me, I am sending you".

Luke 10:1 states that another seventy-two people were also given authority to proclaim the kingdom being near and to heal the sick.

In John 14:12, Jesus prophesies that "anyone who has faith in Me will do what I have been doing (and if that isn't a high enough bar to reach), he will do even greater things than these because I go to the Father". Wow! This was certainly one of the verses high on the list to either cut out or manipulate, I am now frustrated that virtually all of my dozen commentaries on the book of John try to skate around this profound prophetic statement of Christ and dishonestly water it down to mean something else. One interpretation claims that now that we have modern communication technology, we can preach the gospel to so many more people than Christ ever could. But the context is referring to the supernatural works of Christ.

The knock out punch for me was the Great Commission passage of Matthew 28:18-20: "Make disciples of all nations, baptizing them and teaching them (not just doctrine) to obey EVERYTHING I have commanded you (the original twelve disciples) to do".

I was cornered. No way around it. No more excuses. I now saw afresh from a new paradigm that all that Jesus instructed his original disciples to do (love God and one another, forgive, preach the kingdom, heal the sick, cast out demons, raise the dead, minister to the poor etc.) was to be passed on to future generations of disciples to also do. His commission gave us the authority and His promise, that we too would receive power when the Holy Spirit came on us to be His witnesses at home and abroad. (Acts 1:8) All the necessary resources of heaven would be available to serve with.[2]

Aside from walking us through the Word of God on this issue and giving humourous stories of his own stumbling journey, John Wimber also helped us to honestly face our attitudes toward healing. Using the following diagram of steps, we were to find where on this scale we would say we were:

```
                                    _____
                        _____ Fruitful
            _____ Obedient
_____ Timid
_____ Interested
Unbeliever
```

First attitude is one of not knowing or believing that God desires to and indeed does heal today.

Second attitude is one of not believing but wanting to and interested in the subject.

Third attitude is one of believing but too shy/timid to act on that belief.

Fourth attitude is one of believing AND now acting on that belief in obedience, but not seeing positive results.

Fifth and last level on the scale is one of believing in divine healing today, acting on that belief, and seeing positive results.[3]

Where are you on this scale? What is the Lord asking you to do about it?

Jesus preached the good news of the Kingdom but He also demonstrated the power of the Kingdom. And He has called us to follow both His example and His mandate, to do both the words and works of Jesus in the power of the Holy Spirit. It is a matter of obedience. The apostle Paul declares that "the kingdom of God is not just fancy talk (logos); it is living by God's power (dunamis)." (1 Cor. 4:20)

Mark Stibbe and Marc Dupont write: "Separating logos and dunamis in our walk with God is truly dangerous. It should carry a health warning. The opposite is, however, just as true. Combining God's Word and God's power is extraordinarily potent, both within the church and outside. Those who revere and know the Scriptures, and who also know and minister in the manifest power of God, are really the hope of the world" [4]

I should also mention that we are not only called to pray for healing of the body but to also see people set free of demonic bondages and addictions. Sometimes we find that the root problem behind someone's physical problem actually is demonic. And so to see them physically healed, it will involve casting out demons. This is a big topic that we cannot do justice here. There is a plethora of very helpful books and teaching materials now available on inner healing and deliverance. Let me just say that in dealing with the demonic, we must realize that we must first remove the legal ground for the enemy to wreak havoc in that person's life. That will usually involve the need for repentance and forgiveness. The person may very well need some emotional healing and then deliverance. Think of the wounds of the heart as a pile of garbage and demons as flies.

To more effectively get rid of the flies long term one needs to see the pile of garbage dealt with first.

In recent years, aside from ongoing inspiration watching my spiritual mentors, John and Carol Arnott being used by the Lord in healing and deliverance, Bill Johnson, pastor of Bethel Church in Redding, California, has challenged the body of Christ to contend for more of the supernatural power of God in signs and wonders. Bill has become a prolific writer and father figure who has, like Wimber and Arnott, been calling the church to partner with God in seeing the Kingdom of God and His manifest presence break into our daily life and world. I recommend his many books to you.

Of course, I must mention Rolland and Heidi Baker, of Mozambique, who have seen a vast number of healings, miracles, resurrections, tens of thousands of conversions to Christ and thousands of churches planted in their organization called Iris Ministries over the last decade or two. At the time of writing this chapter, my wife and I are presently at their Malawi mission center for 3 months.

We are living in the last days where the glory of God is increasing upon the earth and lives, communities, and cultures are being radically transformed. And the awesome news is that you don't need to be a superstar Christian to participate in this supernatural work of the Holy Spirit. As our minds and hearts get freed up from the lies of the enemy, the Holy Spirit won't be bottle necked or imprisoned in "unbelieving believers" but rather be flowing out of human conduits of grace as rivers of living water. If you are a born again Christian who desires to be continually filled and available to the Holy Spirit, have a passion for Jesus and His Kingdom, a love for others, and are willing to keep learning (stay childlike rather than an expert) and take risks of looking foolish, you my friend, qualify to get in on this wild ride and Kingdom adventure of "being naturally supernatural"!

Let me just give you some practical advice:

Regarding healing, don't hold back with the complacent attitude that "I'll believe it when I see it". You'll only see it when you begin to believe it, and step out and act on it in ridiculously simple faith and obedience.

Settle the issue in your heart to make praying for the sick part of your everyday lifestyle, offering to pray right on the spot. (Having two or three people acting as a prayer team is the ideal but often not possible.)

Ask permission to lay hands on them and do so sensitively and respectfully, seeking to protect their dignity.

Pray with your eyes open, attentive to what is happening with the person and what God may be doing.

Be yourself, don't get religious on anybody or try to be some super spiritual person or super healing evangelist.

Check to see if there is any kind of difference. Have them move around or do something that they weren't able to do before because of the health problem.

If there is little or no difference, briefly praying again may be the way to go, if they are willing.

Remember that healings are not always instantaneous but often gradual and progressive over the coming hours or even day or two. Don't let the devil discourage you.

And finally, remember, God is responsible for the results. Our job is to be obedient in following the Father's initiatives and seeking to represent Jesus well in the power of the Holy Spirit. So, if you stepped out and went for it, congratulations! It is a win/win situation if we are loving, kind and honouring. They see that you are for them, that you value them as a person and that there is a God in heaven who does too.

By the way, I've repented of my teenage ridicule of the Pentecostal tent meetings and healing evangelists. The Lord has graciously forgiven me and ironically enough has even given me opportunities to encourage and challenge a few Pentecostal churches to forget looking for respect from man and seek to regain their lost heritage of believing for and walking in the anointing for signs and wonders. The Lord gets the last laugh.

Not only does God love to laugh, He also loves to talk with His kids. In the next chapter we will explore this realm of learning to hear the voice of God.

Recommended Resources

Books:

Power Healing, John Wimber & Kevin Springer, Harper & Row, 1987
Authority to Heal, Ken Blue, IVP, 1987 Surprised by the Power of the Spirit, Jack Deere, Zondervan, 1993 Breakthrough, Discovering the Kingdom, Derek Morphew, Struik Christian books, 1991 Performing Miracles & Healing, Roger Sapp, All Nations Pub., 2000 How To Pray for Healing, Che Ahn, Regal, 2004
Healing Today, Mark Stibbe & Marc A. Dupont, Authentic Media, UK, GA USA, 2006 When Heaven Invades Earth, Bill Johnson, Destiny Image Pub., 2003 (and his other books)

Websites, DVDs, You-tube:

It's Supernatural, Sid Roth: www.sidroth.org
DVD: Finger of God, Wanderlust productions presents a Darren Wilson film, 2007
You-tube video clip: "Grocery Store Healing Outreach" interview with Chad Dedmon, 4:53 min., uploaded Aug. 21, 2007.

Notes:

[1] Ken Blue, Authority to Heal, Ken Blue, InterVarsity Press, 1987, pp 27-29.
[2] John Wimber's notes and lecture from the Signs and Wonders & Church Growth conference, Vancouver, B.C. May 1985.
[3] 5 attitudes toward healing chart: Healing 87 conference notes, John Wimber, copyright Mercy Publishing 1987, p 7.
[4] Mark Stibbe & Marc Dupont, Healing Today, Mark Stibbe & Marc Dupont, Authentic Media, 2006, pp. 11, 12.

Chapter 8

Learning to Hear God's voice

"...and the sheep listen to his voice. He calls his own sheep
by name and leads them out...and his sheep follow him
because they know his voice." John 10: 3, 4

"I can't afford to think differently about my life than God does."
Bill Johnson

*M*y worldview growing up was that the Lord could speak to
you through the Bible but anybody claiming to hear from
God outside of the written Word of God was seriously suspect. If in
conversation with a Christian I heard them say "God told me this" or
"God told me that", I would have major red flags go up and be rather
irritated with them. After all, how do you argue with that? It seemed
to me to be irrefutable in a discussion and therefore, not fair. I pre-
sumed those kind of Christians lived up in the clouds of super spirituality without much grounding and accountability in their lives.

But in the early 1980s I found myself, at least intellectually and
theoretically, entertaining the possibility that maybe God is still infi-
nitely creative and communicates in many and varied ways such as
through dreams, visions, angelic visitations, and prophetic words
and pictures and that all the spiritual gifts of the Spirit referred to
in Scripture might not have ended after the last apostle died. Books
like, Those Controversial Gifts, by George Mallone, one of my

profs at seminary, helped me to re-evaluate my assumptions on this issue. I came to the realization that I was actually disobeying 1 Thessalonians 5:20 that commands us not to despise prophecy. I had to repent of my unbelief, my cynicism, and my despising of such a gift for today.

The Bible even takes it a step further by actually commanding us to covet prophecy. (1 Corinthians 12:31; 14:1-5, 39) We are to eagerly and passionately desire and pursue this gift of hearing God's heart and God's voice for ourselves and the benefit of others. And since the outpouring of the Spirit at Pentecost, according to Acts 2, we are to expect God to be communicating to His people, not only through the written Word but through dreams, visions and prophecies throughout "the last days". This truth is even more applicable for those of us in the last of the last days. Joel 2:28-31 indicates that prophecy will be intensified during the period immediately preceding the second coming of Christ. We should be prepared for a tremendous surge of prophetic revelation as the Lord is fashioning a prophetic people, the corporate Elijah. (Malachi 4:5)

Sure there have been times I have seen a poor and pathetic representation of this gift. I have heard so called prophetic words that are agitatedly loud, laced in old King James language, and so vague that it doesn't seem to be communicating anything of real substance or meaning. I've also heard supposed words from God that were really coming out of the bitterness, rejection and anger in someone's heart and God gets blamed for the verbal vomit. Rather than producing the fruit of conviction, encouragement and hope, it would spawn heaviness, condemnation, confusion and an all round yucky feeling in your spirit.

While pastoring in the early 1990s in Stratford, Ontario, Canada, I had such an experience. I was on the organizing committee that was formed by the city ministerial to put on a one night drama presentation of the Gospel of Mark to be held at our Shakespearean Festival Theater. After many months of work, the night finally came and I was looking forward to enjoying the play that evening with my wife, without any responsibilities attached. It was a very powerful and moving performance. But as we all began to get up out of our seats and put on our coats to leave the building, a tall wiry young man appeared on stage. With a strong and compelling voice he belted out "can I have your attention please" and then proceeded to ask us to sit down as he had something to tell us. Everyone looked around a little confused but quickly complied, thinking this was part of the program. This man, whom I did not recognize, then began to rant and rave about how the church in the West was self-promoting and worldly and needed to repent.

We were all stunned and paralyzed. Other committee members in the audience turned to me (I suspect because they knew I was not only the one pastor on the committee, but I was a pastor of a "charismatic church" that probably deals with this kind of stuff all the time!) and with their animated body and facial language were obviously pleading with me: "Jerry, do something". I finally got up the courage to get out of my seat and begin the long walk down the steep aisle towards the stage. Lining the front of the stage was an army of women ushers in red blazers whose job it was to keep unauthorized personnel off this sacred stage. World-renowned actors like Christopher Plummer and William Shatner (Captain Kirk) performed early in their careers on this very stage. After convincing an usher to let me go on, I nervously walked out on stage while this young man continued "prophesying" up a storm to a packed out sheepish looking crowd.

As I approached him, I was still not sure what I was going to say or whether I was about to get punched in the nose. I stood in front of him, blocking his view of his captivated audience, looked him in the eye and gently but firmly stated that he was going to have to stop immediately and that he and I should both go off to the side and talk further about what was troubling him. To my relief he instantly obeyed and I then turned to the audience and thanked them for coming, expressed hope that they enjoyed the evening's presentation and bid them good night.

I spent a good part of an hour talking off stage, over to the side, with this intense and angry young man in his twenties. The Lord gave me an infusion of grace, patience and compassion for him. After he got his burden fully off his chest and felt I had truly listened to him, I expressed my thoughts and feelings. I shared with him that much of what he was saying was indeed true but that the platform (literally) In which he was seeking to communicate it was totally inappropriate and that not only did he not have authority to speak out at this occasion but that the spirit in which he was proclaiming these things was one of anger and condemnation. His ranting was flowing out of a very wounded and rejected heart and not from the loving, grace-based and life transforming spirit and heart of God for His church. He admitted to me that he was not in relationship with any fellowship and that he had been kicked out of every church in the neighbouring city in which he had visited in an attempt to bring them "the word of the Lord".

I was hoping that after our conversation and a measure of trust established that I might have a future connection with him and possibly help him get his heart healed as well as see him mentored further in the prophetic. I saw amazing potential and sincerity in this man. Unfortunately, I never heard from him again.

A few awkward and yucky experiences like that could have totally turned me off to "prophecy" and having someone give a "word from God" but over the years I have come to so value and appreciate this precious gift when it flows from a healed and yielded heart. This real live God loves to speak to His kids, not just through His "best seller", the Bible, but in such a variety of creative ways. We can't put the God of the universe in a box and dictate to Him as to what He can and cannot do based on our "enlightened" western worldview and our personal preferences and comfort levels. I'm coming to realize that He really is God and I'm not!

We often laugh about a word being "pathetic" rather than "prophetic". But the body of Christ is on an amazing journey of learning to hear God's voice and heart.

A dear friend of ours, Maria, was coaching her teenage daughter, Leah, in learning to hear God's voice by sitting quietly and journaling, writing down the spontaneous flow of thoughts that comes to them, as taught by Mark Virkler in his Communion with God seminars. One day Leah was writing her thoughts down but then had a wave of doubt come over her. She responded by saying to the Lord, "is this really you God?" She immediately heard a Scripture reference pop into her head, "John 4:26". She quickly looked up the verse and to her amazement found it quoting Jesus addressing the woman at the well, saying: "It is I who am speaking to you"!

Learning to hear God's voice is like any skill. It takes motivation and practice over time. Years ago I heard the story of a Native American being invited by a friend to come visit him in his hometown of New York City. As they walked the streets of Manhattan and saw the tall steel and glass towers and heard the hustle and bustle of the crowds, buses and taxis, the native visitor stopped all of a sudden and said, "I hear a cricket". The New Yorker shook his head in disbelief as he watched his visiting friend look around then bend over and reach his hand in a small patch of grass growing in the cement sidewalk and pull out a small cricket. "That is unbelievable", he exclaimed. "How on earth could you have heard the sound of that cricket in all this noise"? His visiting friend answered by pulling out a coin from his pocket and tossing it up in the air. As the coin bounced on the cement walk, instantly a score of pedestrians stopped and turned to search out the whereabouts of what they were trained to be attentive to.

Jesus, the Great Shepherd, said that His sheep would hear His voice and follow Him. (John 10) We don't always get it right. We all are on a learning curve needing much grace and patience. But as 1 Thessalonians 5:21 instructs us, we are to test everything, including prophetic revelations and words, so that we can grow up and mature. In judging prophecy, we must ask:

Does it line up with the Bible? (2 Tim. 3:16,17; 1 Cor. 14:37-38);
Does it lift up Jesus Christ? (John 16:14; Rev. 19:10);
Does the word bring strength, encouragement and comfort or does it bring confusion, heaviness, and discouragement? (1 Cor. 14:3);
Is the character of the person Christ-like? (2 Cor. 11:13-15; 2 Pet. 2:1-5; Gal. 5:22-23; 1 Cor. 13:2).

Character must come before giftedness and the fruit of the Spirit is foundational for the gifts of the Spirit to flow appropriately. Problems arise when the foundation in our character cannot bear the weight of the anointing and glory God releases. People can begin to idolize the gifted person (especially the prophetically gifted) making excuses and exceptions for them in regards to issues of moral failure and the need for accountability. We so value and desperately need the gifts and power of the Holy Spirit but it is imperative that they be operative in tandem to Christ-like character. God can anoint a person in a split second but the fruit of the Spirit grows and is proven over time. If a person's heart is critical, arrogant, wounded, independent and self-seeking, there will not be a pure flow of the gifts of the Spirit and the heart of God.

We desire that any communication the body hears from the Head, the bride hears from the Groom and the army hears from their Command-in-Chief, is truly an accurate, life giving word, as He intends it to be.

I've also come to realize that, like nuclear power, the greater the gift for potential blessing, the greater seems to be a corresponding potential for things blowing up in your face if not properly pastored and facilitated, leaving a possible trail of hurt and fall out. So I understand why some church leaders insist on keeping their churches a "charismatic-free" zone in hopes of avoiding potential disasters. But to avoid misuse of a gift by banning its use is not the biblical solution. That leaves us at a serious disadvantage, handicapped, not only in our relationship with the Lord but also in knowing how to navigate through treacherous waters in the perilous days ahead.

Rick Joyner points out that in our information age, knowledge is a valuable commodity and accurate knowledge of the future is even more valuable. He was grieved, as we should be, when he heard the statistics of how many Americans twenty years ago were turning to astrology and palm readers to know about their futures. The statistics back then ranged between ten and fifteen million people a year who were dependent on spiritually dark sources to get a glimpse about the future. And the most shocking part of the statistic was that most of them were evangelical Christians who had been taught that God doesn't speak to them anymore.[1]

In days that are becoming more turbulent, uncertain, and stressful, the human spirit longs for insight and direction and if we have concluded that God leaves his children in the dark on specific matters pertaining to them, I guess it is not surprising they will even turn to the dark side for a "heads up" that might give them a measure of peace and security.

Pastors and church leaders, how much of this sad state of affairs are we going to be accountable for? To legitimately claim to be a church that obeys all of God's Word and truly experiences the vibrant and Spirit-filled Christian life that Christ died for us to have, we need to be willing to take risks and trust Christ enough to be the communicating Head of His body. Pastors with control issues take note, He really wants His church back!

John Eldredge, in his helpful book, Walking with God, says:

"I assume that an intimate, conversational walk with God is available, and is meant to be normal. I'll push that a step further. I assume that if you don't find that kind of relationship with God, your spiritual life will be stunted. And that will handicap the rest of your life."[2]

He goes on to talk about Jesus as the great Shepherd and that we, the sheep, live in dangerous country because of the thief who seeks to kill, steal and destroy so it is imperative to stay close to the Shepherd and listen for His voice and let Him lead us.

I heartily agree with Eldridge when he says that God speaks first and foremost through the Bible. It is the unchanging Word of God to us for all cultures and for all time and is the foundation for our covenant relationship with Him. With God's written Word in black and white, we have an objective reference point in which to test all supposed revelations. If it contradicts the Scriptures, it is not to be trusted or embraced.

John Eldridge addresses the sad fact that so many Christians believe that God *only* speaks today through the Bible:

"The irony of that belief is that's not what the Bible says. The Bible is filled with stories of God talking to his people...Now, if God doesn't also speak to us, why would he have given us all these stories of him speaking to others? "Look-here are hundreds of inspiring and hopeful stories about how God spoke to his people in this and that situation. Isn't it amazing? But you can't have that. He doesn't speak like that anymore." That makes no sense at all. Why would

God give you a book of exceptions? This is how I used to relate to my people, but I don't do that anymore...No, the Bible is a book of examples of what it looks like to walk with God."[3]

In the Gospel of John, Chapter 15, Jesus speaks of us being organically linked and dependent on Him, like branches to a vine. He then goes on to declare, "I no longer call you servants, because a servant does not know his master's business. Instead, I have called you friends, for everything that I learned from my Father I have made known to you". (John 15:15) So we should fully expect the Lord to continue to speak to us, His kids, today in all the ways we see Him communicate in the Word of God: through the Scriptures, through dreams, visions, angelic visitations, quiet whispers and promptings in our heart, words of wisdom and knowledge, prophetic utterances, and even the audible voice of God.

On October 3, 2007, I believe I experienced the audible voice of God, for the very first time. I don't see this as a badge of spiritual superiority at all. Rather, I suspect it is a combination of God just being God and my inability to be listening very attentively when He is trying to get my attention. I was riding my bicycle to the church office downtown when all of a sudden I heard this booming voice in stereo coming from the sky saying two simple words to me. I was stunned to say the least and almost fell off my bicycle! And of course my analytical mind was racing to process this experience and find some natural explanation so that I not be conned or deceived. But as the realization began to sink in that it was probably God speaking to me, I then started arguing with Him, while peddling on, that if He was going to speak to me directly, He probably should find something more profound to say. The two words spoken were: "Hi Jerry".

But then I felt God speak to me quietly in my heart that that was profound and significant: the Lord of the universe speaking my name. And then I began to realize the tone in which He spoke those words. Though it was a booming and authoritative base voice as if coming from loud speakers in the sky that brought an element of the fear of the Lord to me, it also had this tender and loving tone of invitation as if to ask: "Jerry, could you slow down a little and let's hang out together more?" This was a time in my life where I was quite distracted with all the challenges in ministry and my time of simply enjoying being with the Lord had substantially shriveled. And so this experience shook me to the core and woke me up to how much of a priority this is to the Lord and should be to me. God is a God of relationship, of friendship, and He loves to creatively communicate and share His heart with us.

According to the New Testament, God's primary intention for the gift of prophecy is to help find the treasure, not the trash in people's lives. Anyone can dig down and find trash. Prophecy is to "lift up, cheer up and build up". (1 Cor. 14:3) It is calling out the greatness and destiny that the Lord has placed in each person. We are made in God's image and have been redeemed by the blood of the Lamb. We are to honour the Christ in another Christian brother or sister. We are to know each other after the Spirit and call forth the gifts and anointings that God has given each believer and honour that.[4]

The accuser of the brethren is constantly seeking to intimidate, downsize and emasculate us. So we need personal prophetic words of encouragement over our lives in order to fight the good fight of faith as Paul tells Timothy. (1 Tim. 1:18) This vital gift of hearing God's prophetic words of affirmation helps break the lies of the enemy that we have believed and empowers us to dare to rise up into our true identity and destiny in Christ.

But some may argue that this will cause pride to rise up in our hearts. Usually those concerned about this are insecure people themselves. Joseph's and David's older brothers verbally accused them of arrogance when in fact it was God ordained confidence that they walked in. Here's a working definition of pride and humility that has helped me:

Pride is an estimation of yourself that is out of touch with reality. Humility is when we agree with God as to who we are in Christ.

Any prophetic words given to me over the years (and thankfully it has been many), I have diligently recorded and transcribed in a journal. Whenever I am discouraged or disoriented or about to venture out by faith on a ministry assignment, I not only read and meditate on the Scriptures, I read through my personal prophetic words, ponder them in my heart and pray into them, reminding both the Lord and myself of what He has said about my life and calling. I don't seek to make any of the words happen (who wants an Ishmael?) but I aggressively use them in the battle to step into my calling and destiny in Christ with faith and confidence.

Someone may ask: "Shouldn't prophetic words bring correction or judgment from God such as we see so frequently in the Old Testament?" God raised up a small handful of Old Testament prophets whose primary assignment was to bring a corporate word from God to the people of Israel, calling them to repent and return to the Lord. If they would not respond, God would have to deal with them accordingly, because He loved them and He would spell that out clearly for them so there was no misunderstanding. It was usually brought in a spirit of tender love yet firmness and with a strong ray of hope if they would respond to God's overtures appropriately.

In the New Testament, the gift of prophecy is available to the whole body of Christ, as is the gift of the Holy Spirit available to all. But prophecy is described as a gift of the Spirit that is primarily for the edification of others, both unbeliever (prophetic evangelism) and believer. (1 Cor. 12-14) Prophetic words are not to be despised but valued, cherished and "coveted" as well as properly tested by the objective written Word of God. (1 Thess. 5:19-21; 1 Cor. 12-14)

Pastoral wisdom suggests that directional and corrective words are best left for the more seasoned prophetic person (or one in the office of a prophet) who has been well established in their gifting, is in relationship and recognized by the body of Christ, and ideally given with pastoral input and involvement. This way the word may be more wisely and sensitively communicated and better received, hopefully resulting in good and lasting fruit.

Knowing the voice of God is not a luxury for God's people who desire to live a vibrant Christian life, especially in the coming days of both chaos and glorious revival. We will increasingly need His specific and tangible guidance that will bring us peace, joy and confidence in our journey of faith.

My wife, Pam, and I and our children have been blessed enormously by personal prophetic guidance and encouragement given to us over the years from other believers and from hearing God's voice ourselves. Receiving a clearer sense of direction, identity and destiny have empowered us to follow the Lord with greater joy and confidence. Here are a few instances where we felt the Lord speaking to us:

Years ago, Pam had a dream about me going to drive for a bigger bus company in Vancouver but that it wouldn't turn out to be a very friendly working environment for me. She didn't know I was considering leaving the small bus company for a unionized company that pays a little bit more. So, after hearing this timely dream I decided to stay where I was and within a month I was stunned to see God catapult me to being the number one driver with all the best paying trips and perks, including a raise in pay!

In January 2011 Pam attended a Mark Virkler "Hearing the Voice of God" seminar hosted by our dear pastor friends, Zak and Karen-Marie Gariba in Orillia, Ontario. In one session Mark had everyone journal, asking the Lord about any dormant dreams that had been buried. As Pam was journaling, the Lord brought up the matter of Pam's dream when she first went into the nursing field some thirty-five years earlier, that of using her nursing skills overseas on the mission field. Pam has missionary blood in her with her parents, grandparents and great grandparents being missionaries in China. She married me during nursing school, and I had a vision for revival and pastoring churches in Canada. Early in our marriage we sought to do a mission venture in South America but it did not work out. Her dream quietly got buried.

When Pam came home from this seminar and like an excited little girl, shared with me this dormant dream the Lord had awakened, I heard the Lord clearly speak to me to listen to her and to stop what I was doing in my life and serve her dream. This actually resolved an impasse that she and I were in. We were thrilled that we had gotten out of credit card and line of credit debt but I was feeling compelled to also sell our cute little home and get out of our mortgage debt as well. We had little equity in the home and if real estate prices were to drop in Canada in the future (the U.S. has already seen about a thirty-three percent national average plunge since 2006 with the buttom not yet in sight), even by ten to twenty percent, we would quickly be underwater.

With my willingness to explore the prospects of both of us going on a short term mission venture for three to four months, without batting an eye, my wife was more than willing to sell our house! We are now completely debt free with enough dollars left to cover our mission trip so we didn't have to do fund raising. And thanks to generous friends who wanted to participate financially and prayerfully in our trip, we have some dollars left for an emergency fund. With Pam's dream coming true, I have not seen her this alive, this joyful and this fulfilled in a very long time.

Also, in April of 2011, just after finalizing our upcoming mission trip to Africa slated for September, a pastor, John Irving, from a neighbouring town prayed and prophesied over me when I visited his church. We don't know each other and he only knew that I was a pastor in a nearby city. To my amazement, he began to prophesy that the Lord was about to give me a sabbatical from my church that I pastor. He didn't know whether it would be two, three or four months but he saw my wife and I traveling and that God was going to have me write a book on this sabbatical. In fact, he said that the Lord had been on my case about writing a book for several years but I had been distracted by other commitments and had been procrastinating and questioning whether I really had anything to say of substance to warrant putting another book on the market. He saw me on this sabbatical sitting in front of a computer and finally getting on with this assignment.

And so as I write this, I'm sitting under a round thatched roof hut on a mission base in Malawi, Africa, with a beautiful but very warm breeze blowing, typing on my wife's Mac laptop. This prophetic word (the latest among a string of words over several years prodding me on to write) has given me more resolve to make this project my top priority and seek to get it completed. I want to be careful however, to make it clear that in sharing this prophetic word, I'm not claiming in any way that what I write is somehow more inspired or accurate than any other book. It simply shows that I needed considerable prodding from the Lord to help get me past my intimidation and procrastination of writing. In spite of all the imperfections of what I am sharing in this book, God seems to think it may have something helpful to say to others.

Of course hearing God's voice is not always about being a blessing to us. Often the Lord will prompt and speak in order that we can touch and bless others with the grace and heart of God.

On one of several occasions that I had the privilege of speaking at the renewal meetings at the Toronto Airport Christian Fellowship in the mid 1990s, the Lord nudged me with a "word of knowledge". After my message was finished, we directed those who desired to receive prayer ministry from the prayer team to line up along the sides and the back of the auditorium. We may have been ten minutes into this time of prayer and worship and as I was going down the line and praying for people, I heard these words in my head or heart: "Go to the microphone and invite those with serious eye conditions to come to the front for prayer for healing". I brushed this thought aside immediately because I had just preached on the story of Jesus healing the blind man from John Chapter 9. But that phrase kept coming to me several times over the next few minutes. I couldn't shake it. I began to believe it could actually be God speaking to me. I then went to the microphone and gave that specific invitation. Within minutes there were about forty people standing in front of me anticipating God to move on their behalf. I asked for a handful of prayer team people to come join me in ministering.

I had the privilege of praying for five of these precious people. As I stepped up to the first person, all of a sudden a rush of faith came upon me, what I believe the Bible calls the "gift of faith", and I felt like a kid unleashed in a playground! All five that I prayed for claimed to be healed of their eyesight problems. Two of them were women who not only were both age forty, but both had been born blind in one eye. And both claimed that they could now see out of that eye for the first time. One of them at first could only see shadows out of that blind eye so I did what Jesus had to do on one occasion when a blind person saw people like trees walking, pray again (Mark 8:22-26), and this time she could see fully! One lady was from Connecticut and the other from Cornwall, Ontario.

Of the other three people I prayed for, one said to me that that morning she was working in her garden and the Lord told her to go to the Toronto Airport church that night because they would be praying for people with eyesight issues. That boosted my faith in praying for her! And another one of the three told me that as she came in to the evening service the Lord told her to make sure she stays until the very end of the meeting because there would be a specific invitation given for prayer for eye sight.

Of course the most exciting thing was that God brought salvation to several that night. That is the greatest miracle of all. But I must admit that I was very encouraged because even I, a rookie in all this, actually heard the Lord's voice and obeyed His prompting and had the joy of seeing our big and loving God do what He does so well, restore people!

And you and I get to partner with Him in this Kingdom venture as we learn to hear His voice and follow His lead, in the power of the Holy Spirit. Fasten your seatbelt. Though things will get a bit bumpy, we are in for the ride of our lives! He has promised that in the last days He will pour out His Spirit on all flesh and prophecy, visions and dreams will be a common occurrence. We will need to hear His still small voice for personal guidance but we will need to hear what the Spirit is saying to the church at large.

God is raising up a prophetic church, the priesthood of all believers. But He is also raising up seasoned prophetic voices that have a credible track record of hearing the Lord accurately. I will be quoting many words from these prophetic voices in the coming chapters of this book that I believe the Lord is giving for the church to be forewarned and further prepared for the exciting but wild days ahead. They are not a substitute for Scripture but are to be tested by Scripture and further confirmation of Scripture.

Let me end this chapter with a prophetic word given by Elaine Tavolacci, posted January 29, 2011 on her website: www.awordinseason.info (used with permission)

A Season of Acceleration

"As we are in a season of changing and shifting the Lord says I am bringing you in to a time of great acceleration. I desire to move you ahead expeditiously into the calling that I have for you. Do not be afraid to move forward into what I have created you to do. Allow Me to fine-tune your hearing to hear My voice with clarity. Listen for My voice and My leading as I open up your ears to hear the direction that I would have you to go.

I have many gifts to release to you. I will speak to you in the daytime and in the night seasons as you allow Me to. I will speak to you in dreams and visions and reveal My plans and purposes to you.

Seek My face diligently. I desire to abide in your midst, to walk with you, to talk with you just as I walked and talked with Enoch. Allow me to be in your every day affairs, to be with you on your jobs, to be with you in the marketplace, to be with you in your homes and your families. Make Me part of your daily life. Watch for My leading and the unique ways that I will speak to you in this time of acceleration. As you lay down your life I am about to do exceedingly abundantly above and beyond all you ask or think. Stay in that intimate communion with Me and cut off anything that would restrain you so that the process of acceleration will not be hindered as I move you forth into the calling that I have for you. As My anointing increases in your life, your ministry will also be enlarged and will expand as you move forward in obedience to the calling on your life says the Lord".

Amen. Let it be so Lord

Recommended Resources:

Books:

Surprised by the Voice of God, Jack Deere, Zondervan, Grand Rapids, 1996
The Beginner's Guide to the Gift of Prophecy, Jack Deere, Regal Books, 2001
Growing in the Prophetic, Mike Bickle, Kingsway Pub., 1995
The Prophetic Ministry, Rick Joyner, Morningstar Pub.,Charlotte, N.C., 1997
You May All Prophesy! Steve Thompson, Morningstar, 2000

If This Were A Dream, What Would It Mean? Murray Dueck, Freshwind Press, 2005
Voices: Understanding and Responding to the Language of Heaven, Steve Witt, Destiny Image Pub., Shippensburg, PA., 2007
Prophecy and Responsibility, Graham Cooke, Brilliant Book House, 2007
Approaching the Heart of Prophecy, Graham Cooke, Brilliant Book House, 2009 Walking with God, John Eldridge, Thomas Nelson, Nashville, TN., 2008,
Communion With God Study Guide, Mark and Patti Virkler, Destiny Image, 1990
Revised manual: 4 Keys to Hearing God's Voice, Mark Virkler, 2010 (companion DVDs)
Ecstatic Prophecy, Stacey Campbell, Chosen Books, 2008

Websites:

Mark Virkler, Communion with God website: www.cwgministries.org
Rick Joyner's Morningstar website: www.morningstarministries.org
John Paul Jackson, www.johnpaul.streamsministries.com

Notes:

---

[1] Rick Joyner, Prophetic Perspectives on Current Events, on his website, www.morningstarministries.org May 16, 2011.
[2] John Eldridge, Walking with God, Thomas Nelson, Nashville, TN., 2008, p. 7.
[3] Ibid., pp. 13-15.
[4] Kris Vallotton and Bill Johnson, The Supernatural Ways of Royalty, pp. 103,4.

Chapter 9

The Coming Monster Waves of Revival and Awakening (Part 1)

I believe we are living in a kairos moment, a unique window of time in history whereby an unprecedented visitation of the glory of God is bearing down upon us like a tidal wave. We need to wax our surfboards and get properly positioned and poised to ride this imminent tsunami of the Spirit! This involves getting prepared theologically, emotionally and spiritually for such an extraordinary acceleration of God's Kingdom power and presence.

However, the late Dr. John White, in his book, When the Spirit Comes with Power, makes this astute observation:

"From a safe distance of several hundred years or several thousand miles, revival clearly looks invigorating...But if we find ourselves in the midst of revival, rather than being invigorated, we may be filled with skepticism, disgust, anger or even fear...The irony of revivals is that they are so longed for in times of barrenness, but they are commonly opposed and feared when they arrive...The hostility is never to the idea of revival, which is ardently prayed for, but to God's answer to our prayers and the unexpected form it may take".[1]

I don't think any of us are fully prepared for what God will bring next but I believe more believers are more prepared than a decade or two ago. Many of us have been stretched by previous waves of the Spirit (the Charismatic movement and Jesus movement of the late 60s and 70s, the "Third Wave" of the 1980s and the "Toronto Blessing" and Pensacola outpourings that began in 1994 and 1995 respectively). We have tasted of the manifest presence of God and we are ruined for anything less. God has captured our hearts afresh and has dealt with some of the control issues in our lives and churches but, I fear, so many of God's people are totally ill-equipped for what is coming. Their mindset and assumptions of what revival would look like when it comes need to be radically changed so they can more readily process and embrace what God is about to do rather than get upset, criticize and oppose it.

So, in hopes of further preparing folks for the "new thing" God is about to do, we will seek to answer the following questions:

What is revival?
Why is revival needed?
When has revival occurred before?
Why should we expect to see revival again soon?

In Revival Part 2, we will seek to answer the questions:

Why is revival often bitterly opposed by believers?
And how on earth can we promote, pursue and partner with God in revival?

What is Revival?

The classic term, "revival", as a noun, is not technically found in the Scriptures. But neither is the term "Trinity" for that matter! And yet both concepts are clearly found throughout the Bible. Various forms of the verb "revive" are found frequently as are words like "restore, renew, awaken and refresh". In Psalm 85:6 we find this prayer request: "will you not revive us again that your people may rejoice in you?" In Isaiah 57:15 we find this promise from God, "I revive the spirit of the humble and revive the heart of the contrite".

The subject of revival is also described in various phrases or metaphors such as: "an outpouring of the Spirit" (like rain or fire falling or wind blowing), "the renewing of God's mighty deeds", "times of refreshing", "the glory of the Lord returning to his temple", "God healing the land" and "the time of God's visitation".

J. I. Packer defines revival as a time, "when God comes down, God's Word comes home, God's purity comes through, God's people come alive and outsiders come in".[2]

I love D.M. Panton's description of revival as, "the inrush of the Spirit into a body that threatens to become a corpse"![3]

Arthur Wallis states that, "revival is man retiring into the background because God has taken the field. It is the Lord making bare his holy arm and working in extraordinary power on saint and sinner".[4]

Summarizing David Bryant's words, it is, "God's kingly presence intensified (fullness) and God's kingdom purposes accelerated (fulfillment)".[5]

"It is a more comprehensive unveiling of King Jesus to His church, with dramatic repercussions. Shaken from our apathy and fears, we are launched afresh into kingdom work on all fronts... We're waking up to all Christ wants to be for His church. It's like the beginning of a brand new day".[6]

C.S. Lewis, in his children's books, The Chronicles of Narnia, powerfully portrays this revelation of King Jesus and His manifest presence being restored again among His subjects. Aslan, the Lion, has been absent from his kingdom for some time and the White Witch has made Narnia a place where "it is always winter but never Christmas". With rumours rumbling around that Aslan is on the move in the land, Mr. Beaver recites this prophecy:

"Wrong will be right, when Aslan comes in sight,
At the sound of his roar, sorrows will be no more,
And when he bares his teeth, winter meets its death,
And when he shakes his mane, we shall have spring again".[7]

When the manifest presence of God intensifies, creating a divine "radiation zone" of the Holy Spirit, it releases a greater revelation of the amazing love and holiness of God as well as the sinfulness of man, causing many to come under awesome conviction. Widespread repentance is the result, usually among Christians first then unbelievers. And it is not limited to the four walls of churches but spills out into the public marketplace.

Let me give you two examples from the 1857-1859 revival:

In the town of Coleraine, in Ulster a young boy in school became very agitated in his soul to the point that the teacher sent him home, escorted by an older boy who happened to be a Christian. They had not gone too far before the older one had brought relief to the boy by leading him to faith in Christ. The two of them then returned to the school and the new little convert reported to his teacher how happy he was now that he had Jesus living in his heart. The great revival historian, J. Edwin Orr tells the amazing story of how those few simple words of testimony were used by the Spirit to release an astounding effect upon the other children: "boy after boy rose and silently left the room. Going outside the teacher found these boys all on their knees, ranged along the wall of the playground. Very soon their silent prayer became a bitter cry, it was heard by another class inside and pierced their hearts. They fell on their knees, and their cry for mercy was heard in turn by a girls' class above. In a few moments, the whole school was on their knees! Neighbours and passers-by came flocking in and all as they crossed the threshold came under the same convicting power. "Every room was filled with men, women, and children seeking God".[8]

The other example would be "during the same 1859 revival in America, ships entered a definite zone of heavenly influence as they drew near port. Ship after ship arrived with the same talk of sudden conviction and conversion. A captain and an entire crew of thirty men found Christ at sea and arrived at port rejoicing. This overwhelming sense of God bringing deep conviction of sin is perhaps the outstanding feature of true revival. Its manifestation is not always the same, to cleansed hearts it is heaven; to convicted hearts it is hell".[9]

Why is Revival Needed?

Throughout biblical and church history, the hearts of God's people perpetually cool off and harden towards Him, creating the need for a spiritual awakening and reviving. Nehemiah 9:25-28 (and many times in the book of Judges) describes the cycle of spiritual decline and renewal which seems to involve about 6 stages:

1. The people of God are alive and passionately in love with Him
2. Spiritual decline sets in and hearts are quietly and subtly cooling off
3. The hearts become like stone
4. The Lord disciplines those He loves, such as when the Israelites were taken into exile
5. The people of God cry out for mercy in intercession and repentance (2 Chron. 7:14)
6. God comes to their rescue and revives His people again (since the day of Pentecost revivals not only involve a return to the Lord but an outpouring of the Spirit upon His people)

Revival Cycle

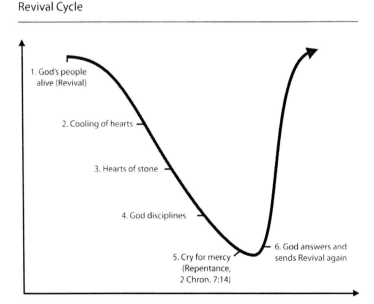

However, let me qualify this description of the "revival cycle" with some challenging words from the well-respected contempo rary revivalist and apostolic father, Bill Johnson. He argues that just because most revivals have only lasted a few years, we shouldn't simply assume that revivals are "only meant to last long enough to give the church a shot in the arm". He urges us to aim higher, believing the Word that declares that God's government, by nature, should only be advancing and increasing. (Isaiah 9)

We must be careful not to just "build monuments to the past but take the advancement to the next level in the next generation...The only safe place to be is in the place of occupation and advancement. The moment we work to maintain rather than increase what we've been given is the moment we begin to lose what was given to us".

Johnson calls for an understanding and practice of the Kingdom principles of honour and inheritance in order that a revival culture would be established and a move of the Spirit could be sustained and not fizzle out. In an environment of mutual honour, he believes that the inheritance of mantles and anointings can be passed on to each succeeding generation and they can stand on their spiritual parent's shoulders. "The ceiling of one generation must become the floor of the next".[10]

I suspect too that being at the end of the age, we are coming into the transition stage of childbirth into the age to come (at Christ's return) and the labour pains of global trouble and revival will be increasing in both intensity and frequency. Waves (or contractions) of revival that came about every one hundred years in previous centuries, have been coming every decade over the last half a century and soon could very well be virtually constant.

When has Revival Occurred Before?
(a snapshot of revivals in recent history)

Rick Joyner makes this wise observation: "Many think of history as dates and dead people. Unfortunately, uninspired teachers often reduce it to that. However, those who are inspired will not only glean wisdom and understanding from the past, but they will also be given a remarkable compass for navigating through the present while they prepare for the future".[11]

Similarly, Winkie Pratney argues, "The great need of the church is a sense of her history and destiny. How do you 'boldly go where no man has gone before' unless you first know where you really are and where you come from?"[12]

The Bible records at least a dozen revivals within its history. Since the outpouring of the Spirit in Acts Chapter 2 in the first century, we see many moves of God to renew and refresh his people throughout church history. Many of these seasons of visitation were prior to the **Protestant Reformation** of the 16th century but we will focus on some of the major moves of God since.

In the 17th century God graciously worked through the **Puritan and Pietist movements** of Europe. Over the last three hundred years we have seen a string of major revivals that have shaped much of our western civilization and our expectations of historic revivals.

Below is a chart showing the waves of revival:

Revival Cycles - last 300 years

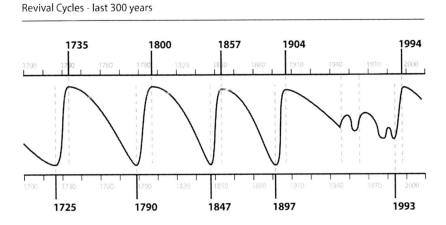

The **"Great Awakening"** of the 18th century in Europe and America is probably the most famous and classic example of a historic revival. This awakening involved leaders like Count Zinzendorf of Germany, with the outpouring which began in 1727 and the amazing twenty-four hour prayer vigil that lasted over one hundred years and hundreds of radical lovers of Jesus going to mission fields throughout the world, carrying the motto: "To win for the Lamb that was slain the reward of his suffering". In Great Britain, John Wesley (who was powerfully impacted by Zinzendorf) and George Whitfield were greatly anointed outdoor preachers and revivalists. In the thirteen colonies of America, God used the brilliant theologian, teacher and pastor, Jonathan Edwards to lead and articulate this work of God.

Not only were there massive numbers of spiritual conversions and believers revitalized in their faith on both sides of the Atlantic, but also over the coming years, major social reforms took place. In Great Britain it included the abolition of slavery through the efforts of William Wilberforce. Some historians credit the Great Awakening with saving England from a bloody revolution like in France.

At the beginning of the 19th century revival fires were burning again in America in what some have called "**the Second Awakening**". On the east coast it was on college campuses. On the western front it was outdoor camp meetings. Charles Finney, a lawyer, became a very influential evangelist, revivalist and social reformer throughout much of this century.

In 1857, "**the Prayer Revival**" broke out, first in Hamilton, Ontario, Canada when Dr. Walter and Phoebe Palmer visited and did some meetings. But it soon went south of the border to New York City where they were from. Jeremiah Lamphier, a businessman, began noon hour prayer meetings in New York and within six months saw up to ten thousand businessmen praying daily for revival. It is worth noting that the social context for this divine work was financial turbulence that led to most of these business men being unemployed and desperately crying out to the Lord.

J. Edwin Orr states, "Revival went up the Hudson and down the Mohawk. The Baptists had so many people to baptize they could not get them in the churches. They went down to the river, cut a square hole in the ice and baptized them. When the Baptists do that, they really are on fire!"[13]

This "Third Awakening", as some call it, spread throughout the United States, with many noon hour prayer meetings in major cities. It also spread to Wales, Scotland and Northern Ireland and saw upwards of two million converts as well as social reforms in society such as the abolition of slavery in America, and prison, labour and education reforms.

In November, **1904, revival fires broke out in Wales** under the leadership of Evan Roberts, a twenty-six year old man. Leaders came from around the world and were humbled to see how God used teens and children. G. Campbell Morgan, pastor of Westminster Chapel in London, visited some of Robert's meetings and later relayed to his church that it was "Pentecost continued", referring to the second chapter of Acts, and said, "We had better keep our hands off this work". He also made mention of the fact that there was no advertising; "The whole thing advertises itself".[14]

Evan and others were not eloquent preachers but were sensitive followers of the Spirit. Robert's vision of seeing one hundred thousand come to Christ in Wales was fulfilled in less than a year. People got converted just reading about the revival in the newspapers! Crime dropped off to the point where many courtrooms and jails were empty and judges and police had very little to do.

Horses in the coal mines had to be brought out and re-trained. They were accustomed to being handled roughly and following commands that involved verbal abuse and cursing. Since the vast majority of coal miners had come to Christ, the horses were confused with the new commands that were so humane and wholesome!

Prior to the revival, Wales was in a frenzy over their favourite sport, football (called soccer in North America). With the revival, the stadiums stood empty. No one preached against the sport, the players and fans had simply become so captivated with the Lord that they were no longer interested in the game.[15]

The Welsh revival fire spread throughout Great Britain, Scandinavia, Europe, Africa, India, Korea, as well as the U.S. The pastors of Atlantic City, New Jersey, reported only fifty adults not converted in a population of over fifty thousand.[16]

In California, hunger for a move of God intensified in the hearts of leaders like Frank Bartleman, William Seymour and Joseph Smale, as they were impacted by the reports and booklets on the revival in Wales in 1905. Smale had visited the Welsh revival and Bartleman corresponded with Evan Roberts. **On April 9, 1906 the**

Holy Spirit was poured out in Los Angeles in a little cottage prayer meeting led by Seymour in a home at 214 North Bonnie Brae Street. With all the commotion, crowds formed outside and Seymour ended up setting up a make shift pulpit on the front porch. After a little over a week, the meetings needed to be re-located due to unmanageable crowds (the city had been stirred) and the floor caving in. William Seymour, a one-eyed black man, ran daily meetings for about three years in a run-down abandoned "barn" (Jesus seems to like showing up in barns!) at 312 Azusa Street in the ghettos of L.A.[17]

God seems to love orchestrating and paying attention to details. "Azusa" is a native term meaning blessed miracle. Los Angeles means city of angels and at the time, Los Angeles was considered the most cosmopolitan city in the world. Like the Day of Pentecost, the Holy Spirit was poured out with the nations present to witness and experience it. The Holy Spirit is truly a missionary Spirit!

The founder and leader of a holiness denomination who lived in Los Angeles at the time, never took the time to visit the Azusa Street outpouring but predicted those meetings would have as much impact in the world as tossing a pebble into the ocean. This move of God turned into the great Pentecostal Revival that saw about five million converts over the next few years and continues to impact hundreds of millions of lives around the world even to this day.

Leaders like C. Peter Wagner have called the twentieth century "The Century of the Holy Spirit". God has been bringing wave after wave of revivals and renewal movements to His church.

In the late 1940s and 50s we saw the **Latter Rain Movement** in western Canada and the U.S. God also unleashed what has been called **"the Healing Revival"** during this same time frame. Billy Graham and the **Evangelical Movement** also exploded on the scene during these post World War II years. On the other side of the Atlantic, revival broke out in the **Hebrides Islands** in Scotland in 1949 with seventy-five percent of the converts coming to Christ outside of the church walls.

The 1960s and 70s saw God do a fresh work in the mainline and Catholic churches with the **Charismatic Renewal Movement**. The Spirit was also poured out among the youth and hippies during this same time period, in what has been called **the Jesus Movement.**

Through Christian evangelistic coffeehouses, Jesus festivals, beach ministry and communes, hundreds of thousands came to Christ, bringing much fresh blood, fresh worship, informal dress and body life ministry into the institutional church. During this time frame we have also seen the birth and growth of the **Messianic Movement** around the world of Jewish people embracing Jesus as their Messiah.

In the 1980s we saw a fresh emphasis upon intimate worship and the power gifts of the Spirit, particularly divine healing and culturally sensitive evangelism, to the baby boomer generation in the **Third Wave or Signs and Wonders Movement**, led by the California Vineyard leader, John Wimber.

Starting January 20, 1994, a powerful outpouring of the Spirit took place in a little church at the end of the airport runway in Toronto, Ontario, Canada that the British media later dubbed **The Toronto Blessing**. Pastors John and Carol Arnott, of the Toronto Airport Vineyard Christian Fellowship (presently called Catch The Fire, Toronto) had just returned from the Argentina revival as well as invited Vineyard pastor, Randy Clark, of St. Louis, Missouri, and his team to come minister for four nights of meetings. Randy had been powerfully touched by the Lord through the ministry of Rodney Howard Browne a couple of months earlier.

After the four nights of very powerful meetings, John Arnott was insistent that Randy stay on for an indefinite period of time of protracted meetings, thinking God's manifest presence may keep coming for several weeks. Word got out that God was showing up at this little church at the end of the runway and hungry believers from all around started showing up. Over the coming weeks and months they were scrambling to look for a larger venue to handle the crowds as dry and desperate Christians started flying in from around the world. Extra flights had to be added between London and Toronto because of all the folks from the United Kingdom flocking to the meetings. A secular Toronto tourist magazine declared the Airport church as Toronto's "most notable" tourist attraction for the year!

Eventually they were able to acquire a nearby conference facility for a fraction of it's worth that could house several thousand people rather than just several hundred.

They continued with daytime pastor's meetings for several years and nightly revival meetings every night except Mondays for approximately twelve years. The Toronto church has also hosted about a half a dozen major conferences each year that continue to this day, almost nineteen years later.

Several million visitors have come from every corner of the globe. They have seen the Lord do amazing things: thousands of conversions, physical, emotional and relational healings, an increase in people's passion for Jesus, for His Word, for evangelism and for the kingdom of God. Aside from nightly meetings and numerous conferences, they have sent out hundreds of ministry and mission teams to do conferences, leadership training schools, soaking schools and planting of churches among the nations.

One high profile ministry that has been impacted by this outpouring is that of Heidi and Rolland Baker, founders of Iris Ministries in Mozambique. This American missionary couple came to Toronto burned out and exhausted from their work with orphans and a few struggling churches in Mozambique. Since getting revived and restored with the Father's love and freshly anointed with the Spirit of God, they have seen their mission work explode exponentially over the last fifteen or so years. They, and the Christian world have marveled at what God has done through and among them - tens of thousands of converts and baptisms, pastors raised up, over ten thousand churches planted, thousands of orphans embraced and loved to life and hope, stunning signs and wonders of healings, resurrections (over one hundred), supernatural multiplications of food and Iris orphanages and mission bases springing up in many nations of Africa and beyond. Heidi has written several books and there have been numerous documentaries and various You-tube videos produced such as: "Heidi Baker: Intimacy for Miracles - CBN.com", telling of the amazing things God has been doing there in our day.

In the 1990s countless hot spots of revival broke out. For instance, on Father's Day, 1995, a powerful move of God broke out in **Pensacola, Florida**, with Steve Hill, the visiting evangelist, at pastor John Kilpatrick's Brownsville Assembly of God church.

And on October 20, 1996, a stunning visitation of God's manifest presence took place, starting with the dramatic shattering of the plexiglass pulpit in the Christian Tabernacle in Houston, Texas, with pastor Richard Heard and Tommy Tenny, the visiting evangelist. Both the fear of the Lord and the joy of the Lord were released with much good fruit for the Kingdom.

I have had the privilege of being a part of what God did through the Jesus Movement of the 70s, the Third Wave Movement of the 80s as well as the Toronto Blessing of the 90s and beyond. I had been an assistant pastor with the Arnotts just prior to the revival at the first church they planted in Stratford, Ontario and then senior pastor of that church once they moved to Toronto in 1992 as the Lord positioned them for what was coming. I was also privileged to be at the Vineyard pastor's all day meeting the next day (January 21st, 1994) that had been previously scheduled with Randy Clark, where God met me in a fresh and powerful way. Since then, my family and I have gone to the Toronto meetings and conferences countless times.

Randy and the Arnotts also came to our Stratford church the first weekend of February to lead meetings with us. To our delight, the manifest presence and power of God came dramatically. They and we were like excited little kids playing in mud, realizing that this fresh and powerful anointing was contagious and easily transferable. We had been praying for God to move for years.

I must confess however, that as pastor of this church of over two hundred and fifty people, it was momentarily quite overwhelming and stressful for me to see the auditorium floor strewn with bodies like the slain upon a battlefield! It was one thing to see all the unusual phenomena that often accompany revivals of the past happening in Toronto where I wasn't pastorally responsible. It's another thing for a pastor to see his flock: adults, teens and children alike, falling, shaking, jerking, laughing, crying, having visions, seeing angels, prophesying, and being healed in heart and body, all at the same time. It is a lot to process, scrambling for understanding and discernment to be sure we are not being deceived. But, over time we have searched the Scriptures, studied revivals in church history, and have been "fruit inspectors" of the lives of those we know and pastorally care for to be confident that this is indeed God on the move.

In the first few years of this renewal/revival I was also privileged to take ministry teams to various parts of Canada, the U.S. and a half a dozen other nations and see God do wondrous work in thousands of precious people. I've taught on this subject of revival and church history, which is a passion of mine, first at the Toronto Airport Church's School of Ministry and then later at their School of Revelation over the years. I also wrote a twenty page booklet called, Preparing for Revival Fire, in 1994 (revised in 1995), which I am drawing from for this chapter

Why Should We Expect To See Revival Again Soon?

We need to keep in mind that there are many revival fires that have been burning for years in various parts of the world and other pockets of revival are breaking out all the time. God is increasingly on the move, and there is much to be encouraged and excited about.

For instance, the 2001 edition of the World Christian Encyclopedia, edited by David Barrett, states that in 1900, Africa had about nine million born again believers (about five percent of the continent) but by the year 2000, it was more like three hundred and sixty million (closer to fifty percent).

In Latin America, the same time period saw growth from about one million true Christians to over one hundred and seventy million. And in recent decades the momentum continues to grow. Worldwide, the number of those considered true disciples of Christ is growing by about eight percent per year. Guatemala is now close to fifty percent born again Christians. Argentina has seen several national revivals in the 1950s, 80s, and 90s. Brazil today is seeing a surge of evangelical Christianity.

Several million Muslims have come to Christ in the last decade or two through signs and wonders, visions of Christ, radio ministry and are being discipled in underground house churches. The conversions in the last couple of decades are more than the total conversions over the past thousand years! Reports from Iran now indicate there could be upwards of four to seven million new believers in Jesus as Messiah.

Joel Rosenberg tells the story of an abused Muslim woman who attempted suicide by taking sleeping pills. Before she went unconscious, she had a vision of something called "Living Water". She wanted to know more so she threw up the pills, found a Bible, and read the book of the Gospel of John. When she got to chapter 4, she read about the troubled Samaritan woman at the well and about living water that Jesus was offering. She received Jesus, found a group of believers and got discipled. Since then she has led four of her sisters and her parents to the Lord and has a house church in her home with twenty some Iranian believers.[18]

And of course the church of China has seen explosive growth from one or two million in 1949 when communism took over to somewhere between one hundred to one hundred and fifty million today. God has given them a vision and a movement called "Back to Jerusalem" of one hundred thousand Chinese missionaries being trained and mobilized to take the gospel west through the Muslim, Buddhist and Hindu nations and on to Jerusalem to reach the Jews, making the promise of Acts 1:8 - from Jerusalem to the uttermost parts of the earth- come full circle before the end of the age. They are being trained on how to suffer and die for Jesus, how to witness for the Lord, how to speak another language, and how to escape from prison with skills such as learning how to jump from second story windows handcuffed without injuring themselves! Hundreds have already left China on their mission.[19]

Even with all the astounding reports of God's Kingdom advancing around the world in recent decades, we are anticipating even greater, wider, stronger moves of God, a tsunami wave or waves to come bearing down on the world in the very near future, leading ultimately to the return of Christ.

What signs are there that point to such a possibility?

1. Biblical texts that create such an expectation:

Numbers 14:21: "But truly, as I live, and as all the earth shall be filled with the glory of the LORD..." (English Standard Version, NIV translation has present tense rather than future tense)

Habakuk 2:14: "for the earth will be filled with the knowledge of the glory of the Lord as the waters cover the sea."

Joel 2:28: "I will pour out my Spirit on all people...(vs. 31) before the coming of the great and dreadful day of the Lord."

Joel 2:23: "He sends you abundant showers, both autumn and spring rains."

Early rains (autumn) soften the ground, making it suitable for ploughing and sowing. With the approach of the harvest, heavy rain (latter rains in the spring) returns to swell and mature the grain and fruit in preparation for the time of reaping. The latter rain is in preparation for the day of harvest. "The spring rains are considered such a natural blessing that they assume an eschatological significance (Joel 2:23; Zech.10:1)".[20]

Malachi 4:5: "See, I will send you the prophet Elijah before that great and dreadful day of the LORD comes. He will turn the hearts of the fathers to their children, and the hearts of the children to their fathers..."

An Elijah revival or revolution is promised before the return of Christ, restoring hearts and relationships. Whether Elijah literally shows up or whether the spirit of Elijah comes (as the case with John the Baptist who prepared the way for Christ's first coming), we will see a significant increase of what he represents, the prophetic and supernatural power encounters against spiritual darkness.

Acts 2:16-21: "No, this is what was spoken by the prophet Joel: "In the last days, God says, I will pour out my Spirit on all people... shall prophesy...see visions... dream dreams...vs. 19: I will show wonders in the heaven above and signs on the earth below, blood and fire and billows of smoke. The sun will be turned to darkness and the moon to blood, before the coming of the great and glorious day of the Lord. And everyone who calls on the name of the Lord will be saved".

Peter sees the outpouring in his day on Pentecost as a fulfillment of Joel's prophecy but evidence points to that day being a partial fulfillment of Joel, the first installment, with more to come towards the end of the last days, before the coming of the Day of the Lord.

Acts 3:19, 20: "repent then, and turn to God, so that your sins may be wiped out, that times of refreshing may come from the Lord and that He may send the Christ". This appears to be a promise of revival before the return of Christ.

John 14:12: "anyone who has faith in me will do what I have been doing. He will do even greater things than these".

I have a pile of biblical commentaries that seek to lower the bar of expectation, to water Christ's promise down to mean things such as taking the gospel all over the world in ways Christ could not because of our advanced technologies. But the text is clearly referring to Christ's miraculous works and deeds. (See verse 11) The prophetic promise remains to be fulfilled and therefore beckons us to set the bar of expectation high for what He will yet do in and through His disciples.

. In Christ's priestly prayer in John 17, Jesus prays for Christian unity. I don't believe He is referring to organizational or denominational unity but rather relational unity and camaraderie. This prayer waits to be fully answered and of all the prayers the Father would answer, would not His only Son's prayers, prayed in the power and agreement of the Holy Spirit, be? Rick Joyner states, "Jesus is coming back for a bride, not a harem."

In Ephesians 5:26 and 27, we see that Jesus is preparing a bride to be presented to Himself when He returns. She will be pure, holy, radiant and passionate for only Him. To be prepared for this grand moment, she needs an extreme makeover - a purifying. Nothing a little persecution and revival fire couldn't fix!

2. Based on previous patterns:

Revival usually occurs in a day of deep moral and spiritual bankruptcy in society. Mario Murillo argues, "Before a great awakening, there must come a rude awakening". The worst of times, in other words, precipitates the best of times.

Who could deny the desperate need for a mighty move of God in our day?

Anyone keeping tabs on current world events would know we are facing overwhelming global challenges of famines, increasing natural disasters of floods, droughts, hurricanes, tornadoes, earthquakes, tsunamis, environmental issues of pollution and climate

changes, wars, ethnic cleansings, terrorism, abortion, AIDs, potential for a global disease pandemic, the threat of weapons of mass
destruction, mass murder of the unborn, the sex slave trade, drug
and alcohol abuse, divorce and family breakdown, growing unemployment and global economic unraveling, the eroding of the middle
class and an ever increasing sense of fear, terror and hopelessness
in the air.

3. Church historians and leaders have been sensing it:

Many of God's leaders have discerned that God is up to something big. He is preparing new wineskins for the new wine, a fire-
place for the fire and barns for the harvest. Many even say that
previous revivals are but a mere rehearsal for the big ones to come.

David Bryant, catalyst for "concerts of prayer", emphatically
states: "I believe, with unshakeable conviction, that we are on the
threshold of the greatest revival in the history of the church."[21]

Bill Bright, founder of Campus Crusade for Christ, stated,
"Lately, I have sensed that the Body of Christ is on the verge of the
greatest spiritual breakthrough in the history of Christianity."[22]

Church historian, Richard Lovelace, claims that, "Our study of
awakening movements only turns up what appear to be rehearsals
for some final revelation of the full splendor of God's kingdom...it
is hard to believe that God will not grant the church some greater
experience of wholeness and vitality than has yet appeared in the
stumbling record of her history."[23]

4. Many prophetic voices of our day are predicting it:

Larry Randolph, an American Christian prophet, believes the
Lord has shown him that a great release of the Spirit is coming,
an unprecedented wave of revival that would forever reshape the
face of modern Christianity. With this conviction, Randolph has
felt compelled to inform believers about critical changes needed
that will help transition believers and churches into this new era of
revival. As a result, he wrote a book called The Coming Shift. At the
risk of sounding like a broken record regarding change and the need

for preparation discussed in my introductory chapters, let me quote
Larry Randolph:

"Old paradigms of thinking must die; new vision must be embraced.
Practically speaking, the difference between success and failure for
many will be determined by a willingness to accommodate change."[24]

Rick Joyner had a vision in 1987 of two waves of revival
coming. He believes the world has been experiencing the first wave
of revival and a harvest of souls over the last two decades, which
provides more workers for the coming revival and harvest that
will be unprecedented in history. He believes we are in the quiet in
between time with the big tsunami revival and harvest about to hit
any time. [25].

On April 6th 1987, David Minor had a powerful prophetic word
about two winds of the Spirit. The first wind is called "Holiness unto
the Lord" and the second "the Kingdom of God", which is characterized by Kingdom government, order, and miraculous power. It is
required of any one wishing to flow in the second wave of power to
have first experienced the first wind of holiness.

In April 1984, Bob Jones heard the Lord tell him that in ten years
(1994) there would be the first of three waves of revival. This was
shared with Mike Bickle, who was quite disappointed that he would
have to wait another ten years for revival. The first wave would be
characterized by new wine, which would release refreshment and
joy. Sometime later a wave of fire (conviction, passion, holiness,
signs and wonders) would hit, then a wave of wind (open heavens,
angelic visitations, major miracles, translations etc.), leading up
to the second coming of Christ and the end of this evil age. This
sequence of wine, fire, and wind would be the reverse order that we
see on the Day of Pentecost in Acts 2. These waves will build on
each other, not replace each other.

Bob Jones was shown that this first wave of wine would not
only bring refreshment and healing of hearts, but would be used by
the Lord to offend the mind to reveal the heart. The Lord is seeking
hungry and humble hearts. Many people will be offended by the
first wave of new wine and miss out and may find it very difficult to

transition into the later waves of fire and wind. We are still waiting for the fire and wind but sense the next wave is imminent. This sig nificant prophetic word given in 1984 by Bob Jones to Mike Bickle can be heard in session # 7 of Bickle's October 2002 teaching CDs that tell of their prophetic history in Kansas City.

I first heard about this prophetic word of Bob Jones in 1988, while living in Vancouver, and began to grow in faith and anticipation about what might come in 1994. Little did I know that when the Lord directed my wife and me to move back to the religiously conservative province of Ontario in 1990 (even with half a dozen prophetic words to do so, we came back to our home province kicking and screaming all the way) to work with John Arnott, that we would be privileged to see this word of the first wave come to fruition in January 1994 before our eyes.

Elaine Tavolacci gave this significant prophetic word in 2010 that speaks of both a move of God as well as troubling days, entitled: **"We are entering the Days of Shock and Awe":**

"As we are entering into a new decade we are coming into the days of Shock and Awe in the world as well as the Kingdom of God.

"There is a spiritual awakening on the horizon and it is time for the body of Christ to shake off all spiritual lethargy and seek the Lord in prayer and fasting for what He is about to release to us this year. The Lord is going to visit us in floods of glory as He has promised and we must prepare our hearts to receive what we have been contending for. For those of you that are submitted to Jesus your greatest days are ahead. Many of you have been through the fires of affliction and you have been saying how long Lord? The Lord is going to visit those of you that have been seeking Him in the secret place. You are coming into a greater dimension of His glory.

"Yes things in the natural will continue to grow darker but don't look to the media, keep your eyes on Jesus. He is your source and He is your deliverer.

"Yes there is a changing of the guard. Some of you are confused because you have also been hearing many prophetic words from credible prophetic voices that seem to be contrary to one another. **We are hearing that we are coming into a season of a great move of the Holy Spirit but we are also hearing that we are coming** into the worst days in history. Who are we to believe? Both are accurate.

"It is like looking into a diamond. The Lord is showing some people one facet of the diamond who are seeing the brilliance of it, some are seeing the transparency of it but there are others that are looking into the other side and seeing the flaws. As you stay connected to the giver of life you will be safe in the secret place and experience the awe of God in your life."[26]

Jim Goll believes the Lord showed him the words "The Beginning of the Third Great Awakening". Jim points out a distinction between revival and an awakening. A revival renews God's people and tends to only last two to four years. But some revivals spill out to not only bring mass conversions but also bring community and societal transformation in what some have labeled "an awakening". Goll believes the next revival will take us into the third great awakening, which will also include a youth awakening and an Israel awakening![27]

Bob Jones has recently released a prophetic word called "2012: The Return of God's Glory to the Church", where he describes the coming move of God as a "glory train" that will soon be arriving. Dec. 29, 2011, Bob was given Haggai 2:9 and told that peace and prosperity would be given to those who know their God during a tough time of judgment.[28]

5. The growing emphasis upon prayer for it:

Church history demonstrates that revival is always preceded by a groundswell of prayer. The revivalist and theologian, Jonathan Edwards claimed that "When God has something very great to accomplish for His church, it is His will that there should precede it, the extraordinary prayers of His people."[29]

And prayer mobilization in recent years is unprecedented in history. C. Peter Wagner claims that the global prayer movement is now totally out of control! The Korean and Chinese churches have been intensely praying for decades. According to David Barrett, leading demographer of Christianity worldwide, back in the 1980s one hundred and seventy million Christians were praying regularly for revival and world evangelization, with twenty million of them believing that intercession to this end was their primary calling. Scores of women's intercessory groups and citywide pastor's prayer fellowships and concerts of prayer have been established.

In the 1990s we saw the phenomena of the praise and prayer on the streets with March for Jesus, the "10-40 Window" global prayer project (which has seen astounding fruit of millions of conversions of Muslims and Hindus) and the Promise Keepers men's movement. When you get men together to worship and pray and seek the Lord to be better husbands and fathers, something is up!

In more recent years God has also raised up "The Call", which are intensely passionate and focused younger generation prayer gatherings. As well, the Lord has raised up the "harp and bowl" ministry (intimate worship mingled with intercession) with fasting, of "24/7 houses of prayer" in Kansas City (the International House of Prayer), the UK and all over the world, with a longing for the increase of the glory of the Lord, the coming great end time harvest and the return of the Lord. As in the Old Testament with the Tabernacle of David, the night and day ministering of the priests in the temple and in church history with the three hundred year prayer movement of the Bangor Monastery in Ireland and the more than one hundred year twenty-four hour prayer movement of the Moravians in Germany in the 1700s, God is again raising up Spirit-filled, joy-filled activity of passionate and intimate worship and prayer on the earth that reflects what is happening 24/7 in heaven.

Mingled in with the growing worship, prayer, and fasting for the reviving of the church and a global harvest, we have seen an increase in recent decades of Christian persecution and martyrdom around the world. David Barrett's research concluded that in the 1980s two hundred and seventy thousand died every year as Christian martyrs. By 1990 the number reached three hundred and twenty-five thousand who died for their faith in Christ, and he projected that the numbers in the coming years will only increase.

In Rev. 6:9-11, we find those who have already been martyred crying out "how long, sovereign Lord, holy and true, until you judge the inhabitants of the earth and avenge our blood?...They were told to wait a little longer, until the number of their fellow servants and brothers who were to be killed as they had been was complete".

If what the church father, Tertullian, said is true: "the blood of the martyrs is the seed of the church", then God must be sowing for a massive evangelistic harvest and explosive church growth![30]

6. It's God's heart to bring revival:

The Lord longs to renew, restore and awaken His bride into her royal destiny in Christ and see mankind redeemed much more than we ever could. And God, without violating the precious gift of free will and free choice, is committed to renew His bride and see the nations come to Him (Psalm 2:8: "ask of me and I will make the nations your inheritance"). He has poured out His Spirit freely before, surely He is willing and more than able to do it again and in greater measure as we come to the grand finale of history.

In the following chapter, Revival Part 2, we will seek to answer the questions:

Why is revival often bitterly opposed by believers?
And how on earth can we promote, pursue and partner with God in revival?

(Resource Recommendations will be found at the end of the next chapter)

Notes:

[1] John White, When the Spirit Comes with Power, InterVarsity Press, Downers Grove, Illinois, 1988, page 39.
[2] J.I. Packer, Keep In Step with the Spirit, Fleming H. Revell Co., Publishers, Old Tappan, New Jersey, 1984, pp. 244-245.
[3] Arthur Wallis, In the Day of Thy Power, Cityhill Pub., Columbia, MO, 1956, p. 46.
[4] Ibid., p. 20.
[5] David Bryant, The Hope At Hand, Baker Books, 1995, pp. 72-91.
[6] Ibid., p. 52.

7. The Lion, The Witch, and The Wardrobe, pp. 74-75, cited in The Hope at Hand, p. 77.

8. Edwin J. Orr, The Second Evangelical Awakening, Marshall Morgan, 1949, p. 44 (cited in Winkie Pratney, Revival, Huntingdon House Pub., 1994, p. 24).

9. Winkie Pratney, Revival, p. 25.

10. Bill Johnson & Kris Vallotton, Supernatural Ways of Royalty, Destiny Image, 2006, pp. 187-201.

11. Rick Joyner, Shadows of Things to Come, Thomas Nelson Inc., 2001, p. 5.

12. Winkie Pratney, Revival, in his preface to his book.

13. J. Edwin Orr, cited by Mary Stewart Relfe, Cure of All Ills, League of Prayer, Montgomery, Alabama, 1988, p. 48.

14. G. Campbell Morgan, Lessons of the Welsh Revival, Revell, 1905, p. 3., cited by Richard Riss, A Survey of 20th Century Revival Movements in N. America, Hendrickson, 1988, p. 41.

15. Rick Joyner, The World Aflame, MorningStar, 1993, p. 51.

16. Nate Krupp, The Church Triumphant, Destiny, 1988, p. 22.

17. Richard M. Riss, A Survey of 20th Century Revival Movements in N. America, Hendrickson, 1988, pp. 47-54.

18. Joel C Rosenberg, Inside the Revolution, Tyndale House, 2009, 2011, pp. 389-390.

19. Christian Brother Yun, with Paul Hattaway, The Heavenly Man, Monarch Books, UK, 2002, pp. 289, 290.

20. J.D. Douglas, Merrill C. Tenney, editors, NIV Compact Dictionary of the Bible, Harper Paperbacks, Zondervan, 1989, p. 494.

21. David Bryant, The Hope at Hand, p. 42.

22. Ibid., cited on p. 27.

23. Richard Lovelace, The Dynamics of Spiritual Life, I.V. Press, 1980, p. 425.

24. Larry Randolph, The Coming Shift, MorningStar, 2006, p. 12.

25. Rick Joyner, Nov. 22/11, http://www.morningstartv.com/featured-video-week/harvest-revival-tsunami-imminent

26. Elaine Tavolacci, We are Entering the Days of Shock and Awe, Jan. 1/10, her website: http://www.awordinseason.info/

27. Jim Goll interviewed by Matt Sorger, You-tube, "Power for Life - James Goll: Third Great Awakening, uploaded Jan. 4, 2012, http://www.youtube.com/watch?v=6wdc2H57Ebw

28. Bob Jones, "2012:The Return of God's Glory to the Church", the Elijah List website, Jan. 16/12.

29. Jonathan Edwards, Works, 1:426.

30. cited in David Bryant, Hope at Hand, pp. 31, 123.

Chapter 10

The Coming Monster Waves of Revival And Awakening (Part 2)

"See, I am doing a new thing! Now it springs up; do you not perceive it?" Isaiah 43:19

Why Is Revival Often Opposed By Believers?

*W*e have already quoted Dr. John White at the outset of the previous chapter about this strange irony in history of Christians fervently praying for God to come and revive His church and bring sinners to Himself, yet when God answers their prayers, they often find themselves being skeptical, fearful and even angry.

Why all this opposition? John White goes on to say "We grow angry when we are scared. We fear what we cannot understand".[1]

First, we fear change and the feeling of losing control. We are creatures of habit and changes unsettle us. We fear the unknown, the unfamiliar, and the unpredictable. We seem to have an affinity toward the status quo. We are not risk takers by nature and so we hesitate to embrace something new, especially if it looks different than we expected. This can make us feel very insecure and way out of our comfort zone.

Secondly, we fear emotions. We should wish to avoid emotionalism, that is, the manipulation of people's emotions, but God-given emotion naturally springs up when we receive fresh revelation and understanding. When God awakens people to the truth of their sinfulness and to God's astounding love and mercy, people's emotions are appropriately stirred. Jonathan Edwards called emotions "holy affections" and said they are essential for spiritual life. After all, Christianity is very much about one's heart. A hard heart is an unaffected heart, a heart not moved by divine truth and revelation.

Charles Swindoll argues: "Since when is the Spirit's work limited to our minds and our wills but not our hearts? Why is it that so many of us evangelicals are so afraid of feelings? What has happened to us? Why must our theology and the expression of our faith be devoid of emotion?...There should be a lot of room in our theology for feelings of loss and tears, just as there is room for lighthearted, joyous feelings and great laughter. The Spirit of God prompts both. I have been concerned for years that too many so-called mature evangelical Christians have little room in their lives for either".[2]

Swindoll goes on to add: "Church gatherings that restrain Spirit-led emotions can become dull and routine...God gave you a mind, use it to know Him better...God gave you a will, use it to obey Him...And God gave you emotions. Don't be afraid of them. Let them out. Allow your heart to show through. Exercise your emotions! If we refuse to open up, to allow the full prism of His love and truth to shine through our lives, we will miss much of the color life has to offer".[3]

Thirdly, many people have a fear of disorder. Understandably we prefer peace, decency and order. We say, "God is a God of order", but we must realize that to bring in order is sometimes a disorderly process. If someone suddenly goes into cardiac arrest and they fall off their chair at the restaurant, it may look pretty disorderly and even violent for a child at the next table to watch a paramedic use defibrillator pads on the man's chest. Desperate times demand desperate measures.

We don't like it when meetings get messy, unpredictable and lengthy. It is embarrassing and offensive to most of us. But John

White reminds us that "revival is war, and war is never tidy. It is an intensifying of the age-old conflict between Christ and the powers of darkness".[4]

The great Baptist preacher, Charles Spurgeon declared that "revival is a season of glorious disorder."[5]

Again, John White argues that "if we insist that revival must be 'decent and orderly', as we define those terms, we automatically blind ourselves to most revivals. Like the dwarfs in C. S. Lewis' children's story, The Last Battle, we may spit out heavenly food, for to us it looks like, smells like, tastes like dung and straw".[6]

Fourthly, many have a fear of controversy. However, the fact remains, "renewal has always been controversial and will always be controversial. We must be ready for it".[7]

Jonathan Edwards said, "It is probably that many of those who are thus waiting, know not for what they are waiting. If they wait to see a work of God without difficulties and stumbling blocks, it will be like the fools waiting at the riverside to have the water all run by. A work of God without stumbling blocks is never to be expected".[8]

John Wesley prayed, "Lord send us revival without its defects but if this is not possible, send revival, defects and all".[9]

Remember, wherever Jesus or the apostle Paul went there was confrontation, riots and controversy. Martin Luther, Wesley, Whitfield and Edwards were extremely controversial characters in their day - some kicked out of their churches! But once the dust settled centuries later, they have come to be highly revered and seen as champions for orthodox Christianity.

Chuck Swindoll advises us not to live life so cautiously and safely, "You can abstain from tea, coffee, and all other stimulants, eat health food, avoid night life, avoid involvement in other people's problems, stay away from controversies so no-one takes offense, and still break your neck in the bathtub and serve you right!"[10]

Fifthly, people fear the bizarre behaviour and manifestations
(Such as: shaking, jerking, falling to the ground, weeping, screaming, laughing, prophesying, trances, visions and being intoxicated or "drunk in the Spirit").

This is perhaps the mother of all objections. Because it is so unusual, so foreign to our experience and so bizarre looking and sounding, it is easy to conclude that this must be, at best, silly emotionalism and group manipulation, or at worst, a crazy circus of demonic bedlam.

So, it may be helpful to ask **some simple questions**:

Have these manifestations been reported in previous revivals (is there biblical and historical precedence)?

What is the fruit of it?

How do we explain this phenomenon?

Have These Manifestations Happened In Past Moves Of God?

Yes, they definitely have occurred during seasons of heightened spiritual activity. Martyn Lloyd-Jones points out, "these phenomena are not essential to revival...yet it is true to say, that on the whole, they do tend to be present when there is a revival".[11]

Let's look at some **biblical texts** that seem to give evidence of some manner of unusual emotional and/or bodily reactions to an encounter with the manifest presence and power of God or one of his angelic agents:

In 1 Samuel 10:11, we find Saul in a trance, prophesying when the Spirit came upon him. In 1 Sam. 19:23, 24, Saul lay naked on the ground all day and night prophesying.

Examples of people falling down in some kind of divine encounter:

2 Chron. 5:13, 14: "the glory of the Lord filled the temple so the priests were unable to stand to minister." (NASV)

Ezekiel fell face down in the glory of the Lord. (Ezekiel 1:28, 3:22-23, 44:4)

Daniel collapsed and sank into a deep sleep during a vision and an angelic visitation (Daniel 8:17, 18) and in Daniel 10:7-11, Daniel sees a vision and claims "I had no strength left, my face turned deathly pale and I was helpless...I fell into a deep sleep, my face to the ground. A hand touched me and set me trembling..."

On the Mount of Transfiguration, the disciples fell face down to the ground. (Matthew 17:6) Luke 9:32 tells us that they also became heavy with sleep.

When the soldiers came to arrest Jesus, they fell to the ground as they approached him and he spoke the words "I am He". (John 18:6)

On the morning of Jesus' resurrection, the Roman guards at the tomb "shook and became like dead men" at the presence of an angel. (Matthew 28:4)

Saul, on the road to Damascus, fell to the ground, blinded by the glory (Acts 9:4) and later, had an experience of being in a trance-like condition and taken up into the third heaven. (2 Cor. 12:1-4)

And the apostle John, while in exile on the island of Patmos, had a divine encounter with the exalted Christ. In Rev. 1:17, we read, "When I saw him, I fell at his feet as though dead."

Some argue that they always fell face down in the Bible, not backwards as we see today. It is true that some texts clearly state that they fell face down but some texts merely describe the loss of strength and collapsing, as though dead, which could be forward or backward.

The manifestations of weeping, moaning and crying out, though they still make many uncomfortable in a meeting, are usually considered to be the only "kosher" emotional responses in a revival. After all, many are coming under agonizing conviction of their sin and a revelation of God's holiness. We see this emotional response from the people as they heard the public reading of the "Book of the Law of God" in Nehemiah Chapter 8. We see Nehemiah and Ezra and the Levites urging the people: "Do not mourn or weep...do not grieve, for the joy of the LORD is your strength."

Speaking of the joy of the Lord, what about the manifestations of joy and laughter?

Psalm 16:11 declares, "You will fill me with joy in your presence". Psalm 126:2 states, "Our mouths were filled with laughter, our tongues with songs of joy".

In Isaiah 51:11 we see the promise that "gladness and joy will overtake them" and Isaiah 60:1-5, speaks of the glory of the Lord coming upon His people and, among other things, "your heart will throb and swell with joy". The question I have is: what would that look like and sound like when "your heart throbs and swells with joy" and "joy overtakes" you?

And of course there is a strong biblical co-relation between joy and the Holy Spirit:

"filled with joy and with the Holy Spirit (Acts 13:52), "joy through the Holy Spirit" (Luke 10:21), in the midst of signs and wonders with people shrieking when delivered of demons and many getting healed, "so there was great joy in that city" (Acts 8:8), and of course joy is one of the precious fruit of the Spirit. (Galatians 5:22)

On the Day of Pentecost, the outpouring of the Spirit created quite a commotion and attracted a large crowd. Some jokingly concluded that they must be drunk. Though not explicitly stated, there is an inference that the behaviour of the disciples appeared to onlookers to involve intoxication or drunkenness. Peter responds by saying it is too early in the morning for this to be behaviour attributed to alcohol consumption but rather it was the outpouring of the Holy Spirit that caused "what you see and hear". (Acts 2:33)

The apostle Paul would later urge believers, "do not get drunk on wine...instead, be filled with the Spirit". Why the connection between the two? Could it be that some get so saturated in the sweet presence of the Spirit of God that they feel overwhelmed and intoxicated in the glorious, joyful and euphoric "liquid love" of the Lord?

Examples from past revivals in church history of these strange manifestations:

Jonathan Edwards, the brilliant theologian and leader of the Great Awakening of the 1730s and 40s in New England, wrote to a friend saying, "many of the young people and children appeared to be overcome with a sense of the greatness and glory of divine things...and many others at the same time were overcome with distress about their sinful and miserable state and condition; so that the whole room was full of nothing but outcries, faintings and suchlike. Others soon heard of it and came...many of them were overpowered in like manner."[12]

His wife, Sarah Edwards, documented her experiences of joy and drunkenness in the Spirit for seventeen consecutive days, beginning January 19, 1742. One time she was on a chair but kept sliding off onto the floor. Another time, a Tuesday, a Mr. Buell was present at the dinner table and talking about heavenly things, Mrs. Edwards was greatly affected at that point apparently fell face first into her supper". A one-line testimony from Sarah sums up her ecstatic experiences: "I was very aware of His nearness to me and my dearness to Him."[13]

John Wesley and George Whitfield spoke of the strange physical phenomena that took place in their meetings in England as well. Wesley describes in his Journal:

"Monday, Jan. 1, 1739 - Mr. Hall, Kinchin, Ingham, Whitfield, Lane, with about sixty of our brethren. About three in the morning, as we were continuing instant in prayer, the power of God came mightily upon us, insomuch that many cried out for exceeding joy, and many fell to the ground. As soon as we were recovered a little from that awe and amazement at the presence of his Majesty; we broke out with one voice, "We praise thee, O God; we acknowledge thee to be the Lord."[14]

Following his Aldersgate conversion experience and this New Year's divine encounter, the supernatural dimension became more pronounced in Wesley's ministry for the next fifty years. One comical story involving Wesley is early in George Whitfield's preaching career. Whitfield saw people being "slain in the Spirit" in some of

Wesley's meetings and decided to write Wesley a letter of protest: "I cannot think it right in you to give so much encouragement to these convulsions which people have been thrown into in your ministry".

Ironically enough, later when Whitfield came in person to challenge Wesley on this matter, Wesley had Whitfield preach and while he did so, he had four people near him simultaneously sink to the ground, some trembling or convulsing and others groaning or crying out. Wesley writes in his Journal on July 7, 1739 in response to this "in your face" reprimand of Whitfield, "I trust we shall all suffer God to carry on his own work in the way that pleaseth him".

By the time Whitfield was making trips to America to preach, he was seeing people falling out on the ground as a regular occurrence in his ministry. "Some were struck pale as death, others were wringing their hands, others lying on the ground, others sinking into the arms of their friends."[15]

Bishop Francis Ashbury, appointed by Wesley in 1771 as a missionary to the American colonies, was a very disciplined man who insisted on meetings being conducted in a proper fashion, yet his meetings were often characterized by shouting, falling, crying, and the "jerks".[16]

One observer at the 1801 Cane Ridge camp meetings, which featured mostly Presbyterian preachers, gave this graphic report: "The noise was like a roar of Niagara. The vast sea of human beings seemed to be agitated as if by a storm...Some of the people were singing, others praying some crying for mercy in the most piteous accents...While witnessing these scenes, a peculiarly-strange sensation, such as I had never felt before, came over me. My heart beat tumultuously, my knees trembled, my lip quivered, and I felt as though I must fall to the ground...Soon after, I left and went into the woods, and here I strove to rally and man up my courage...After some time I returned...At one time I saw at least five hundred, swept down in a moment as if a battery of a thousand guns had been opened upon them, and then immediately followed shrieks and shouts that rent the very heavens."[17]

Peter Cartwright, one of the prominent camp meeting evangelists in the Kentucky area, spoke of the phenomenon of the "jerks": "No matter whether they were saints or sinners, they would be taken under a warm song or sermon and seized with a convulsive jerking all over, which they could not by any possibility avoid, and the more they resisted the more they jerked...the first jerk or so, you would see their fine bonnets, caps and combs fly; and so sudden would be the jerking of the head that their loose hair would crack almost as loud as a wagoner's whip."[18]

And Charles Finney, at the village schoolhouse near Antwerp, N.Y., described the phenomenon of falling under the awesome power of God's presence and conviction: "...the congregation began to fall from their seats in every direction and cry for mercy. If I had a sword in each hand, I could not have cut them down as fast as they fell. I was obliged to stop preaching."[19]

One report described the Azusa Street revival resembling "a forest of fallen trees". Charles Parham, William Seymour's previous mentor, came to visit Azusa and was horrified with the mingling of whites and blacks as well as the room given to the bizarre manifestations.

Oh, and don't forget the revival in the 1600s with the English dissenter, George Fox and the "Quakers and Shakers" or the revival in the 1730s among the French Jansenist movement with those who were called "Convulsionaires". It doesn't take much imagination to figure out where these mocking nicknames came from!

Under the unction of the Spirit some fell into ecstatic trances and prophesied. Some, like sixteen year old Isabeau Vincent of France, starting in 1688, and Major Perry, an illiterate African American farmer, starting June 16, 1880, would bolt up in their beds in the middle of the night and, with near photographic memory of the Bible, deliver impassioned sermons that resulted in hundreds of conversions. While in a trance, Major Perry preached a different message in perfect English every night for forty-five years. His wife took him on "sleep tours" to various towns. Skeptics would twist his hands, hold fire to his skin, pinch him and do anything to try to break his trance to no avail. He died in his sleep in the middle of a sermon November 8, 1925 at the age of ninety-four![20]

What Is The Fruit Of All This? ("By their fruit you will recognize them" Mt. 7:16)

Jonathan Edwards, claimed by many to be the authority on revival, wrote a treatise in 1741 called, The Distinguishing Marks of a Work of the Spirit of God. Edwards encourages his listeners to discern the Great Awakening by looking past the enthusiastic behaviour and see the ultimate spiritual fruit. In other words, patiently take the time to become objective "fruit inspectors". He argued that the authenticity of God's hand in the revival was demonstrated by five "sure, distinguishing, scripture evidences": it raises the esteem of Jesus in the community, works against the kingdom of Satan, it stimulates a greater regard for the Holy Scriptures, is marked by a spirit of truth, and manifests a renewed love of God and of man.[21]

In his concluding section, Edwards exhorted his readers not to oppose the Spirit of God in the revival for this is to commit the unpardonable sin of Matthew 12:22-32. Edward's warning went unheeded by and large. By 1742 a majority of the New England clergy had come to the conclusion that the Great Awakening was merely an epidemic of emotionalism and what was needed was a return to sound theology.

Rev. Charles Chauncey of Boston became the brilliant champion against the revival. He effectively articulated all the doubts, fears, and criticisms of the revival. "When Whitfield arrived in 1744, practically all the pulpits were closed to him, and the wind had gone out of the Awakening."[22]

It is worth "inspecting the fruit" at the end of the lives of these two prominent figures, Edwards and Chauncey. In 1757, Edwards became president of Princeton but when he arrived in the area, there was a threat of a smallpox outbreak. To set an example, he was quick to volunteer to take the experimental vaccine. He became ill and died. Chauncey, the great critic of the revival, went on to become one of the founding theologians of Unitarianism which discarded the Trinity and advocated universal salvation. Chauncey is no longer considered a hero who saved the people from emotionalism. He is now "seen as a religious bureaucrat who defended the status quo without comprehending the deeper issues of revival."[23]

How Do We Explain These Phenomena?

It is important to recognize the element of mystery in God's dealings with man. We can't fully figure it all out, but God has given us a mind and He wants us to use it, in spite of its limitations, to grasp the spiritual and supernatural realms. We need to stay humble and teachable in the process.

For those who simply chalk it up to the demonic, Lloyd-Jones poses this question: "Here is the Church in a period of dryness, and of drought, why should the Devil suddenly do something which calls attention to religion and the Lord Jesus Christ?...If this is the work of the Devil, well then the Devil is an unutterable fool. He is dividing his own kingdom; he is increasing the Kingdom of God... There is nothing which is so ridiculous as this suggestion that this is the work of the Devil."[24]

Let me add that we discern at times that a portion of the manifestations would be of the flesh, the person's own need for acceptance and attention. And at times could very well be demonic. When the powerful presence of Jesus shows up, people can be set free of demons. We see it in the Gospels that Jesus goes into the synagogue and demons cry out. (Luke 4:33-37) But both John White and Lloyd-Jones conclude that the bulk of unusual manifestations in revival result from the power and glory of God.

When God sovereignly visits a person or group of people, His manifest presence and power often affects their bodies in some way. God is present everywhere but there are times that we find He is more intensely present. John White articulates it this way: "He seems to draw aside one or two layers of a curtain that protects us from Him, exposing our fragility to the awesome energies of His being."[25]

Jonathan Edwards states: "We are all ready to own that no man can see God and live...therefore, it is not at all strange that God should sometimes give His saints such foretastes of heaven, as to diminish their bodily strength."[26]

Bob Sorge, in his wonderful book, Glory: When Heaven Invades Earth, provides a very insightful diagram for people like me who find a visual enlightening.[27]

This Glory Continuum (below) shows that once the presence of God begins to intensify and we enter into the manifest presence or glory of God, we have actually stepped through the "sensory threshold" whereby at least one of our five senses are impacted. If the manifest presence of God continues to increase, we could be getting dangerously close to the "survival threshold". If you go through that threshold you will no longer be living in this earthly life!

Degrees of God's Presence (a continuum)

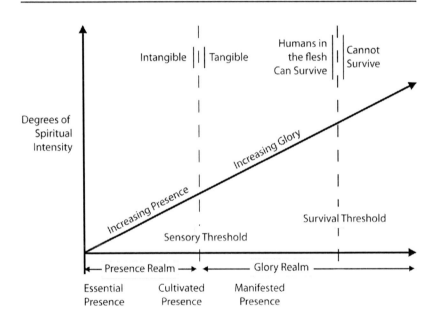

According to David Bryant, the Puritans spoke of God's presence having three levels of intensity: God's essential presence, God's cultivated presence and God's manifest presence or glory.

His essential presence describes the fact that God is everywhere. He is "omnipresent". Psalm 139 says how we cannot get away from God's presence whether you climb the highest mountain or go to the deepest sea. He is essentially everywhere.

They also spoke of God's "cultivated presence". Whether individually or corporately, we have all experienced times when we were worshipping, praying, or meditating on the Word and just sensed God's nearness. Jesus promised that where two or three gather together in His name, He promises to be in their midst. (Mt.18:20) That is rather redundant if He is already there. It must mean He will be there in a fuller or more intense way or dimension.

Lastly, we see in Scripture that there are times God's manifest presence or glory comes and someone or a group is profoundly affected in at least one of their five senses. We see it in Acts chapter 2 on the Day of Pentecost. They would have felt the wind blow and the building shake, seen fire on their heads, and heard the praises of God in foreign languages. In Exodus 33 we find Moses having an audible conversation with the Lord. He is in the manifest presence of God but in verse 18, he has the audacity to ask the Lord to show him more of His glory. The Lord warns him that no man can see God face-to-face and live but comes up with a creative solution to fulfill Moses' request. God suggests Moses hide in the cleft of the rock and God will cover him with His hand and allow Moses to see God's back.

So for frail humanity to be exposed to the raw glory and energy of God's magnificence and goodness is a very dangerous and delicate matter. No wonder God's glory shows up and some of our bodies are affected as if we had stuck a finger in an electric socket! I suspect that for us to live in the full on glory of God's presence in eternity, we really are going to need our glorified and resurrected bodies to handle it!

I believe the unusual manifestations provide another opportunity for us to be humbled. God wants to know if we are willing to play the fool for His glory. It is often said: "God often offends the mind to reveal the heart."

It is best not to be fixated on the manifestations, either fascinated or offended by them. They are not a trophy of spirituality but simply bodily reactions to the intense presence and power of God. We need to focus on the person of the Lord Jesus Christ and what He is doing. We often interview folks after their time on the carpet to hear what they sense the Spirit was doing on the inside and we are often simply amazed to hear what work God was sovereignly accomplishing that was tailor-made to the needs of that person at that time.

I remember our last session at a renewal conference our team led in Germany in 1995. One of the pastors on our team was slated to do the teaching so we looked around for our very gifted German translator, a pastor from Berlin, to come forward to help. We kept calling his name but he did not respond. Finally someone found him under the pew towards the back totally out of it. We desperately wanted him to translate for us. It was the grand finale meeting. So four of us each grabbed a limb and we carried him to the stage, hoping he would come around by the time we got him there. He continued to be in some kind of trance so we laid him on the stage floor and requested another interpreter.

Someone else graciously offered to fill in but they were not nearly as good as our official translator. Since our best man for the job was laid out on the carpet, I decided to sit beside him and continue to soak him in prayer, as we often do with people. While the teaching went on and I prayed for this German pastor, in my heart I found myself getting more and more frustrated and offended at God. Here is our best translator out cold, under the power of the Spirit, and actually drooling and grinning like a drunken sailor, creating this pathetic puddle on the carpet.

I was fit to be tied on the inside but of course looking really spiritual on the outside. How come Lord? I protested. We needed this guy to translate for the final teaching. And of course he finally comes around and sits up just as the teaching is finished. I at least had the presence of mind to interview him, asking him what God was doing during this time. With his face aglow, he just grinned from ear to ear and said that God gave him a series of powerful visions, showing him first each of his children and the plans and destinies God has for them. Then God revealed creative ideas, solutions and strategies for his church he pastors and finally God downloaded to him some citywide church strategies for Kingdom advancement in his city. After he shared with such joy and gratitude, I was totally humbled and quickly repented to the Lord for taking offense and settled it again in my heart that He is God and I am not!

So we want to be careful not to domesticate God and seek to put Him in a box. We are not experts on how God works. His thoughts are not our thoughts and His ways are not our ways (Isaiah 55:8, 9).

We should fully expect to have difficulty understanding and agreeing with the way God does things at times. And with the fact that God seems to add a new and unique feature to each successive revival (with Whitfield and Wesley it was outdoor preaching, with Finney it was altar calls, with Seymour it was mixed races and speaking in tongues), we have a further challenge to not take offense.

Tragically we see that the first people to be offended and criticize a new move of God are usually the leaders of the previous revival. They assume they know how God does things and also if He was to do a new thing it is easy to assume He would start it with them since they are the seasoned ones with experience and expertise.

The conservative biblical scholar, Walter C. Kaiser Jr., concludes that, "Every one of our preconceptions and built-in limitations concerning what God can or cannot do or what He is likely or not likely to do in exact detail must be jettisoned."[28]

Jonathan Edwards warns us: "The Holy Spirit is sovereign in His operation; and we know that He uses a great variety; and we cannot tell how great a variety He may use, within the compass of the rules He Himself has fixed. We ought not to limit God where He has not limited Himself."[29]

We are wise to take the advice of Martyn Lloyd-Jones: "we must be careful in these matters...What do we know of the Spirit falling on people? What do we know about these great manifestations of the Holy Spirit? We need to be very careful 'lest we be found fighting against God, lest we be guilty of quenching the Spirit of God.'"[30]

How On Earth Can We Promote, Pursue And Partner With God To See Revival?

Taking a survey on the street, a reporter asked a hurried pedestrian, "Sir, do you know the two greatest problems in the world today?" The man responded, "I don't know and I don't care." Without missing a beat, the reporter declared, "You got them both." (ignorance and apathy)!

How can we promote revival?

We need to care that God's Kingdom truly advances and as quickly as possible, especially in light of us now coming into the end times where everything intensifies. We are in a real war with real lives at stake. We need to have our hearts beating in tandem with the heartbeat of God. Feel what He feels, love what He loves, hate what He hates. Like Nehemiah, who had a pretty cushy job as a cupbearer to the king, but was compelled to leave to rebuild the walls.

We also need to be hungry enough to get informed. We need to get the bigger picture. Reading the Bible as well as biographies of leaders of past revivals can stir your heart and imagination as to what is possible. Learn from past revivalists and be sure to honour them and thank the Lord for them. If we would deliberately study past revivals and the price those leaders paid and follow the biblical command to honour our fathers, both physical and spiritual, then God is in a position to release a measure of their anointing in our day to our generation.

Getting off our duffs and actually visiting places where the fire of God is reportedly ablaze today is strategic as well. It is irresponsible to criticize that which we know nothing about first hand. And we should not just go to one meeting with our hands folded and our hearts closed as tight as a fist.

We need to have more confidence in God's ability to lead and minister to us than in the devil's ability to deceive us. He promises that if we ask for bread He will not give us a stone or a snake. (Mt. 7:9-11)

And we must guard our hearts from any jealousy that God would bless some other group and place before He would us and our church and city. Rejoice with them and honour them as they seek to steward the outpouring as best they know how. And with hungry and child-like hearts, we should also ask them to pray for us to receive a fresh touch of God's reviving grace in our lives as well as our loved ones back home.

One of my favourite Bible characters is Barnabas. Barnabas was a phenomenal encourager (even his name means "son of encouragement") with people like Saul, the ruthless persecutor of Christians who actually became one of them. We also see Barnabas in Acts chapter 11 being sent by the Jerusalem church to investigate a very strange and unconventional thing happening down in Antioch.

It all started when God prepared Peter through a vision to "not call anything impure that God has called clean". (Acts 10:15) Peter then received a request to travel to Caesarea to meet with a God fearing Gentile, named Cornelius. He ended up preaching the gospel to Cornelius and his friends. And while still sharing the gospel, "the Holy Spirit came on all who heard the message. The circumcised believers who had come with Peter were astonished that the gift of the Holy Spirit had been poured out even on the Gentiles. They heard them speaking in tongues and praising God". (Acts 10:44-46) So God shattered Peter's narrow thinking and he opened his arms wide to accept Gentiles as candidates for the gospel.

And as other Jewish followers of Messiah, those who had been scattered due to persecution, began to "gossip the gospel" to Gentiles in places like Antioch, a great number of Gentiles were turning to the Lord Jesus. (Acts 11:19-21)

This was quite a significant stretch, a paradigm shift, for the Jewish followers of Jesus. So Barnabas was assigned to go to Antioch to check things out. Acts 11:23 states, "When he arrived and saw the evidence of the grace of God, he was glad and encouraged them all to remain true to the Lord with all their hearts. He was a good man, full of the Holy Spirit and faith, and a great number of people were brought to the Lord."

Barnabas could readily recognize and rejoice in the moving of God in ways that were culturally challenging for him and his friends. And if that's not amazing enough, in the next verse we see that he went down to Tarsus to track down this dangerous man named Saul. He had heard that Saul had had an encounter with the resurrected Christ and even though others suspected this may be a trap, Barnabas, the man full of the Holy Spirit and faith, was quick to embrace this new convert and want to encourage, disciple and include him not only among the brethren but also as his teaching partner. We too, need to be like Barnabas and check things out, be on the look out to see what God is doing, see the evidence of the grace of God, even if it challenges our prejudices and comfort levels and learn to embrace and rejoice in it.

We need to cultivate daily intimacy with the Lord. This is what John Wimber calls, "developing a personal history with God". It is vital we develop personal disciplines that cultivate a passion for Jesus, such as: prayer, worship, fasting, Bible study, and prompt obedience in the small things. Jack Deere urges us to pray the following prayer on a daily basis, "Father, grant me power from the Holy Spirit to love the Son of God like You love Him". (John 17:26) [31]

We must not "despise the day of small beginnings". Let me quote from Jeff Olson, author of the book, The Slight Edge, "If only you were aware of the slight edge. If only you knew what it was doing in your life and how easy it is to have the Slight Edge working FOR you- instead of AGAINST you. If only you were making the right choices, doing those simple, little disciplines that would change your life for the better forever...where would you be 5 years from today?...Remarkable successes in life rarely happen immediately. We want to "leap tall buildings in a single bound" when in fact, the truth is it's baby steps, small incremental steps done over and over again. Success happens through the slight edge, over a period of time".[32]

The principle of sowing and reaping is relevant: "Sow a thought, reap an action, sow an action, reap a habit, sow a habit, reap a character, sow a character, reap a destiny."

So the small but intentional things we do daily and privately are like compound interest at work that bear exponential fruit over time. We need to tuck in close to the Lord and learn to hear His voice and catch His heart and get spiritually prepared so that when God's zero hour strikes, we are fit for action!

We can participate in the groundswell of intercessory prayer for revival. In 2 Chronicles 7:14, we are promised that if we "humble ourselves, pray, seek God's face and turn from our wicked ways that God will hear from heaven, forgive our sins and heal our land."

Wesley said, "God does nothing but in answer to prayer." John Knox cried, "Give me Scotland or I die." Luther claimed, "Prayer is not overcoming God's reluctance, it is laying hold of his highest willingness." Historian, David Wells, declared, "Prayer is rebellion against the status quo."

A.T Pierson, of Fuller Seminary stated, "There has never been a spiritual awakening in any country or locality that did not begin in united prayer."[33]

And Jonathan Edwards claimed that "When God has something very great to accomplish for His church, it is His will that there should precede it, the extraordinary prayers of His people."[34]

Some argue that revival is sovereign and you cannot do anything to make it happen while others say that it is a biblical formula, meaning we can pray and bring it about. Mike Bickle claims, and I agree, that God initiates the prayer and He then responds to our response. And in recent decades, as mentioned earlier, God is stirring the church to be united, aggressive and persistent in prayer for God to act and move again. While passionately seeking the Lord to move in greater power, we must not get distracted from continually obeying Christ's commands to evangelize the lost, heal the sick, deliver the demonized, minister to the poor and plant new churches, in the power of the Holy Spirit that is presently available.

Lastly, we need to be willing to pay the price for revival. The Holy Spirit has a ministry of comforting the disturbed and disturbing the comfortable. And in our day where there is much complacency, we need the Holy Spirit to come and disturb us. He first produces a spiritual restlessness and dissatisfaction with our "business as usual" and a deeper realization that we really are quite ineffective and our version of Christianity quite sub-standard. He causes a hunger and thirst to grow for more of Him and His power and glory to be displayed. We begin to ache for all the signs and wonders that were normal in the early church and in revivals of the past. And as Arthur Wallis describes, "There is a sensing that the 'no miracles today' theory is a clumsy attempt to cover up our own unbelief and spiritual deficiency."[35]

Are you willing to be childlike again? Are you willing to receive a divine "baptism of desperation," a "holy dissatisfaction" that puts your reputation, dignity and personal peace at risk?

The church statesman, Dr. Jack W. Hayford, offers these wise words, "The Lord still only lavishes His grace and glory on those who admit they are poor. The 'poor in spirit' are recipients of the Kingdom (Mt. 5:3); the ones willing to admit 'I don't have it all'...

Such priority is something I dare never outgrow. The minute I ever believe that the depth of riches I've come to know in Christ are a bank account, securing me from the constant need of a simple, teachable heart and a childlike, seeking soul, I've become duped by false definitions of maturity, discernment or knowledge."[36]

We need to have the courage to be honest with God and say with Oswald Chambers, author of My Utmost For His Highest, that, "If what I have is all the Christianity there is, then the thing is a fraud... We must force a crisis in our lives...when our very being aches with desire for His visitation, when we are consumed with hunger for his reality, when we radically cut back on other activities in order to seek his face, then we are ripe for transformation - then the breakthrough will come."[37]

A.W. Tozer writes, "Acute desire must be present or there will be no manifestation of Christ to his people. He waits to be wanted."[38]

We need to surrender our puny agendas and our need for security, safety and comfort. Hebrews 11 tells us not to shrink back and displease the Lord but to step out in faith (which is spelled "r-i-s-k"). "Christians ought to be old friends with risk and when a church or an individual Christian builds a wall of safety, something very basic to the Christian faith has been violated...Christians ought to be the most gutsy people on the face of the earth."[39]

Revivalist, Arthur Wallis, urges that, "If you would make the greatest success of your life, try to discover what God is doing in your time and fling yourself into the accomplishment of His purpose and will."[40]

Jesus insisted that His disciples cross the Sea of Galilee to Gennesaret. In the process a furious storm developed (being in God's will does not automatically bring smooth sailing). We, like the apostle Peter in the boat during a storm, need to hear Jesus' reassuring words, "do not be afraid" and His personal invitation to "come" which will involve the thrill of a supernatural life of walking on water. As we keep our eyes fixed on the Prince of Peace, we get to participate in the miraculous right smack in the middle of a violent storm.

God's gracious disposition is always toward revival and, I believe, even more so as we enter into the last and final show down between the Kingdom of light and the pseudo-kingdom of darkness, before our victorious King Jesus rides in to town. The unveiling of the coming Elijah revolution is upon us.

Revivalist, John Crowder, declares,

"The greatest harvest the earth has ever seen is just at hand. And it will largely come through a radical movement of love-crazed, end-times martyrs, whose ecstatic lives will usher in the Last Great Awakening...Forerunners have seen what is on the horizon...There are dispensations of God throughout the course of time when the hand of the Almighty moves with untold zeal and fury to showcase His glory to the nations of the earth...These were times of revolution...**This last-day revival will be like every preceding great awakening combined, super-sized and coupled together with miracles never before seen by the human eye.**"[41]

Much excitement and anticipation is stirring in heaven for what is about to take place on earth. Our Warrior King is looking to see if there is a people, a generation who dares enough and cares enough to pay the price. Like the Israelites poised to enter the Promised Land, we too need to hear the strategic instructions of the Lord to:

First, keep our eyes focused upon the ark of God's presence.
Second, follow His presence "then you will know which way to go, since you have never been this way before".
And third, "Consecrate yourselves, for tomorrow the LORD will do wonders among you". (Joshua 3:3-5)

You and I were born for such a time as this. So fasten your seatbelt. Let the revolution begin.

Recommendations for further exploration:

Books:

The Church Triumphant at the End of the Age, Nate Krupp, Destiny Image, 1984, 1988

Revival:Its Principles & Personalities, Winkey Pratney, Huntingdon House, 1994

Floods Upon the Dry Ground, Charles P. Schmitt, Destiny, 1998

2000 Years of Charismatic Christianity, Eddie L. Hyatt, Hyatt Intl. Min., Tulsa, 1996

The Harvest, Rick Joyner, Morningstar Pub., 1989

Visions of the Harvest, Rick Joyner, Morningstar, 1998, 2012

The God Chasers, Tommy Tenny, Destiny Image, 1998

Welcoming a Visitation of the Holy Spirit, Wesley Campbell Creation House, 1996

The World's Greatest Revivals, Fred, Sharon Wright, Destiny, 2007

The Century of the Holy Spirit: 100 Years of Pentecostal and Charismatic Renewal, Vinson Synan, Thomas Nelson, 2001

God's Generals, 1, 2, 3, Roberts Liardon, Albury Pub., 1996; Whitaker House, 2003; Whitaker House, 2008

Visions Beyond the Veil, H.A. Baker, Whitaker, 2006

The Rising Revival, C. Peter Wagner & Pablo Deiros, editors, Renew Books, Ventura, California, 1998, (recent revival in Argentina)

When God Shows Up, R. T. Kendall, Renew Books, 1998

The New Mystics, John Crowder, Destiny Image, 2006

The Ecstasy of Loving God, John Crowder, Destiny Image, 2009

Visions of the Coming Days, R. Loren Sandford, Chosen, 2012

Free Falling, True Stories of One Man's leap into the miraculous, Chuck Parry, 2010, printed in the U.S. Copies can be ordered from: https://www.createspace.com/3475080

DVDs:

The Finger of God, a Darren Wilson Film, Wanderlust Productions, 2007

Furious Love, focusing on spiritual warfare, Darren Wilson, 2009

Father of Lights, 3rd in the trilogy, Darren Wilson film, Wanderlust Productions, 2012, fatheroflightsfilm.com

Articles, websites, You-tube:

Rick Joyner sharing of his vision of two waves of revival in 1987. He believes we are in the quiet in between time, with the big tsunami revival and harvest about to hit any time. http://www.morningstartv. com/featured-video-week/harvest-revival-tsunami-imminent Nov. 22, 2011
Rick Joyner, MorningStar Prophetic Bulletin #69, The Great Tsunami, http://www.morningstarministries.org/resources/prophetic-bulletins/2011/great-tsunami Catch the Fire TV, Toronto, http://www. youtube.com/user/catchthefiretv?feature=results_main
www.GodTV www.bethelredding.com www.ihopkc.org
high level Rabbi Yitzhak Kaduri, died at age 108 in Jan. 2006, he supposedly left a note before he died with the name of the Messiah, Yehoshua, whom he met through a vision, http://tulisanmurtad. blogspot.ca/2012/07/rabbi-kaduri-reveals-name-of-messiah.html

Notes:

[1.] John White, When the Spirit Comes with Power, IVP, p. 41.
[2.] Chuck Swindoll, Flying Closer to the Flame, Word Pub., 1993, pp. 154, 157.
[3.] Ibid., p. 173.
[4.] John White, p. 35.
[5.] Mary Stewart Relfe, Cure of All Ills, League of Prayer, 1988, p. 8.
[6.] John White, p. 45.
[7.] George Mallone, Canadian Revival, It's Our Turn, Welch, 1985, p. 42.
[8.] Jonathan Edwards, Works, Vol. 2, Banner of Truth, 1974, p. 273.
[9.] John Wesley, cited in Azusa Street, Frank Bartleman, Logos Intl, 1980, p. 45.

10. Chuck Swindoll, in his sermon at First Evangelical Free Church in Fullerton, California, July 18, 1993.

11. Martyn Lloyd-Jones, Revival, Crossway Books, Wheaton Ill., 1987, p. 134.

12. Jonathan Edwards, "Letter to Rev. Thomas Prince of Boston" in Goen, The Great Awakening, p. 546, cited in Quenching the Spirit, by Wm. DeArteaga, Creation House, 1992, pp. 39,40.

13. Sarah Edwards, cited by Guy Chevreau, Catch The Fire, Harper Collins, 1994, pp. 75-85.

14. Cited in Francis MacNutt, Overcome By the Spirit, Chosen Books, a division of Baker, 1990, p. 98.

15. Dallimore, George Whitfield, Vol 11, Crossway Books, 1980, pp. 392,3; cited in Francis MacNutt, p 104.

16. Francis MacNutt, p 107.

17. Charles Johnson, The Frontier Camp Meeting, S. Methodist Univ. Press, 1955, pp. 64,65; cited in MacNutt, p. 109.

18. Peter Cartwright, Autobiography of Peter Cartwright, Abingdon Press, 1956, pp. 17-18.

19. Winkie Pratney,Revival, p.24.

20. John Crowder, The Ecstasy of Loving God, Destiny Image, pp. 221,222, also Google Isabeau Vincent & Major Perry.

21. Jonathan Edwards, The Distinguishing Marks of a Work of the Spirit of God, Banner of Truth Trust, 1st pub. 1741, reprinted 1984, pp. 109-115.

22. Wm. DeArteaga, Quenching the Spirit, p. 52.

23. Ibid., p. 54.

24. Martyn Lloyd-Jones, Revival, pp. 141, 142.

25. John White, When the Spirit Comes with Power, p. 23.

26. Jonathan Edwards, Works 11, pp. 261, 263.

27. Bob Sorge, Glory: When Heaven Invades Earth, Oasis House, 2000, p.p. 56-58.

28. Walter C. Kaiser, Jr., Quest for Renewal, Moody, 1986, p. 25.

29. Jonathan Edwards, Works II, p. 261; cited in Catch The Fire, p 101.

30. Martyn Lloyd-Jones, cited in When The Spirit Comes with Power, John White, p. 13.

31. Jack Deere, Surprised by the Power of the Spirit, Zondervan, 1993, p. 201.

32. Jeff Olson, The Slight Edge, Momentum Media, division of VideoPlus, 2005.

33. David Bryant, Concerts of Prayer, p 40.

34. Jonathan Edwards, Works, Vol. 1, p. 426.

35. Arthur Wallis, Rain From Heaven, Hodder & Stroughton, 1979, p. 111.

36. Jack W. Hayford, Stanced Before Almightiness, 1995.

37. Oswald Chambers, cited by Michael Brown, Whatever Happened to the Power of God, Destiny, 1991, pp. 28,29.

38. A.W. Tozer, The Pursuit of God, Christian Pub., 1948, p. 17.

39. Stephen Brown, If God is in Charge, Nelson, 1983, pp. 113-14.

40. Arthur Wallis, In the Day of Thy Power, 1956, p. 10.

41. John Crowder, The Ecstasy of Loving God, Destiny, 2009, pp. 293, 314, 316.

Chapter 11

The Adventure of Apostolic and Kingdom Expansion
(fivefold ministry and new wineskins)

"If you don't like change, you're going to like irrelevance even less." General Shinseki

"A spiritual stronghold is a mind-set impregnated with hopelessness that causes us to accept as unchangeable, situations that we know are contrary to the will of God."
Ed Silvoso

"*W*e are in the midst of a megashift in paradigm and practice. It is nothing less than a kingdom revolution authored by God that is changing the way we perceive and "do" church...What a great time to be alive...where the expression of Christianity in the West shifted dramatically from what we've had to something more radically biblical, creative, simple, and fiery than anything we've seen...Not everyone is able (or willing) to see this shift of epic proportions. But more and more can - and will. The church in the West has been fast asleep, but she is being awakened by her Lover", so American pastor, Mark Perry, so aptly observes in his book, Building Kingdom Churches.[1]

In September 1982, while in Cairo, Egypt on a forty day fast and global tour to get God's heart for the poor, Mike Bickle heard the Lord clearly speak into his spirit these thunderous words verbatim: "I will change the understanding and the expression of Christianity on the earth in one generation".[2]

Among other things, this calls for a radical commitment to both the authority of the Word of God and to "keeping in step" with the Spirit of God (Gal. 5:25) and His agenda for this hour, which requires that our comfortable mindsets, traditions, wineskins and sacred cows become subservient and dispensable.

Church consultant, George Barna puts it this way: "Let's cut to the chase. After nearly two decades of studying Christian churches in America, I'm convinced that the typical church as we know it today has a rapidly expiring shelf life...Today's church is incapable of responding to the present moral crisis. It must reinvent itself or face virtual oblivion by mid-21st century. Merely tinkering with processes and structures will not do...we now require major reconstructive surgery".[3]

Apostolic New Testament Church Life Returning

C. Peter Wagner, the well-known church growth specialist and missiologist, observes various paradigm shifts in the church in recent decades:

Firstly, there is a shift from denominational government to **apostolic government with fivefold equipping leadership**. For over three hundred years, denominations have been used by God to evangelize and disciple many in the world. During this time however, we have not fully functioned in all five equipping offices that Paul speaks of in Ephesians 4:11-13. The foundational offices of prophet and apostle were not recognized or valued. We are now moving from the unbiblical "doctrine of democracy" of committees, councils, general assemblies in church government to Holy Spirit delegated authority among spiritual fathers and mothers. We are seeing new apostolic missional networks forming, not around a featured doctrine but around godly and anointed apostolic fathers and mothers who lead with decisiveness, servanthood and teamwork to empower all the saints for their callings and destinies.

Secondly, there is a shift from the church being on the defensive (and just hanging on for dear life till Jesus gets here) to going on the offensive in dealing authoritatively with the pseudo-kingdom of darkness and utilizing **new and flexible wineskins** in the process.

Thirdly, there is a shift from church vision to **Kingdom vision**. Instead of thinking Christian ministry is pretty much confined to the four walls of the local church, it is now seen as both in the church gathered on Sundays (or whatever day they choose to meet) and the church scattered Monday through Saturday, in what we call, "**marketplace ministry**". Jesus sent out his disciples to proclaim the good news of the Kingdom, not just the good news of the church.

Fourthly, associated with this emphasis upon marketplace ministry is the shift from focusing almost exclusively on evangelism and church growth to equally focusing on the **cultural mandate**. It is not a matter of either/or but both/and. This involves seeking the transformation of every sector of society for the Kingdom of God, what some have called "**the seven mountains**" of: religion (church), media, politics, education, family, business (economy) and arts and entertainment.[4]

In this chapter we will address the restoration of the prophets and apostles and the full operation of the fivefold equipping team as well as the need for new and flexible wine skins (particularly the house church phenomenon).

In the following chapter we will focus upon the third and fourth aspects of this apostolic expansion, that of marketplace ministry and the seven mountain teaching.

1. With the Restoration of Prophets and Apostles, the Fivefold Equipping Team is making a Come back

The apostle Paul, under the inspiration of the Holy Spirit, writes in Ephesians 4:11-13 that:

"It was he who gave some to be apostles, some to be prophets, some to be evangelists, and some to be pastors and teachers, to prepare God's people for works of service, so that the body of Christ may be built up until we all reach unity in the faith and in the knowledge of the Son of God and become mature, attaining to the whole measure of the fullness of Christ."

And Paul informs us in Ephesians 2:20 that God's household is "built on the foundation of the apostles and prophets, with Christ Jesus himself as the chief cornerstone."

Jesus, the Great Shepherd, Teacher, Evangelist, Prophet, and Apostle, wants His church back! This will involve the restoration of the function of prophet and apostle in order for the church of Jesus Christ to shift from neutral (or reverse in some cases) into forward gear and ultimately into overdrive. Apostles and prophets help release the dynamic of the manifest presence and power of God, which changes everything. God is committed to transforming His church from being simply a nice but irrelevant institution in survival mode to becoming a Holy Spirit empowered agent of change and healing in our broken communities and world.

It has generally been agreed that the prophetic and apostolic movements began to re-emerge in the late 1980s and 90s respectively. In this second decade of the 21st century we are beginning to see these two foundational ministries grow in greater synchronization and maturity.

While we rejoice in this development, which has God's fingerprints all over it, we need to mention that unfortunately we have also had a slew of self appointed prophets and apostles jump on the band wagon, demanding title, turf and treasure. Demonstrating a serious lack of humility, sanctified ambition and sense of team work and accountability, these so called leaders, what the apostle Paul calls false prophets and false apostles, have spiritually and financially abused many impressionable folks as well as turned off many others from embracing the real deal that God is raising up.

When God initiates something fresh and vital, it doesn't take very long for the deceiver to seek to discredit, counterfeit or push the new thing to unhealthy extremes. He is very predictable and unoriginal in his modus operandi. This sad state of affairs demonstrates once again how critically important it is to have solid biblical teaching, relationally accountable fivefold leadership teams, as well as a greater dose of heavenly wisdom and discernment imparted to and exercised by God's people. These protective measures will be needed even more so as we enter days of increasingly heightened spiritual activity, both divine and demonic, and multi-faceted upheaval on the earth.

Johnny Enlow, in his book, The Seven Mountain Prophecy, argues that, "We could probably weed out ninety percent of so-called apostles just by informing them they can't use their title anymore. The love of the title is perhaps the first evidence of not really being one. The natural instinct of anyone who knows the responsibility associated with the call would be to run in the opposite direction."[5]

New Testament scholar, Brian Dodd, wrote an article challenging both those who think that today's apostles are super stars and others who don't believe apostles are for today.

He claims that the New Testament apostles "would not have considered the gifting a title, status or privilege. What we need is not leaders grasping for a title that bolsters their desire to be in charge of their church or network of churches while living in the comfort of some Christian bunker. But rather, to be an apostle is to become expendable, low status, and exposed to ridicule and insecurity in this life, while out on Christ's mission to the lost and broken."

Notice how Paul puts it: "For it seems to me that God has put us apostles on display at the end of the procession, like men condemned to die in the arena. We have been made a spectacle to the whole universe, to angels as well as to men. We are fools for Christ." (1 Cor. 4:9,10)

They are being released in these last days for the final push of acceleration of the Kingdom and harvest. They are little "a" and little "p" apostles and prophets, not superstars and celebrities in a hierarchical system. God is building his dream team that has all five equipping ministries humbly serving and learning to "submit to one another out of reverence for Christ". (Eph. 5:21) [6]

Jesus, the suffering servant King, came to serve not be served and Christian leaders are no greater than their master. And yet, while having a servant's heart is crucial to lead, the Lord no longer calls any of us servants but friends. Out of intimate friendship and living in the presence of God found in the secret place, we become conduits and facilitators of God's presence, grace and power to others wherever we go. This brings great joy and pleasure to our Lord. Christ in us really is the hope of glory. It's not what we can do for God in our own striving, it's all about what the Spirit of Christ can and will do in and through us in these last days. God is about to show Himself extraordinarily strong through those whose hearts are fully committed to Him. (2 Chron. 16:9)

How did the fivefold ministry team of the early church get shut down and dismantled in the first place?

The apostolic expansion of Christianity had an impressive start out of the gate on the Day of Pentecost and throughout the Roman Empire in the first and second centuries. This came about via Spirit ignited revival, fivefold equipping teams, every member ministry, rabbit-like multiplication of simple churches, and waves of fiery opposition and persecution that only poured gasoline on the grass fire. But over time, incremental steps of institutionalization crept into the primitive and charismatically dynamic church, often by leaders who were dealing with threats of heresy and the like. But by the beginning of fourth century, something even more catastrophic happened to shut it all down.

Shortly after Constantine, the Roman emperor, was reportedly converted to the Christian faith in 312 AD, he cancelled the search and destroy program targeted against Christians and legalized the Christian faith. What at first glance looked like a welcomed godsend of favour and recognition, turned out to be a demonic slight of hand, a Trojan horse of massive proportions. High octane biblical Christianity combined with its dynamic priesthood of all believers had impacted much of the empire while outlawed. Now, with it being formally legalized and eventually declared the official state religion, the pagan world and pagan practices flooded the Christian church and overtook it from within.

The dynamic fivefold leadership combo, which had already been in decline thanks to the gradual introduction of a single professional pastor/bishop per church in the late second and third centuries, was now officially and thoroughly taken out of service and replaced by the professional clergy one man show that was financed by state taxes. And the massive army of God's marketplace ministers who had turned the world upside down, was stripped of its potency, status and mission and demoted to a mere crowd of subdued and castrated spectators sitting in large cathedrals and tagged with the disempowering label of laity (meaning the uneducated people), just for re-enforcement.

After centuries of this paganized, institutionalized and neutralized version of church stumbling its way around the dungeon of the Dark Ages, God raised up reformers and freedom fighters who began the process of injecting the fresh air of God's grace and the fresh light of biblical truth to awaken and revive His own.

With the Bible being placed back into the hands of the common folk once again along with the liberating truth of salvation by faith in Christ alone, a critical turning point had been reached. Over the coming centuries, a portion of the church began its long climb out of spiritual darkness and religious bondage to discover afresh, step by step, piece by piece, long-forgotten precious truths, divine encounters, and grace based practices that are her birthright in Christ Jesus.

After the Protestant Reformation of the 16th century, which was a good start, the church continued to be led and shaped by the solo pastor model but with a measure of Bible teaching included. In the 18th and 19th centuries we saw the office of evangelist playing a significant role, particularly throughout various waves of revival with guys like Wesley, Whitfield and Finney. By the 20th century the function of teacher was making a notable contribution of depth and substance. But without the foundational equipping gifts of the prophetic and apostolic fully operating, the church has remained quite handicapped and visionless.

As the prophetic and apostolic nature of the church more fully recovers and matures, releasing more of the vision, presence and power of God, the people of God will once again rise up to become a Spirit Ignited and Spirit directed force to be reckoned with for the transforming and discipling of both neighbourhoods and nations.

The fivefold ministry has been aptly compared to the five fingers of the hand.

The apostle is the thumb, giving stability, holding the counter-balance, and can touch all the other fingers.
The prophet is the index finger who points at you and says, "you're the guy".
The evangelist is the middle finger, the one that sticks out the furthest to touch the world.
The pastor is the ring finger, married to the church and caring for the relationships within the church family.
The teacher is the little finger, which can worm its way deep into any ear and share the truth of the Word of God. [7]

Can you imagine a hand trying to do everything with just three fingers, the middle finger, ring finger and baby finger? Living with such a handicap is what the church has been doing for centuries. Can you imagine how much more the hand will be able to accomplish with all four fingers and a thumb fully functioning?
We are about to see exponential increase in what the church of Jesus Christ is capable of doing. We are getting a sneak preview even now in such apostolic centers as Bethel Church in Redding California, Harvest Rock Church in Pasadena, IHOP in Kansas City, Morningstar in Fort Mills, South Carolina and Catch the Fire in Toronto, Canada. Those are just the apostolic centers that I am familiar with. I suspect there will be many more rising up in this hour.
House church planter and consultant, Wolfgang Simson, in his book, Houses that Change the World, provides some very helpful insights into the complementary but distinct roles of the fivefold ministry team, all of which flow out from Jesus, the Great Shepherd, Prophet, Evangelist, Teacher, and Apostle.
The **pastor**, a term (in noun form) used only once in the New Testament, is by nature a loving and caring shepherd who stands

among the flock. His strength of nurturing would have a corresponding weakness however. The pastor tends to lose sight of the big picture. To him, healthy relationships are everything.

"The **prophet** is way ahead of the flock of sheep, perhaps five miles beyond the next hill. He is on the lookout. There he hears God's voice and sees visions, enters the throne room of God and glimpses something...few really understand him. He is interested not so much in people and what they think of him, but in God's voice for the situation...A prophet's perspective is radically different from that of the pastor. He hears from God and quite mercilessly questions everything, including the pastor, from God's perspective. That, however, is his healthy and God-given duty. For that reason, there is also a historical tension between the pastor and the prophet."[8]

Both views are valid and both are necessary.

A prophet's chief role is not to prophesy, but to teach God's people how to hear the voice of God for themselves and for others. That process will certainly involve prophesying and modeling how the gift should be correctly used.

The **apostle**, as described by Wolfgang Simson, is one who is not as far away from the flock as the prophet would be, perhaps only three miles away on top of the next hill. From this vantage point he can see the big picture and study the map and keep an eye out for future pastures for the sheep to graze. The word, apostle, literally means to be sent out, and like the apostle Paul, an apostle considers the world to be his mission field and church and is always looking for new challenges and strategies.

The apostle is very much like an army general who sets things in order and carries the vision, burden and risks of advancing the cause. He can also be likened to a pioneer or a wise builder who problem solves, initiates, expands and builds new projects, churches, networks and ministries. This spiritual father/mother figure is also gifted by God to identify others to train and invest in and release.

Apostles, like the other equipper roles, are called by God and over time recognized by the body of Christ. They need not promote themselves but let God do that in due time. Let me further add that according to Scripture, suffering and opposition as well as signs, wonders and miracles all come with the territory of those called to be apostolic.

Though the New Testament conveys the fact that the original twelve apostles are unique and in a class of their own, we find possibly ten other individuals who were also apostles in the early church. These include: Matthias (Acts 1:26), Paul (1 Cor. 15:8), Barnabas (Acts 14:3, 4, 14), Silas (Acts 15:22; 1Thess.1:1; 2:7), James the brother of Jesus (Gal. 1:19; 1 Cor. 15:7), Andronicus (Rom 16:7) and Junias (who may have been a woman). Though the biblical data is much less definitive, Timothy (Acts 19:22; 1 Thess. 1:26; 2:7), Apollos (1 Cor. 4:6-9), and Epaphroditus (Phil. 2:25) might have been in this leadership category as well.

Scripture also indicates that all five ministries would be needed indefinitely ("until we all reach unity in the faith and in the knowledge of the Son of God and become mature, attaining to the whole measure of the fullness of Christ" Eph. 4:13) to continually equip the saints and build the church. It appears the foundational ministries of apostle and prophet were the first offices to be stolen by the enemy and the last to be restored at the end of the age.

The **teacher** could be described as one who lives about a half a mile from the flock. He is close enough to deal with any sheep that may stray or misbehave. The teacher gives attention to quality, precision and detail, which interests him, more than the big picture of the apostle. His passion is to communicate truth and for believers to get grounded in the Word and have a foundation of understanding. He has a passion for teaching and empowering others to teach.

The **evangelist** hangs around just outside the flock, just enough to not smell like the sheep pen which could scare the wild sheep away but close enough so that when he finds a lost sheep he can direct them into the fold. The evangelist has a passion for the lost and that they come to know the Great Shepherd. He helps to cultivate a measure of that same passion in the flock, creating a healthy outward focus so that all the sheep develop sensitivity to lost sheep and a desire for them to meet the Shepherd and join the flock.[9]

So the question to ask is not how many people were saved through an evangelist's ministry but how many more evangelists did he raise up and how many churches have become more effective in touching their community and world with the love of Jesus.

Each fivefold equipping office is called to inject its unique DNA into the church, creating a church that carries all five flavours or characteristics. The result will be a pastoring, prophetic, apostolic, teaching, and evangelistic church that shifts from being static to dynamic, from growth by addition to multiplication and from being intimidated to being gutsy and dangerous against the forces of darkness on the earth.

A helpful chart used by John Wimber of the Vineyard movement in his training conferences many years ago caused light bulbs to go off in my understanding of spiritual gifts and the equipping ministries and offices:

obedience -> occasional gracelet - > ministry - > office

witness for Christ	of evangelism	evangelist
encourage	of prophecy	prophet
teaching each other	of teaching	teacher
caring for each other	of pastoring	pastor
each sent out on mission	of apostolic	apostle
pray	of intercession	intercessor

We see that in the process of stepping out in obedience to the Lord, He occasionally graces us with anointing for the task. If or as that anointing grows and seems to evidence itself frequently, the body of Christ may recognize that the person has a ministry in that area. Some people, after years of exercising and maturing in that gift and ministry, may be recognized by the church as being called by God to be in that office. It has been said of the prophetic office that it often takes about twenty years of refining and grooming by the Lord for this role. By the time someone is in the ministry or office of an area, the primary role they are to play is in the mentoring and reproducing of that gift in other individuals as well as raising the water table level of that gift within the whole church.

Fivefold Servant leadership team versus solo pastor

Ephesians 4:11 makes it clear that these five leadership ministries are to work together as a servant leadership team. That means that "the traditional model of a pyramid with a pastor perched precariously on its pinnacle, like a little pope in his own church" is a seriously flawed historical development and deeply contradicts the biblical pattern.[10]

Fivefold team purpose and function

Not only is the more biblical fivefold leadership team emerging to replace the flawed solo pastor model, but so is its true purpose and function coming to light.

Ephesians 4:11 expressly states that these roles are "to prepare God's people for works of service, so that the body of Christ may be built up..."

The New King James Version and English Standard Version state that the fivefold team is: "to equip the saints for the work of ministry, for the building up (edifying) of the body of Christ..."

Tragically, the four hundred year old King James Version placed what scholars have called "the fatal comma" after the word saint, "for the perfecting of the saints, for the work of the ministry, for the edifying of the body." This comma makes it appear that the leaders have three purposes: to perfect the saints, do all the work of the ministry themselves as well as edify the people. This punctuation has no linguistic authority to be there but demonstrates aristocratic clergy bias that seeks to maintain "ministry" status among the elite few. After all, they, not the common saints, are considered educated, competent and responsible enough for the "work of ministry."

We rejoice that one of the core teachings of the Church Renewal movement that emerged in the 1970s has been regarding this vital issue of all God's people being called and valued as ministers, not just the elite few. Church leaders are not to be like the owner of a sports team who is usually obsessed with revenue and attendance, nickels and noses. Rather, they are to be like coaches of a sports team, riveted on the crucial job of equipping and empowering the players on the team to bring out their full potential and to work together with the objective of victory over the opposition. If the team consistently performs poorly, it is evidence that the coaches are not successfully doing their job and they could end up fired.

But traditions and old mind sets die hard so to see this critical truth of everyone being a true minister fully etched into our hearts and minds and lived out in practice is yet to be fully realized.

I remember the time a busload of our church people went to a Saturday night Benny Hinn rally in Toronto in the 1990s. I was close to completing a four-week Sunday preaching series on Ephesians 4 and seeking to drive the point home that we are all ministers. During the meeting, Benny Hinn asked for all the ministers in the crowd of some fifteen thousand to stand up. As I stood, I looked around at the forty or so of our people, hoping they would enthusiastically jump to their feet with me. They would not stand even though I was prompting them to do so. They knew and I knew that Benny was really asking for pastors to stand and identify themselves. But I wanted to hammer home a point. It may be semantics but words have powerful ideas behind them. We are all ministers. My ministry just happens to be that of pastoring, teaching and equipping other ministers. Needless to say, the next morning in church, that Saturday night episode created some interesting interaction in my final sermon on the subject!

God's agenda for this prophetic and apostolic hour will not be thwarted or held back by those who resist change in this and so many other issues. The Lord is increasingly on the move and He is raising up a remnant within His people who are passionate about what is on His heart and agenda and determined to step out and track with Him no matter what the cost.

I agree with Bill Hamon who states that, "The full restoration and activation of all fivefold ministers will bring about the teaching, training, activating, mentoring and maturing of the saints...There is another Saints Movement coming in the 21st-century church. The great harvest that will soon take place will not be reaped by just a few great apostles, prophets and evangelists, but by God's prepared and anointed saints."[11]

Southern California church planter, Rick Warren, rightly argues that our church success must not be measured by our "seating capacity" but by our "sending capacity."

We will expand on this matter of marketplace ministry, of God's people taking the Kingdom of God into the seven mountains or sectors of society in the following chapter.

But before we do, I would like to address the delicate issue of church wineskins since they have had a powerful effect to either enhance or hinder the actual exercise of every member ministry and their development. My experience has been that I can preach until I'm blue in the face about the priesthood of all believers, that every member is to be a minister, but church structures can shout louder.

2. New And Flexible Wineskins, With Particular Focus On House Churches

I am convinced that our God, who is a God of variety, is creating alternative wine skins in these last days that are streamlined, simple, flexible, easily reproducible, and more conducive to what He is seeking to accomplish in and through His people.

One such wineskin is the house church model, preferred by some to be called "simple church", "micro church", or "organic church". Some prefer to avoid the word church altogether since it can carry baggage for many.

God personally tapped me on the shoulder in 2001, during a time of recovery from pastoral ministry burnout, and said this was the direction He wanted me to go. I came kicking and screaming, thinking I had gone through all the paradigm shifts necessary this side of heaven! But in making a commitment in this direction, I knew that it was not necessarily for everyone, or at least not now. So, I have had no need to crusade or have a theological axe to grind on this issue. As I address house churches in this chapter, it is not with the intent of trying to convert anyone. I recognize that the God of variety and creativity has each of us on different journeys, assignments and timings.

But one aspect of the book is biographical. I'm seeking to articulate the many paradigm shifts God has taken me through in hopes that this will:

- Encourage those who may have gone or are in the process of going through similar mindset changes, which tend to create much pain and upheaval in your life.
- Further prepare you to be more alert and informed on various issues that you may face in the future and be able to respond with grace rather than react.
- Build your faith and confidence that God is not only good, but also that He is clearly in charge and has an eternal purpose. So if you belong to Him you will not need to fear or panic in days of increasing change, turmoil and uncertainty.
- And to be a catalyst for God to challenge and change you in some of these areas so that you will be more able to run hard after Him and His agenda for you with much joy and abandon in these incredible days of Kingdom opportunity.

Aside from the fact that God spoke to me about making this shift, here is a brief list of some of the factors that nudged me along as I reached the tipping point regarding the simple church wineskin:

1) Biblical evidence:

The Greek word for "church" in the New Testament is "ecclesia", which is found more than a hundred and ten times. Fifteen times it refers to the Universal church, eighty-one times to the City church (the church of Rome, Corinth, Ephesus) and fourteen times to the house church. In Romans 16:5 Paul urges them to "greet the church that meets at their (Priscilla and Aquila) house." In Colossians 4:15 Paul makes reference to "Nympha and the church in her house" and in Philemon verse 2, Paul addresses "Philemon...and to the church that meets in your home".

1 Corinthians 14:26 is one of the few New Testament passages that gives us instruction as to what we should do when we gather together as believers Paul commands that "when we come together,

EVERYONE (not just the professionals) has a hymn, or a word of instruction, a revelation, a tongue or an interpretation. All of these must be done for the strengthening of the church..." It is very difficult, if not impossible to obey this command in our congregational service format due to our unbiblical clergy/laity mindset as well as the logistics of dealing with large numbers in a limited timeframe.

Also, the New Testament gives us "one another" commands approximately sixty times. These are best facilitated in smaller and more intimate fellowships where informal, spontaneous, grace-based every member ministry can take place.

2) Historical evidence:

As we have already stated, for the first three centuries Christianity rapidly expanded throughout the Roman Empire. This apostolic expansion of the Christian church was a combined result of the manifest presence of God in revival power with signs and wonders, a little persecution (separates the men from the boys) and the flexible and easily multipliable wineskins of mutual ministry in house churches being the norm.

But just after 300 AD, the church tragically got sidetracked. It turned from being a revolutionary band to a respectable establishment, which defended the status quo. With the Roman emperor, Constantine, ending the persecutions and allowing Christianity to be legal, in the process he outlawed house church gatherings and began erecting church buildings. A few decades later it actually became the state religion where all were forced to be "Christian".

The church ceased being an interactive family and army and was turned into a large and passive audience in big cathedrals in which folks stared at the back of the heads in front of them and watched the professional clergy on stage put on "the show". It was like going backwards to the Old Testament priestly system again. Gone were the days of the warm, intimate, interactive meetings in someone's living room or under a tree. "It institutionalized and split into clergy and laity, turning itself into a top-down pyramid with 99% of its members relegated to peon status."[12] The professional clergy, financed by the state, performed the pomp and ceremony and the masses turned into "pew potatoes."

We see in church history that in seasons of revival, the small group structure would again be dusted off and pulled into service for discipleship and "body life" purposes. John Wesley is probably the most famous leader who utilized the small group wine skin for extremely effective spiritual growth and accountability of his tens of thousands of new converts, many of whom were coming out of various bondages and addictions. Forming his "bands" and "classes", Wesley was one who "organized to beat the devil" and his method of using small group structures came to be known as the "Methodist" movement.

In recent decades we have seen a major return to church life being expressed in more intimate and informal gatherings. In the charismatic movement of the 1960s and 70s, many precious saints entered into the delightful realm of the Spirit with fresh worship and prayer and the spontaneous flow of the gifts of the Spirit. With minimal opportunity in formal churches to share their enthusiastic testimonies or express these newfound spiritual gifts in a spontaneous and free fashion, many found themselves meeting in "body life" informally in people's homes. Over time, in Great Britain, many of these "house churches" grew larger in number and went from living room Christianity to renting halls and buildings. Much of this house church movement evolved into the "Free Church movement", which is basically back to the congregational model but has considerable freedom from century old traditions and a strong missional and charismatic side to them and God is using them.

In the last few decades we have also seen an incredible explosion of cell groups or home groups within traditional congregations, bringing fresh life and growth to believers at the grassroots level and spurring some congregations to grow into mega churches of thousands. Those who have deliberately formatted their church with cells as a high priority are called cell-based churches. They have gleaned the best elements of "church in rows" and "church in circles."

The newer movement of house churches often organize themselves as a network of house churches that relate to each other and may even gather together once a month or so for a larger celebration event.

In the 1990s and into the 21st century, we have seen unbelievable growth and momentum in the house church or simple church movement around the world. In fact, it is safe to say that there are more Christians in the world today who experience Christian fellowship and worship in the house church model than in the larger professionally led congregational model. That may be a surprise to Christians in the West who think that the traditional congregational model is the standard model of church life.

For many believers who live in countries hostile to the Christian faith, meeting under the radar in underground house churches is their only option. Many are persecuted and even martyred for their faith in communist, Muslim and Hindu nations. God is moving in revival and signs and wonders in places like China, India, Bangladesh and Arab nations like Iran with whole extended families coming to Christ and discipleship taking place in organic house churches that are multiplying like rabbits.

Below is a diagram to show the slight differences:

Organizational Diagram

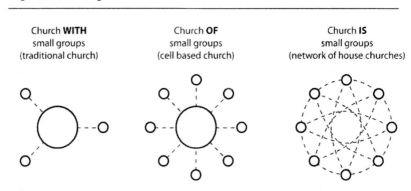

| Church **WITH** small groups (traditional church) | Church **OF** small groups (cell based church) | Church **IS** small groups (network of house churches) |

3) Respected and informed Christian leaders are observing this global house church phenomenon and are recognizing God's fingerprints all over it. Here is a sampling:

Larry Kreider, apostolic leader of the international network of churches called Dove, declares, "It is happening again. A new species of church is emerging throughout North America...Hungry for community and relationship, people are learning the values of the kingdom by first-hand participation. They meet in small groups in homes, offices, boardrooms or restaurants. For them, church has become a way of life where discipleship and growth occurs naturally as everyone develops their gifts and "learns by doing", under the mentorship of spiritual fathers and mothers. I like to call this fledgling grassroots phenomenon "house church networks". Within the next ten to fifteen years, I believe these new house church networks will dot the landscape of North America just as they already do in other nations of the world."[13]

Don Finto, pastor of Belmont Church, Nashville, Tennessee, writes, "For years I have been seeing this house church movement coming. I see groups of people who do not fit into church the way we are doing it."[14]

Mike Bickle, director of International House of Prayer of Kansas City, declares, "God is going to change the forms and expressions of church within one generation to a great degree. I believe the house church network is a vital ingredient in that change..."[15]

C. Peter Wagner, world renowned church growth consultant, writes in the forward to Larry Kreider's book, "They (house churches) are in the process of becoming a permanent and very visible feature on the landscape of faith these days...For growing numbers of the new generation, house churches, not the traditional church, will most likely draw them to God...of all the different kinds of churches, house churches will be most closely attached to the marketplace."[16]

4) Many credible contemporary prophetic voices have been declaring for years that there are still new wineskins yet to come that will be simple, organic, relational, easily adaptable, more persecution resistant and readily multipliable. Also these wineskins will be capable of more fully containing the new wine that is yet to be poured out as well as accommodate the great harvest yet to come in.

Published In 1989, in his landmark book, The Harvest, in which he describes the visions he feels God has given him about the future, Rick Joyner writes:

"There will be world-wide 'house church' and 'Christian community' movements which will help prepare the saints for both the persecution and the harvest...A great anointing will be upon these home meetings and some of the greatest visitations of the Lord will take place in them. Leaders and ministries will be raised up through them just as Stephen was in the first church. Some will even send out apostolic teams. Large congregations will be giving themselves to making home meetings the very center of church life. Even without knowing it, most of these are being prepared for the time when all large meetings will be banned, or the targets of violence and persecution." [17]

Graham Cooke, in his book, The Divine Confrontation, is seeking to help prepare the church for the major transitions God is now taking us through. He sees that God is raising up a prophetic and apostolic church that will learn to be dependent upon God's prophetic word and develop apostolic strategies to fulfill them. He too is claiming that God is calling for flexible, simple, and multipliable wineskins, "prototype" churches verses "stereotype" churches that will allow for spontaneity and creativity. As well, God is raising up a faceless and nameless generation of saints who will be an equipped and mobilized Kingdom army for these last days of harvesting.[18]

5) Studies have shown that our western culture is transitioning from a "modern" society to a "postmodern" society.

Leonard Sweet, professor of Evangelism at Drew University, has written prolifically on this subject. In his book, Postmodern Pilgrims, he makes a case that we need "EPIC churches for this EPIC Time". EPIC stands for: Experience, Participation, Image-driven and Community.[19]

In this post-modern era, experience of spiritual reality and power is highly valued verses intellectual pursuits. Participation is also highly desired. Being mere spectators will not be tolerated. In our day of the television and computer screen, people are more drawn to images than word and print. Furthermore, this post-modern mindset highly values community and relationship. The simple church model fits well with helping to meet these needs of this post-modern era that we are transitioning into.

Of course wineskins are only secondary. What is primary in meeting the needs of the post-modern pilgrim is a personal encounter with a living and supernatural God through His Son, Jesus Christ and continually living in His dynamic love and manifest presence and a sense of community among friends.

The current house church movement, with all its strengths, also has vulnerabilities and dangers, particularly in the West, that threaten its usefulness. Hurt and disgruntled Christians have left their church and formed house churches with others who are wounded and negative. If the house church is founded on a reactionary anti-church, anti-authority critical spirit, rather than a proactive focus upon the beauty and majesty of Christ as well as a desire to foster a culture of honour towards the body of Christ, the favour of God cannot remain and the enemy renders them ineffective for the Kingdom.

Bob Fitts Sr., a Youth with a Mission leader and simple church advocate and author, shared this statement with us a number of years back in a simple church seminar:

A Declaration of Unity:
I belong to everything that belongs to Jesus
And everything that belongs to Jesus belongs to me.
It's not "us and them." It's just us!
For there is only one Body of Christ and the problems of
the Church,
the whole Church, are OUR problems!
For WE are the Church. And we can do more together
than we can do alone.
"One shall chase a thousand, and two shall put ten
thousand to flight."

Another weakness or danger in the house church movement in the West is that many of the Christians who have left their church have brought a "program mentality" with them into the simple church. Already, some house churches have become simply conventional churches held in a home. Some have humorously called this scenario, "Honey, I shrunk the church!" Our belief is that house church, properly understood, is much more than a mere change in venue. It is, in fact, a "whole different animal."

Here are a few characteristics of simple church:

- For success, everyone needs to take ownership and come expecting to contribute (not unlike Alcoholics Anonymous): highly interactive sharing, prophesying, digging into the Word together, laughing, crying, praying and worshiping.
- Though there are regular gatherings, often revolving around eating a meal together, it is more about doing life together as an extended family - learning to "be the church" not just "do church." Graham Cook argues that we "must get past our obsession with everything revolving around meetings. Jesus did not come that we might have meetings and have them more abundantly! He came to give us life."[20]
- Meetings tend to be spontaneous versus programmed. A program is man's best efforts to accomplish God's purposes. But Jesus is working preveniently in people's lives. This changes everything. It is no longer our job to make something happen in our meetings or as we encounter folks in daily life. Out of intimacy with Jesus, we are to see what He is already doing and ask how we might join Him. This principle of prevenient grace is key to the organic nature of church. It is important not to put the cart before the horse (horse equated with intimacy with God, living from the heart, and listening to the Spirit while cart is equated with mission).[21]
- The house church is a church in its own right, not just a cell within a church or an appendage that is considered optional. It's the real meal deal, not just a vitamin supplement!

- It needs however, to be part of something bigger than itself, a network of house churches as well as the citywide church (including missional ministries, healing rooms and houses of prayer and worship) for apostolic input and occasional joining in with larger celebrations and training events.
- With apostolic and prophetic input and a Kingdom mindset, the potential for multiplication is comparable to the reproduction of rabbits versus the reproduction of elephants!
- Any leader or leaders are like spiritual mothers and fathers, facilitators of God's grace and body life together.
- Simple church is fairly decentralized and more like a starfish than a spider. A spider has a central body with legs. Cut off the head and it dies. A starfish has no head. It is a decentralized network. Major organs are replicated throughout each arm. Cut it in half and you get two starfish. Starfish type churches not only empower the little guy, but their grass roots structure makes them harder to kill off (like a terrorist cell), making them more persecution proof.
- Voluntary mutual submission is a superior form of government to top down forms of control and accountability.
- Shift of priority from church in rows to church in circles, platform ministry in a building to face-to-face interactions in living rooms, restaurants, schools, at work and in the marketplace.
- With a simple and flexible wineskin, it is able to be freer from bureaucracy and red tape so it can rapidly respond to needs that arise and whatever God is doing.
- Minimal or no overhead so dollars can go directly into meeting needs in the church family or in the community and beyond.
- Involves a forming of apostolic missional networks of simple churches with a Kingdom mindset and mandate to evangelize, minister in the power of the Holy Spirit, disciple and empower each other and others.
- Highly values marketplace ministry and taking the presence of the Kingdom to every mountain or sphere of influence in our society.

Orville and Wilbur Wright invented the airplane over a century ago. Their prototype was very crude and simple and required much trial and error to perfect but it started with a paradigm shift. Likewise with those of us who have been taking baby steps in this new wineskin called simple, organic, prototype church, it will be a bit crude and primitive.

It may be the next generation who will perfect it to maximize its potential usefulness. We need to be patient through the awkward process of transition. We are torn between running back to the safe, predictable and familiar and moving forward to the new. Issues of integration of children, spontaneity, being real, raising up new kinds of leaders, and developing a strong apostolic missional focus all need to be grappled with as we learn to think from a fresh new paradigm. The next generation may very well take the ball and run with it so much farther than we will.

As in the natural, so it is in the spiritual. Businesses are streamlining and downsizing to be more cost effective and competitive and home schooling has become a promising trend in education. So the Lord is trimming the church back to basics and saying to many "it's time to come home", to "living room Christianity", which is where the New Testament church was first birthed.

Yet, ironically, there have been a number of prophetic words describing the coming days in terms of "stadium Christianity". I suspect we will see a combination of both because each brings different strengths and dynamics. Small units of fellowship combined with citywide gatherings of thousands will beautifully complement each other, not unlike what we have seen with the men's movement called Promise Keepers, which has utilized both the stadium gatherings and the ongoing small accountability groups.

Whether the Lord has you involved in the simple church paradigm, the cell based congregational model, or some other alternative wineskin, we need Christian communities that give greater priority to being "cloud-sensitive, than crowd-sensitive", that is, more "Spirit sensitive than seeker sensitive." We can no longer afford to settle for the omnipresence of God when the manifest presence is accessible to those who are hungry. As Graham Cook states it, "We want to build a church that is so attractive to God that He cannot stay away."[22]

Cook also gives us this excellent advice; "it is always good to check ourselves for signs of domination, manipulation, and control. Are we threatened when people speak their mind? Are our people allowed to have an opinion without being labeled subversive? Do we encourage our people to hear from the Lord? It is usually more implied than stated that leaders hear from God and followers obey but the best leaders are facilitators to empower all their people to hear the Lord and obey."

Graham Cook further claims that, "In the next dimension of church, we must prepare ourselves to walk with the God of the unreasonable. He will call us to do the impossible, to take on projects that are inconceivable to our mindsets. These projects will have their roots in the prophetic...Without that revelatory rationale to guide and help us we will miss the grandeur of the wider purposes of God. We will be trying to take a neighborhood while He wants to give us the city...the nation."[23]

On that note, let's now turn to the issue of marketplace ministry and the seven mountain strategy.

Recommended Resources:

Books:

House Church/City Church/Presence based church:

Houses that Change the World, Wolfgang Simson, OM Pub., 2001
House Church Networks, Larry Kreider, House to House Pub., 2001
The Global House Church Movement, Rad Zdero, Wm. Carey Library, 2004
Nexus: the World House Church Movement Reader, editor, Rad Zdero, Wm. Carey, 2007
Organic Church, Neil Cole, Jossey-Bass Pub., 2005
Permission Granted to Do Church Differently in the 21st Century, Graham Cooke & Gary Goodell, Destiny Image, 2006
Mega Shift, James Rutz, Empowerment Press, 2005

Revolution, George Barna, Tyndale Press, 2005
Pagan Christianity, George Barna and Frank Viola,
Building Kingdom Churches, Mark Perry, Xulon Press, 2005
The Presence Based Church, Terry Teykl, Prayer Point Press, 2003
Hosting the Holy Spirit, Che Ahn editor, Renew, 2000
Hosting the Presence, Bill Johnson, Destiny 2012
Keepers of the Presence, Murray Dueck, Fresh Wind Press, 2010

Websites:

HouseChurch.Ca (www.housechurch.ca)
House-2-House Magazine (www.house2house.com)
(What is Simple Church? You-tube)
Robert Fitts Ministries (www.robertfitts.com)

Notes:

[1] Mark Perry, Building Kingdom Churches, Xulon Press, 2005, pp. 1,2.
[2] Mike Bickle, stated in various books, as well as Bickle's CDs on the prophetic history of IHOP Kansas City, 2004.
[3] George Barna, cited by Mark Perry, p. 9.
[4] Peter Wagner, from class and conference notes of recent years.
[5] Johnny Enlow, The Seven Mountain Prophcey, Creation House, 2008, p. 67.
[6] Brian Dodd, article by Brian Dodd, author of Empowered Church Leadership, IVP., 1991.
[7] Wolfgang Simson, Houses that Change the World, OM Pub., 1998, citing Gerald Coates, pp. 112,3.
[8] Ibid., pp. 113,114.
[9] Ibid., pp. 114-116.
[10] John R. W. Stott, God's New Society, The Bible Speaks Today, Commentary on Ephesians, IVP, 1979, p. 167.
[11] Bill Hamon, Apostles, Prophets, & the coming Moves of God, Destiny Image, 1997, p. 245.
[12] Jim Rutz, The Endgame of God, p. 31.

[13.] Larry Kreider, House Church Networks, a Church for a New Generation, House to House Pub., 2001, p. 1.

[14.] Don Finto, part of his endorsement of Larry Kreider's book.

[15.] Mike Bickle, part of his endorsement of Kreider's book.

[16.] C. Peter Wagner, forward to Kreider's book.

[17.] Rick Joyner, The Harvest, Morningstar Pub., 1989, pp. 92-5.

[18.] Graham Cook, A Divine Confrontation: Birth Pangs of the New Church, Destiny Image, 1999.

[19.] Leonard Sweet, Post-Modern Pilgrims, Broadman and Holman Pub., 2000.

[20.] Graham Cook, p. 115.

[21.] John White, article called The Spontaneous Church, White leads a home church network in Denver, Colorado.

[22.] Graham Cook, pp. 5,345.

[23.] Ibid., p. 310.

Chapter 12

Apostolic Expansion

Marketplace Ministry and the Seven Mountain Teaching

"Enemy occupied territory, that is what the world is. Christianity is the story of how the rightful King has landed in disguise and is calling us all to take part in a great campaign of sabotage."
C. S. Lewis

*T*he god of this age does his sinister work basically in two realms or battlefields:

1. Micro level: the flesh, that is, in the hearts of men (which we discussed in chapter five)
2. Macro level: the world, that is within the structures and fabric of society and culture

In the macro level, during these last days, the "prince of this world" is pursuing global conquest. He is subtly seeking to establish his counterfeit New World Order that consists of a global tyrannical government, global economy and a one-world religion. Through various demonic principalities dominating geographical areas and the top of the major mountains or spheres of influence, Satan appears to be quite successful at present in employing these structures towards his diabolical objectives.

We, the church, have lost much ground in recent generations, largely due to our disengagement with culture as salt and light and by our own compromises with the ungodly values of our culture. Sadly, we have not been a thermostat but rather a thermometer in our environment.

We have not been called however, to a pessimistic defeatism and escapism in which we merely hunker down in survival mode until Jesus shows up on the scene to beam us up and gets us out of this mess. Astonishingly, you and I are invited to join our Warrior King in a much bigger story.

It is a daring but adventurous quest of enforcing His victory at the cross and empty tomb and seeing His righteous and grace-drenched kingly rule break in and permeate here on earth as it is in heaven. We desire to see God's restoring love, life and justice not only impact the hearts of men but also the very fabric of society and the nations.

Christ has called His followers to live "in the world" but not "of the world" system (John 17:15,16). While fully engaging with our culture, we are to refuse to allow the pressure of this anti-God world system to squeeze us into its mold of thinking and behaving. Instead, we are to be transformed by the renewing of our minds (Rom. 12:1-2) and learn to "practice the presence of God". Through a lifestyle of intimacy, thanksgiving and gazing upon His beauty, we reflect His glory and manifest presence wherever we go. The fragrance of Christ, the treasure in our earthen vessels, spills over to those we come into contact with. We desire to be carriers of the glory and watch His light and love dispel darkness and hatred.

The best defense is a good offense, as the saying goes, and we are instructed to "be about our Father's business", and "occupy until He comes". (Luke 2:49; Luke 19:13) Again, this is not us working for God, but rather allowing God and His sweet presence and Kingdom to fill us and flow through us - loving the person in front of us and receiving God's heavenly solutions to problems in people's lives and in the workplaces of the seven sectors of culture.

"Calling" and Marketplace Ministry

"Answering the call" has been a long standing expression for becoming a priest or a nun. In protestant circles, it entails "going into full time ministry" and becoming a pastor or missionary. Thankfully, the Spirit of God is in the process of smashing this unbiblical "sacred/secular" or "first class/second class" mindset that has dominated the church for centuries. This damaging perspective claims "ministry" is what the clergy do in the church and "work" is what the regular people do out there in the world. But God is calling forth "marketplace ministers" who see both the value and dignity of their work in and of itself as well as the unique opportunity to partner with God in seeing the Kingdom invade every sphere of life, work and culture.

Followers of Christ are waking up to the fact that the Lord has a specific calling, ministry and destiny that is custom made for each of them. And with a harvest of salvations as well as social transformation on God's agenda, much of that ministry will be outside the four walls of the church and out in the marketplace.

Let us look at this matter of marketplace ministry, of God's people taking the Kingdom of God into the seven mountains or sectors of society.

Seven Mountain Teaching Revealed To Leaders

Bill Bright, founder of Campus Crusade, and Loren Cunningham, founder of Youth With a Mission, had lunch together in Colorado in August 1975. Days earlier God had given each of these influential leaders a message to give to the other. Around the same time frame the Lord gave a similar message to Francis Schaeffer, founder of L'Abri, and Pat Robertson of Regent University and CBN.

That message was that if we are to truly disciple the nations for Jesus Christ, then Christians would need to be agents of influence within the seven spheres or mountains of society. These seven mountains are: business, government, media, arts and entertainment, education, the family and religion. It is in these sectors or mind molders of society where culture would be won or lost. The divine assignment was to raise up change agents to scale the mountains and bring the Kingdom of God and His righteousness.[1]

The seven mountains initiative is not an initiative to establish dominion over all the earth or in governments. Os Hillman, in his book, Change Agent, claims that, "I do not believe God's intent is for Christians to rule the earth; rather, I believe the New Testament calls us to serve the culture...Jesus never sought to have dominion; rather, He encouraged others to love and obey God. It is better that we avoid the word dominion in our culture today due to the connotation that comes with this word of control and manipulation of others."[2]

The world is fearful that Christians want to rule the world through a right wing political agenda, similar to Muslims seeking to impose shariah law upon the nations. What the world is really looking for are solutions to societal problems. Christians should be about networking together to solve problems with heavenly solutions. The seven mountain strategy is merely a way to be salt and light among strategic spheres of influence which shape and define values and beliefs in the culture.

We have already briefly discussed the family mountain in chapter five as well wrestled with some key issues to do with the church, which is in the religion mountain, in the previous chapter. Let me touch on the remaining five mountains.

Mountain of Government

The shining historical example of a Christian seeking to make a difference for Christ and His just and righteous Kingdom in society through the political arena was an ugly little man with a long nose. William Wilberforce, "came within a hair's breadth of missing his grand calling altogether - a 'near miss'"!

When converted in 1785 at the age of twenty-five, Wilberforce's first reaction was to give up politics for "the ministry". He thought the "spiritual" affairs were far more important than "secular" affairs. Thankfully, John Newton, the converted slave trader who composed "Amazing Grace", convinced Wilberforce that God wanted him to stay in politics rather than enter "the ministry". After much prayer,

Wilberforce concluded that Newton was right. God was calling him to fight on behalf of the oppressed - as a "Parliamentarian."[3]

William Wilberforce's accomplishments were achieved in the face of enormous odds. In his day, very few Englishmen considered the slave trade to be evil. Most saw it as foundational to the welfare of the economy. The intense and ongoing opposition he faced came from every direction, including Admiral Lord Nelson and most of the Royal family. Wilberforce and his evangelical faith were despised and yet he persevered tirelessly for nearly fifty years before he finally succeeded.[4]

The slave trade in the British Empire was abolished by 1807 but slavery itself remained legal until 1833. By the time Wilberforce died, he had championed many social justice issues and reforms, including the most famous, the Slavery Abolition Act of 1833, which he received the good news about three days prior to his passing. An excellent film of Wilberforce's life and battle against slavery, Amazing Grace, came out in 2006.

Mountain of Arts and Entertainment

In the 1930s, the Communist party began to strategically seek inroads into the Hollywood film industry. By the end of World War II, more than six hundred prominent film producers, directors, writers, and actors had become members of the Communist party. Ronald Reagan took up the battle when he woke up to this shocking reality and almost single-handedly defeated their infiltration of Hollywood.

This was at a time, according to William Dyrness, when a producer at 20th Century Fox wrote letters to several evangelical colleges urging them to send graduates to become screenwriters in hopes of helping to make wholesome films. The response was deeply disappointing. One college president even wrote back stating he would rather send his young people to hell than to Hollywood. Such a fortress and retreat mentality among Christians has significantly contributed to Satan and his forces having free reign to shape and dominate this mountain of influence.[5]

In recent years we have seen some promising signs in the right direction in both Hollywood and the arts and entertainment industry in general. Such faith based movies as the Passion of the Christ, Lord of the Rings trilogy, Chronicles of Narnia, Amazing Grace, Faith Like Potatoes and two shoe-string budget films, Facing the Giants and Fireproof have all contributed to a possible tipping point.

People like Karen Covell, who have had a career in Hollywood for years, are making a difference. She began a prayer group almost three decades ago that has now grown to hundreds of Christian Hollywood professionals who see themselves as marketplace ministers. Ten years ago she began the Hollywood Prayer Network to pray for Hollywood missionaries, for those who don't know Jesus yet, and to encourage gifted Christians to come to this mission field.[6]

I got a tiny glimpse of some of the prayer activity behind the scenes when the Christian rock band, Hawk Nelson, in which our oldest son, Jonathan, is the lead guitarist (and now lead singer), had the privilege of performing two of their songs in the Hollywood movie, Yours, Mine, and Ours, in 2005. At the end of the two days of filming on the set, one of the lead actors, Rene Russo, found out they were a Christian band and wished they knew that ahead of time so they could have been invited to join the many Christians involved in the filming of the movie who met every morning to pray together.

Yes, Hollywood has been guilty of dumping destructive moral pollution and trash into the nations for decades. But rather than being part of the Christian community that is calling on God's judgment to be unleashed on Hollywood and have the ground swallow it up, maybe there is still time to be like Jonah who obeyed, albeit reluctantly, and went to Nineveh, where God desired repentance and redemption to have the last say.

Mountain of Media

Media refers to the powerful news outlets that report and create the news. Francis Schaeffer said, "Whoever controls the media controls the culture."[7]

Mainstream media in the West is owned primarily by powerful corporations and the global elite and empowered by demonic forces. They have people, most with a humanistic and liberal bent, reporting partial truth often designed to create fear and hopelessness as well as shape viewers' perception of reality. Johnny Enlow argues that, "They can turn a non-story into the big story and turn what should be huge stories into non-stories...Bad News is Satan's specialty, and twisting news is his delight."[8]

We need to pray that a new generation of uncompromising journalists would rise up with a biblical worldview and that the airwaves would be filled with truth, righteousness and praiseworthy stories that bring a redemptive purpose to our world.

Mountain of Education

The top disciplinary problems in American schools in 1940 are quite different from 1990:

1940	1990
talking out of turn	drug abuse
chewing gum	alcohol abuse
making noise	pregnancy
running in the halls	suicide
cutting in line	rape
dress code infractions	robbery
littering	assault [9]

This list reflects the moral decline in America, which has only intensified with the removal of prayer from the schools in 1963 and Christian values in general over the decades.

We have also had humanism, atheism and rationalism flood our educational systems in the West and indoctrinating our young minds. And the more education a student gets, the more analytical and left-brain dominant they become, at the expense of the right-brain intuitive and creative side. "Such left-brain dominance rules out supernatural answers to anything." But with the coming moves of God coupled with His temporal judgments, we will see a release of the fear of the Lord, which is the beginning of true wisdom. Enlow confidently claims that, "God is going to raise up a new breed of Elijah Revolution teachers to invade the mountain of education. On-fire, passionate, Holy Spirit-filled teachers who are gifted and empowered will give education an extreme makeover."[10]

Mountain of Business or Economy

The strongholds over the economies and marketplaces of the world appear to be greed, pride, mammon and Babylon. Jehovah Jireh is in the process of shaking everything that is not based on trust in Him and His Kingdom provision. We are in the midst of an economic crisis that will continue to sift and shake things. Revelation 18:1-6 tells us that we need our hearts and souls to come out from being under the seductive influence of this principality and system of Babylon which is about to fall and collapse. We need to be cleansed of the love of money, which is the root of all evil, and yet see its usefulness. John Wesley had it right, "earn all you can, save all you can, give all you can".

God will entrust the resources of earthly wealth to those who are Kingdom-minded to bring provision to the world. God will be raising up Josephs who can be trusted, business men and women who have been refined in the fire and prepared to partner with Him to do great exploits, bringing heavenly solutions to global problems.

We have heard prophetic words that God will release innovations as well as raise up Joseph companies that will be used by God to meet a very real need, with wealth as a byproduct, not the goal. Such Joseph companies will not be driven by greed but by compassion.

An interesting example of a new trend in business is what is being called "social entrepreneurship". This involves companies, whether owned and operated by Christians or not, using the 'for-profit' business model and harnessing it for humanitarian purposes. Let me give a few inspiring examples:

Blake Mycoskie was vacationing in Argentina in 2006 and became aware of the pervasive social problem of many children in villages who had no shoes to protect them from disease or to make it possible for them to attend school. He went home and built a shoe business which gives away one pair of shoes to a child for every pair purchased. As of 2010, the company has given away over one million pairs of shoes to children in need around the world.

A growing number of other companies are launching out in similar ways. I am aware of at least two nutrition supplement companies who have launched initiatives to combat the massive global problem of malnutrition among children.

I am so excited to be part of such a new venture with the nutrition company with which I am associated. They are seeking to be good stewards of the advanced and patented nutritional technologies that are real food sourced. Whenever people purchase the nutrition for themselves, the company provides plant-based nutrition to a child at risk, a "donation by consumption" strategy. Their goal is to radically improve the quality of life and health of at least five million orphans and "at risk" children of the world on an ongoing basis.

This unconventional thinking has the potential of becoming a further win/win scenario by becoming a sustainable source of revenue for various charitable organizations and churches as partnerships are established. The recent shift in the global economy has negatively impacted the level of donations of many not-for-profit organizations, which were already struggling to meet growing social needs. Nic Frances, author of the book, The End of Charity,[11] writes that if lasting and effective change is to occur in solving social and environmental challenges we need partnerships between charitable organizations, governments and corporations using the value driven market economy. Sustainable funding will have to come from the structure of markets and social enterprise if they wish to keep up with addressing ever growing needs in the coming years.

Another promising strategy developed to fight global malnutrition and extreme poverty involves combining sustainable organic farming and natural medicine. It involves training folks to grow their own high nutrient foods with simple tools and little rain with bio-intensive mini-farms.[12]

Let me mention one further inspiring development that first began in the business mountain. A Christian ministry called La Red has been impacting the world with values-based curriculum and ethical leadership training for some twenty years. For the first fifteen years this organization focused on serving the business world, particularly in Central and South America. Then governments (including the military and prison systems) began to ask for assistance in training their employees and leaders in these principles and values of wisdom and integrity found in the Word of God. Educational systems and churches are now asking for this values-based curriculum. La Red is now touching over forty nations of the world with astonishing results in terms of social transformation in justice and righteousness. Many of these people have also become disciples of Christ in the process.

We are living in days of acceleration where God is on the move. As Johnny Enlow states, "Rise up, Josephs! First invade the heart of the Dreamgiver, then get and take His dreams and make Him famous in all the earth!"[13]

Recommended daily prayer as a marketplace minister:

"Lord, give me a divine appointment today with someone who is hungry for You or in need, and give me grace to minister the love of Jesus in the power of the Holy Spirit."

Recommended Resources:

Books:

The Apostolic Ministry, Rick Joyner, Morningstar Pub., 2004
The Gift of Apostle, David Cannistraci, Regal Books, 1996
Dreaming with God, Bill Johnson, Destiny Image, 2006
Culture of Honor, Danny Silk, Destiny Image, 2009
Informed Intercession: Transforming Your community Through Spiritual Mapping and Strategic Prayer, George Otis Jr., Renew Books, 1999
The Church in the Workplace, C. Peter Wagner, Regal Books, 2006
Anointed for Business, Ed Silvoso, Regal, 2002
The Reformer's Pledge, editor, Che Ahn, Destiny Image, 2010
Seven Mountain Prophecy, Johnny Enlow, Creation House, 2008
The Seven Mountain Mantle, Johnny Enlow, Creation House, 2009

Change Agent, Os Hillman, Charisma House, 2011
There is Always Enough, Rolland & Heidi Baker among the poor
Be a Hero, Wesley Campbell, Stephen Court, Destiny, 2004
Operation World:The Definitive Prayer Guide to Every Nation, 7th edition by Jason Mandryk, Biblica Pub., 2010
Akiane: Her Life, Her Art, Her Poetry, W Pub. Group, a div. of Thomas Nelson, 2006 (stunning artwork & poetry by the young girl, Akiane Kramarik)

Websites

La Red (www.lared.org)
Reclaiming the 7 Mountains of Culture, http://www.reclaim7mountains.com/

DVDs
7M Revolution, Lance Wallnau, Lancelearning Group, 2008, www.lancelearning.com

Notes:

1. Os Hillman, Change Agent, Charisma House, 2011, p. 7.
2. Ibid., p. 20.
3. Os Guiness, The Call, Thomas Nelson, 2003, pp. 28, 29.
4. Ibid., p. 97.
5. Os Hillman, pp. 140-141, citing "Visual Faith: A Christian Recovery of the Arts, A Conversation with Dr. William Dyrness," Cutting Edge 6, no. 1 (Winder 2002), 9-11, referenced in Cunningham, The Book That Transforms Nations, 62.
6. Ibid., p. 148.
7. Ibid., p. 155; citing Francis Schaeffer, How Should We Then Live? Crossway, 1983.
8. Johnny Enlow, The Seven Mountain Prophecy, Creation House, 2008, pp. 47-48.

9. Os Hillman, p. 179, citing Congressional Quarterly, quoted in William Bennett, Index of Leading Cultural Indicators, Simon & Schuster, 1994, p. 83.

10. Johnny Enlow, p. 90.

11. Nic Frances, The End of Charity, Griffin Press, 2008.

12. www.organics4orphans.org

13. Johnny Enlow, p. 97.

"My people are destroyed from lack of knowledge." Hosea 4:6

"Everything is permissible but not everything is beneficial."
1 Cor.10:23

"One-quarter of what you eat keeps you alive. The other three-quarters keeps your doctor alive." Ancient Egyptian Proverb

"Let your food be your medicine, and your medicine be your food." Hippocrates, father of western medicine, founder of the Hippocratic School of Medicine

"The human body heals itself and nutrition provides the resources to accomplish the task." Roger J. Williams PhD. 1971

Chapter 13

Making Wise Lifestyle Choices In a Growing Nutritional Famine

(In order to live long enough and healthy enough to fulfill your God-given destiny)

*G*rowing up in a non-charismatic Christian family and church background, I learned by osmosis that the medical community was really our only source of help when it comes to matters of physical health. Of course we would pray in a general way at church for Aunt Betsy that the Lord would touch her or would "guide the hands of the surgeon".

But as I shared in chapter seven, in 1985 the Lord challenged and shattered this narrow paradigm of mine. I saw that the Lord is the "Great I Am", not the "Great I Was". He didn't do supernatural acts of healing and miracles back in Bible days and then stop. The One who is the same yesterday, today, and forever still calls us to partner with Him in seeing His supernatural Kingdom come. A major part of that partnership entails proclaiming the good news of the Kingdom, casting out demons, healing the sick and raising the dead in the power of the Holy Spirit.

But in the mid 1990s the Lord began challenging me on this improved two dimensional health paradigm of the medical plus divine healing, saying that it was still incomplete. With a few health challenges cropping up as I came into my forties and a small nudge from the Lord I began doing a little investigating about the things we eat (and don't eat) in our modern diet and how that can compromise our health. I didn't radically change my eating habits but I had been sobered enough by the realization of declining nutrition and increased toxins in our modern western diet that I made at least some moderate changes. I consciously chose to cut back on sugar, salt, white flour, white rice, dairy, meat as well as drink more water (and more purified water at that). I also tried to make a more conscious effort to eat more fresh fruit and vegetables. And I noticed some encouraging progress in my level of health and wellbeing.

But after about ten years of a moderately improved eating lifestyle and now into my fifties and struggling with more health challenges, I believe the Lord shouted louder than ever about this health paradigm of wise lifestyle choices.

In the summer of 2005, Suzanne, a Christian friend gave me some materials for me to check out regarding the place that nutrition and the wellness industry can play in the health equation. I had read stuff before and had taken various vitamin supplements from the health store for several years with what seemed to be of some benefit. But she was insistent that I needed to be aware of some fairly new patented and scientifically validated plant-based nutritional technologies that were now available to the public. I begrudgingly said I would take a look at the material and get back to her.

Although my basic stance was one of skepticism, I was motivated enough to check it out because 1) my friend was persistent 2) as a seeker of truth, I love to learn and discover things I didn't know before and 3) I was dealing with over a dozen health challenges, a few of which I had had for over ten years and specialists were saying I needed to just learn to live with as nothing medically could be done. I had gotten prayer for some of these ailments many times and had seen a measure of temporary relief. But I wasn't winning the war.

In checking out this material I was quite stunned with what I found. It wasn't long before I was putting my money where my mouth is - literally ingesting these plant-based and nutritionally dense supplements. My dozen or so ailments all cleared up within six months and I have, over time, seen at least a dozen other health benefits in my body such as: more energy, younger looking skin, fewer colds and flues, thicker and faster growing hair, better cognitive functioning in terms of memory and concentration (although some may contest that!).

This definitely got my attention and has led me on a fascinating journey of discovery through courses, seminars and several thousand hours of study over the last seven years. I love to research and learn. I have since received a certificate as an "Integrative Wellness Representative" from Proevity, an American based group for continuing education of medical professionals and lay people in some of the latest scientifically validated nutritional technologies. I have also established a small home based business in helping others with their health and wellness choices through plant-based yet standardized nutritional supplementation. My wife is a nurse in the medical community and we both love to pray for the sick by faith in the name of Jesus. We really do want to utilize every weapon at our disposal in our battle for our health.

In fact, while I'm writing this, my wife, Pam, is the acting nurse at a mission base in Malawi, Africa for three months. I'm teaching at the mission base Bible school, writing a portion of this book and helping to set up daily distribution of plant-based vitamin/mineral and glyconutritional supplementation for the sixty children. We are also taking every opportunity to pray for supernatural healing for folks.

Quite early in this process of making this change in worldview, the Lord gave me what I believe were several prophetic visions or pictures that impacted me, of which I will share two.

The Lord said to me that just as a country like Canada went to war in WWII, it sent the army, navy and the air force with the ultimate objective of victory over the enemy, so in our battle for our health, we need to use the navy (medical community), air force (prayer for divine healing) and the army (God's ground troops of various plants for nutritional support and wise lifestyle choices). And whether it is the army, or navy or air force that plays the more significant role in any given battle is practically immaterial. The objective is victory over the enemy. They were all working as a team for the same cause.

So we too should not pit these three weapons in our arsenal against each other but see them as complementary and integrative.

Another picture the Lord gave me involved me standing at the top of a cliff. As I stood there I watched as people in mass were walking towards the edge of the cliff. There was fog or clouds that kept them from seeing clearly the danger ahead and so they were falling off the cliff in epidemic numbers. I looked down at the bottom of the cliff and saw a fascinating scene. I saw a row of ambulances with their back doors open and people in white uniforms placing injured people on stretchers into the ambulances to take to hospital. I also saw small groups of people at the bottom who were praying over the injured. But the numbers were quite substantial and those seeking to help either by prayer and/or with medical care appeared quite overwhelmed.

Then I heard the words "Why not build a nutritional fence at the top of the cliff?" I then immediately saw a fence along the top that kept many people from falling over but it was not high enough to prevent everyone from falling. I looked again over the cliff and saw that those below still had plenty of people to care for, but it was not of epidemic proportions as it was earlier. There would always be people to hospitalize and pray for.

However, in conversing with various Christian friends or acquaintances in the coming months on this subject of health through proper nutrition and exercise, I wasn't quite prepared for some of the reactionary responses.

One repeated argument that arose in conversation was that I was no longer walking by faith in Jesus for my health. I was trusting in nutrition instead and making it an idol, a god in my life. I must admit that I had become quite passionate about this new paradigm that I had come to embrace not only because of the compelling data in my research but also the substantial health improvements I was personally experiencing after years of challenges. So, while some folks may have been reacting more to my enthusiasm, I wanted to address issues of assumptions and paradigms.

I would usually ask the person questioning my faith because of my use of nutritional supplements, if they were on any kind of medications. They either were, had been, or were quite prepared to do so because they did not see this as a conflict with their Christian faith. Of course I don't see a conflict either but for the sake of the argument, I would then challenge them for not having faith in the Lord for their healing. They would usually respond with saying that it is different and yet they were at a loss as to why. Some would try to dismiss it by saying the nutritional approach is New Age and thus suspect while medications were a gift from God.

While recognizing the need for discernment because of some New Age influences in the wellness movement, I've come to realize that natural nutritional products are actually more directly from the Lord (from plants in God's creation for our benefit) than man-made synthetic drugs. Medications given for chronic ailments tend to be more about managing symptoms caused by some breakdown in the body while nutrition brings resources to support the body's own ability to heal, mend and repair itself as God designed it to do. I've heard one allopathic doctor make an interesting comment, "To drug is human, to nourish is divine".

So although it is not my intention to argue that those depending on the medical community do not have faith in God, I am not willing to let those folks claim that I don't. It comes down to a matter of paradigms and **the need for a shift to a more comprehensive paradigm. We don't need to pit them against each other but rather be thankful to the Lord for them and take advantage of all the weapons in our God given arsenal in our battle for our health.**

The Navy

Having said the preceding statement with all sincerity, I do wish to express some concern with how we in the West seem to have stepped across a line in giving the medical field unquestioned authority in our lives. **As much as it is an amazing gift from God, I believe we also need to realize its limitations.** We are grateful for the "navy", the medical community of doctors, nurses and specialists. We marvel at their skills, courage and dedication. In emergency rooms, intensive care units, hospital wards, clinics, trauma centers and disaster scenes, they work tirelessly, saving lives and mending bodies. Modern medical science has made astonishing advances over the years, which have alleviated much pain and suffering. When it comes to diagnostic capabilities, surgical technique and trauma care, the contribution they bring to humanity is impossible to measure. If I get hit by a Mack truck, please don't take me to the health store, get me to the nearest ER!

However, at the risk of stepping on some toes, we must grapple with the data and not bury our heads in the sand. The modern medical paradigm and our present health care systems are tragically failing in many respects. While health care systems in the West are flirting with bankruptcy in their spending of trillions of dollars each year, obesity, chronic disease and illness continue to climb to epidemic levels. The medical paradigm, on its own, is demonstrating it is not only inadequate, it appears to be quite inept and impotent to address and help solve this health crisis of sky rocketing cases of chronic disease.

Something is drastically wrong when, for instance, there are approximately seven hundred thousand doctors in the U.S. (according to the US census) doing their best, with a cost of well over one trillion dollars a year for their health care system and yet according to the World Health Organization, in their 2000 report, the US now ranks only seventy-second out of one hundred and ninety-one countries in overall health.[1]

A 2007 IBM report called "Healthcare 2015: win-win or lose-lose?" states: "The U.S. healthcare system is on an unsustainable path that will force its transformation". It claims that U.S. healthcare expenditures per capita are 2.3 times higher than that of other developed countries and are projected to increase eighty-three percent over the next ten years.[2]

Nicholas J. Webb, a chief executive officer at several health-care companies, advisor to hospitals and medical research organizations and the recipient of twenty seven patents for medical inventions, in his book, The Cost of Being Sick, argues that "Americans are adapting way too easily to unhealthy lifestyles in full confidence that if they get sick there's a miracle pill a phone call away that will cure what ails them. It's a mindset that the medical-industrial complex is only too happy to accommodate". He goes on to argue that "our lifestyles, the medical-industrial complex, and our health-care system have converged to the critical point where they're actually working against us. They're doing so by focusing our health-care efforts on post disease pills rather than prevention and on treating illness rather than promoting wellness".[3]

We should be particularly concerned about Big Pharma, the massive and very powerful government lobbying pharmaceutical industry that is profit driven and regulated by the FDA (Food and Drug Administration) that is supposedly an independent and objective government agency.

April 15, 1998, the Journal of the American Medical Association reported that there are more than two million drug "adverse reactions" every year in the US and that more than one hundred thousand of those reactions are fatal. This makes properly prescribed drugs the fourth leading cause of death in the United States. And that is not taking into account the patients who were accidentally given the wrong drug or dosage or who died from drug reactions but whose death was mistakenly or deliberately attributed to other causes.[4]

For even more sobering statistics, check out on-line the 2003 abstract by Dr. Gary Null and others which compiles American statistics from various peer-reviewed medical journals, called "Death by Medicine". It confirms the above statistic, claiming there are 2.2 million in-hospital, adverse reactions to prescribed drugs each year but also claims there are over twenty million unnecessary antibiotic prescriptions per year. "The most stunning statistic, however, is that the total number of deaths caused by conventional medicine is an astounding 783,936 per year. It is now evident that the American medical system is the leading cause of death and injury in the U.S. (By contrast, the number of deaths attributable to heart disease in 2001 was 699,697, while the number of deaths attributable to cancer was 553,251)."[5]

In stating such information, this is not meant to be an attack on medical personnel who are committed to saving lives and alleviating suffering but rather a call to critically evaluate the medical paradigm, the financially unsustainable health care systems and the pharmaceutical industry. Something is wrong when the profit-driven pharmaceutical industry goes over the health-care providers and straight to the American people with their persuasive television commercials, spending as much money on advertising as they do in research and development.

The medical paradigm, with it's many centuries old view of the human body as a mechanical machine that can be diagnosed, classified and repaired just like any other machine, works exceptionally well in the realm of surgery and trauma care. But when it comes to chronic illness and disease, predominantly managing the symptoms and not effectively resolving the root cause, it is woefully inadequate. And when using a drug to relieve or manage a symptom, because of various negative side effects, often the person is put on other drugs to address that. The average person over sixty-five in the US takes fifteen plus medications a day.[6]

That seems quite shocking and unrealistic but I remember two years ago when my eighty-two year old father and his ninety-year-old wife, my stepmother, both passed away within weeks of each other. In cleaning out their house, we collected up all their prescription and over the counter medications and dropped them off at the nearby drug store. We completely filled two large garbage bags and half filled a third.

Revelation 18:23 states, "for by sorceries were the nations deceived." The Greek word for sorceries is "pharmekia", where we get our word "pharmacy" or "pharmaceuticals."

Is it possible that the majority of today's citizens, including most Christians, have been deceived concerning the widespread use of drugs? They rightly stand against illegal drugs such as heroin, cocaine and amphetamines due to their obvious harm, but what about the blind acceptance and unthinking consumption of a plethora of prescription drugs taken over years or even decades? "Prescription drugs now represent the single largest monthly expense for most over sixty-five U. S. citizens, approximately $300 a month."[7]

Again, most drugs tend to suppress symptoms but not really address the cause. They silence the symptoms that your body is trying to use to communicate to you about a problem. "They merely hush the voice of nature's protest", says Daniel H. Kress, M.D. Dr. Joe Barton poses the question: "If your kitchen faucet was turned on and water was overflowing from the sink, would you grab a mop or turn off the faucet? Drugs can be like a toxic mop!"[8]

There can be a very valid place for drug medications, at least short term, which has saved many lives and alleviated much suffering but there is often a trade off that can be lethal, especially when used in combination with other medications and for long-term management of symptoms of chronic disease.

With the increase of chronic illnesses, aging populations, prospects of end time wars and natural disasters, escalating medical care costs, and unprecedented stress on the earth, the medical care system will not be able to cope financially or otherwise. Not only is radical reform within the medical care system itself (navy) crucial, but so is a growing partnership with the wellness industry with its emphasis on prevention through natural means (army) and with prayer and God's supernatural intervention (air force).

The Air Force

The weapon of divine healing and signs and wonders has already been addressed in an earlier chapter. God has made it clear that He is still very much in the healing and restoring business and He calls His church to partner with Him in this Kingdom mandate. I am thrilled every time I see the Lord's healing compassion and mercy demonstrated in a tangible way in someone's physical body, whether it be the removal of a head ache or a cancer or a creative miracle such as the recovery of someone's sight or mobility.

However, I deeply appreciate and agree with the point Larry Randolph makes in his book, The Coming Shift. Randolph honestly admits that he, along with many other Christian leaders who have had an anointing for healing the sick, have become "super-spiritual" and have often neglected and abused their own bodies by living a lifestyle that lacked proper rest, exercise and a healthy diet, with serious consequences.

He went to see his doctor about an irregular heartbeat and the doctor said, "You are a prime candidate for a heart attack. I don't know what you do for a living, but it seems to be bad for your health. So you better stop before it kills you". Randolph was too embarrassed to tell the doctor about his occupation as an itinerant and prophetic preacher who often sees the sick healed through prayer. The doctor's advice drove him to his knees where he asked the Lord to show him what he could do to avoid premature death. He expected God to say he should fast and pray more but the Lord said, "If you want to live and be a part of the next spiritual outpouring, you must get in shape".[9]

Larry Randolph goes on to mention a litany of revivalists and faith healers of the past who were used by God to heal many but they themselves fell prey to this mindset of neglecting one's body which has resulted in their suffering poor health and premature death. A few names mentioned were Wm. Seymour, who died of a heart attack at age fifty-two, Aimie Semple McPherson who died at age fifty-three, A.A. Allen at age fifty- nine, and the overweight Jack Coe who died at age thirty-nine.[10]

Why were they vulnerable to the same illnesses as they healed and died prematurely even though some of them raised others from the dead?

Sickness is the vengeance of nature for the violation of her laws. We often take better care of our cars! And many Christians and particularly Christian leaders are guilty of workaholism and a performance mentality that leads to exhaustion and premature breakdown of the body.

Randolph goes on to say that: "Many falsely assume that a healthy anointing can flow from an unhealthy source. This is especially true of those who believe that occasional manifestations of the Holy Spirit in and through their ministry can somehow compensate for the imperfections of a vessel weakened by neglect and abuse. As a result of this deception, believers often push their minds and bodies beyond the limits of human endurance. Worse yet, many believe this abuse is a sacrificial requirement for an anointed ministry and often preach that the neglect of the human body is necessary to reach a higher status of spirituality. With great pride, these misguided ministers boast about their infirmities and weaknesses as though they are a requirement for receiving the anointing...In many instances the Lord is blamed for our infirmities and the premature death that often follows".[11]

We should never underestimate the role of how our physical health plays in God's purposes for our lives. If we neglect proper stewardship of our bodies, which are temples of the Holy Spirit, we are risking not living long enough or healthy enough to fulfill our God-given destinies.

George Malkmus, former Baptist pastor, promoter of the Hallelujah Diet, and author of several books on the crucial need for healthy eating, cleansing and exercise, also speaks frankly regarding this matter of Christians getting sick and experiencing premature deaths. He hears the standard answer among Christians, as "it must have been God's will". He raises the question: "Could it be possible that we are attributing sickness to 'sin', or 'the will of God' when, in reality the cause of that sickness might be the violation of some natural laws of God?"[12]

So yes, let's make praying for the sick in the name and authority of Jesus a "naturally supernatural" part of our daily Christian lifestyle (and take advantage of what the medical world might have to offer). But let's not get super spiritual and ignore our personal responsibility of good stewardship and wise lifestyle choices in regards to these fragile earthen vessels the Lord has given us.

Our church heads up a walk-in clinic in our city's downtown called "The Barrie Healing Rooms". We have trained volunteers from various churches who form prayer teams to pray for the sick at no cost. We have seen God heal everything from headaches to cancer. It has been wonderful and we say "Yea God"!

Now if someone comes in and asks for prayer for healing from dehydration we could pray for them and God in His mercy could supernaturally heal, that is hydrate them. But if they come in a few days later and say they have mysteriously lost their healing and request that we pray for them again, it would be more than appropriate to say to them that they need a "wisdom encounter", not a "power encounter" and point them to the water fountain across the room. This leads us to our next discussion.

The Army: Wise Lifestyle Choices

There is a myth our western culture strongly embraces, the myth that all these modern diseases we are experiencing are simply an unexplainable mystery that we simply have to tolerate ("it comes with our age") until the day a cure is found.

However, mounting scientific evidence is showing that the vast majority of these modern chronic diseases are directly related to our modern western lifestyles of: stress, electromagnetic pollution from high tech communication gadgets, nutritionally deficient but calorie packed refined foods, an increase of toxins in our food, water and air and a lack of exercise and rest.

Psalm 139:14 tells us that we are fearfully and wonderfully made. God has designed our bodies with over sixty trillion cells, which require constant nourishment for rebuilding as well as constant cleansing from toxins. If we have healthy cells, then we have healthy tissues, which give us healthy organs, which provide us healthy systems, which lead to a healthy body. If we are healthy at the micro level, the odds are very high that we will be healthy at the macro level. If these cells are not provided the proper nutritional building materials and kept cleansed of toxins, optimal health of our bodies is compromised and we will probably experience premature and unnecessary breakdown.

A picture is worth a thousand words. Dr. Jon Barron of the Baseline of Health Foundation provides an extremely helpful graph called "the Baseline of Health":[13]

Level of Health | The Line of Optimal Health
                | _____
                |
Feel Great |
                |
                |
                | The Line of Symptoms
                | _____
                |
                |
                |
Don't feel so good |
                | The Death Line
                I   _____

    Dead   Immune System   Heart   Cancer   etc

As long as all the body's organs and systems function above the Line of Symptoms, a person will feel fine and there are no worries. He may feel healthy but in fact he could be quite a distance from true optimal health. But as soon as any part of the body drops below the Line of Symptoms, problems surface and we begin to take notice (and probably be quite baffled because we thought we were fine specimens of vibrant optimal health). If those problems persist and drop low enough, we will need to take more drastic action. If any part of our health line touches the Death Line, it is all over.

The goal then is to raise every area of one's personal health line, not just above the symptom line, but as close to the optimal health line as possible, which increases the odds in one's favour.[14]

I see a parallel with the times we take our automobile to the mechanic. We go to him when we are aware of a "symptom", a problem with our car. We ask him to fix it, which he is willing to do, but he may also point out to you a list of other issues that will soon become an expensive repair, if not attended to very soon. The mechanic (if he is honest) is looking at things from a more comprehensive view to keep your vehicle purring along at minimal expense and maximum lifespan. But human nature tends to be narrow-minded and shortsighted, dealing with only the pressing issue at hand. We are into "crisis management" instead of "preventative or maintenance" care. So we need to do ourselves a big favour and adjust our perspective to a more comprehensive and long term one, both with our cars and our bodies.

To aim higher than the mere line of symptoms towards the line of optimal health, we need to look at all the areas, which can make a difference. We should seriously cut back on modern junk food we tend to eat, consume all the daily nutritional resources the body needs, cleanse the body of toxins, seek to get adequate exercise and give attention to our emotional and spiritual well being.

We need to be quick to forgive, cultivate a personal relationship with God, develop friendships, learn to be a loving and generous giver, and laugh and play so much more. Did you know that children laugh about four hundred times a day while the average adult only about six to eight times a day? It's a scientific fact that exercise, laughter, play, and having fun cause endorphins to be released in your brain that gives a sense of well being, fortifies your immune system, and decreases the stress hormones of cortisol and adrenaline.[15]

With increased days of trial and turbulence coming our way in the end times, it's all the more crucial that we learn to stay child-like, playful, not take ourselves too seriously, and maintain a good sense of humour. Over the twenty-five years of pastoring churches, I have usually tried to add a few jokes into my sermons. The folks in one church use to tell me that I tithed my jokes - one in ten was actually funny! My wife just shared some jokes with me today that she found on Facebook that brought lots of oxygen to my brain and most seem relevant to a book about perspectives as well as this chapter on health. Hope you enjoy them.

I sat up all night wondering where the sun went. Then it dawned on me.

They laughed at me when I said I wanted to be a comedian. Well, they're not laughing anymore.

It's all about perspective. The sinking of the Titanic was a miracle to the lobsters in the ship's kitchen.

Funny new trend at the office. People putting names on food in the company fridge. Today I had a tuna sandwich named Bob.

I was wondering why the frisbee was getting bigger and bigger, til it hit me.

I let my imagination run wild! That way at least some part of me gets some exercise.

I have a hunch that my posture is not the best.

Whatever you do, always give 100 percent. Unless you're donating blood.

I used to think the brain was the most interesting part of the body. Then I realized what was telling me that.

Even the Bible tells us that laughter is therapeutic, "A cheerful heart is good medicine" (Prov. 17:22). When the Hebrew people were brought out of captivity the Scriptures testify that "our mouths were filled with laughter, our tongues with songs of joy". (Ps. 126:2) I also recommend spending time soaking in the presence of the Lord often. The joy of the Lord really is our strength (Neh. 8:10).

Nasty Things to Avoid Putting in Your Body

According to the USDA, Americans spend less than ten percent of their incomes on food today, compared to eighteen percent in 1966. That is good news. But the bad news is **that ninety percent of the money Americans do spend on food today buys cheap processed food that is high in calories and low in actual nutrition, a major contributing factor to our modern obesity and chronic disease epidemics.**

Much of this processed food consumed is very inexpensive, largely thanks to the government subsidized corn and wheat industry. One of the byproducts of corn is the low cost sweetener called high fructose corn syrup that is found in everything from soda pop to hot dogs. Production of corn is up from four billion bushels a year in 1970 to over twelve billion bushels today. A study in the American Journal of Clinical Nutrition found that a US dollar could buy 1,200 calories of potato chips, 875 calories of soda, but only 250 calories of vegetables or 170 calories of fresh fruit.[16]

George Malkmus tells us "Most Americans just take it for granted that if it is a product sold for food that it is safe to eat. Not so!" The recent documentary film, "Food Inc." calls this processed food "edible food like substances"![17] This edible food like substance has not only be refined, stripping it of its nutrition and fiber that the body needs, but has had all sorts of chemical ingredients added to it. Such **chemical additives** are used as preservatives for longer shelf life, artificial colouring (for presentation), and addictive additives for flavour (for further sales and profits) such as sugar, salt, MSG, and artificial sweeteners like Aspartame.

Sugar in the form of **sucrose** has become a man-made addictive drug. The heat used in this process changes it from natural glucose into unnatural simple sucrose. This refined product has been stripped of vitamins, minerals, proteins and enzymes, making it a calorie rich and nutrient empty simple carbohydrate. This sugar is quickly released into the blood stream causing harmful "sugar spikes" and messes with proper blood sugar balances. Sugar temporarily impairs your immune system. Eating 100 grams of simple sugar, like cookies, cake, or doughnuts, can reduce the ability of your white blood cells to destroy microorganisms by fifty percent for a few hours. Furthermore, sugar actually feeds cancer cells, is linked to behavioural disorders such as ADHD, promotes osteoporosis, yeast infections, type 2 diabetes, and accelerates the aging process.[18]

At the turn of the 20th century, the average annual consumption of white table sugar was about five pounds per person in the US. Today it has reached one hundred and seventy pounds per person per year. That is around fifty teaspoons of sugar per day. One twelve ounce soft drink contains over ten teaspoons of sugar.[19]

Refined table **salt** is another additive that we consume way too much of. This inorganic addictive drug is a form of sodium chloride, which is a deadly poison. Refined salt contributes to hardening of the arteries, higher blood pressure and hypertension. The recommended maximum daily salt limit is 2,400 mg, which is about one teaspoon.[20]

MSG (monosodium glutamate) is a common processed food additive that can potentially be addictive. This dangerous and well-disguised ingredient doesn't alter the actual taste of the food but enhances it, stimulating your taste buds and your appetite. Manufacturers have also been creative in using other names in the labeling in hopes that you don't notice its presence. MSG can cause various adverse reactions as well as promote obesity and neurotoxicity.[21]

Aspartame is a sweetener found in over six thousand products such as: diet soda pop, coffee sweetener, sugarless gum, and is consumed by seventy percent of Americans, including forty percent of children. Aspartame is made up of three components: aspartic acid, phenylalanine, and methanol (wood alcohol). Methanol, converts into formaldehyde (embalming fluid) and can cause eye and neurological damage. Aspartic acid excites nerve cells and may cause permanent nervous system damage. It is also associated with brain abnormalities, including brain tumours in animals. In spite of all the damnable evidence that keeps mounting against this deadly additive, the FDA continues to refuse to rescind its approval of Aspartame for public consumption.[22]

Aside from those harmful additives to our food and drinks, let me also address the popular drug called **caffeine**. Caffeine is not only a diuretic, meaning it removes water from your body, but is a popular stimulant that excites the nerve-centers into unusual activity as the body makes every effort to reject and repulse it. Your blood vessels constrict and your heart will beat faster, causing adrenalin to be released into your system. This toxic poison can damage the lining of the stomach as well as your liver and kidneys, let alone produce irritability, insomnia and depression. If you don't think caffeine is addictive, just try going off caffeine "cold turkey" and wait for the withdrawal headaches you will experience. Caffeine is found in coffee, cola soft drinks, chocolate (though dark unprocessed chocolate has some health benefits) and some teas.[23]

Then there are the toxic chemicals of insecticides, herbicides, fungicides that are used to help protect the food while it is being grown. "The average American consumes over seven pounds of these poisons annually."[24]

Toxic heavy metals have found their way into our bodies as well. Mercury is accumulated in the body from such sources as fish, dental fillings and vaccinations (with controversial and inconclusive rumours of a possible connection between mercury laced vaccinations and autism). Aluminum, which may be a culprit in brain function issues like Alzheimer's disease, is found in under arm antiperspirants. Some studies also indicate a possible connection between breast cancer and the long-term use of antiperspirants and/ or deodorants with parabens.

We can't ignore the problem of **hazardous toxins in our municipal drinking water.** Not only heavy metals and other contaminants are in our tap water, but it has also been chlorinated (to kill bacteria), often fluoridated, and tests have shown startling levels of a host of non-biodegradable medications.

Chlorine in our drinking water, bath water and swimming pools kills harmful microorganisms but there is a health trade off. Chlorine can combine with organic materials to form trihalomethanes - a cancer-promoting substance. Bladder cancer has been linked to chlorinated water as well as issues related to pregnancy. I would recommend filtering not only your drinking water but also your shower/bath water since absorption through your skin and the inhaling of chlorinated vapours may be a greater health issue than chlorinated drinking water.

Throughout Europe (with the exception of Ireland), authorities will not allow the use of **fluoride** in drinking water. They know the health hazards of this poison and that it is unethical to medicate citizens without their prior informed consent. But in America it is a different story.

According to Dr. Paul Connett, a university professor of chemistry in New York State, in his document, titled "50 Reasons to Oppose Fluoridation", claims fluoride is a cumulative poison. On average, only fifty percent of the fluoride we ingest each day is actually excreted through the kidneys. The remainder accumulates in our bones, pineal gland, and other tissues. He gives a litany of possible health concerns related to such important issues as DNA, nerve, brain, thyroid, hyper and hypoactive behaviour, enzymatic interference, infertility, and bone cancer.

Methodically flawed trials first began in the US in 1945, but before any of the trials were complete, the practice of placing a concentration of one part fluoride per million in drinking water began. This was under the guise of preventing tooth decay and was endorsed by the U.S. Public Health Service in 1950. The chemicals used to fluoridate water in the U.S. are not pharmaceutical grade (except in animal studies). Rather, they are classified as hazardous wastes contaminated with various impurities including relatively high levels of arsenic. And yet fluoridation continues to be enthusiastically promoted by U.S. health officials as being "safe and effective" for fighting tooth decay, even though other countries that have not succumbed to this practice have teeth just as good, if not better. Today, about seventy percent of Americans drink fluorinated water.[25]

According to other sources, such as journalist Christopher Bryson, author of Fluoride Deception, a man named Edward L. Bernays was instrumental in promoting fluoride to the American people. Bernays, a double nephew of Sigmund Freud, was a propaganda and persuasion expert, graciously called the "father of public relations." He was hired to make bacon and eggs a standard breakfast, to persuade women to take up smoking, to convince the American public to join the efforts of WW I, and also to initiate a national campaign to fluoridate America's drinking water supply.[26]

Sodium fluoride, a waste by-product of the production of aluminum and phosphate fertilizer, is a poison that is not allowed to be dropped into the sea but is allowed to be placed in drinking water and toothpaste. Its toxicity level is between lead and arsenic and has shown to increase attention deficit disorder, reduce I.Q. of children, and cause stiff joints. Adolph Hitler first introduced it into drinking water in Nazi concentration camps, knowing it can help control the population in terms of compliance and dumbing-down.

Very rarely talked about is the horrific disaster developing in our drinking water due to the over use of **non-biodegradable drugs** (and personal care products) over the years. I remember flying from Vancouver to Toronto several years ago and got chatting with a middle-aged man across the aisle. I found out he worked for the government in testing water quality in rivers, lakes and streams, particularly in northern Ontario. When I mentioned that I had come across some news articles that revealed quite shocking information regarding toxic chemicals and medications in the drinking water of various European and North American cities, he had a very somber look on his face. After looking around to see if others were listening to our conversation, he affirmed that indeed the situation is getting extremely serious and admitted that they did not have any real solutions to this growing crisis. The articles I have read spoke of alarming traces of such non-biodegradable medications as antibiotics, anti-depressants, anti-seizure meds, pain- killers, and high levels of the hormone estrogen, from birth control products. In Lake Mead in Nevada, pharmaceutical estrogen is so high that male fish are producing female egg protein.[27]

Margarine, shortening and fried products are very unhealthy hydrogenated products that the public uncritically devours.

White flour has been processed, removing the germ because it gums up their machinery, then removing the bran because it leaves brown specks in the flour, then bleaching it to make it nice and white, then adding coal tar derived chemical vitamins to supposedly enrich it. It is best to avoid **white rice** as well and focus on consuming brown rice that has not been stripped of its fiber and nutrition.

Most **meat** on the market shelves contain sobering levels of **antibiotics and growth hormones** that have been given to the animals that live in very crowded accommodations as a preventative measure for maximum profitability. The Union of Concerned Scientists estimates that about seventy percent of antimicrobial drugs used in America are given to animals, not people.[28] We just get them after consumption!

Add to that the disturbing fact that the FDA has allowed meat (as well as some imported fruit and vegetables, juices, and grains) to be irradiated, that is, zapped with radiation, killing some of its nutritional value, and who knows what else it may cause.

Humans are omnivores (designed to eat meat and plants) but most of us act like we are carnivores (meat only eaters). According to the 2011 documentary film, Forks over Knives, the average American in the early 1900's consumed 120 pounds of meat each year while in 2007 it climbed to 222 pounds per person per year.

One of the scientists featured in this film, Dr. T. Colin Campbell of Cornell University argues both in the film and in his book, The China Study, that there is a distinct difference between the diseases of the affluent in western cultures (heart disease, cancer, diabetes, stroke, obesity) and the diseases of poverty in non-western populations. Through his own rat and mice laboratory experiments and a comprehensive study done in China, Dr. Campbell has come to the conclusion that the major culprit of modern chronic illnesses, particularly cancer, in the West, is our excessively high protein consumption from animal products, meat and dairy. Not only has our meat consumption doubled in the last one hundred years, but also our dairy intake, from 294 pounds per person per year to 605 pounds in 2006.

In a culture that strongly advocates getting enough protein Dr. Campbell warns that the fifteen to sixteen percent protein in the average American's diet is far too high. Ten percent is adequate for our needs. We need to not only cut back our protein intake, but the real kicker is that we should get it from plants not animals. He therefore calls for a radical change in our eating habits. He recommends people reduce and preferably cut out altogether their consumption of all **meats and dairy products**[29]

Dr. Caldwell Esselstyn, a former cardiac surgeon, is also featured in the film, Forks over Knives, and author of the book, Prevent and Reverse Heart Disease. Dr. Esselstyn claims that if we would change our ways and begin to follow a radical plant-based diet, we could abolish the heart-disease epidemic and other chronic illnesses and thereby cut health care costs by seventy to eighty percent.[30]

And as if this is not enough of a challenge to chew on (pardon the pun), seeking to avoid or at least reduce consuming refined foods, poisonous additives, meat and dairy, a Dr. William Davis, a cardiologist in Wisconsin, in his eye-opening 2011 book, Wheat Belly, gives a compelling case for eliminating or at least reducing **wheat** from our diet.

He states in his introduction, "I recognize that declaring wheat a malicious food is like declaring that Ronald Reagan was a Communist...But I will make the case that the world's most popular grain is also the world's most destructive dietary ingredient". He blames the mass consumption of wheat for today's epidemic of obesity, which then leads to various health challenges such as diabetes and cardiovascular disease.

You might be thinking: yea but Jesus encouraged us to pray the Lord's prayer which includes the petition, "give us this day our daily bread". But Dr. Davis points out that our modern wheat, which is found in thousands of our breakfast, lunch, supper and snack products, is not really wheat but the transformed product of man made genetic engineering (for the purpose of higher yields and profits) of the last fifty years.[31] Since our wheat has been hybridized and cross-bred multiplied times in recent decades (without being tested for safety), increasing evidence points to this so called wheat being guilty of being addictive and dangerous for human health.

Of course he would say the hybrid whole grain products are better than refined wheat products but he would not say whole grains are healthful for you. Dr. Davis points out that wheat carbohydrates convert to blood sugar more efficiently than just about any other carbohydrate, including table sugar (sucrose). In fact, he claims that whole wheat bread has a glycemic index of seventy-two while sucrose has a glycemic index of only fifty-nine.[32]

This easy conversion to blood sugar causes greater extremes of roller coaster highs and lows, of sugar spikes and sugar crashes. The rise in blood sugar causes a high insulin response, which leads to excess blood sugar being converted to fat. In my estimation, Dr. Davis provides a fairly convincing case that the primary culprit of virtually all the large bellies in our day are the direct result of our love affair with wheat. The USDA and other health authorities have been sending out a message since the 1980s that we need to consume more whole grains and cut out fat. And since 1985 the problem of obesity has been skyrocketing. One third of Americans are now overweight while another one third are considered obese.

Dr. Davis also argues that wheat is highly addictive and it affects neurological and cognitive functions. He has found about thirty percent of the thousands of patients he has worked with experience substantial withdrawals as they come off wheat. And studies have shown an increase of problems related to brain function and behaviour for people struggling with schizophrenia, ADHD, and autism. Wheat is also a contributing factor to fatigue and brain fog.[33]

With the fat belly comes an increase in the production of the hormone, estrogen, in both men and women. In men it is responsible for the growing phenomenon of larger breasts. I kid you not. Rather than recommending the reduction of wheat from one's diet to deal with a cascade of health problems, including enlarged male breasts, you can go get various medications to manage your symptoms and even take advantage of a new and booming industry across America of having male breast reduction surgery![34] Maybe the price tag on that bagel is much more than you ever bargained for.

I don't mean to depress you or get you mad at me. I am only trying to tip you off to information that I've stumbled upon and encourage you to check things out for yourself so you can make informed decisions that affect your life and the lives of your loved ones. We cannot afford to do what the majority do, naively assume that government agencies and big business will always have our best interests in mind. Governments often buckle under the pressure from various powerful lobbying groups such as: the meat, sugar, dairy, corn, wheat, and pharmaceutical industries. The almighty dollar is usually the bottom line.

Ignorance is not bliss. We must do our homework and take personal responsibility for our health and well being, even if it involves some substantial and unpopular changes in lifestyle and possible accusations of having a "healthy eating disorder" called "orthorexia nervosa." This laughable label is now being pinned on people who are considered to have an unhealthy fixation with eating healthy food, rather than just going with the flow and eating whatever the food industry dishes up for us.[35]

This is not just theory for me. In recent months, my family and I have all been researching these matters of meat, dairy, and wheat and have been making some significant changes to our eating habits. Unfortunately, we often don't make changes until we have had a rude wake up call of some kind. Our daughter, who is almost twenty five years old, is pregnant with our first grandchild but was recently diagnosed as having an aggressive form of Hodgkin's Lymphoma, a form of cancer in the lymph nodes. You can bet that as we look to the Lord, we are seeking to take advantage of all the resources God has put at our disposal: the army, the navy, and the air force.

It is amazing that the average person, including the average Christian, rarely associates his physical health problems with what he eats or drinks. George Malkmus bemoans the fact that, "We poison our food while it is growing, harvest it green before much of the nutrition develops, remove any nutrients in processing, add toxic preservatives to it, cook it, and then we are baffled as to why we get sick...When we get sick from the drugs in our drinking water and from taking drugged, so called food substances into our body, we call the medical doctor, the doctor licensed to practice the prescribing of drugs, writes a prescription for some more drugs...We cannot be drugged or poisoned into health..."[36]

Christians are challenged by God to not be blindly following the crowd, being conformed or squeezed into the world's mold and patterns of thinking or lack of thinking. (Romans 12:2) And yet we buy into the enticements of our advertising industry like everyone else. We (and I include myself) thoughtlessly consume what everyone else does and simply assume it couldn't be that bad for us. We forget there are consequences to our actions or inactions. We reap what we sow. We are what we eat. And so without realizing it, we play Russian roulette with our health.

There is an increasing urgency to wake up and smell the coffee (someone please help me find a healthier expression!) and take greater personal responsibility for our health and well being. Let's learn to read not only the price tag but the ingredient labels on food products and seek to avoid things that have words you can't pronounce.

Further, I recommend we begin to think local and take advantage of local farmer's markets, where some produce may not be harvested green or transported long distances and stored for lengthy periods of time, which allows for oxidation. We may also want to consider organically grown food more. Some websites state that if the sticker on the fruit or veggie has four numbers, it is conventionally grown. If it has five numbers and starts with the number nine, it is organic. If it has five numbers and starts with the number eight, it is genetically modified. Some sources question the reliability of this labeling system. Regardless, we vote three times a day with what meals we choose to eat.

For some, this long list of nasty things to avoid makes it seem like we are robbing life of so much joy and pleasure. I understand that concern. But thankfully, our choice is not simply enjoyment of food vs. joylessly eating healthy. My wife and I are learning to be more creative and are having fun with it all. It is interesting how your taste buds change (not controlled and manipulated by addictive additives) when one switches to a more natural diet and you discover all kinds of new foods that actually taste amazing. And learning to slow down and thoroughly chew your food not only allows you to savour each bite, but aids in the digestive process and a healthier outcome.

Let me add as well that we should recognize that there are legitimate times for celebration and festivity on special occasions. I just came back from a family gathering for Easter Sunday where I ate turkey and homemade apple and pumpkin pie and yet on a regular basis I am eating a lot less meat, dairy, wheat, or conventional desserts than I use to. I don't want to get religious, self-righteous or legalistic about it all. I want to stay joyful, light-hearted, thankful, a guy who still has friends, and yet in these challenging last days, is informed and intentional in how I take care of this body that is a temple of the Holy Spirit. Without this earth suit, I'm no earthly good to anyone.

We've taken a glance at so-called food items that we should consider reducing or avoiding altogether. Now let's take a look at healthy stuff that we need to get into our bodies.

Healthy Things to Put into Your Body

For starters, we need to be drinking **adequate amounts of pure water**. Many folks in western cultures are chronically dehydrated and don't know it. If we only drink when we are thirsty, we are probably dehydrated. To determine how much your body needs, take your body weight and divide it by two. That is how many ounces of water you need. That is usually about two to three liters a day. Fortunately, some of our daily water intake comes from the fruit and vegetables we eat. However, unfortunately, the UN predicts that by 2025, two-thirds of the world's population will be suffering from water shortages.[37]

I encourage you to do some research on various forms of water purifiers due to sobering levels of a wide array of harmful pollutants in tap water. Don't always trust bottled water. There is no guarantee it has been purified. Random tests have revealed some bottled water to actually be worse than tap water. Regulations in the bottled water industry are sadly lacking. I use a filtered water bottle that has been tested to remove 99.999 percent of all contaminants. Not only can I be assured of high quality drinking water but I'm not adding to the environmental problem that comes from billions of disposable plastic watei bottles (Google the "Great Pacific Garbage Patch" to see the problem of our oceans becoming "plasticized").

Also we may want to factor in the pH level of our water. On the pH scale of 1 to 14, a pH of 7.0 is considered neutral. Under 7.0 is acidic and over 7.0 is alkaline. Your blood has a constant pH of 7.4, which is alkaline. Disease seems to flourish in a more acidic environment so it is healthier for you to take in more alkaline water (can get alkalizer filters) and food, such as fruits and vegetables. Meat is more acidic.

The USDA (United States Department of Agriculture) recommends between 7-13 servings of **fresh fruit and vegetables** daily. In 1995, their recommendation was only 5-7 fresh fruit and vegetables each day. It's up because they know that the nutritional levels in our mass-produced fruit and vegetables continue to decline and so we need to eat more fruit and vegetables.

With our modern and big business farming practices, large quantities of cheap food are produced and great profits generated by corporations, but it is now evident it is at the expense of nutritional quality and the public's health. We have the problems of:

- Depleted soil (often only three petroleum-based fertilizers: phosphorus, nitrogen, and potassium are utilized to grow crops fast),
- Corn, wheat and other crops genetically modified by corporations like Monsanto,
- Crops picked green so they don't spoil before consumed (but most nutrition, particularly phytochemicals, are developed in the last days of maturation),
- Toxic pesticides and herbicides are used to protect their investments,
- Produce traveling great distances and with the passage of time, plants oxidize (rust),
- Poisonous gassing of some produce, such as turning green tomatoes to red before reaching market shelves,
- Then we cook much of it, destroying even more nutrition.

Even if we take all or most of the harmful items out of our diet listed earlier, and are willing to consume more fresh fruits and vegetables, we still need to ask the following questions regarding the USDA's recommendations of 7-13 servings a day:

Who is actually going to eat that many servings of raw fresh fruit and vegetables every day?

Who can afford it?

And who has the time to chew it all?

The answer is probably a small minority of the public. But even if more and more of us are able to attain that goal fairly regularly, the goal posts may need to be changed again due to a further decline of nutrition in our fruits and vegetables in the days ahead. And in today's toxic world, there's no guarantee you are getting every nutrient at the levels that your body needs to function at its best. Gone are the days when it was "an apple a day keeps the doctor away". It's more like a dozen or two and don't forget to scrub them thoroughly to remove the wretched toxins!

So, we need to ask a further question:

If it is extremely difficult to get what our bodies need every day in our modern diet, should we be taking nutritional supplements to make up the difference?

I believe the answer is a resounding yes, but with qualifications.

This topic of nutritional supplementation is a fairly big subject to discuss and warrants its own chapter.

Recommendations:

Books:

The Seven Pillars of Health, Dr Don Colbert, Siloam, Lake Mary, Florida, 2007

What You Don't Know May Be Killing You! Dr. Don Colbert, Siloam, 2004

The Hallelujah Diet, George Malkmus, Destiny Image, 2006

Super Immunity: The Essential Nutrition Guide, Dr. Joel Fuhrman, HarperCollins Pub., 2011
Eat to Live, Dr. Joel Fuhrman, Little, Brown & Co., revised edition 2012 (healthy weight loss)
How to Survive on a Toxic Planet, Steve Nugent, Alethia Corp. 2006
The China Study, T. Colin Campbell & Thomas M. Campbell, Benballa Books, Dallas, 2006
Wheat Belly, Dr. William Davis, Rodale Books, 2011

DVDs:

Supersize Me, directed & starred by Morgan Spurlock, distributed by Samuel Goldwyn Films, 2004
Food Inc., American documentary directed by Robert Kenner, 2008
Forks and Knives, documentary, Monica Beach Media, Virgil Films, 2011
Hungry for Change, new documentary from Food Matters, youtube trailer, http://www.youtube.com/watch?v=3MvAM97VDE8

Websites:

Death by Medicine, abstract by Dr. Gary Null and others http://www.wnho.net/deathbymedicine.htm
Natural News.com, "GlaxoSmithKline pleads guilty to criminal fraud charges, pays massive $3 billion in fines", Ethan A. Huff, July 8, 2012, http://www.naturalnews.com/036416_GlaxoSmithKline_fraud_criminal_charges.html

You-tube clips:

Death by Medicine, documentary trailer on youtube: http://www.youtube.com/watch?v=CPNDL4M4qC4
War on Health (Teaser), Dr. Gary Null, http://www.youtube.com/watch?v=0j_WOpioHuw
Cancer: Forbidden Cures, documentary film, http://www.youtube.com/watch?v=BTGye7kA6rM

Industry FoodBusters, uploaded Aug. 31/12, http://www.youtube.com/watch?v=PkEPshJUBD0
The Blueberry Deception, uploaded Feb. 11/11 http://www.youtube.com/watch?v=WEKldNyBhbM
"Vitamin water Deception", Aug. 21/11 http://www.youtube.com/watch?v=Z8lLp26HaZY
"The World According to Monsanto - GMO Documentary, uploaded May 18, 2011, http://www.youtube.com/watch?v=Rml_k005tsU

Notes:

1. Dr. John Barron, Lessons from the Miracle Doctors: a Step-by-Step Guide to Optimum Health and Relief from Catastrophic Illness, Baseline of Health Foundation, LA., 2002, pp. 6, 7.
2. 2007 IBM report: "Healthcare 2015:win-win or lose-lose?"
3. Nicholas J. Webb, The Cost of Being Sick, Sound Concepts Inc., 2003, (intro., pp IV, VI).
4. Dr. John Barron, p. 3.
5. Dr. Gary Null and others, "Death by Medicine" extract.
6. Living a Health Lifestyle, Did you know that? # 86, http://www.living-a-healthy-lifestyle.com/did-you-know.html
7. Paul Zane Pilzer, The Next Trillion, Video Plus, 2001, p 10.
8. Joe Barton, 10 Deadly Health Myths of the 21st Century, Golden Keys Mentoring Group, LLC, 2004, pp. 8-10. PDF, http://www.simpleandbetter.com/pdf/ebooks/health/10myths.pdf
(One promising exception is an old drug called DCA, which appears effective with cancer cells. Since it can't be patented, drug companies not interested in doing expensive clinical trials). http://www.dca.med.ualberta.ca/Home/Updates/2010-05-12_Update.cfm (accessed April 4/12); See also You-tube on DCA.
9. Larry Randolph, The Coming Shift, Morningstar, 2006, p. 57.
10. Ibid., 59.
11. Ibid., p. 55.
12. George Malkmus, Why Christians Get Sick, Destiny Image, 1989, pp. 16, 20.
13. Barron, Jon. Lessons from the Miracle Doctors, pp. 6, 7.

14. Ibid, p. 7.
15. Dr. Francisco Contreras, The Hope of Living Long and Well, Siloam, 2000, pp. 80,81.
16. Bryan Walsh, Time Magazine, Aug. 31, 2009, Vol. 174, No. 8, article, pp. 30-37, cited on website, http://www.meatlessmonday. com/the-secret-cost-of-cheap-food/
17. Robert Kenner, director, filmmaker, Food Inc., 2008.
18. Dr. Don Colbert, The Seven Pillars of Health, Siloam, a Strang Company, Lake Mary, Florida, 2007, pp. 80-82.
19. George Malkmus, The Hallelujah Diet, Destiny, 2006, p. 122.
20. Ibid., pp. 124, 125.
21. Dr. Don Colbert, pp. 77-79.
22. Ibid., pp. 82,83; also article by Dr. David Stewart, The Truth about non-nutritive Sweeteners, The Very Essence Blog, Sept 25, 06, http://aromatherapy4u.wordpress.com/2006/09/25/the-truth-about-non-nutritive-sweeteners/ (accessed Apr. 18/12)
23. George Malkmus, Hallelujah Diet, pp. 127,128.
24. George Malkmus, Why Christians Get Sick, p 43.
25. Dr. Paul Connett, "50 Reasons to Oppose Fluoridation", 2000/04/11, pp. 2,3. http://www.fluoridealert.org/50-reasons.htm
26. Christopher Bryson, "Fluoride Deception", 2006 & You-tube by same name, uploaded June 29,06; also Jan. 8/11 article, "Did the Father of Propaganda Convince America that Fluoride is safe?" georgewashington2.blogspot.com/2011/01/did-father-of-modern-propagandasell.html; also You-tube: Propaganda's Founding Father Edward Bernays Exposed, Derrin McBreen, Apr. 1/12.
27. Steve Nugent, How to Survive on a Toxic Planet, the Alethia Corp., 2006, pp. 49-55.
28. http://www.meatlessmonday.com/the-secret-cost-of-cheap-food/
29. Forks over Knives, US documentary, 2011 & T. Colin Campbell, The China Study, Benballa Books, 2006.
30. Forks over Knives & Dr. Caldwell B. Esselstyn, Jr., Prevent & Reverse Heart Disease, Penguin Group, 2007.
31. Dr. Wm. Davis, Wheat Belly, Rodale Books, 2011, intro. p. x
32. Ibid., pp. 8, 9; also Dr. Davis interview Macleans Magazine article,"The Evils of Wheat", Sept. 20/11, http://www2.macleans. ca/2011/09/20/on-the-evils-of-wheat-why-it-is-so-addictive-and-

how-shunning-it-will-make-you-skinny/;also Google Denise Minger who sees the China Study as incomplete, not taking into account the wheat factor.

[33.] Dr. Davis, Wheat Belly, pp. 44 – 51.

[34.] Ibid., pp. 63 - 65.

[35.] "orthorexia nervosa", Psychology suite 101, http://suite101.com/article/health-food-obsessions-a25402

[36.] George Malkmus, Why Christians Get Sick, p. 53.

[37.] CNN   http://edition.cnn.com/SPECIALS/road-to-rio/secret-life-drinking-water/index.html?hpt=hp_bn7

Chapter 14

Filling the Nutritional Gap

"Most people do not consume an optimal amount of all vitamins by diet alone...it appears prudent for all adults to take vitamin supplements."
Journal of American Medical Association 2002

"It is virtually impossible to get the optimal amount of antioxidants from food alone." Dr. Lester Packer, The Antioxidant Miracle

"When it comes to obtaining the micronutrients your body needs, your best possible source is food, especially fruits and vegetables. But circumstances may prevent you from eating optimally every day. The main reason I take nutritional supplements is for insurance against gaps in my diet. I take supplements faithfully and encourage my patients to do so as well." Andrew Weil M.D.

*I*n a perfect world, we would be able to get all of our nutritional needs met by the food we eat. We no longer live in a perfect world. Our food is calorie packed and nutritionally challenged. So, if it is extremely difficult to get what our bodies need every day from our modern diet (even if we are avoiding the harmful stuff and eating more fresh fruit and vegetables), **should I be taking nutritional supplements to make up the difference?**

The answer is a resounding yes, but with qualifications (which I'll talk about in a minute).

Taking nutritional supplements is no longer a luxury in the 21st century with nutritional levels much lower in our so-called healthy foods than they use to be (thanks to depleted soils, new crop breeding practices, genetic modification, and green harvesting). As well, toxins in our environment are substantially greater than they have ever been.

Here are just a couple of examples of nutritional loss:

The RDA amount of Vitamin A that a woman needs daily could be acquired from eating two peaches in 1951. Today, however, you would have to eat about fifty-three peaches to get the same amount of vitamin A. And today it would take sixty-five cups of spinach to equal the amount of iron in one cup in 1951.[1]

If you consider yourself to be healthy, or at least feel healthy now (though none of us can know exactly what is going on inside of us short of having an autopsy), why not do everything you can to maintain that level of health? Too much is at stake. Health is a necessity - something you cannot afford to be without. Complacency that leads to inaction can lead to premature aging and your early demise. With the depletion of nutrition in our modern diet, one of the smartest things you can do to support your body's ongoing ability to maintain health as well as heal it self is to use "edible health insurance" in the form of nutritional supplements. I consider them a part of one's monthly grocery budget. Yes, we must not overlook other important factors like adequate exercise, rest, cleansing of toxins, healthy relationships, laughter and so on. But filling the nutritional gap with supplements proactively and preventatively, I believe, is crucial in the day in which we now live.

I urge you to go against the flow of the crowd, which holds to the shortsighted and narrow approach of merely focusing on finding a nutritional supplement that will address a particular symptom (the sickness paradigm). But rather we must look at the big picture of what our bodies need daily in our pursuit of optimal health. Remember good ole Ben Franklin's proverb: "An ounce of prevention is worth a pound of cure"!

When we have healthy cells, we have healthy tissues. When we have healthy tissues, we have healthy organs. When we have healthy organs, we have healthy systems and inevitably healthy bodies. It would be the better part of wisdom to ask this critical question:

What categories of daily nutrition are vital (not merely beneficial) for the cells in my body in order to gain and maintain optimal health?

Scientific research points to the reality that our bodies regularly need the following micro nutritional components for healthy cellular structure and function:

- **Food based vitamins and minerals** (to nourish cells)
- **Food based antioxidants** (to protect cells in our fight against free radicals)
- **Phytosterols** (for support of our endocrine system and to regulate cells)
- **Omega 3 fatty acids** (supports brain & heart health)
- **Glyconutrients** (for cell to cell communication and immune system modulation)

We will, in turn, discuss these foundational and vital nutritional categories.

1. Vitamins and Minerals

Today, nutritional supplements have become big business. Many pharmaceutical companies have jumped on the bandwagon and along with thousands of nutrition companies are producing countless supplements that crowd the shelves of our stores and leave the average consumer overwhelmed and confused as to what is best for them.

Roughly one hundred and fifty million Americans take some form of vitamin and mineral supplement and Americans are spending billions every year on supplements for their health and wellness and yet, strangely enough, the rates of many forms of chronic diseases have not improved but rather have massively increased. Supplement shopping and consumption therefore should never be mere guesswork but well researched and thought through.

We must realize that not all supplements are created equal.

Real Food Supplements Versus Chemical (Synthetic) Supplements

Whole foods are known to be much better for you than refined foods. I don't think there is much of an argument there. Most folks would agree that brown rice is better for you than white rice. Why should it be any different for a vitamin supplement?

It's a bit odd that most naturopathic doctors or nutritionists, who would give people lengthy and detailed educational talks on the value of whole foods versus refined foods that have been stripped of their natural nutrition and fiber then proceed to advise someone to purchase plenty of isolated and refined chemical vitamins to take.[2]

The vast majority (ninety-five percent) of vitamin and mineral supplements on the market today are isolated and synthetic products, first generation technology. They are inexpensive to make in the laboratory and in theory they chemically constitute what the bottle says (this vitamin or that mineral) and are able to be standardized. They may also say on the label that it is all natural but that can be very misleading because synthetic vitamins come from natural petroleum or coal tar and minerals mostly come from natural rocks, often limestone. Check out a recent You-tube video, Industry FoodBusters, which addresses this very issue both in our supplements and many foods.

But recent studies are showing that there is very limited utilization of these products (often less than ten percent) because the body is looking for and only recognizes real food (which include the necessary cofactors, enzymes and phytochemicals that accompany the vitamins and minerals found in a food matrix).

With synthetic supplements we are in fact producing "expensive urine", money down the drain. Don't believe me? Ask someone at the local sewage plant about the "tablet" bricks in the fecal material that are undigested vitamins. In the sewer system in Tacoma,

Washington, more than two hundred and fifty thousand pounds of undigested vitamin and mineral pills are filtered out every six weeks, some with the brand name still readable! And in Salt Lake City, over one hundred and fifty gallons of vitamin and mineral pills show up in their filters every month.[3]

The body can only absorb about four percent of a calcium carbonate supplement and six percent if it is a calcium citrate supplement (treated with citric acid).[4] If the mineral supplement is chelated, it can trick the body into absorbing and utilizing a little more of the ground up rocks. But our bodies were designed by God to benefit from real whole foods, not petroleum and rocks. Three rules we must keep in mind: rule # 1: plants eat dirt, rule # 2: people and animals don't eat dirt, and rule # 3: animals and people eat plants. It was God's design all along that plants should eat minerals from rocks and man should eat plants. Violating these basic rules and bypassing this perfect design is proving to have its shortcomings.

Synthetic Supplements Can Cause More Harm Than Good

Recent studies are now coming out showing not only quite limited bioavailability of synthetic and ground up rock supplements but that there can even be harmful effects over time and even premature death.

A 1994 study that appeared in "The New England Journal of Medicine" gave 29,000 smokers synthetic beta-carotene and synthetic vitamin E. The study aimed to evaluate the cancer-protective properties of these vitamins. After ten years of taking the synthetic beta-carotene, participants had an eighteen percent higher rate of lung cancer and more heart attacks than the group of participants given the placebo. And those taking synthetic vitamin E had more strokes than participants given the placebo. The study also showed that participants who regularly ate fruits and vegetables containing these nutrients had greater protection against cancer, stroke and heart disease than participants who did not regularly consume food sources of these vitamins.[5]

In November 1995, The New England Journal of Medicine published a study in which 22,748 pregnant women were given synthetic vitamin A. Researchers had to cancel the study only four years into it because of a 240 percent increase in birth defects in babies of women given 10,000 international units daily of synthetic vitamin A. They also discovered that the women taking 20,000 international units daily of synthetic vitamin A had a four 400 percent increase in birth defects in their babies. The study also concluded that eating plant sources of vitamin A does not cause these increased birth defect rates.[6]

Dr. Bjelakovic, of Copenhagen University Hospital, Denmark, and his colleagues did a study in which they did a meta-analysis on research published before October 2005. This study was published in 2007 in the Journal of the American Medical Association. Results of the study demonstrated that Vitamin A increased death risk by sixteen percent, beta carotene by seven percent, and Vitamin E by four percent. The results for Vitamin C were unclear but suggested it increased death risk by six percent with selenium showing it might reduce death risk by ten percent. The overall conclusion of vitamin C and selenium was that they needed further study. It must be pointed out however, that all supplements used were synthetic.[7]

A nineteen-year study ending in 2004 and conducted by researchers from the University of Minnesota shows similar concerns about synthetic supplements. The data analyzed was from an ongoing study with more than 38,000 women from Iowa who were approximately age sixty-two. They found that the women who took supplements had, on average, a 2.4 percent increased risk of dying, compared with women who did not take supplements. Supplements taken included multivitamins, vitamin B6, folic acid, iron, magnesium, zinc and copper. Iron particularly increased the risk of death while calcium actually lowered it. Again, it needs to be pointed out that we are talking about synthetic vitamins and ground up rock minerals, not food sourced supplements.[8]

If there is limited bioavailability and potential harm in taking synthetic vitamins and minerals, then why don't they make the supplements out of real food? It has been a real challenge for the wellness/nutrition industry to try to produce supplements from real food because of cost as well as the fact that minerals are only found in very small quantities in our vegetables. So they continue to manufacture this first generation synthetic supplement (since most of the general public is still in the dark on this matter). Second generation supplements include whole food extracts and single exotic fruit juices or "super juices". This is a step forward because, as whole food extracts, they are bioavailable to the human body but are not standardized nor have they adequate levels particularly of minerals. Some super juice companies claim their product is the silver bullet, meeting all of your nutritional needs. Don't buy into their hype. God didn't put all we need in simply one plant, no matter what the advertising tells you. The public needs to demand to see the science to back up such claims.

However, the good news is that third generation technology is now available that provides plant sourced and standardized vitamins, minerals, and phytonutrients. A laboratory out of New Jersey in the last decade has patented this new technology using the Indian Mustard plant, or Brassica juncea, which is a little-known member of the broccoli family. It's been nicknamed "nature's magnet" because it has a unique ability to absorb metals and minerals like a super vacuum cleaner.

This plant has been used by Russian scientists to de-contaminate the ground of harmful radioactive heavy metals from the Chernobyl nuclear reactor disaster of 1986 in the Ukraine.[9]

Someone has since had the revelation that this super hyper accumulating plant, which has been used to remove bad metals from the ground, should also be able to vacuum up needed healthy minerals for man's benefit.

Using state-of-the-art biotechnology, the Indian Mustard plants are being grown hydroponically, in water infused with the right ratio of nutrients. The plants absorb the minerals, storing it in their stalks and leaves ready for harvesting. Plants naturally convert minerals into phytominerals, a bioavailable form that the body can easily use. But this plant's ability to uptake minerals is many times higher than other vegetables like spinach and regular broccoli, thereby making it feasible to produce a plant based multi-mineral supplement. Utilizing other plants to provide the full spectrum of vitamins the body needs daily, we now have, for the first time, a real food multi-vitamin, mineral and phytonutrient supplement on the market that is a patented, scientifically validated and standardized technology. It is just that most people don't know it yet (including most naturopathic doctors) nor appreciate what this breakthrough represents.

An increasing number of synthetic vitamin and mineral supplements on the market today have been put into a fruit and vegetable powder base (second generation technology), giving the impression that the whole product is food based. Adding synthetics to a food base is mostly marketing and much less effective than supplement companies would like to admit. Don't be misled.

You may be fooled into buying it but your body can't be fooled into utilizing the synthetic and ground up rock components within it. I encourage you to read the ingredients on the label. The vitamins are synthetic if their names end with:

acetate, Hydrochloride, Mononitrate, Palmitate, Succinate. Additional specific vitamins may be listed as: Vit. C - ascorbic acid, beta carotene (if source not given), Vit. B 2 - riboflavin, niacin, Pantothenic acid -calcium D-pantothenate, Folic Acid - pteroylglutamic acid, Vit. D - calciferol, Vit. E - dl-alpha tocopherol, and Vit. K - menadione or phytonadione.

Regarding minerals, you can identify commonly used mineral salts or mineral/organic acid mixtures in a supplement by reading the ingredients on the label.

The rock mineral will have a name that usually ends in one of the following:

Ascorbate, Aspartate, Carbonate, Chloride, Citrate, Gluconate, Glycerophosphate, Hydroxyapatite, iodide, Lactate, Malate, Methionine, Disulfide, Orotate, Oxide, Dibasic phosphate, tribasic phosphate, Picolinate, Pyrophosphate, Silicon dioxide, Stearate or Sulfate.[10]

Two fun tests to determine synthetic vitamins from real food:

1. take eight ounces of warm water, add eight tablespoons of distilled white vinegar (simulate stomach acid) and drop your vitamin pill in the mix. How long does it take to dissolve? Does it even completely dissolve?

2. bake several vitamin brands in the oven. If they are synthetic they will ooze black tar stuff. If they are truly food based, they will brown like any food would. Below is a picture from Ron Roy with brand names left out. Used by permission.

95% of all Multi-Vitamins contain synthetics and are derived from petroleum or coal tar!

After baking for
10 min. @ 350°F

1 - one of the most recommended

2. Men's Formulae

3. Women's Formulae

4. A Prenatal Vitamin

5. Multi complex

6. Real Food V/M

7. Popular Child's chewable

8. Real Food child's bears

What does baked petroleum look like?

Again, I encourage you to check out the eye-opening You-tube video, Industry FoodBuster, which shows synthetic supplements being baked in the oven.

The problem of taking nutrients in isolation

Taking these isolated nutrients (ie. Vitamin A, C, D or E supplements on their own), especially at ultra high doses found in many formulas today, creates imbalances in the body and is more like taking a drug. Studies demonstrate that the body treats these isolated and synthetic nutrients like foreign substances. You see, nature does not produce any nutrient in an isolated form. Nutrients in foods are blended together and work in synergy. They are highly complex structures that combine an array of enzymes, coenzymes, antioxidants, phytochemicals, minerals, trace elements and many other unknown factors all working together synergistically, to empower this vitamin complex to do its job in your body.

Nutrients from within this complex cannot be isolated from the whole and then be expected to perform in the body the same as the whole complex is designed to do. Every nutrient needs other nutrients as synergistic partners or co-factors. No nutrient is an island unto itself. For example, a car is an amazingly complex machine that needs all its parts to function properly. You can't take off the wheels or pull out the engine and call those separate parts a car or expect them to function like a car. Vitamin E requires the mineral selenium to function correctly and selenium, magnesium, and zinc all need vitamin B 6 to perform their role correctly. They cannot do the job of the entire complex by themselves. They need their synergistic partners.

Although your typical synthetic multivitamin and mineral supplement on the health store shelves is not one nutrient in isolation, it would be comparable to going to a junk yard, finding all of the separate parts you would need to make up an entire vehicle, throwing them together in a heap (or in this case, capsule) and expecting that heap of car parts to drive like a car. Synergy means the whole is greater than the sum of its parts.[11]

It is not the amount of a nutrient you put in your mouth that is important but its form (food sourced vs. synthetic, complex vs. isolated) and bioavailability that counts.

2) Food based Antioxidants

Since 1930, over seventy-five thousand synthetic chemicals have been introduced into our global environment and only about seven percent have been tested for safety. No one on the planet is exempt from these chemical toxins. We are bombarded from every direction. They are in the air we breathe, the water we drink, the food we eat, and the homes and workplaces we live and work in. The reality is that we are all carrying toxins. Scientists have even found pesticides and industrial chemicals in polar bears at the North Pole and in the fatty tissues of penguins at the South Pole. Most toxins are fat-soluble so the more fat you have, the more toxins you are able to store.

On January 30, 2003, the Environmental Working Group (EWG) published the first study to analyze the amount of synthetic chemicals in the human body. They found an average of ninety-one different chemical agents in the people they tested and believe that number is on the rise.[12]

This toxic burden in our bodies creates various problems, including excessive free radicals that attack our cells. This free radical activity can also be described as oxidative stress. It is like rust developing on our cells. Free radicals attack and damage our cells speeding up the aging process and if unchecked, can cause cancers, heart disease, nervous system issues and a host of other illnesses. In fact, one antioxidant researcher, Dr. Bruce Ames, estimates that the average person today takes about ten thousand free radical hits to every cell of their bodies every day! Your first line of defense against free radical attacks is antioxidants.[13]

In today's toxic world, attempting to reach the RDA (required daily allowance) of antioxidants (or vitamins and minerals in general) from the food you eat is virtually impossible. And RDA is simply the minimum level of nutrition required to keep people from eventually becoming victims of nutritional deficiency diseases.[14]

But mega dosages of antioxidants are not the answer either. Synergy is the key to maximum protection.

A four-year study concluded in 2003 found that some proven individual antioxidants, taken in isolation and in large dosages had a neutralizing or even a pro-oxidative harmful effect in the body. Some of them are as bad as smoking cigarettes! Vitamin A, C, and E serve as antioxidants but Vitamin A and E are fat-soluble and therefore can be toxic and harmful at large dosage levels.[15]

The gold standard in the industry for accurately measuring the level of protection from free radicals in the body is called ORAC serum testing, which stands for oxygen radical absorption capacity. This blood test has demonstrated that the synergy of various antioxidants in the right ratio can provide an impressive level of protection against free radical damage in the body.

The researchers of this four-year study have developed an antioxidant supplement that can increase free radical protection in the blood by thirty-seven percent. That may not seem like much but when compared to only a thirteen percent increase in free radical protection by consuming an additional five servings of fresh fruit and vegetables daily that is almost a three hundred percent improvement.[16]

Please don't misunderstand me. I am not trying to discourage anyone from taking more servings of fresh fruit and vegetables but rather wanting to encourage you to take as many servings as practically possible then supplement with a synergistic blend of food based anti-oxidants to be assured of maximum protection from the extraordinary stressful days and toxic environment that we live in today.

3) Phytosterols or Phytohormones (plant hormones)

Phytohormones or phytosterols are another crucial nutrient category but very few people have heard of them let alone know much about them. Because modern western diets are typically very low in phytohormone nutrition, the average person is only consuming about two to four mg per day while the body needs at least thirty to fifty mg per day just to support and maintain endocrine system health. That is less than ten percent of what is needed.[17]

Recent studies suggest that phytosterols, of which beta-sitosterols, saponins, and phytoestrogens are perhaps the most important, may provide health benefits such as helping to protect against the development of some cancers (particularly breast and prostate), cardiovascular disease, osteoporosis, and premenopausal and menopausal symptoms. In terms of cardiovascular health, they appear to help lower blood cholesterol and triglyceride levels and raise HDL (good) cholesterol levels, reduce blood sugar, and decrease inflammation.[18]

Great sources for these nutrients include soy protein (non-GMO, non-genetically modified organisms), rice bran or nutritional supplements from Dioscorea Villosa, the Mexican wild yam root.

4) Omega 3 Essential Fatty Acids

Omega 3 essential fatty acids are also vital for those who seriously desire to achieve optimal health. They are called essential because the body is not able to manufacture them. They must come from our diet. We want to avoid harmful fatty acids such as: saturated and trans-fatty acids (hydrogenated margarine and shortening for example) but consume helpful fatty acids such as monounsaturated fats (olive, canola, peanut oils) and polyunsaturated fatty acids (omega 3 and 6). We get enough omega 6's (maybe even too much) in our diet but definitely not enough omega 3's.

A great source of Omega-3 fatty acids is cold-water fish. Scientists believe the most effective way to consume sufficient omega-3 is by directly obtaining DHA (docosahexaenoic acid) and EPA (eicosapentaenoic acid) from fish. DHA helps protect the brain and EPA protects the heart and decreases inflammation.[19]

Some people seek to get their omega 3s from eating flaxseed and other foods that provide ALA (alpha-linolenic acid) but the body must then convert the ALA into DHA and EPA and that conversion is energy taxing and inefficient for most. It is better to get Omega 3 directly from a fish source but because of heavy metals and toxins in our fish, it is recommended not to eat fish very often (limit of once or twice a week?). Taking an Omega-3 purified, fish-sourced supplement appears prudent. Though more expensive, choose a fish oil supplement that has gone through a molecular distillation process to pharmaceutical grade so you are not ingesting toxins and heavy metals such as PCBs, dioxins, mercury, and lead. If the product has been purified, they will brag about it on the label. Don't nickel and dime it. You get what you pay for.

5) Glyconutrients - the Sugar Code of Life

Paracelsus, the father of pharmacology is quoted as saying: "Everything man needs to sustain health can be found in nature. It is the job of science to find them".

Sounds a bit like Proverbs 25:2: "It is the glory of God to conceal a matter; to search out a matter is the glory of kings".

It is not very often that a scientific discovery of a new class of nutrients comes along. Dr. Allan C. Somersal claims that this discovery, called glyconutrients, represents a revolutionary breakthrough in nutrition, science and medicine that will have worldwide ramifications. A secret of nature has now been revealed that appears overwhelmingly simple, yet profound, providing a disruptive technology that will be a 21st century wellness solution.[20]

This paradigm shift, according to Dr. H. Reg McDaniel, is "critical to all cellular biochemistry and physiology for defense, repair, healing and homeostasis (balance) within and between cells".[21]

Being a Canadian, I can't help but want to call glyconutrients the Wayne Gretzky on the nutritional hockey team!

"Glyconutrients are so vitally important to your life that the only difference in human blood groups O, B, A and AB is the glyconutrient combination attached to each molecule. It is almost a certainty that your doctor doesn't know that."[22]

Human Blood Groups (or types) determined by sugars

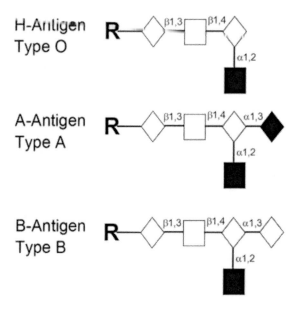

R represents the linkage to protein in the secreted forms, sphingolipid (ceramide) in the cell-surface bound form.

Carbohydrate or sugar chains:

open diamond = galactose, open square = N acetyl-glucosamine (GlcNAc), filled square = fucose, filled diamond = N acetyl-galactosamine (GalNAc)

(the linkage in the glycolipid form may include a glucose in a B1,3 or B1,4 to the initial galactose residue)[23]

In 1996, Dr. Robert Murray, microbiology professor emeritus of the University of Toronto, Canada, first published a chapter in Harper's Biochemistry medical textbook, which identified eight saccharides (glyconutrients) as instrumental in glycoproteins for cell-to-cell communication within the body. "Glyco" is the Greek word for sugar. No, we are not talking about the "white death" kind of sugar. These glyconutrients, which do not taste sweet, are special structural carbohydrates that support normal physiological structure and function. They provide the building blocks that enable the roughly sixty trillion cells in your body to communicate effectively.

Since the development of the electron microscope a few decades ago, scientists have been able to look closely at an individual cell. What they found were little hairs growing out from the cell surface. At first they didn't think these little hairs really had a function other than looking pretty like ornaments on a Christmas tree. But over time they realized that they actually function as "cell towers" (pardon the pun) for the cells to communicate with each other. On further investigation, they found that these towers were actually made of a protein molecule at the cell surface followed by a string of sugar molecules. These glycoproteins and glycolipids constitute the "sugar code" or "language of life".

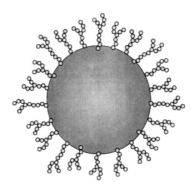

According to the Harper's textbook (as of its 1996 edition), there are over two hundred known saccharides in nature but only eight have been identified as essential for cellular communication and recognition. The eight known sugars necessary for healthy structured and functioning cells are:

- Fucose (not to be mistaken for fructose)
- Galactose
- Glucose
- Mannose
- N-acetylgalactosamine (GalNAc)
- N-acetylglucosamine (GlcNAc)

- N-acetylneuraminic acid (NeuAc)
- Xylose

In 1996 as well, Dr. Bill McAnally, a toxicologist from Dallas, Texas developed a plant-sourced supplement of this new class of nutrition that has come to be called glyconutrients. He, along with Dr. Reg McDaniel, former Director of Pathology & Laboratories and Director of Medical Education at Dallas-Fort Worth Medical Center, were presented with the "Discovery of the Year Award" by the American Naturopathic Medical Association.[24]

The 27th edition of Harper's Illustrated Biochemistry textbook of 2006 carefully states: "...there is evidence that the other sugars (other than glucose) may be beneficial in some circumstances when added to the diet. This has led to the development of glyconutrient supplements, containing either members of the sugars listed in Table 46-4 (excluding glucose) or precursors of them. The efficacy of such supplements is under study."[25]

It is fascinating to know that most if not all of these eight sugars are found in mother's breast milk. These sugars make up one third of the solids in mother's milk. And studies have shown the many health benefits (fewer allergies, higher cognitive function, overall health) of infants being breast-fed versus bottle-fed.[26]

Let me mention two of the eight sugars.

Many folks are somewhat aware of **glucosomine**. By itself, this sugar is known for its benefits for people with joint and cartilage issues of pain, stiffness, and inflammation. In a supplement, it is best to have this sugar in its pre-curser form, N-acetylglucosamine, so that it is not destroyed by stomach acids.

Possibly less known but one of the key sugars is **mannose**. The aloe vera plant has an abundance of this sugar. The Bible mentions the aloe plant at least five times. Alexander the Great went into his battles taking wagons full of the aloe plant to help heal wounded soldiers. We probably have all tried aloe products from the drug store for cuts or sunburn, with limited success, and yet if we have ever cut into an aloe plant and smeared the fresh gel onto our damaged skin, we would have seen impressive results. That is because the mannose sugar which gives it its healing properties, mostly dies within forty-eight hours after being exposed to oxygen. Dr. McAnally developed a patented procedure to stabilize and keep the mannose sugar "bioactive" for at least two years. Mannose, on its own, has been shown in laboratory studies to be an anti parasitic, antiviral, antibacterial and anti fungal. Collagen synthesis is stimulated by mannose, which is the reason why mannose has helped out so much with skin enhancement.

The discovery of these eight biological sugars began with Dr. McAnally being assigned to a research project working to find the healing ingredient within the aloe plant in the 1980s. He expected it to be a protein molecule but to his surprise found it was a sugar molecule, mannose. After stabilizing the gel to keep it bioactive, he and Dr. McDaniel did immune system related pilot studies with this stabilized aloe juice (not to be confused with the cheaper unstabilized aloe juices on the shelves) with astonishing health benefits. By 1996 the mystery was unraveled of not just one but at least eight biological sugars that are required for proper structure and function within the body. They and their associates then scoured the earth and found various plants and tree gums that had high concentrations of these sugars which resulted in a safe, standardized and patented technology being made available to the public.[27]

Science has shown that as cells roll over each other they actually read the brail of these sugars to communicate. For instance, the immune cell (such as B cell scouts) would read the sugars of a cell to determine if that cell belongs in the body or whether it is a foreign invader. If it were a foreign invader (bacteria, virus, fungus, or cancer cell) then a message would be sent for the T cells to come kill and destroy that cell. If it turns out to be a good cell that belongs, it would be asked if it needed any nutrients.

It was discovered, however, that if any of these sugars were missing on the glycoproteins (or glycolipids, which are fat molecules attached to a sugar structure), then a miscommunication would inevitably take place. It is similar to a far distant friend or relative giving you their long distance telephone number or email address and you get one number or letter incorrect. No matter how close to being correct you are, your call or email is not going to reach them.

So if any of these sugars are missing, the immune system cell will potentially make a misdiagnosis or miscommunication about a cell basically in one of two possible ways. If it thinks a cell is one of the good guys when in fact it is a bad guy (a foreign invader or cancer cell), it will not destroy it and, over time, infection or "dis-ease" can develop in the body. Or if in reality it is a good guy cell, but the immune system cell misdiagnosed it as a bad guy and has it attacked and destroyed, you may have the development of what we call an "auto-immune" disease, which is the immune system in overdrive and attacking good cells that belong to you. Where in the body this is happening will determine what autoimmune disease it will be classified as.[28]

Two important questions must be addressed.

Do we get adequate amounts of these eight sugars in our modern western diet?

Previous generations probably did but in recent decades there has been a serious and sobering decline in all categories of nutrition in our food chain, including six of the eight vital sugars (we get adequate amounts of glucose and possibly galactose).

And does the body make these eight sugars by converting our glucose sugar?

The liver can actually do a conversion process to produce all eight sugars, however the liver, which is an amazing multi-task organ, was never intended to do the large number of enzymatic steps involved in the conversion process on a regular basis, but rather as an emergency mechanism.[29]

I liken it to your starter under the hood of your car. Its function is to start your engine and then the starter's job is done and it rests. It would burn out if it were running all the time. This conversion process done by the liver is very energy consuming and complicated and for various reasons (a sickness/disease, aging, toxins, stress and a host of other factors) it can break down and become less efficient, leaving the cells not fully "glycosolated" or "sugar coated".

The significance of this discovery of a new class of nutrients

Some scientists are claiming this could prove to be the most important health discovery of the last fifty years or more because it is foundational to all other nutritional requirements of the cells of the human body. If the various nutritional categories could be likened to software programs, glyconutrients would actually be the operating system of the computer.

Dr. John Rollins, former award-winning U.S. Trademark and Patent Office official for twenty-three years and who reviewed thousands of products in his career, calls glyconutrients one of the most important healthcare discoveries of the 21st century and a disruptive technology that brings hope to healthcare.[30]

Since 1996 a plethora of research and clinical studies have been done and continue to be done to increase our understanding. Recent independent clinical studies have shown impressive improvements to the digestive system, cognitive function, immune system, and even evidence of stimulating the growth of adult stem cells in bone marrow to enable the body the potential of healing and regeneration.[31]

The pharmaceutical, medical, and educational communities have even developed a new branch of scientific research called the field of "glycobiology". They are spending millions of dollars in research seeking to create these eight essential sugars synthetically in hopes of then patenting them and introducing them into medications to make them more powerful and effective.

Dr. Gerald Hart, biochemist of John Hopkins University on October 23, 2002, claimed, "This is going to be the future,,,We won't understand immunology, neurology, developmental biology or disease until we get a handle on glycobiology."

MIT's Technology Review magazine in their February 2003 issue claimed that glycobiology/glycomics, the study and application of these vital sugars, to be one of ten emerging technologies that will change the world.[32]

The great news however, is that the world does not have to wait for the field of glycobiology to develop synthetic sugars. These sugars are available now in a non-toxic plant based, standardized and patented nutritional supplement. They have been shown to bring benefit to the body and as of this writing there are no known contraindications with medications a person may be on. And we have heard of testimonies from people whose doctor eventually reduced their drug dosage and in some cases, took them off completely.

Dr. Glen Hyland, an oncologist, did a pilot study with cancer patients undergoing chemo and radiation treatments. They were given plant based antioxidants and glyconutrients and saw very encouraging results. Not only was the nutrition not harmful in conjunction with the conventional treatment, but also the chemo and radiation was more effective against tumour cells. They also found that normal cells were provided a measure of protection from treatment damage and adverse side effects of hair loss, nausea, vomiting and immune system devastation were minimized.[33]

It must be made clear, however, that glyconutrients or any other nutritional technology do not cure, heal or mitigate disease. Rather they are nutritional tools to support the body's own physiology, that of structure and function.

I am aware of a concerted effort in recent years to discredit the plant based nutritional side of this discovery. One could say it appears like the pharmaceutical industry wants to protect their research costs and future profits in the field of glycobiology. It would seem as though they do not want this nutritional disruptive technology to reach a tipping point, even though it has great promise to bring unmeasured health benefits to the world. As well, it has the potential of complementing the conventional medical approach and contributing to a solution for the financial crisis of the existing health care systems of the world.

One of the main arguments that some have used in their attempt to discredit this patented discovery is to say that the body is not capable of assimilating the sugars into the cells of the body so it ends up being expensive fiber that may give you nothing but gas, suggesting that the public gets exploited, again.

I am encouraged to see, however, that in just the last few years hard scientific data from laboratory and clinical studies has proven that indeed these plant based glyconutrients do get absorbed through the good bacteria in the gut and uploaded into the bloodstream and assembled into the glycoforms on the cell surface. These scientific findings have now been presented at recognized glycobiology conferences and published in scientific peer-reviewed journals.[34]

Dr. Ben Carson, one of America's top ten medical doctors, according to CNN, and world famous for his successful surgeries of separating Siamese twins, is a strong proponent of this glyco-nutritional technology and calls for a move towards "integrative medicine," using the best of the medical community with the scientifically validated and regulated nutritional technologies coming forth from the wellness industry.[35]

Aside from the five foundational nutritional categories mentioned above that are vital for our health, let me mention just a few other nutritional components that I believe can be of benefit.

Taking a probiotic supplement is a smart thing to do. With stress, toxins, aging, drugs (especially antibiotics), our probiotics or good bacteria in the gut get depleted. The good flora or bacteria is critical for nutrient uptake into the body from our food and supplements.

Super green foods such as chlorella can nourish, detoxify, and energize the body.

Regarding the electro magnetic pollution we are all hit with everyday in our high tech communications world, you may want to research for possible shield protection.

Essential oils are natural aromatic compounds extracted from seeds, bark, stems, roots, flowers, and other parts of plants. They can be powerfully fragrant to people, bringing rest and relaxation to the brain, emotions and body. Essential oils have been used throughout history in many cultures for their medicinal and therapeutic benefits. The Egyptians were some of the first people to use aromatic essential oils in medical practice, beauty treatment and food preparation. Frankincense, sandalwood, cinnamon and myrrh were viewed as valuable cargo along caravan trade routes. The Greeks got the idea from the Egyptians, using essential oils in their practices of therapeutic massage and aromatherapy. The Romans also used aromatic essential oils to promote health and personal hygiene.

A fairly recent technology on the market is called silver sol. This mid 1990s technology is not to be confused with colloidal silver, which has been used for over a hundred years. Producers of silver sol claim it to be a safer, more effective, and advanced technology particularly in our fight against infection and pathogens in the body, including malaria.

As we seek to prepare for the challenges of the last days, I strongly encourage you to get fit and aim for optimal health by making substantial, if not radical changes to your lifestyle. Build a good habit of:

- Getting physical activity (don't just sit around staring like zombies at the boob tube and computer, get out doors, hike, have fun, play and laugh lots with friends),
- Cutting junk food from your diet,
- Eating more fresh fruit and vegetables,
- Recognizing that we still need to fill the gap with nutritional supplementation, not with cheap synthetic and potentially dangerous stuff, but food or plant based, standardized, and scientifically validated nutritional technologies that are now available in the wellness industry.

We are under siege. The thief comes to steal, kill and destroy and he is doing a thorough job on many fronts - relationships, finances, and our spiritual, emotional and physical health. Because it is so gradual and subtle, it is easy to be naive and complacent about this. But we are at war and it really is a matter of life and death. It behooves us to step up and take a more active and responsible role for our own health and be looking at things preventatively, not just when our body begins to break down (although that is human nature to do so). We want to be pro-active not reactive. In the long run, it is wiser, involves less misery, and is actually less expensive. Let's not play Russian roulette with our health then expect the person in the white coat or God to always fix us after the fact, due to our negligence and self-destructive behaviour.

Good health is not the result of just one single action. It is the result of doing your homework, thinking comprehensively, making a series of right decisions and a commitment to action on a daily basis for the long haul. It is the power of "the slight edge" over time.

We can no longer afford to live with the assumption that government agencies and corporations will hold our hand and take care of us. We must wake up and realize that in the 21st century we live on a very toxic planet and consume food that has been seriously compromised nutritionally thanks to man's greed and lack of foresight. We reap what we sow.

By God's grace we need to have the courage to go against the crowd and take responsibility for our own health. Even if it means we have to put up with bullying tactics of being labeled with an eating disorder called orthorexia nervosa!

We want to not only live long lives, but also have optimal health and vitality along the way. One of my personal goals now is "to live healthy enough and long enough to fulfill my God-given destiny". I consider it part of my ministry to help others do the same.

As I am writing this chapter today, (October 6, 2011), in Malawi, Africa, I'm saddened to read the headlines on the internet that Steve Jobs, the U.S. computer engineer, genius and co-founder and former CEO of Apple, died yesterday of cancer at the young age of fifty-six. We all wish he had lived longer. In honour of this "out of the box" creative thinker and innovator, let me end this chapter by echoing a quote of his that certainly applies to him and maybe someday it will be said of us:

"Here's to the crazy ones, the misfits, the rebels, the troublemakers, the round pegs in the square holes...The ones who see things differently - they're not fond of rules. You can quote them, disagree with them, glorify or vilify them, but the only thing you can't do is ignore them because they change things...They push the human race forward and while some may see them as the crazy ones, we see genius, because the ones who are crazy enough to think that they can change the world, are the ones who do."[36]
(Steve Jobs 1955-2011)

Recommended Resources:

Books:
How to Survive on a Toxic Planet, Steve Nugent, 2nd edition, Alethia Corp., 2006
(Nugent is past President of the American Naturopathic Medical Association and author of "Nugent's Physicians Desk Reference for Applied Clinical Nutrition")
The Seven Pillars of Health, Dr. Don Colbert, Siloam, a Strang Co., Florida, 2007

What You Don't Know May Be Killing You! Dr. Don Colbert, Siloam, 2004
The Maker's Diet, Jordan S. Rubin, Siloam, 2004
The Hallelujah Diet, George Malkmus, Destiny Image, 2006

You-tube clips:

Industry FoodBusters, http://www.youtube.com/watch?v=PkEPshJ UBD0&feature=plcp (uploaded Aug. 31/2012) highly recommend this video that exposes the synthetic junk (fortified vitamins & minerals) put in many of our foods, baby foods & supplements
Sweet Language of Life, produced by Willen Wellness Center and Synapse Productions, 2005, DVD copies can be ordered on: www. glycotools.com

Notes:

[1.] Jeffery Christian "Charts: Nutrients Changes in Vegetables and Fruits, 1951 to 1999" July 5, 2002. CTV.ca
[2.] Dr. Daniel H. Chong, ND., article, "Real or Synthetic: The Truth Behind Whole-Food Supplements" posted by Dr. Mercola Jan. 19/05, http://articles.mercola.com/sites/articles/archive/2005/01/19/whole-food-supplements.aspx p. 1.
[3.] "Natural vs. Synthetic Supplements", http://www.priestman-wellness.com/wellness_supplements.html (accessed March 13/12) quoting a 1998 article in Chiropractic Economics
[4.] Dr. Steve Nugent, (former Pres. American Naturalpathic Medical Association) nutrition training lecture, Cambridge, ON Can., Dec. 1/07.
[5.] Jessica Jacobs, Studies on Synthetic Vitamins Versus Natural Vitamins, Livestrong.com Sept. 4/11, The Limitless Potential of You, http://www.livestrong.com/article/535137-studies-on-synthetic-vitamins-versus-natural-vitamins,
References: Schachter Center for Complementary Medicine: The Vitamin E-Beta Carotene Cancer Study in Finland; Michael B. Schachter, M.D.; 1996

The New England Journal of Medicine: Teratogenicity of High Vitamin A Intake; Kenneth J. Rothman & et al; Nov/95.

6. Ibid

7. Medical News Today, Feb. 28/07, "Some Vitamin Supplements increase Death Risk Say Researchers", study in JAMA 2007;297:842-857. Vol. 297 No. 8, Feb. 28/07 http://www.medicalnewstoday.com/articles/64100.php

8. Joseph Brownstein, "Some common vitamin supplements could increase death risk, study finds", Vitals on msnbc.com, Oct. 10/11, MyHealthNewsDaily, http://vitals.msnbc.msn.com/_news/2011/10/10/8256866-some-common-vitamin-supplements-could-increase-death-risk-study-finds

9. http://www.mhhe.com/biosci/pae/botany/botany_map/articles/article_10.html (accessed Apr. 3/12).

10. Proevity Continuing Education Group, pamphlet on "How to Evaluate Vitamin and Mineral Products: What Healthcare Professionals Want to Know", 2009, p. 14.

11. Dr. Daniel H. Chong, p. 2.

12. Dr. Steve Nugent, How to Survive on a Toxic Planet, Alethia Corp., 2006, pp. 17-19.

13. Ibid., pp. 103, 116.

14. Ibid., pp. 108, 109.

15. Ibid., p. 113.

16. Ibid., pp. 122, 123.

17. Thomas H. Gardiner, Eileen Vennum, Shayne McAnalley, Bill H. McAnalley, Choices: Choosing the Right Dietary Supplements for Optimal Health, Talking Stick Pub., 2004, p. 54.

18. Ibid., pp. 55, 59.

19. Dr. Don Colbert, The Seven Pillars of Health, Siloam, a Strang Co., 2007, pp. 97, 98.

20. Dr. Allan C. Somersall, editor, The Healing Power of 8 Sugars, The Natural Wellness Group, LLC, Mississauga, Canada, 2005, intro. pp. viii, x, xi.

21. Dr. H. Reg McDaniel, Forward to the book "The Healing Power of 8 Sugars, p. ii.

22. Dr. Steve Nugent, How to Survive on a Toxic Planet, p. 79.

[23.] chart of Blood types A,O,B, that shows sugar chains, "Clinical Significances of Glycoproteins", http://themedicalbiochemistrypage.org/glycoproteins.php, further info & chart at "Blood Type" Wikipedia, http://en.wikipedia.org/wiki/Blood_type

[24.] Dr. George V. Dubouch, Chapter 1: "The Discovery of Glyconutrients", The Healing Power of 8 Sugars, p. 7.

[25.] Dr. Robert Murray, one of editors, Harper's Illustrated Biochemistry, 27th ed., McGraw-Hill, 2006, Ch. 46, pp. 523-552.

[26.] Dr. Vicky Arcadi, Ch. "Glyconutrients for Babies and Children", in The Healing Power of 8 Sugars, 2005, pp. 85, 87; also Dr. Rita Elkins, Miracle Sugars, Woodland Pub., 2003, p. 10.

[27.] Dr. George V. Dubouch, The Healing Power of 8 Sugars, Ch. 1., pp. 5 - 9.

[28.] Dr. Steve Nugent, How to Survive on a Toxic Planet, p. 88.

[29.] Dr. George V. Dubouch, Ch. 1: The Discovery of Glyconutrients, The Healing Power of 8 Sugars, p. 13; also: DVD "Sweet Language of Life", produced by Willen Wellness Center & Synapse Prod., 2005, copies: www.glycotools.com ; You-tube.

[30.] Dr. John Rollins, interview, The Atlantic Voice, Aug. 27/04.

[31.] Dr. Gary Anderson, Ch.19: "Clinical Trials, Stems Cells & the Future of Glyconutrients", The Healing Power of 8 Sugars, pp. 257-263.

[32.] Dr. George V. Dubouch, Ch. 1, p. 11.

[33.] Dr. Steve Nugent, p. 93.

[34.] 9th Annual Jenner Glycobiology & Medicine Symposium, Brussels, Belgium, Sept. 13-15/09; by Royal Society of Medicine (U.K.) in assoc. with Rega Institute for Medical Research, Catholic Univ. of Leuven, Belgium.

[35.] Interview with Dr. Ben Carson on Integrative Health, You-tube, May 18/11.

[36.] Steve Job's quote, http://www.quotationspage.com/quote/38357.html (accessed Oct. 6/11).

Chapter 15

More Economic Trouble Ahead

"Confront the most brutal facts of your current reality, while, at
the same time, retain faith that you will prevail in the
end, regardless of the difficulties."
(Admiral Stockdale, in the book, Good To Great, by Jim Collins)

*T*he U.S. Federal Reserve announced in June of 2012 that the
recession of 2008 and 2009 wiped out nearly twenty years
of Americans' wealth. The median net worth of families plunged
thirty-nine percent in just three years, with the middle class bearing
the brunt of it. "Home ownership, once heralded as a pathway to
wealth, became an albatross."[1]

Even though the pain has run deep, many have given a big sigh
of relief that we narrowly missed taking a fatal bullet in terms of a
total economic meltdown. Thanks to all the global emergency bailouts and manipulations, we have supposedly seen a recovery, albeit
slow and modest. But putting bandaids on a terminal disease is like
trying to hide a herd of elephants under your living room carpet.
It's just a matter of time. 2008 may well have been a practice run, a
warning shot across the bow, compared to what is coming over the
next few years.

The coming trouble may very well be deeper and more painful
the more politicians and the financial elite seek to keep the world
economy on life support to delay the inevitable. And seeking to bail

out the banks by using more taxpayer's money only further strips the middle class of any remaining wealth.

In spite of all the attempts to trick the masses by putting a positive spin on things, we are seeing the Greek sovereign debt and political crisis intensify and the rest of the PIIGS nations (Portugal, Ireland, Italy, Greece and Spain) even more precarious. The world economy is intimately tied in with this European financial crisis. If a little economy like Greece can give the global financial system the jitters, how much more will Italy and Spain, much larger economies, unravel things in the coming months and years?

And aside from debt crises the world over (U.S. government debt is roughly sixteen trillion dollars, increasing by almost four billion a day), we are now beginning to see a global economic slow down (including the BRIC nations of Brazil, Russia, India and China) and words like recession and depression being nervously whispered about once again. The artificial resuscitation and financial steroids used are wearing off and we will soon be forced to face brute reality.

We need not follow the crowd and be "sideswiped" again. We need to get our heads out of the sand, face the signs that indicate a massive economic storm is brewing and prepare accordingly with God's help and wisdom. Let's look at some of the signs:

1. Scriptures That Indicate Coming Economic Trouble
(as a consequence of our foolish actions)

Romans 12:2: "Do not be conformed any longer to the pattern of this world (don't follow the crowd) but be transformed by the renewing of your mind".

Galatians 6:7 "Do not be deceived: God cannot be mocked. A man reaps what he sows. The one who sows to please his sinful nature, from that nature will reap destruction..." (eg. greed, recklessness and lack of meekness and self control in finances and economy, that is, living beyond your means).

Proverbs 22:7 "the borrower is slave to the lender".

Proverbs 22:3 "A prudent man sees danger and takes refuge, but the simple keep going and suffer for it".

Collectively we have not demonstrated being like the "men of Issachar, who understood the times and knew what to do". (1 Chronicles 12:32) Rather, we have been like the simpleton, the mocker, the foolish who did not listen to Wisdom shouting in the streets as recorded in Proverbs 1:20-33. The result would be catastrophe and disaster:

"Wisdom calls aloud in the street...How long will you simple ones love your simple ways? How long will mockers delight in mockery and fools hate knowledge? If you had responded to my rebuke, I would have poured out my heart to you and made my thoughts known to you. But since you rejected me when I called and no one gave heed when I stretched out my hand...I in turn will laugh at your disaster; I will mock when calamity overtakes you...like a storm, when disaster sweeps over you like a whirlwind, when distress and troubles overwhelm you...they will eat the fruit of their ways and be filled with the fruit of their schemes. For the waywardness of the simple will kill them, and the complacency of fools will destroy them; but whoever listens to me will live in safety and be at ease, without fear of harm."

An insightful Christian author and teacher in the body of Christ (and mentor and friend), Craig Hill, had a profound biblical teaching on the Jubilee cycle on his website: www.familyfoundations.com. This two part video teaching is called "Jubilee Cycle, are you prepared?" (Unfortunately, as of 2012 I do not see it posted any longer but I would recommend his new book, Five Wealth Secrets that 96% of Us Don't Know, which covers and elaborates on some of it.) I am indebted to Craig for much of what I am going to share on this subject of Jubilee.

In Leviticus 25:8-17, we see that the year of Jubilee is God's way of purging excess debt. Israel was commanded by Yahweh to practice this purge of national debt every fifty years. We have no such debt purge mechanism in our society.

In a Jubilee year, all debt is cancelled/forgiven, slaves are set free and all property goes back to the original owner. This sounds very upbeat and exciting until we look at the contemporary terms to describe this process: bankruptcy, repossession and foreclosure! With no pre-set Jubilees in place every fifty years, we may inevitably experience an unplanned Jubilee cycle, which today is called a "depression". Though it appears we can delay it for a time, it will inevitably come. We have not experienced a depression in our lifetime. We have only heard about the "Great Depression" of the 1930s.

Craig Hill points out that whether it is a planned or unplanned Jubilee, every purge involves a transfer of wealth. Proverbs 13:22b declares: "But the wealth of the wicked is stored up for the righteous". But before we get too excited about this verse, we need to ask ourselves: "Who are the financially wicked and who are the financially righteous, according to Scriptural definitions?"

Psalm 37:21 states: "The wicked borrows and does not repay; but the righteous shows mercy and gives". So, here it appears that the wealth of the one who borrows and does not repay is stored up for the one who shows mercy and gives.

The New Testament declares that, "Blessed are the meek for they shall inherit the earth." (Mt. 5:5) Meekness is not weakness, but rather "power under control". If someone has margins in their life, that is, a spare amount held back for contingencies, they are considered meek.

Most people live beyond their means, including many Christians (violating Rom. 12:2 command to not be conformed to the patterns of this world system). Statistics indicate that many in the West run on close to 140 percent of what they earn/have. Debt results from a person using more than 100 percent of their power or resources. Meekness is foreign to our culture and to many Christians and yet Jesus invites those who are weary and burdened down to take up His yoke and learn of Him, for He is meek and humble of heart (Mt. 11:28-30). A meek person gives generously, saves and invests then spends what is left. A person in debt, with a poverty mindset, usually spends first then gives, saves and invests what's left (which isn't usually very much if anything).

According to Robert Kiyosaki (and quoted in Craig Hill's book), if one hundred people were given $10,000 each, about 80 percent of the people would only be good at subtraction - spending all of it, about 16 percent would be good at addition, earning a little perhaps in a bank account, and about 4 percent would practice meekness by living within their means and using their resources for multiplication. The 4 percent would value knowledge and wisdom over wealth, power and position. They don't buy into the myth that real estate only goes up and economies only expand so they anticipate and prepare for cycles in the economy.[2]

Craig Hill also compares the last Jubilee cycle of the 1930s Great Depression with today's jubilee cycle. The 1929 stock market crash saw the Dow fall 49 percent from its high in a couple of months. The 2008 cycle had the Dow drop 47 percent in a few months. After rallying 52 percent from its low, the Dow then lost a total of 86 percent over the next two years in the early 1930s. We have seen a strong rally (though with some jittery ups and downs) in the stock market since late 2009 (thanks to all the artificial stimulations and manipulations of governments and Wall St. bankers) but we anticipate a serious drop again in the near future. If we were to repeat a total drop in the Dow of 86 percent as in the last Jubilee cycle that would take the Dow to under 2000.

Craig Hill believes, and I agree with him, that we are in the beginning stages of a serious Jubilee cycle, a depression, with huge amounts of wealth presently being transferred. In a depression, "cash is king" while debt enslaves.

The financially righteous and meek or the financially wicked and enslaved - which camp are you in?

If the latter, I urge you to repent, that is, change your mind and behaviour and seek the Lord for a game plan to get out of debt as promptly as possible. For some, that may include, among other drastic action, a "plastictomy", cutting up your plastic credit cards! Time is ticking and it may be that by the time this book is published and in your hands we could be seeing the financial and economic systems unraveling, if not collapsing all around us.

My wife, Pam, and I have been helped tremendously by Dave Ramsey's financial teachings. Our oldest son, Jonathan, gave us a gift of one of Ramsey's very practical books with a plan for getting out of debt. Our son's wise counsel (which was a healthy humbling experience) as well as this book empowered us to work on a disciplined as well as full game plan to get out of credit card and line of credit debt in just over a year and it worked! We also experienced the favour and wind of God under our wings to make this happen. We are so relieved to be out of this debt, after almost ten years of enslavement.

After this victory, we also took a further step and got off the "housing prices go up forever" bandwagon by getting out of mortgage debt. We sold our home in which we only had about twenty percent equity based on its present peak value. If or when Canadian real estate values follow the American housing market and begin their descent, it wouldn't have taken too much for us to be "underwater" with our mortgage.

Now we are completely out of all debt and have some cash (again, "cash is king" during a deflationary period) for the bumpy ride ahead and are free and mobile as a couple, who are now "empty nesters", to do whatever the Lord might ask of us. So far that has meant a three month sabbatical in Malawi, Africa in the fall of 2011 and in the spring of 2012, a move to Stratford, Ontario to rent a home with our pregnant daughter and her husband to support them as she battles with cancer and gives birth to their first baby, our first grandchild (a personal experience of the best of times and the worst of times simultaneously).

What freedom and relief to not only be out of debt, but to also be learning the discipline of living with margins and having fun becoming a more "cheerful giver" (literally means "hilarious", 2 Cor. 9:7) in obedience to the Lord. And He can do it for you.

Don't, however, just automatically do what we have done and sell your home. Seek the Lord as to what he might have you do particularly with investments or a home. He may wish that you keep your present house and be prepared to make it a house of refuge for others in need. Individually we really need to hear His voice and follow His promptings in preparation for and during the coming turbulence.

Let me mention one further way that Scripture might possibly be pointing to coming economic trouble; through what is called the "Bible code". According to Michael Drosnin, a secret code has been hidden in the Bible for some three thousand years but has been unlocked by computers in recent years. Sir Isaac Newton had searched for it three hundred years ago, calling it "a cryptogram set by the Almighty," the "riddle of the Godhead, the riddle of past and future events divinely fore-ordained." But a world famous Israeli mathematician, professor Eliyahu Rips, broke the code and it was confirmed by a senior code-breaker at the U.S. National Security Agency.

In Drosnin's third book, Bible Code III: Saving the World, he claims that he and professor Rips discovered a year before the 2008 election that the code predicted that Barack Obama would be president. He also claims it predicted the 2008 Great Recession when the stock market was at an all time high as well warns of a second Great Depression.[3]

2. Christian Prophetic words Warning to Prepare

It appears God has been raising up not only a prophetic church in which all believers are privileged to learn to hear His voice but also those who are learning to walk in a more mature and seasoned ministry or office of the prophetic. Here and in other places in this book I will be mentioning prophetic words from people who I have tracked for some time and believe they are credible and authentic prophetic voices that deserve to be taken seriously (which also includes testing the words as Scripture instructs us to). Amos 3:7 states, "Surely the Sovereign LORD does nothing without revealing his plan to his servants the prophets".

As early as May of 2008, **John Paul Jackson** went public with his "Coming Perfect Storm" prophecy. He had hesitated in sharing it because he did not want to be known as a prophet of gloom but felt the strong nudge of the Lord to do so. You can see the full video coverage on You-tube or purchase the DVD.

Jackson saw a convergence of geo-physical, economic, military, political and religious dimensions creating a coming perfect storm for at least the next ten years.

Several months after giving this word of a coming perfect storm, we watched in horror as the stock market crashed and the financial system seemed to unravel. We have also been seeing wacky weather getting more extreme in America and around the world. We will talk about this in the next chapter. In follow up words, John Paul Jackson has shared in more detail as well as challenged believers to really listen to the voice of God for what they are to do. He believes that we have been given grace of a little more time to get out of debt and get our house in order before greater economic challenges hit.

In 2005, **Larry Randolph** had a vision in which he saw the American economy go down a long dark hill. December 30, 2010, at a Morningstar conference, Randolph shared that we are in "the eye of the storm" right now. He sees many with a false sense of security, believing that everything is recovering when in fact, the back wall of the storm will be hitting soon.

"It's going to rain!" he cried (in a dream in Sept 2010). The rain went from threat to promise, rain of harm and then rain of blessing, back and forth - the best of days and the worst of days. And he said it is time to posture ourselves for the coming rain. If we humble ourselves and listen to God, we will change history. Joseph faced catastrophic disaster in Egypt and he postured himself right with God. The word tested him and he was found faithful. (Psalm 105:16-19) He brought provision of blessing to a world in a time of famine.[4]

Rick Joyner had a dream in December 2010 where he saw a horrendous raging fire underneath the foundations of a cabin. He believes that judgment is coming to America if we don't repent. We should not live in denial. He shared this vision on Sid Roth's TV show called "Naturally Supernatural" on Jan. 3, 2011.[5]

And since the Japanese earthquake and tsunami of March 2011, on his website, Rick Joyner has been warning that we have now crossed the line and will soon be going into an American economic unraveling and meltdown of some kind which has serious global economic consequences. At some point in the future he expects we will also be doing transactions by the barter system for roughly a few months.

Pat Robertson has also given a sobering prophecy:

"Your country is in great peril. In two years will come a time of reckoning, there will be turmoil but I will protect my people...Warn them now about what is coming. Tell them to get out of debt and restrict purchases now...If you own your house and have no debt against it, you get to keep it. But if you have debt against it, you lose...My glory will shine throughout the earth...It's not a time of happiness but of revolutions, increasing turmoil..."[6]

The Apostolic Council of Prophetic Elders meets towards the end of each year to seek the Lord for that coming year. January 12, 2010 they released their prophetic word for 2010 of which part of it stated:

"We felt that the Lord had given us an "eye of the storm" time period to get out of debt. In fact, as we discussed the many prophetic warnings about a second economic shaking, we felt that the Lord in His mercy had extended a period of grace to His people because many were not ready for another shaking. Supernatural ability to get out of debt is being released. If you will start paying your debts, even in very small amounts, God will supernaturally get behind your efforts and help you get out of debt".

Norm Franz believes the Lord gave him this word on August 7, 2010:

"All order is about to be lost. Financial order, civil/political order, family order and religious order. Society is about to be thrown into financial chaos and war. So prepare, prepare, prepare. Prepare in spirit, prepare in soul and prepare in body. Prepare mentally, prepare emotionally and prepare physically, for the next great shaking is about to come upon this world's order of things. Repent and prepare your hearts, for yet another shaking is about to remove more of what can be shaken, so that more of what cannot be shaken may remain. So return, return, return- return to Me says the Lord, "with all your heart and soul and might, and walk in My ways and not your own. Return to Me and I will return to you, and I will save you and deliver you, and you will not be shaken in the troubling days ahead".

Franz believes that 2011 may be the year or one of the last years to be able to get ready. When the crisis really unfolds, those not prepared will suffer so he urges people to get out of debt and get close to the Lord.[7]

Curt Landry, of Oklahoma, has given a prophetic word found on the Elijah List website entitled: "Entering into a New Season - Foundations for the Next Ten years". Let me quote just a portion of it:

"2012 will be marked as a year of numerous catastrophic events throughout the world, from natural disasters to financial disasters, wars and rumors of wars. Everything that can and has been shaken will be shaken. However, there is good news! If the church will hearken unto the Word of the Lord and will remain true to His instruction, we will find ourselves witness to the greatest corporate awakening the church has ever seen, as she rises up into a season of unprecedented power and authority...This warning comes to the church, not to bring fear and panic, but in order that we can prepare..."

The Apostolic Council of Prophetic Elders met in late November 2011 to seek a word of the Lord for the coming year of 2012 of which a small portion of it stated:

"Things are going to 'crack open' financially. There will be a shaking of economic systems across the face of the earth. However, during this time, God will raise up his Josephs who have been prepared for this hour. The Lord was clear to us that we were not to get into fear. We asked how to prepare and He said that we must have 'crisis preparedness'. This, we felt, meant that it was good to have some sort of provision, such as one would have in the event of an earthquake or some other disaster. While storing some amount of provisions was felt wise, there was a caution against hoarding motivated by fear. Joshua 1:10-11 says: "Pass through the camp and command the people, saying, 'Prepare provisions for yourselves, for within three days you will cross over this Jordan, to go in to possess the land which the LORD your God is giving you to possess.'"

There were three important things to remember in this season. First, face your fears. Secondly, prepare provisions. And thirdly, realize that the Kingdom of Heaven cannot be shaken.[8]

Rabbi Jonathan Cahn, in his riveting book called The Harbinger, claims that America is now under God's judgment, not unlike ancient Israel in the Old Testament. And as God gave Israel a series of specific warnings or harbingers in hopes that they would humble themselves, repent and return to Him, so He has been giving America very similar warnings.

Cahn sees a strong connection between Israel's judgment in Isaiah 9:10 with the destruction of the symbol of America's economic system, the World Trade Center, on 9/11 and subsequent events, including the 2008 Wall St. stock market crash. With the proud and defying responses that came after these warnings, more devastating judgments can be expected. I recommend you hear this man out. The specific details of each warning are sobering and quite stunning. Rabbi Cahn has been on the Sid Roth show, the Jim Bakker show, and on Benny Hinn's program.[9]

Loren Sandford, son of John and Paula Sandford, in the spring of 2012, has given this prophetic warning:

"Know that the outcome of the 2012 election will have a significant effect on how much or how little time we in the body of Christ yet have to prepare for the very difficult days that must inevitably come. No matter who wins, America and the world are in serious trouble. The church must awaken spiritually, morally and biblically and we have a limited amount of time in which to do it. We must grow in numbers, in grace, in righteousness and in love in order to be ready to minister to those made desperate by the coming collapse. Neither presidential candidate has the power or the wisdom to prevent this. We are witnessing and will soon see the catastrophic collapse of a once great culture. The effect in human suffering will be enormous... The promise: For those who will receive it, a determined remnant is about to experience an unprecedented outpouring of the Holy Spirit that will prepare and propel us into these coming days as a people ready to shine as lighthouses of hope, healing and salvation in the midst of growing darkness".[10]

3. Evaluations of Our current Economic Situation From a Few financial Experts

"U.S. and many global consumers gorged themselves on the Big Macs of all varieties; burgers to be sure, but also McHouses, McHummers, and McFlatscreens, all financed with excessive amounts of McCredit created under the mistaken assumption that the assets prices securitizing them could never go down. What a colossal McStake that turned out to be." (**Bill Gross**, CEO of PIMCO, World's largest fixed income manager.)

According to **Kevin Freeman**, in his book, Secret Weapon: How Economic Terrorism Brought Down the U.S. Stock Market and Why it Can Happen Again, the primary culprit behind the 2008 economic crisis was economic warfare. Freeman is considered a top financial expert who has briefed members of Congress, the U.S. Senate, CIA, FBI, as well as other agencies with his findings.

Freeman claims the evidence points to America's foreign enemies, Communist China and Islamic finance in particular, deliberately seeking to exploit Western economic weakness and push it over the brink. This weakness has been a consequence of spiritual and moral failure in our society as well as unbridled greed and corruption in Wall St. and government. He also claims that the economic system of America and the West continues to be extremely vulnerable to financial terrorism and unless some things drastically change, we should expect a further attack in the future with even greater devastation.[11]

A Financial Post article June 8, 2010 by **Jonathan Ratner** is entitled: "Double-dip Recession Practically Inevitable: UBS". He observes that although there has been quite an impressive rebound since the summer of 2009, a number of investors are beginning to believe we might be heading for a double-dip recession. Ratner argues that, "Politicians and central bankers can delay the bust with ever more interventionary policies. But what they cannot do, is prevent it from happening altogether...What is worrying, however, is the observation that the bigger the stimuli and the longer the period of delay the bigger the eventual recession will be."[12]

A Dec. 5, 2011 article on the Automatic Earth website speaks of a coming "sovereign debt train wreck". It quotes **Peter Schiff**, president of Euro Pacific Capital, in describing the seriousness of the financial trouble that the U.S. is in, with characteristic bluntness:

"Our government doesn't have enough spare cash to bail out a lemonade stand. Our standard of living must decline to reflect years of reckless consumption and the disintegration of our industrial base. Only by swallowing this tough medicine now will our sick economy ever recover."[13]

An article on CNN Money on February 24, 2012 came out entitled:" A New Recession Seems Inevitable", stating, "**Lakshman Achuthan**, co-founder of the Economic Cycle Research Institute, said on Friday that his research firm is sticking with the forecast it made in September: A new recession is inevitable...ECRI is one of the more widely respected firms on economic recessions, as it has never been wrong when forecasting that a recession would start, or failed to predict a recession well before it was widely accepted.

"Achuthan predicts the recession will happen even without a new shock to the economy, such as a spike in oil and gas prices or a Greek sovereign debt default sparking a financial meltdown. If those things occur, he says they will simply make an inevitable recession more painful. In fact, Achuthan said data gathered since his September forecast only confirms his view that economic growth has slowed to such a degree that a downturn is now unavoidable..."[14]

In an interview with Newsweek Magazine, Jan. 23, 2012, the eighty year old investor guru, **George Soros**, expressed his concerns, "As he sees it, the world faces one of the most dangerous periods of modern history—a period of 'evil'. Europe is confronting a descent into chaos and conflict. In America he predicts riots on the streets that will lead to a brutal clampdown that will dramatically curtail civil liberties. The global economic system could even collapse altogether."

"I am not here to cheer you up. The situation is about as serious and difficult as I've experienced in my career," Soros tells Newsweek. "We are facing an extremely difficult time, comparable in many ways to the 1930s, the Great Depression. We are facing now a general retrenchment in the developed world, which threatens to put us in a decade of more stagnation, or worse. The best-case scenario is a deflationary environment. The worst-case scenario is a collapse of the financial system."[15]

As of the spring of 2012, we have a dozen countries in the European Union that have fallen back into recession, including the UK and Spain. Unemployment among the youth of Spain is over fifty percent. And China's economy, second largest in the world after the U.S., is slowing down, largely due to Europe's low demand for their products.[16]

Between 2000 and 2006, home prices in the United States basically doubled. So far, between 2006 and 2012, they've lost about 32 percent of their value. In Canada, home prices in our major cities climbed 125 percent over the past twelve years. In recent months (summer of 2012) sales and prices have begun their descent in the largest cities of the west coast while other major centers across Canada have peaked and are now beginning to show signs that the "real estate prices always go up" party has come to an end.[17]

In the United States, with municipal revenues dropping due to such factors as real estate value slumps that translate to lower property taxes, we have seen municipalities cut back on their services such as police and fire, and as of July 2012, three cities in California have declared bankruptcy - Stockton, Mammoth Lakes, and San Bernardino, with other cities expected to follow their lead.[18]

Harry S. Dent Junior does not consider himself a doom and gloomer by nature but is forecasting very dismal days ahead. This prediction takes various factors into consideration but one in particular that he gives serious attention to is demographic trends as a key driver to economic ups and downs. Dent declares that every boom has a bust, every bubble has a burst and that it inevitably takes you back to the start of that boom or bubble, if not a bit lower.

In his 2011 book, The Great Crash Ahead, Dent claims that we have experienced the greatest real estate and credit bubble in modern history and that de-leveraging and deflation are ahead for the foreseeable future where cash will be king. The stimulus plan created to address the first crisis of 2008/09 is now facing demographic and debt saturation head winds and that an even greater crash is just around the corner, probably some time between late 2012 and 2014.

Dent accurately forecasted the U.S. real estate decline that began in 2006 as well as the 2008/2009 stock market crash and great recession. He has been boldly forecasting for some time that the real estate prices will drop a further 30 percent during the 2012-2015 time frame with no turn around until some time after 2020. Dent sees the Dow dropping possibly as low as 3,300 by the end of 2013 or 2014 at the latest.[19]

Nicole Foss argues that, "2008 did not demonstrate what a liquidity crunch really means, but this time we are going to find out. As with many aspects of financial crisis, Greece is the canary in the coal mine, demonstrating what happens when liquidity disappears and it ceases to be possible to connect buyers and sellers or producers and consumers...money is the lubricant in the engine of the economy in the way that motor oil is the lubricant in the engine of your car, and you know what will happen to your car if you drive it with the oil warning light on.

"Greece stands on the verge of an energy crisis caused not by lack of energy, but lack of money within the energy sector. This will become a common refrain throughout Europe and beyond in the coming months and years. Loss of liquidity has a cascading effect on supply chains, causing them to seize up.

"For a long time, money will be the limiting factor, and finance will be the key driver to the downside, just as was the case in the Great Depression of the 1930s. Resources will remain available, at least initially, but no one will have the means to pay for them during a period of economic seizure...Europe is at the epicenter at the moment, but contagion will ensure that the dynamic will spread."[20]

The American economist and former bank owner, **Larry Bates** and his team did a survey of banks nationwide asking them if one percent of their customers demanded their money in cash, could they provide it. Not one bank answered that they could.[21]

Jerry Tuma, an American financial advisor, in his fascinating and highly perceptive 2009 book, From Boom to Bust and Beyond, looks at how demographics play a significant role in the global economy. He argues that with the seventy-six million American baby boomers (those born between 1946 and 1964) now past their peak spending age and heading for retirement, the unprecedented thirty year wave of economic prosperity we have enjoyed has now crashed on the shore and we have entered into an "economic winter" or bust that will probably last ten to fifteen years.

This is compounded by the fact that the global humanist agenda of recent decades has promoted de-population throughout the world. He, as well as many other experts, argues that you cannot have economic expansion with dwindling populations and seventy countries of the world are now well below the replacement rate of 2.1 births per female (including the U.S., Canada, and Europe). We have set ourselves up for big trouble.[22] Tuma, as well as Harry Dent Jr., sees the economic downturn in Japan since 1990 largely due to an aging population and a preview of what we will be experiencing.

Other dynamics are adding insult to injury. Tuma warns "a rising peril exists, a peril so great that it threatens all of our lives, our futures, and our destinies...We've gone from self-reliance and hard work toward government dependency...from saving and investing to debt dependency and consumer addiction...In just about every area, America has moved toward the moral gutter".[23]

The economic school of thought originating with John Maynard Keynes, a 19th century agnostic and member of a group of Fabian socialists at Cambridge, was the first to strongly push for government intervention in a troubled marketplace. We have seen massive government spending, bailouts and increased control of private industry in the past few years that have artificially propped things up and have given the illusion of a true recovery. In reality, however, such actions are setting us up for a greater fall down the road.

Jerry Tuma writes his book to give a clarion call regarding not just another "bear market" but rather a coming "grizzly bear" market that we have never experienced in our lifetimes and to help prepare others financially and otherwise by making informed rather than panicky decisions. The twenty-five year borrowing binge is over. "Like partygoers on a drunken binge, the hangover for this mega top of consumer spending and borrowing will stay with us for awhile".[24]

I also agree with Tuma on the following issues, which also line up with other financial forecasters like Harry Dent Jr. and Nicole Foss.

First, that the real problem is not just the real estate bubble popping and consumer spending decreasing (seventy percent of a nation's economy consists of consumer spending), but the entire financial system. With massive doses of stupidity and greed, leverage was piled on top of leverage by the banks, using the financial tool known as derivatives (or Credit Default Swaps, CDSs for short), which has created a nightmare that we are only now waking up to.

As an aside, Joseph P. Farrell, in his book, *Babylon's Banksters*, mentions that a Chinese mathematician, David X. Li, while living in Canada for his schooling and work, developed a formula called Gaussian copula formula. This formula appeared to be a godsend to the Wall Street and London financial manipulators who made a ton of money as the markets expanded out of nothing to unimaginable levels with derivatives, credit default swaps and bundles of brand-new triple-A securities. But his popular formula proved seriously flawed and may go down in history as quite instrumental in bringing the global financial system to its knees. Dr. Li quietly went back to China in 2008 where he is high up in financial risk management. Farrell, like Kevin Freeman, raises the question of economic warfare being a major factor in the 2008 crisis.[25]

Secondly, that we'll probably see a heart sinking deflationary scenario, a loss of liquidity, for a period of time (with the possible exception of some commodities such as food and fuel) before things kick into an inflationary horror show a few years or so down the road.

Thirdly, that due to economic upheaval that will sideswipe the masses, we could expect to see things turn ugly very quickly with a run on grocery stores and banks, protests, riots, and looting (as we have already seen in parts of Europe). With such a deep mindset of entitlement in our society where many believe they deserve to be taken care of by the government, waves of anger, desperation and lawlessness could quickly unfold, leading to possible martial law in some cities. With that in mind, it would be wise and prudent to take some steps of physical preparedness without being fear based. Joseph stored grain for the upcoming famine and Proverbs 21:20 states that "In the house of the wise are stores of choice food and oil".

And fourthly, that those who continue to follow the crowd, ignoring the signs of a coming category five hurricane and believing business will carry on as usual, will continue to lead high-consumptive lifestyles and indebtedness and be the first to suffer. Challenging and uncertain times can either wipe you out or create amazing opportunities as we saw take place during the last "Great Depression". Potential for a great wealth transfer is before us, from the hands of the unprepared to the hands of the prepared. It is time to develop a strategy and take proactive steps to weather the storm.[26]

In researching this matter of a coming financial perfect storm, I have come across an army of financial experts (including **Robert Kiyosaki**, author of Rich Dad, Poor Dad, see his you-tube video listed at the end of chapter) who are shouting from the rooftops that massive trouble is just around the corner. **Though these experts all agree that we are headed for a major financial storm, two very different camps exist as to how this storm will play out.**

One camp is claiming that we are about to face serious inflation problems as well as the U.S. dollar collapsing. The other camp claims that we are about to hit a massive deflationary crisis (with possible inflation/hyperinflation later). Both agree that you need to get your house in order, get out of risky investments and get out of debt. But in regards to what to do to protect your wealth, each camp will have different advice. Obviously in a deflationary phase where assets plunge and bubbles pop, then "cash is king" but in an inflationary period, cash loses its value and safe havens such as precious metals of gold and silver may be the wiser course of action.

Those pointing to a coming inflation period claim that the printing of money will create inflation and loss of dollar value. Those believing we are in or going in to a deflationary phase would argue that regardless of how much money is printed to try to solve our problems, this will not offset the pace and size of debt bubbles that are imploding. Craig Hill, a proponent of deflation, likens it to a bathtub whereby any printing of money and/or "quantitative easing" is water coming into the tub but the destruction of wealth (real estate, stocks, gold and other bubbles popping or about to pop) is going down the drain at a faster rate and in much greater volume.[27]

Some financial proponents of a deflationary crisis are: Jerry Tuma, Craig Hill, Nicole Foss (Stoneleigh is her writing name), Harry Dent Jr., and Robert R. Prechter.

Some voices that speak of a soon coming inflationary crisis are: Larry Bates, Marc Nuttle, Norm Franz, Gary Kah, Bob Chapman, Mark Faber, Jim Rogers, Lindsey Williams, Gerald Celente, Paul McGuire, Chuck Missler and David Wornom.

I have a high regard for all these people but I find myself leaning towards the deflationary camp, with a probable inflationary phase (and possible collapse of the U.S. dollar) to come a little later.

Coming Lawlessness and Civil Unrest

As just mentioned a moment ago, when citizens have a strong sense of entitlement in which they believe the government owes them, they become dependent on the government to take care of them and when they cannot deliver what is promised, anger, rage and flying bullets are the result (as seen in hurricane Katrina).

Gerald Celente is the founder of Trends Research Institute. In 2011 Celente predicted that some time in 2012 we would see riots on the streets of American cities. Lindsey Williams has also claimed that by the end of 2012, we will first see the collapse of the Euro and then the U.S. dollar with civil unrest following. I suspect such predictions may turn out to be fairly accurate with the exception of their timing. Although riots in the streets of Europe and in Muslim nations are already commonplace, it may be another year or several years before we see serious civil unrest in America.

In an Interview on TruNews Radio May 2, 2012, private investigator **Doug Hagmann** said high-level, reliable sources told him the U.S. Department of Homeland Security (DHS) is preparing for "massive civil war" in America. "We have problems...The federal government is preparing for civil uprising." Recently, requests made by the DHS for the procurement of four hundred and fifty million rounds of hollow-point ammunition only fuels speculation of an upcoming tragic event expected on American soil.[28]

George Soros also senses that anger will rise and that riots on American streets will be inevitable. He is concerned about the handling of this unrest. "It will be an excuse for cracking down and using strong-arm tactics to maintain law and order, which, carried to an extreme, could bring about a repressive political system, a society where individual liberty is much more constrained, which would be a break with the tradition of the United States."[29]

Though not putting a time frame to it, various Christian prophetic voices such as: John Paul Jackson, Rick Joyner, and Terry Bennett are also speaking of coming riots in the streets and an overall sense of lawlessness followed by martial law in some American cities.[30]

Practical Preparations for coming economic turbulence and potential natural disasters:

First, let me say that we don't put our faith in our preparations. We place our faith in the God who advises us to prepare. Proverbs 27:12 states that a "prudent man sees danger and takes refuge, but the simple keep going and suffer for it".

Of course the primary way to prepare is by drawing close to the Lord. Where the church is riddled with compromise and mired in a culture of self-absorption, independence, comfort and materialism, we need to repent. Years of prosperity have lulled us to sleep. Repentance is key to our preparation spiritually. God is calling us to red-hot devotion and intimacy with Himself - to be radical lovers who follow the Lamb wherever He goes. We need to learn to hear His voice, know His heart, be wowed by His greatness and goodness and quick to trust Him and obey His directives.

Secondly, we could prepare in some very practical matters like: store at least a month's supply (some say three to twelve months) of dry food and clean water and emergency cash for yourself and family and anyone else the Lord would have you care for.

According to a CNN article in June 2012, 28 percent of Americans have no emergency savings while 49 percent don't even have enough money saved to cover three months of expenses.[31]

Not only do we need to give priority to having some emergency savings for several months at least, but have an emergency cash fund at our fingertips, under our mattress or in our safe. At some point we may not be able to get much if any money out of the banks (power outage or banks closed to avoid a bank run) and in any type of crisis the food on store shelves will be cleared out within days or even hours.

Other items to have on hand are: flashlights, candles, radio, batteries, and a first aid kit. I'll give a longer item list in the chapter on natural disasters. I have found the book, When All Plans Fail, by Dr. Paul R. Williams, a Christian medical doctor, a wealth of practical information for planning and preparing your family for any type of disaster and emergency.

Our western culture has highly valued rugged individualism, independence, and watching out for number one. These attitudes, inspired by the demonic spirits of mammon, greed and fear, have also permeated the church. And God desires to deal with these spirits (including the spirit of religion) in the church. This will create much upheaval in the natural. Our heart's treasure has been our wealth more than the Kingdom of God, resulting in us thinking of ourselves more as reservoirs than channels of financial blessing to others. The coming upheaval will be a painful stripping and pruning. He is after our hearts and He wants the joy of being our source of provision.

God not only wants us to experience a deeper and closer relationship with Him but also with others in the Christian community in order to survive and even thrive in what is coming.[32] Having a strong sense of community will be critical in the uncertain days ahead. Friendships, that is, relationships of trust, with fellow believers and our neighbours will be invaluable, as we need each other for emotional support, safety as well as in sharing resources and practical skills.

Rick Joyner suggests we not only have practical resources for ourselves in order to love our neighbours but have extra Bibles and Christian reading materials on hand as many will turn to the Lord during a crisis. Joyner sees practical preparation as a significant evangelistic tool in the future and has many in his church who have already gone through training to help in natural or man-made disasters. They had teams help out in the hurricane Katrina disaster and he felt the Lord say that it was the first of many emergencies that the church will be called upon to respond to with the compassion and mercy of God.

So, it appears that life as we have known it is soon to drastically change economically and otherwise. It will no longer be business as usual. We need to be informed and be prepared spiritually and practically. We also need to cultivate a faith-filled expectation of our heavenly Father breaking through with supernatural provision for us on occasion. Like Joseph in the Old Testament, we may get to partner with God in seeing paradigm jarring heavenly solutions for local, national and even global problems. That would apply to the challenges of extreme weather and natural disasters as well, which is the focus of our attention in the next chapter.

Recommended Resources:

Books:

Five Wealth Secrets that 96% of Us Don't Know, Craig Hill, E Book, 2012
From Boom to Bust and Beyond, Jerry Tuma, Excel Books, 2009
The Great Crash Ahead, Harry S. Dent Jr., by H.S. Dent Pub., 2011
The New Economic Disorder, Larry Bates, Excel Books, 2009
Money and Wealth in the New Millennium: A Prophetic Guide to the New World Economic Order, Norm Franz, whitestonepress, 2001
Secret Weapon: How Economic Terrorism Brought Down the U.S. Stock Market and Why It can Happen Again, Kevin Freeman, Regnery Publishing, 2012

While America Stumbles, David Wornom, IT Pub., 2009
More than Enough, Dave Ramsey, Penguin Books, N.Y., 1999 (any book by Dave Ramsey would be good!)
Healing Your Financial Soul: An Interactive Guide to Restoring Your Relationship with Money, David Hicks, Pensario Pub., 2007

Websites:

John Paul Jackson: http://preparingfortheperfectstorm.com/
Terry Bennett prophecies: http://www.terrybennett.net
Rick Joyner: www.morningstarministries.org
Rick Joyner, February 24, 2012 Prophetic Perspectives on Current Events, Managing economic trials wisely http://www.morningstartv.com/prophetic-perspective-current-events/managing-economic-trials-wisely
Nicole Foss (Stoneleigh), www.automaticearth.com,
Dave Ramsey: http://www.daveramsey.com
USdebtclock.org

You-tube videos:

We are Preparing for Economic Collapse - Robert Kiyosaki - Author 'Rich Dad, Poor Dad' uploaded Nov. 20, 2011 http://www.youtube.com/watch?v=lwdKc9a8WfY&feature=related
Nicole Foss aka Stoneleigh - A Century of Challenges - Peak Oil & Economic Crisis, http://www.youtube.com/watch?v=BJKZT5TNjYw
Stoneleigh on Transition, http://www.youtube.com/watch?v=WiOOkb3bXW4&feature=related
6 prophetic words regarding potential American civil war, riots and marshall law in America, uploaded May 5, 2012, (accessed May 10, 2012) http://www.youtube.com/watch?v=4Zv5engRrQo&feature=relmfu

Notes:

1. The Arizona Republic, June 13/12, News: Families lost 39% of worth in recession, http://www.azcentral.com/arizonarepublic/news/articles/2012/06/11/20120611fed-reports-how-much-recession-shrank-us-wealth.html#ixzz1xh96DXQO
2. Craig Hill, Five Wealth Secrets that 96% of Us Don't Know, E Book, as of March 2012.
3. Michael Drosnin, Bible Code III: Saving the World, Weidenfeld & Nicolson, 2010, pp.8, 9, 43-49
4. Larry Randolph, You-tube, Morningstar conference, Dec. 30/10 http://www.youtube.com/watch?v=oyzZ6OEHKSU
5. Rick Joyner on Sid Roth show, Jan. 3/11, http://www.youtube.com/watch?v=1oDKcAQHWrQ uploaded Jan. 16/11.
6. Pat Robertson, video on cbn.com & transcript on Elijah List
7. Norm Franz, Prepare! Prepare! Prepare! DVD, Ascension Ministries, word for 2011, www.ascensionministries.net
8. The Apostolic Council of Prophetic Elders: www.revivalnow.com, word for 2012: http://www.revivalnow.com/eyesandwings/glob_proph/ACPE%20Word%20for%202012.pdf
9. Jonathan Cahn, The Harbinger, Frontline, Charisma, 2011, also Youtube: "Jonathan Cahn 1& 2 on It's Supernatural with Sid Roth - Harbinger the Warning", also on Jim Bakker Show website under the video archive, #2054 -2060, on Benny Hinn's ministry.
10. R. Loren Sandford, prophetic word, Charisma News, May 17/12, http://charismanews.com/opinion/33424-a-prophetic-warning-about-the-2012-presidential-elections
11. Kevin Freeman, Secret Weapon: How Economic Terrorism Brought Down the U.S. Stock Market and Why it can Happen Again, Regnery Pub., Wash. D.C., 2012.
12. Jonathan Ratner, The Financial Post, June 8/10 article: "Double-dip recession practically inevitable: UBS". http://business.financialpost.com/2010/06/08/double-dip-recession-practically-inevitable-ubs/#ixzzOtcfBuen3
13. December 5 2011: Look Back, Look Forward and Look Down, Way Down. www.automaticearth.com Peter Schiff

[14.] http://money.cnn.com/2011/09/30/news/economy/double_dip_recession/index.htm?iid=EL   http://money.cnn.com/2012/02/24/news/economy/double_dip_recession/index.htm

[15.] Newsweek Mag., George Soros on the Coming U.S. Class War, Jan. 23, 2012, The Daily Beast website, Business, http://www.thedailybeast.com/newsweek/2012/01/22/george-soros-on-the-coming-u-s-class-war.html (accessed June 16/12).

[16.] CNN money: Apr. 30/12, http://money.cnn.com/2012/04/30/news/economy/spain-recession/index.htm?hpt=hp_t3

[17.] Garth Turner's blog, The Greater Fool, July 20, 2012 "Outrageous", http://www.greaterfool.ca/ (accessed July 21/12).

[18.] Tami Luhby, Money.cnn.com "California bankruptcies are only the Beginning", July 12/12, http://money.cnn.com/2012/07/12/news/economy/california-bankruptcies/index.htm?iid=Popular (accessed July 12/12).

[19.] Harry S. Dent Jr., The Great Crash Ahead, Free Press, by H.S. Dent Pub., 2011, pp. 15-18, also http://www.boomandbustinvestor.com/pages/bnb/BNB1_NEW.php?&pub=BNB1_NEW&code=LBNBN700 (accessed July 24/12).

[20.] Nicole Foss, Automatic earth: Crashing the Operating System - Liquidity Crunch in Practice, June 4/12, http://theautomaticearth.com/Finance/crashing-the-operating-system-liquidity-crunch-in-practice.html (accessed June 16/12).

[21.] Larry Bates interview, Jim Bakker's show, Apr. 20/11, #1839

[22.] Jerry Tuma, From Boom to Bust and Beyond, Excel Books, Florida, 2009, p. 106-7.

[23.] Ibid., p. 5.

[24.] Ibid., pp. 72-74.

[25.] Joseph P. Farrell, Babylon's Banksters, A Feral House Book, 2010, pp. 21-27.

[26.] Tuma, pp.75, 165, 171,2, 193.

[27.] Craig Hill, Bathtub Economics on You-tube, July 4/10, though not accurate on the timing of next downturn, his teaching is very relevant http://www.youtube.com/watch?v=memM2s40F98 (accessed Feb. 27/12)

[28.] "We are Preparing For Massive Civil War" Says Dept of Homeland Security Informant, by Dominique de Kevelioc de Bailleul, Before

It's News, May 3/12, http://www.youtube.com/watch?v=QTUCWq ZOdKY&feature=related

[29.] George Soros interview, quote on automaticearth Jan. 25/12, http://theautomaticearth.com/Finance/occupy-your-own-space.html

[30.] You-tube, 6 prophetic warnings to America: lawlessness, riots, civil war, and martial law, (Bobby Conner, Bob Jones, John Paul Jackson, Mike Bickle, Terry Bennett, Rick Joyner, uploaded May 5, 2012, http://www.youtube.com/watch v=4Zv5engRrQo

[31.] Blake Ellis, CNNmoney, June 25, 2012, "28% of American have no Emergency savings", http://money.cnn.com/2012/06/25/pf/emergency-savings/index.htm?iid=Popular

[32.] Johnny Enlow, The Seven Mountain Mantle, Creation House, 2009, pp. 7-9.

Chapter 16

Wacko Weather, Devastating Disasters, the New Norm

"There will be famines and earthquakes in various places. All these are the beginning of birth pains." Jesus (Matthew 25: 7, 8)

"But mark this: There will be terrible times in the last days."
2 Tim. 3:1

"A sensible man watches for problems ahead and prepares to meet them. The simpleton never looks, and suffers the consequences."
Proverbs 27:12 (TLB)

"When you get to your wit's end, you'll find God lives there."

The Lord is coming and will be showing all sides of His nature during this transition at the end of the age; sides of Him you may be offended by. He is a God of love but also a God of justice and He balances them perfectly. He is not bringing His wrath unto destruction (at least not yet) but rather His redemptive discipline and corrective judgment, which is designed to bring people to their knees and to God. The awe of God, the fear of the Lord will return. He will not be mocked.

It is not God's desire to have natural disasters unleashed that cause horrific things to happen. He is saddened and agonizes over it. His joy is to see people return to Him and live in His love and blessing.

The earth was created for righteousness and justice. The earth is groaning and convulsing - responding to sin, rebellion, and injustice. It groans and trembles under the accumulating weight of sin and evil on the earth. (Isaiah 24:5, 20; Romans 8:19-22) Sin allows Satan to have legal leverage in our lives and causes God's protective hand to lift, leaving us vulnerable. God allows the discipline of natural disasters and the consequences of our sin to run their course in hopes of getting our attention, removing our idols that hinder His love, and returning to Him.

In Hebrews 12, God speaks of a shaking coming that strips everything but the Kingdom, which cannot be shaken.

We have been seeing an increase in earthquakes and extreme weather patterns in recent years and both prophetic and scientific predictions indicate more is on the way. The challenge is not to react in fear but rather get informed and ready.

Jesus predicted some of the signs of the end of the age in Matthew 24 as wars, famines, and earthquakes in various places, unprecedented stress on the earth, and even heavenly bodies shaken. These signs will be like labour pains, growing in frequency and intensity as we begin the transition from this evil age into the age to come. The grand finale of these end times will be Christ's return in glory and splendour, which will usher in a brand new age and the consummation of the Kingdom of God.

Storms are brewing. Don't be like the ostrich that buried its head in the sand. But don't live in fear either (Google the Stockdale Paradox). Jesus, the Prince of Peace, tells us to take heart because even though we will have tribulation in this world (and more so towards the end of the age), He has overcome the world. (John 16:33)

If we are prepared spiritually (have a personal and up-to-date relationship with Christ, have our lamps filled with the oil of the Spirit, have a Kingdom perspective, are in fellowship with other followers of Christ, and are able to discern the times we are in) and if we take steps to prepare practically, then we not only increase our prospects of weathering the coming storms (surviving), but of helping others and making a difference in this world for the Kingdom (thriving). Great opportunity will be ours to be conduits of God's supernatural grace to see heavenly solutions and provision brought to bear in crisis situations with eternal benefits.

It's interesting that the Chinese word for "crisis" supposedly has a two-fold meaning: "danger" but also "opportunity". Nations will be shaken and we will see an increased opportunity for the nations to turn to the Lord. Rick Joyner, having an eternal perspective, states that the Holy Spirit is urgently calling the church to think eternally, and not be offended at God in all that will be taking place. The Lord promises to be with His children but that does not automatically mean Christians are immune to the coming dangers and challenges. We need to hear the voice of the Lord as to where He wants us to live and how to prepare for the coming turbulence and opportunities. Joyner goes on to say, "Some will be lost and go to heaven. How bad is that?"[1]

We belong to a Kingdom that cannot be shaken. We are called to be an overcoming church and be the hands and feet of Jesus. While Israel was under judgment and captivity in Babylon, the Lord promised His people that He had plans, a future and a hope for them (Jeremiah 29:11) and that is very applicable to us today.

We are responsible on our watch to partner with God in seeing transformation in society. "For God did not give us a spirit of timidity, but a spirit of power, of love and of self-discipline". (2 Tim. 1:7) We are to be anxious for nothing for "the just will live by faith". We need to learn from the hard lesson experienced by one of Christ's disciples, Peter, when he stepped out of the boat and walked on water towards Jesus. We applaud him for stepping out but he took his eyes off the Lord and got very impressed with the wind and waves around him that caused his heart and then the rest of him to sink.

Amos 3:7 states: "Surely the Sovereign LORD does nothing without revealing his plan to his servants the prophets". God does not wish to leave us in the dark, not knowing what is going on. He desires to keep His bride informed so we are not caught unawares and so we can partner with Him in His redemptive purposes in the midst of the calamity.

Many contemporary prophets have been getting dreams, visions and angelic visitations, warning of impending natural disasters. And when more than one prophetic voice blows the trumpet of warning about the same or similar events, it's even more imperative that we heed the word. Of course repentance and intercession could possibly avert, delay or minimize the disaster.

John Paul Jackson has publicly warned us of what God called a "Coming Perfect Storm" for America and the world for at least the next ten years, which includes various natural disasters such as earthquakes, floods, droughts, volcanic eruptions, tornadoes, solar storms, and extreme weather patterns.

Bob Jones believes that Kansas City and area will become one of several "cities of refuge" in America. It will have an "open heaven" and be a "bread basket" for America and the world in the natural as well as the supernatural. There will be many natural disasters. Sadly, he also believes there will eventually be another world war that will involve a limited nuclear exchange on the east coast of the U.S.[2] Mike Bickle claims he is aware of at least twenty-five prophetic voices that have warned of this coming world war and limited nuclear exchange.[3]

Rick Joyner urges, in preparation for the coming times, to start now to actually perform one of the most basic reformation truths, that of the priesthood of all believers. Very few believers understand the reality of their call to be a priest or are walking in this reality. We are entering some of the most challenging times the world has ever experienced. We find this described in Isaiah 60:1-5:

"Arise, shine; for your light has come, and the glory of the LORD has risen upon you. For behold, darkness will cover the earth, and deep darkness the peoples, but the LORD will rise upon you, and His glory will appear upon you. And the nations will come to your light, and kings to the brightness of your rising. Lift up your eyes round about, and see; they all gather together, they come to you. Your sons will come from afar, and your daughters will be carried in the arms. Then you will see and be radiant, and your heart will thrill and rejoice; because the abundance of the sea will be turned to you, the wealth of the nations will come to you."

People will come to the light, not the darkness. We need to get ready for this. And learning to be the priesthood of all believers is a foundational part of that preparation.[4]

2011 - A record year of wacky weather and natural disasters

In the last decade we have seen an increase and an intensification of natural disasters in America and around the world. In particular, the year 2011 has rewritten the record books. It has been a historic year for disasters - from the massive earthquake and tsunami in Japan to famine in East Africa to floods in Australia to the deadly tornado outbreaks, heat waves, fires, droughts and floods in the United States. More than a dozen weather-related disasters in the United States alone have caused more than one billion dollars in damages each, breaking the record of nine billion-dollar disasters set in 2008, according to the National Oceanic and Atmospheric Administration. Altogether, the damage from these events exceeds fifty billion dollars.[5]

2012 - Records continue with more on the way

A CNN article dated July 11, 2012 titled, "Extreme weather: Get ready to see more of it, scientists say", by Moni Basu, states:

"A map of significant climate events for the United States in June looks almost apocalyptic: hellish heat, ferocious fires and severe storms leaving people injured, homeless and even dead...After all, nine of the top ten warmest years globally have occurred since 2000, according to NOAA."[6]

Another CNN article the same day, by Steven Cohen, titled, "Why we should expect more weather disasters", announces that:

"A recent report from the U.S National Oceanic and Atmospheric Administration provides hard data that the first six months of 2012 were the hottest since records began being kept in 1895.

"We need to devote more public resources to pay for emergency response and reconstruction from weather-related catastrophes. In fact, we should no longer deal with these events as if they are emergencies, but start to see them as routine events, requiring standard, programmed responses. This includes setting aside funds for fires and floods each year, just as northern cities budget for blizzard clean-up."[7]

Thunderstorms and a record-breaking heat wave in early July 2012 left over two million Americans in the eastern portion without power for a week or more. After ten days, seventy-five thousand were still without power. By the beginning of August, the record warmest twelve months ever had resulted in the worst widespread drought since the 1930s. Half of the counties in the U.S. have been declared disaster zones by the Department of Agriculture.

A CNN report posted Jan. 24, 2012, quotes Japanese researchers as claiming that the Tokyo metropolitan area, home for forty-two million people, faces the possibility of being hit by a massive earthquake within the next four years. The University of Tokyo's Earthquake Research Institute predicts there is a seventy percent probability that the capital's metropolitan area will experience a magnitude-7 quake or greater within four years and a ninety-eight percent probability within the next thirty years.[8]

Christian prophetic voices such as John Paul Jackson and Bob Jones are also predicting another big earthquake hitting Japan, particularly in the Tokyo region. Jackson also sees Mount Fiji erupting with devastating results.

Many prophetic individuals (Jackson, Jones, Joyner, Bennett) have publicly predicted major earthquakes hitting the west coast of United States, both California and the North West as well the New Madrid fault in central United States. Let me add that it is important that Christians pray for more time and for minimal casualties, for mercy to triumph over judgment.

Wonders in the Heavens

Luke 21:25-28 reminds us "There will be signs in the sun, moon and stars. On the earth, nations will be in anguish and perplexity at the roaring and tossing of the sea. Men will faint from terror, apprehensive of what is coming on the world, for the heavenly bodies will be shaken..."

Blood Moons

Eschatological significance appears to be given to such signs as the moon turning to blood (Joel 2:31). Though caution in making any conclusions is advised, it is an interesting note that scientists expect blood moons in 2014 and 2015 and they appear to be connected to Hebrew holy days. According to various websites, including NASA, the lunar eclipses break down as follows:

Passover	April 15, 2014
Feast of Tabernacles	October 8, 2014
Passover	April 4, 2015
Feast of Tabernacles	September 28, 2015

The two solar eclipses connected with God's Holy Days in 2014-2015 occur:

Adar 29/Nisan 1(new year)	March 20, 2015
Feast of Trumpets	September 13, 2015 [9]

Solar Storms

John Paul Jackson has predicted that sunspots will increase and that this will disrupt the magnetic field, disrupting our communications technologies.[10]

There will also be riots in the streets.[11]

On March 10, 2006, the NASA Science website announced:

"First Solar Storm Warning from NASA", stating: "It's official: Solar minimum has arrived. Sunspots have all but vanished. Solar flares are nonexistent. The sun is utterly quiet. Like the quiet before a storm.

"This week researchers announced that a storm is coming-the most intense solar maximum in fifty years. The prediction comes from a team led by Mausumi Dikpati of the National Center for Atmospheric Research (NCAR). "The next sunspot cycle will be 30 percent to 50 percent stronger than the previous one," she says. If correct, the years ahead could produce a burst of solar activity second only to the historic Solar Max of 1958...A similar maximum now would be noticed by its effect on cell phones, GPS, weather satellites and many other modern technologies".[13]

Then on June 4, 2010, NASA put an article on their website called, "As the Sun Awakens, NASA Keeps a Wary Eye on Space Weather", stating:

"Earth and space are about to come into contact in a way that's new to human history. To make preparations, authorities in Washington DC are holding a meeting: The Space Weather Enterprise Forum at the National Press Club on June 8th...The National Academy of Sciences framed the problem two years ago in a landmark report entitled 'Severe Space Weather Events—Societal and Economic Impacts.' It noted how people of the 21st-century rely on high-tech systems for the basics of daily life. Smart power grids, GPS navigation, air travel, financial services and emergency radio communications can all be knocked out by intense solar activity. A century-class solar storm, the Academy warned, could cause twenty times more economic damage than Hurricane Katrina".[14]

A website called 2012hoax claims the warnings of a 2012 solar storm that will wreak havoc on the earth is overstated. This site states that there are solar flares all of the time but they vary over time in an approximate eleven-year cycle. The Sun was expected to reach a maximum (called "solar max") in its eleven-year cycle in

2011 or 2012 but more recent calculations have pushed this date off to sometime in 2013.[15]

These solar "eruptions" are known as coronal mass ejections, or CMEs. The disturbances they create in the earth's magnetic field are called solar storms. They can interfere with satellites, electrical grids and communication systems as well cause Northern and Southern Lights. The strongest solar storm on record is called the "Carrington Event", after Richard Carrington, the man who reported the solar flare, which occurred in late August and early September of 1859 and damaged telegraph lines in North America and Europe. According to a recent estimate, the likelihood of another Carrington event occurring over the next decade is twelve percent.[16]

Jesse Ventura, former governor of Minnesota, has spoken out publicly regarding his concern that the U.S. government is feverishly building underground bunkers to protect the elite from threats, assuming they have information regarding upcoming natural or man-made disasters that they are not revealing to the public. Ventura specifically focuses on the Denver airport (with its plaque that refers to a "New World Airport Commission" and artistic murals with the theme of death) and the nearby Cheyenne Mountain bunker.[17]

It is interesting that the Bible states that, "Men will flee to caves in the rocks and to holes in the ground from dread of the LORD and the splendor of his majesty, when he rises to shake the earth". (Isaiah 2:19)

Natural Disaster Preparedness

In recent years we have seen an increase of natural disasters: earthquakes in New Zealand, Chile, Indonesia, Japan and floods in Australia, Pakistan and in the U.S. Mississippi basin while there is a major drought and fires in Texas, Oklahoma and Colorado, sprinkled with a heavy dose of hurricanes and tornadoes.

As well we have seen increased volatility and tensions between nations of the world (War on Terror, Arab Spring, a pending Israeli pre-emptive strike against Iran's nuclear sites) and major economic turbulence with accompanying civil unrest in Europe. Combine these present realities with the warnings from Scripture that as we get closer to the end of this age, disasters, wars and rumours of wars will only increase and intensify like a woman in labour, and it no longer seems over-reactionary to be personally taking practical steps of preparation in case of a possible emergency of some kind.

However, many folks, including Christians feel they were duped with Y2K hysteria several years back and they don't want to go through any potential embarrassment and extra costs again of acquiring generators and supplies.

But I believe we need to get past this "Cry Wolf" syndrome and realize that we must take personal responsibility for our families and ourselves and not rely on our governments alone to take care of us. It is sobering to realize that a 2004 American survey showed that only about twenty percent of Americans feel "very prepared" for a catastrophe. The same survey conveyed that only ten percent of US households have actually developed a family emergency plan, have organized an emergency kit, or have received any training in first aid and CPR.[18]

If you are in that eighty to ninety percent who are not prepared, you risk being a paralyzed victim who needs assistance (part of the problem, not part of the solution) and becomes a drain on rescue efforts. You could also miss out on an incredible opportunity to help and love your neighbour from a place of peace, confidence and practicality. Being prepared for disasters will be one of the greatest ways to show the compassion of Christ and be an evangelistic tool in the days ahead.

Dr. Paul R. Williams, a Christian medical doctor who has led medical mission teams to over a hundred nations, many of them stricken by devastation and disaster, has written an exceptionally practical book on preparedness, When All Plans Fail.

In his book he tells the story of a man who worked in the New York City's Twin Towers during the first bombing in 1993. After that attack, he planned an escape route for himself should a similar incident occur again. When the plane struck his building on September 11, 2001, the man was trapped on one of the floors above the level of impact. Following his pre-determined plan of evacuation, he was one of the very few above the point of impact to make it out alive.[19]

Dr. Williams points out that the majority of people have not sufficiently planned for common everyday crises let alone disasters. He then asks simple and practical questions such as:

Do you keep jumper cables in your car? (I actually read this part of the book just ten minutes after having to use cables to get my wife's car started so she could go to work.)
Do you keep at least one flashlight, with extra batteries, on hand?
Do you use surge protectors for appliances and electronic equipment?
Do you take along extra water when jogging or bicycling on long excursions?
Do you change the oil in your car at the recommended schedule?
Do you have health, life, homeowner's insurance?
Do you pray and read your Bible every day?

He assumes we probably would have said yes to most of these questions about practical and everyday things and he urges us, in the same spirit of "no hype, no fear", to prudently prepare for future disasters.[20]

We should learn about our local community's plans for warning and evacuation. Also, we should determine which hazards and emergencies that your area would most likely face (floods, hurricanes, tornadoes, winter ice storms, earthquakes, fires, wildfires, landslides, volcanoes, tsunamis etc.).

Federal governments, the Red Cross, and other agencies encourage citizens to do their part and not depend totally on governments to be able to take care of them in a crisis. They recommend that as a family you discuss and develop a plan, which should include a seventy-two hour emergency kit that can fit in backpacks or a small suitcase on wheels, in case you need to evacuate. A longer-term kit with food and water supplies to last a couple of months or more would also be advisable.

Remember that in the event of an emergency, the shelves of supermarkets would be cleaned out within hours. With generally only a three-day supply of food and other necessary products of inventory, the "just-in-time" delivery systems, which lower costs to business, make us immediately vulnerable to shortages.

Basic items to include in a seventy-two hour kit (and a longer term kit) would be:

Water - store two liters of drinking water and two liters of water for washing per person, per day
Non-perishable food - select foods that are compact and lightweight, non-perishable and require no refrigeration, cooking, preparation or added water. Once per year, check the expiration dates of your food items
Manual can opener
Crank or battery-operated flashlight, with extra batteries
Crank or battery-operated radio, with extra batteries
First aid kit
Cash in small bills
Special needs items - medications, baby formula, diapers and equipment for people with disabilities
Copy of your emergency plan (where to meet or contact loved ones etc)

Additional items to consider:

change of clothing and footwear for each person, sleeping bags or blankets, pet food, garbage bags, toilet paper, basic tools (hammer, wrench, screwdrivers etc), duct tape, scissors or pocket knife, matches, candles, rope, plastic sheeting, personal hygiene items, important documents (birth certificates, passports, wills, land deeds, insurance etc), and alternative sources of energy, heat and light.

Buying a few extra things when regularly shopping or buying in bulk to save money can either do building up emergency supply kits. You can develop a rotation system so that food items don't pass their expiry dates.[21]
A practical tip in what to do during an earthquake is what they call "drop, cover, and hold on". In the event of an earthquake, drop to the floor, take cover under a sturdy desk or table, and hold on to it firmly. Be prepared to move with it until the shaking stops.

Practical Tips in Preparation for a Nuclear Disaster

Contrary to popular myth, most people could survive a nuclear disaster, if educated on basic instruction. Shane Connor, a consultant and developer of civil defense solutions to government, military, and private organizations, claims that ninety percent of potential casualties from fallout can be avoided if trained.[22]

He recommends people:

- "Duck and cover", that is, stay away from windows
- If evacuating, travel perpendicular to the downward drift of the nuclear fallout to avoid contamination, and
- Learn how to effectively shelter or bunker down for a short time.

The good news is that radiation loses ninety percent of its damaging energy and effect in the first seven hours and ninety-nine percent of it within two to three days, so one does not need to hunker down for weeks on end.[23]

In choosing a location for shelter, choose a structure nearby with both the greatest mass and distance between the outside and occupants inside. If there is a basement that may be your best option to build a protective shelter in a corner wall where the above ground level is highest. Use tables, doors, appliances, boxes of books, anything that can act as a protective shield from radiation. You want to place sufficient mass between you and the fallout so it absorbs the radiation, including appliances or whatever on the floor directly above your shelter. It is best to cover windows with whatever material so they don't break and allow fallout dust to come in and to minimize radiation coming through - the thicker and denser the material, the better. To stop ninety-nine percent of radiation, you would need steel five inches thick, concrete sixteen inches, earth twenty-four inches if packed or thirty-six inches loose, water thirty-six inches, or wood fifty-six inches.[24]

Aside from the list of supplies in the emergency kit mentioned above, N95 dust filter masks would be helpful in a nuclear disaster as you want to avoid inhaling or ingesting fallout dust. If you have been outside and may have dust on you, remove outer clothing before going indoors (of course a shower to wash off dust in hair and skin would be helpful).

Connor claims that if proper steps of preparation are taken, you can increase your chances of survival by at least one hundred times. He suggests thinking of it as acquiring medical insurance that hopefully you will never need but if you do, you are able to step up to the challenge of responsibly providing for and protecting your family.[25]

Conclusion

Benjamin Franklin once said, "To fail to plan is to plan to fail". Regarding any kind of disaster or emergency, my wife and I and family are not fully prepared as yet, but we at least have a seventy-two hour emergency kit now established. We are in the process of completing our long-term food, water and other survival supplies to last for at least a month. We want to be able to not only care for our needs as a family but also be able to care for and love our neighbours in a practical way in the name of Jesus. And I am believing for God to provide through miraculous multiplication from time to time as well. How ready are you, both spiritually and practically?

Let me close with some insightful comments from the great churchman, A. W. Tozer, from an article called, "A Scared World Needs a Fearless Church":

"No one can blame people for being afraid. The world is in for a baptism of fire...God declares this by the voice of all the holy prophets since time began- there is no escaping it. But are not we Christians a people of another order? Do we not claim a place in the purpose of God altogether above the uncertainties of time and chance in which the sons of this world are caught? Have we not been given a prophetic preview of all those things that are to come upon the earth? Can anything take us unaware?...A fear-stricken church cannot help a scared world. We who are in the secret place of safety must begin to talk and act like it. We, above all who dwell upon the earth, should be calm, hopeful, buoyant and cheerful. We'll never convince the scared world that there is peace at the Cross if we continue to exhibit the same fears as those who make no profession of Christianity."[305]

Recommendations:

Books:

When All Plans Fail: Be Ready for Disasters, Paul R. Williams, M.D., Mountain View Pub., 2008
Handbook to Practical Disaster Preparedness for the Family, Arthur T. Bradley, Createspace, 3rd edition, 2012
Shane Connor, author of Chapter 2, "Nuclear Armageddon", in the book, How to Overcome the Most Frightening Issues of this Century, editor, Thomas Horn, Defender, 2009
The Harbinger, Jonathan Cahn, Frontline, 2011

Websites:

John Paul Jackson: www.preparingforthecomingperfectstorm.com
Rick Joyner: www.morningstarministries.org
Terry Bennett's prophecies: http://www.terrybennett.net
Jim Baker Show website: http://jimbakkershow.com/
solar storms: NASA website: http://science.nasa.gov/
spaceweather: http://spaceweather.com/glossary/flareclasses.html
Canadian Red Cross, natural disaster preparedness recommendations, http://www.redcross.ca/article.asp?id=33841&tid=001&gclid=CKnovfTPo7ACFSMDQAodxWvNZw
article by Patrice Lewis, The End of the World as We Know it, about what things would be like if the power grid goes down, Aug. 10, 2012, WND commentary, http://www.wnd.com/2012/08/the-end-of-the-world-as-we-know-it/ (accessed Aug. 12, 2012)
free webinar by Kacper Postawski to grow your own food by building a biodome: http://www2.onlinemeetingnow.com/register/?id=55c1f31431

You-tube videos:

The Coming Perfect Storm, by John Paul Jackson:
The Kingdom of God in Turbulent Times, J.P. Jackson
John Paul Jackson, Prophecy Overview, With Details, 1.14.2012
Rabbi Jonathan Cahn, author,The Harbinger, on Sid Roth Show,
http://www.youtube.com/watch?v=tXei0Zb3dxM&feature=related

Notes:

1. Rick Joyner, Prophetic Perspective on Current Events video, www.morningstar.org Aug. 12/11
2. Bob Jones, Revival and WW III coming prophecy, www.friendsofgod.org
3. Mike Bickle, CDs, prophetic history of KC, sessions # 1, 2, Oct. 2002
4. Rick Joyner, Prepared for the Times, Part or Week 49, www.morningstar.org Nov. 29, 2010
5. National Oceanic & Atmospheric Administration. http://www.noaa.gov/extreme2011/index.html ; http://preparingfortheperfectstorm.com/2011/12/11/record-breaking-year-for-disasters/
6. Moni Basu, CNN article, July 11/12, "Extreme weather: Get ready to see more of it, scientists say" http://edition.cnn.com/2012/07/10/world/unusual-world-weather/index.html?hpt=hp_t2
7. Steven Cohen, CNN article July 11, 2012, "Why we should expect more weather disasters", http://edition.cnn.com/2012/07/11/opinion/cohen-extreme-weather/index.html
8. Elizabeth Yuan, "Tokyo sees high quake probability, scientists warn", CNN, Jan. 24, 2012, http://articles.cnn.com/keyword/seismic-activity
9. Blood Red Lunar Eclipses and solar Eclipses on God's Holy Days, http://www.triumphpro.com/blood-red-lunar-eclipses-and-solar-eclipses.htm (accessed August 6/12), see also NASA lunar eclipse website: http://eclipse.gsfc.nasa.gov/LEdecade/LEdecade2011.html and NASA solar eclipse website: http://eclipse.gsfc.nasa.gov/SEdecade/SEdecade2011.html

[10.] J. Paul Jackson, You-tube: Prophetic warning: sunspots, Nov. 28/11

[11.] J. P. Jackson, You-tube: Prophecy for America: mobs will rove America, Dec. 6/11, (accessed Feb. 23/12)

[12.] NASA Science website, March 10/06 Solar Storm Warning http://science.nasa.gov/science-news/science-at-nasa/2006/10mar_storm-warning/ (accessed March 6/12).

[13.] NASA science, June 4/10, As the Sun Awakens, NASA Keeps a Wary Eye on Space Weather, http://science.nasa.gov/science-news/science-at-nasa/2010/04jun_swef/

[14.] 2012hoax website: http://www.2012hoax.org/solar-flares

[15.] Space Weather website: http://www.agu.org/pubs/crossref/2012/2011SW000734.shtml (accessed March 6/12).

[16.] You-tube, Conspiracy Theory with Jesse Ventura - Apocalypse 2012, 5 of 6 parts, uploaded Jan. 14/10, (accessed Feb. 22/12)

[17.] Dr. Paul R. Williams, When All Plans Fail: Be Ready for Disasters, Mountain View Pub., 2008, p. i, Intro.

[18.] Ibid., intro, ii,iii.

[19.] Ibid., pp. 5,6.

[20.] Ibid., pp. 35-39. also Canadian Red Cross website: http://www.redcross.ca/article.asp?id=33841&tid=001&gclid=CKnovfTPo7ACFSMDQAodxWvNZw (accessed May 27/12).

[21.] Shane Connor, Ch. 2, "Nuclear Armageddon", in book: How to Overcome the Most Frightening Issues you will Face this Century, Defender, editor, Thomas Horn, 2009, p. 10.

[22.] Ibid., p. 11.

[23.] Ibid., pp. 18-21.

[24.] Ibid, p. 41.

[25.] A. W. Tozer, This World: Playground or Battleground? Christian Publications, 1989, Ch. 2, cited in an article entitled, A Scared World Needs a Fearless Church.

Chapter 17

Towards a Counterfeit and Temporary New World Order

Part 1

By a European/Anglo-American Global Elite

"We shall have world government whether or not we like it. The question is only whether world government will be achieved by consent or conquest."

James Warburg, son of Paul Warburg, Feb. 17, 1950. Testimony to the United States Senate Foreign Relations Committee

"Why do the nations rage and the peoples plot (conspire) in vain? The kings of the earth take their stand and the rulers gather together against the LORD and against his Anointed One." Psalm 2:1,2

"There is no wisdom, no insight, no plan that can succeed against the Lord." Prov. 21:30

*L*et me ask you a question: How did two planes bring down three skyscrapers in New York City on September 11th, 2001? Your response may be, "What do you mean, three skyscrapers?"

The third tower, WTC7, a forty-seven story steel structured building came down virtually at free fall speed, a little after five p.m. the afternoon of September 11th. Our stunned psyches only have the vivid images from our television sets of the twin towers collapsing so that the third collapse went virtually unnoticed and without serious inquiry. Most people look shocked when I ask them this question because they didn't even know about this third tower, even ten years later.

The tragic events of 9/11 are not intended to be the focus of this chapter (though I'll say more about it in a moment) but they could be considered symptoms or manifestations of what we will be addressing.

I believe it is imperative for the body of Christ today to not only be attentive to the very exciting things that God is doing on the earth, but to also become aware of the sinister plans of Satan, both at the micro and macro levels, as we approach history's grand finale, the end of this evil age.

Some may wish to skip this chapter because they don't want to be frightened or overwhelmed. They may say we can't do anything about it anyway so let's not even go there. But the Bible tells us not to be ignorant of the devil's schemes (2 Cor. 2:11). Ignorance is not bliss. If I had cancer in my body, I'd want the doctor to be honest and frank so I'd know exactly what I'm dealing with. And Jesus insisted that we be watchful and alert at the end of the age so we are not deceived (Matt. 24:4, 10, 11, 24, 25, 42; 25:13; Luke 21:8). We are now entering those increasingly perilous times.

If we remain in an intimate walk with Christ, stay connected in Christian community and alert to the subtle deceptions of the enemy in these dangerous times, we can avoid being sideswiped and paralyzed by shock and trauma as the world experiences future shakings and demonic and sinister manipulations. Instead we will be walking in the supernatural peace, compassion and authority of Christ to make a difference in people's lives. And we will be walking in our destiny and experiencing His joy even while dealing with danger and chaos all around us.

The Sunday after the tragic 9/11 events, grieving Americans flocked to church, creating the fastest church growth ever. But within weeks, we saw the greatest exodus from church. Why? I suspect a major reason would be because the church did not have a clear prophetic voice to address the pressing issues and questions. We were as traumatized and clueless as everybody else. Nor have we, the western church, for the most part, been walking in the healing presence and glory of God to minister to their felt needs in the midst of crisis. This needs to change.

Conspiracy Theories?

This may be the chapter more than any other in this book that the reader suspects the author has really gone over the top with conspiracy theories and the like. I understand that. There are many wild and bizarre theories out there. But there are also some that, under fair scrutiny, may show substantial credibility. The word conspiracy is even found in the Bible.

In Psalm 64:2, King David asked this of the Lord: "protect my life from the threat of the enemy. Hide me from the conspiracy of the wicked." A conspiracy isn't automatically something that is imaginary and made up by the paranoid. The wicked often scheme together to devise a plan, a conspiracy, a snare, to the harm of others.

It can be quite tempting and convenient for someone who wants to discredit or dismiss someone with an alternative view on a complex situation, to just lump it under the term "conspiracy theory". With a roll of the eyes and a smirk on the face, one may condescendingly groan, "Oh, don't tell me you are one of those conspiracy theorists." Once it is ruled out as ludicrous, the person feels justified in not having to bother investigating things thoroughly themselves or risk being threatened by a vastly different view of reality.

But I encourage you to bear with me and seek to be radical, liberal and conservative, in the original sense of those words. Blindfold your prejudices and allow yourself to see things from a fresh perspective. That is, set your own assumptions and emotions aside, seek to be objective and do your own homework. Don't take my word for it, go to the root of the subject, examine as much of the evidence as you can for yourself and be slow to come to firm conclusions.

I believe we must critically evaluate the spin of information we are fed daily by the liberal media, which massively shapes our view of reality and how we interpret life's events. The corporate owned and controlled media has a liberal, humanistic and anti-Christ slant to what it dispenses to the public. On top of that, it would be good to discuss this with others who are serious about seeking truth and not afraid to ask questions and think outside the box. And by all means, stay grounded in the Word of God and the peace of Christ as well as constantly asking the Lord for further wisdom, revelation and discernment.

Again, Scripture warns us not to be naive regarding the devil's schemes. (2 Cor. 2:11) We can no longer afford to go along with the crowd and assume everything we are told is how it is. There's a real war going on. Has been since day one but it is only ramping up towards a climax in these last days. The hour is urgent. The thief comes to kill, steal, and destroy while Jesus comes to bring us life to the full. (John 10:10) "The harvest is the end of the age". (Matthew 13:39) Evil as well as righteousness will grow and mature. Light and darkness will intensify in the end times. (Isaiah 60) While the fullness of Christ shines brighter through His bride, evil will also intensify, including the manifestation of a very deceptive Antichrist and his temporary tyrannical government. Of course, light always wins over darkness.

Thankfully in recent decades Christians have become increasingly aware of and effective in dealing with spiritual warfare on the micro level, that of Satan attempting to neutralize us from our God-given destinies and cause us to self-destruct as individuals and in our relationships. The devil seeks to tempt us, discourage us, get us to doubt God's integrity and Word and believe his lies, get our hearts wounded and offended so that we ultimately ignore or curse God and die in every way possible.

Satan of course also works at the macro or global level, seeking to wreak havoc in God's creation and in social structures with the ultimate goal of achieving world domination. He has a lust for power and glory. Our struggle is not against flesh and blood, but principalities and spiritual forces of evil in the heavenly realms. (Eph. 6:12) But he uses corrupt people and deceptive ideologies for his sinister purposes. It is this macro level that I wish to address in this chapter, at the risk of upsetting some.

Though it may not be politically correct to do so, I wish to go on record as stating that Satan, who knows his days are numbered, is intensifying his efforts in a campaign towards global domination through at least two parallel vehicles.

First, he is operating through a socialist global elite (a small group of powerful bankers, aristocrats, corporate businessmen and political leaders) that is pursuing the establishment of a one world government, economy, and religion. This group is energized by Lucifer who plays on their pride and greed for maximum power and wealth and motivated by a vision for a socialist utopia under their wise leadership.

The second group consists of Islamists within the Muslim community who are bent on imposing shariah law throughout the world and establishing an Islamic state, a caliphate over the nations of the earth under the Madhi, their Islamic messiah and world leader, for the cause of Allah.

The Antichrist spirit seeking world domination has also manifested itself through such ideologies as communism and Nazism which were quite a serious threat in the 20th century but appear to be out of the running. But appearances can be deceiving. We may think that communism has petered out but could it be about to make a comeback in Russia? And could Communist China soon become a/ the leading superpower (economically and militarily) of the world?

Regarding Nazism, most think that it was wiped out at the end of WW II. But there is evidence it only went underground. Many of the Nazi scientists and intellectuals escaped trial and were secretly and illegally distributed to Russia and the U.S. (Google "operation paperclip"). In the U.S. Nazi scientists were assigned to help with the NASA space program or various military programs.

But evidence exists to indicate that many Nazi leaders and scientists were smuggled into South America (possibly with the Vatican assisting with passports). It is quite possible that some of the most classified and advanced technologies (such as anti-gravity) as well as substantial wealth remained in Nazi hands and was taken to

Argentina and other South American countries in hopes of someday making a comeback, the fourth Reich.[1]

It can be quite jarring for those of us who believe things usually happen randomly, that is, by accident, to hear that the Anglo-American global elite helped to orchestrate (assisting Lenin and Leon Trotsky in getting back into Russia) and finance the two Russian revolutions of March and October 1917 and the birth of communism on the world scene (including helping Chairman Mao get into power in China and Fidel Castro in Cuba). What if I was to say that the global elite also financed and provided weapons, equipment and supplies to the Nazi leader, Adolf Hitler to wage World War II?[2]

It can also be a bit jolting to be informed that Adolph Hitler, in 1937, helped finance the Muslim Brotherhood, a strategic Islamic organization with a vision of world domination for Allah that enabled them to spread to over forty countries. So to see occasional alliances and partnerships among these rival groups that all seek global conquest causes one to scratch one's head in bafflement, unless you take into account the philosophy of George Wilhelm Friedrich Hegel.

It appears that the global elite is utilizing Hegel's dialectic theory of historical progress through thesis, anti-thesis and synthesis. The motto "order out of chaos" is its war cry. It involves deliberately planning conflict to bring about change toward a new order. Norm Franz puts it this way, "First, there is 'thesis' which brings 'antithesis' which produces 'synthesis' or the desired outcome."

Many see this game plan used behind the French, American, and Marxist Revolutions, as well as both world wars. "Take World War I, for example - the 'thesis' was Germany and her allies' attempt to conquer Europe. The 'antithesis' was the allied powers that opposed and defeated them. The 'synthesis' was the first open attempt to form a world government through the League of Nations. Since the League of Nations failed, World War II was obviously the next Hegelian model...The 'synthesis' was the successful creation of the United Nations, which appears to be the apparatus of the soon coming new world government."[3]

And we cannot ignore the fact that powerful elite who appear to be behind the instigation of such conflicts in order to move things towards their ultimate objective of a one world order, also profit from both sides of the war.

Over many years, Satan has been orchestrating these and other life sucking ideologies and mechanisms such as: humanism, atheism, post-modernism, the inter-faith movement, New Age movement, freemasonry, the Illuminati, occultism and other "isms." Most if not all of these mechanisms have been useful tools in the hands of the global elite and have empowered them towards their agenda.

Some may argue that the New Age and interfaith movements are a third contender in the race for global domination. The growing New Age and interfaith religious movements gleefully anticipate that come the end of 2012, there will be a world-wide evolutionary leap into their desired global spiritual transformation of a new age of Aquarius. I suspect, however that such religious movements will be shown to be pawns in the hands of the global elite and fuel for their cause.

We have been seeing in recent decades an acceleration of mind-blowing proportions of these two groups, the global elite and Islam, towards their parallel objectives of world dominance. After they have, in some respects at least, worked together (the 9/11 events may very well be one example) in undermining and eroding existing structures of freedom in the West such as: democratic governments (especially the U.S. Constitution), educational and legal systems, economies, and the Judeo-Christian faith and values, they may very well turn on each other for the prize of supremacy.

One school of thought believes that the one world dictator, the Antichrist, will be the prophesied Muslim messiah, the Mahdi, who will oversee the oppressive shariah law imposed on earth's citizens. Another school of thought believes the global elite will triumph over the Islamic competition to install their tyrannical world leader, who will demand exclusive allegiance. In this and the following chapter, we will look at these two options and let you come to your own conclusions.

The Spiritual Battle From a Biblical and Eternal Perspective

Of course the good news is that after a dark dictatorship (whether Muslim or otherwise) briefly oversees a global (or close to global) government, economy, and religion, Jesus Christ will invade this planet in spectacular fashion. He will be accompanied by His host of powerful angels and His saints and will obliterate His enemies, overthrowing the government(s) and setting up His one true and righteous world government. In this new age to come, the Glorious One, King Jesus, will establish His headquarters in Jerusalem and reign for what many Christians believe will be a literal thousand years, what is called the millennial Kingdom, followed by His eternal reign.

But let me back up for a minute and take a brief run through the biblical overview of this spiritual battle.

The Bible makes it abundantly clear that there really is a spiritual war raging on planet earth. Ever since Adam and Eve first sinned, this world has come under the dominion of Satan and his pseudo-kingdom of darkness. In 1 John 3:8 we are told, "the reason the Son of God appeared was to destroy the devil's work." Since the first coming of Jesus, the Messiah, the Kingdom of God has broken onto the scene. "For He has rescued us from the dominion of darkness and brought us into the kingdom of the Son He loves, in whom we have redemption, the forgiveness of sins". (Col. 1:13) With the death and resurrection of Christ, Satan has been defeated. The apostle Paul puts it this way, "having disarmed the powers and authorities, He made a public spectacle of them, triumphing over them by the cross." (Col 2:15)

Jesus did not put an end to Satan's power however. Satan is bound and his counterfeit kingdom is breaking up, yet God has left him room to maneuver. Ken Blue puts it this way: "The most dismal evil in all history found its absolute limits at Calvary. After evil had choked on its own venom, it became forever subject to Christ and to us in his name. There is no absolute dualism between God and satan. The victor at the end of the battle is already crowned".[4]

An illustration from the Second World War can be helpful to describe the situation. Europe experienced two major victories in this war. The first was "D Day" and the second was "VE Day". D Day was June 6th, 1944, when the Allied forces landed on the coast of France. This is considered the decisive victory in the war. The end result of the war was now assured. But the war was not finally over until VE Day, almost a year later on May 8, 1945. Between these two dates were many months of battles and very high casualties but no one doubted the final outcome. Christ won the "D Day" victory at the cross. But the church, as God's army, is called to continue pushing back the counterfeit kingdom of darkness and extending the rule and reign of God until "VE Day" when Christ returns and all darkness and evil will be finally crushed.[5]

The Bible adamantly declares that the government or Kingdom of God will ultimately triumph and rule for eternity.

The prophet Daniel interprets Nebuchadnezzar's dream of a statue with its head of gold, its chest and arms of silver, it belly and thighs of bronze, its legs of iron, and its feet of iron and clay as a series of world kingdoms or superpowers. A rock struck the statue and it smashed to pieces and was blown away by the wind. That insignificant rock became a huge mountain and filled the whole earth. This rock is the indestructible Kingdom of God that would crush all the other kingdoms and last forever. (Dan. 2:28-45)

The prophet Isaiah also spoke of the Kingdom, the government of God so long ago. "For to us a child is born, to us a son is given, and the government will be on his shoulders...(and regarding this) Prince of Peace, of the increase of his government and peace there will be no end...The zeal of the LORD Almighty will accomplish this". (Isaiah 9:6, 7)

The angel Gabriel announced to Mary the news of the coming of Jesus through her and the fact that "His Kingdom will never end". (Luke 1:33)

And the apostle John records that future moment at the end of this present evil age when "loud voices in heaven" joyfully announce that, "The kingdom of the world has become the kingdom of our Lord and of his Christ, and he will reign for ever and ever". (Rev.

11:15) In other words, Jesus Christ ultimately sets up His one world government, His New World Order!

So, armed with a biblical and eternal perspective, we know that the enemy is real and he works through wicked men but that ultimate victory in Christ Jesus is without question. Knowing of their ultimate demise, God merely laughs at them and instructs believers not to fret or be anxious. (Psalm 37) This is not something for us to freak out about or think that God is in heaven breaking out in a sweat over. Ultimately the devil is a pawn in God's hands. The establishment of the New Jerusalem over against Babylon is assured. Light wins over darkness.

We can therefore, with joyful confidence, proceed to look at this sobering issue of a coming, but temporary one world government without it striking fear in our hearts.

The Bible Warns of an End-Time Tyrannical One World Government

The Scriptures clearly warn us of a coming end-time one world political dictator who will lead a totalitarian regime in ruling over many of the nations. The Antichrist, the man of lawlessness, the beast (2 Thess. 2:3,4, 8; 1 John 2:18; Revelation Chapters 13 and 17) will appear and be given great authority by Satan over virtually all the inhabitants of the earth, for three and a half years. (Rev. 13:2-8) In other words, he will be the tyrannical leader of a one world government. Rev. 13:16-18 tells us that everyone will be required to take a mark (possibly on their body) that shows allegiance to this dictator if they wish to do any business transactions in this one world government and global economy. This dictator, who will have a religious colleague along side of him, will claim divinity and demand worship from everyone, indicating an agenda towards a one world religion as well.

If we believe the Bible (and are not of the partial preterist theological camp, who believe that most of these predictions have already been fulfilled in history), then we believe that at some point a demonically-inspired world dictator will arise who will go well beyond the power and tyranny of "shadow antichrists" like a Stalin, a Hitler, a Mussolini, a Chairman Mao, a Saddam Hussein, or a Gaddafi. This final Antichrist or Anti-messiah may be a culmination of them all.

It is very unlikely that this world government leader would just show up in a vacuum, out of the blue, and take over. It is reasonable to suspect that Satan will be quietly working behind the scenes orchestrating structures, people and circumstances over time towards this grand finale. And if we believe we are getting very close to the end of the age (whether we have five years or fifty years remaining), don't you think that upon closer examination, we just might be able to see at least preliminary signs of a stage being set for such a biblical scenario?

As already stated, it appears Satan has been preparing at least two very different vehicles for many years, in hopes of one (or both?) of them being successful in their mission. In this chapter we will look at the European/Anglo-American global elite who seek to establish a New World Order. Next chapter we will look at the Islamic threat.

9/11 and The Anglo-American Global Elite's agenda for a New World Order

We in the West feel sorry for the masses in countries that are not considered free and democratic. The people of communist bent countries like Russia or China or nations with brutal dictatorships are probably fed a constant diet of misinformation from their political leaders. We wonder why the majority who seem to believe their leaders could be so gullible.

But are we in the so-called free and democratic world always fed accurate and objective news information? Could it be that those who own and control the media (a small handful of global elite-owned mega corporations) put a certain spin to things for their own purposes and we are being just as gullible?

So maybe our media and culturally shaped biases need to be exposed and challenged if we are to begin investigating something with any degree of objectivity.

For instance, it is so much easier to take at face value the official line dispensed to us and believe that foreign terrorists were solely responsible for the September 11th attacks on America than to risk people thinking we are being unpatriotic (or even un-Christian) by asking tough questions that might implicate some of our own leaders who could have been accomplices (or even the instigators) in this mass murder. Perhaps there is a legitimate place to apply Benjamin Franklin's advice, "It is the first responsibility of every citizen to question authority".

Are we willing to look at all the evidence?

For starters, how do you solve the mystery of that third tower, WTC 7, coming down that same day about 5:20 p.m.? Steel structured buildings do not suddenly collapse like that because of a few fires in the building. This would be the first in history. There must be another explanation. If it was brought down by professional demolition later in the day because of the fires and concern for people's safety (as some have suggested), how can you explain such a complex project being planned, set up and executed in a matter of hours? Demolition projects would take weeks of planning out, strategically planting explosives and in the right time sequence, to pull off a successful demolition job that perfectly implodes in on its own footprint.

And how does one explain the fact that the BBC announced the collapse of WTC 7 about twenty minutes before it occurred? As the BBC presenters talk of its collapse, it is visible, still standing behind the woman reporter. Oops! Or CNN's Aaron Brown's report at 4:15 p.m. EST that WTC 7 had either just collapsed or was in the process of collapsing. It is possible that it was simply a mistake in the midst of a very shocking and chaotic day. Or did somebody hand out the script a little ahead of schedule?[6]

Further evidence that points to prior knowledge is found in the September 2002 PBS documentary called "America Rebuilds." In this film, Larry Silverstein, the new leaseholder of the towers (who benefited handsomely from the liability insurance), is interviewed regarding WTC 7. He states, "I remember getting a call from the fire department commander telling me that they were not sure they were going to be able to contain the fire and I said, 'We've had such terrible loss of life, maybe the smartest thing to do is pull it.' And they made the decision to pull and we watched the building collapse."[7]

If it were a professional demolition job, as it appears in the video footage,[8] explosives would have had to be put in place before the planes ever hit the towers. And if that is the case, could it be that explosives were also placed in the Twin Towers? Many of us don't want to even entertain such thoughts because it completely rattles us at our core. It puts into question things that we have assumed are solid and trustworthy.

In recent years, sobering information has come out regarding samples of the fine dust taken from the collapsed towers that have been analyzed by a team of scientists in Denmark. In April 2009, Danish chemist and STJ member Niels H. Harrit, of the University of Copenhagen, and eight other authors, some also STJ members, published a paper in The Open Chemical Physics Journal, 2009, 2, pages 7-31, titled, 'Active Thermitic Material Discovered in Dust from the 9/11 World Trade Center Catastrophe'.

The scientists claimed that by placing a torch to the residual material, they could get a further explosion from the red layer of the red/gray chips.

At the end of the article, the authors give this conclusion, "Based on these observations, we conclude that the red layer of the red/gray chips we have discovered in the WTC dust is active, unreacted thermitic material, incorporating nanotechnology, and is a highly energetic pyrotechnic or explosive material."[9]

It has also been claimed that this high tech "super thermite" technology had only been developed and made available in April 2000. The U.S. military and some academic laboratories have had active R & D programs aimed at exploiting the unique properties of nano-materials. The safe handling of a malleable sol-gel of the material allows for easy coating of surfaces (such as steel) either by painting or spraying.[10]

Others have rightly questioned the issue of fire temperature from jet fuel and whether the heat would explain the melting of steel beams. It has been argued that the fire from the jet fuel would have only reached about five to six hundred degrees Fahrenheit, while steel beams would need considerably hotter temperatures to soften and begin to lose strength (over eleven hundred degrees F). Slow motioned video footage also shows liquid steel pouring out in some places as well as little puffs of smoke from explosions in sequence happening just before those floors would begin to implode.

There is also the issue of how to explain the fourteen hundred degree Fahrenheit hotspots at ground zero even a week later and ongoing burning over a month later in spite of massive amounts of water poured in. Could this heat source be from a thermitic chemical reaction?

These claims need to be further investigated and either confirmed or shown to be false. There are many other questions that need to be asked about the 9/11 events.

It is worth noting, however, that the official 9/11 story given by the U.S. government and repeatedly presented on mainstream media over the last ten years is itself a "conspiracy theory." It has never been proven in a court of law and yet it is touted as factual (just as the "theory of evolution" is taught in schools as factual). So, everyone is actually a "conspiracy theorist" in this story!

Yes, a commission was set up and an inquiry done on the September 11th attacks but it is questionable as to how independent it really was and it made no mention of the third tower. It has a similar feel to the Warren commission investigating the assassination of John F. Kennedy in 1963 that seemed determined to cover up the whole truth of more than one shooter.

Many groups have formed, such as Architects and Engineers, Firefighters, Intelligence officers, Lawyers, Medical professionals, Pilots, Scholars, Scientists, Veterans for 9/11 Truth, and others who seem to be making a reasonable request that a totally independent inquiry be done on the matter.[11]

The fact that as time goes on more and more American citizens have begun to question the official version, there appears to be inconsistencies, inaccuracies and glaring omissions (such as WTC7) in the commission's report and that this is the largest mass murder on continental American soil, you would think it deserves to be thoroughly investigated. If the U.S. government has nothing to hide and a growing number of the citizens in this so called free and democratic nation, including a growing number of pilots, university professors, scientists, architects and engineers have serious and legitimate questions and concerns for justice and truth to prevail in these catastrophic events, why would a further and more independent inquiry not be allowed?

Another important question to ask in any murder investigation would be: who else would benefit from such a crime?

Apart from the convenience of having vital documents destroyed in WTC 7 offices of the CIA, IRS and the Secret Service (some of which were criminal investigations of high up and influential people) some would say that such an "event" creates a justification to invade countries in order to get their hands on their oil. That could very well be true but there seems to be a host of other potential benefits as well.

Some say 9/11 was a "false flag operation" (Google this term for some eye-opening information) not only for oil, but for creating higher national patriotism around one's political leaders and higher fear among the American public which leads to a willingness to sacrifice one's personal freedoms in order to feel safe and secure. Keep in mind that both Homeland Security and the freedom-eroding Patriot Act were established shortly after 9/11. Such knee-jerk developments have substantially stripped away personal American freedoms and increased the power of various government agencies. Others have pointed out that this event has created both the Afghanistan and Iraqi wars which feed profits to powerful elite within the U.S. military complex, helps de-populate the world and helps destabilize nations and economies, all of which further the ambitions of a global elite towards forming a New World Order.

I don't have a lot of solid answers, just many sobering questions and grave concerns as I have delved into this controversial matter of 9/11.

For instance, there is the embarrassing case for the Bush administration of Susan Lindauer, who claims to have been a CIA asset for nine years, working as a back channel with Iraq and other Middle East countries. In her shocking 2010 book, Extreme Prejudice, she tells her story. She states that she had personal knowledge of the CIA's advance warnings about the 9/11 attacks on the World Trade Centre and that it was imminent. She had further confirmation when shortly before the tragic events she was advised by her "handler" not to make any more visits to New York because of the danger.

Also, Lindauer's team had successfully negotiated a peace framework with Baghdad, which included full cooperation with having inspectors return to verify that Iraq was not hiding weapons of mass destruction. These negotiations would have achieved all American objectives in Iraq without the need to go to war or fire a shot. Perhaps there were other objectives with Iraq not verbalized?

Going from a CIA asset to being a Washington liability, Susan Lindauer was arrested March 11, 2004 by FBI agents and accused of being an Iraqi agent. The Justice Department argued that she could be detained "indefinitely", without a trial. She was one of the first American-born citizens to be targeted under the Patriot Act, which had been approved after 9/11 to crush terrorism. The horrifying thing is that the Patriot Act is proving to be a perfect tool to silence whistle-blowers and crush anyone who does not agree with government policy, stripping them of basic protections under the U.S. Constitution.

Susan Lindauer was held in Carswell prison within Carswell Air Force Base in Texas for seven months, where her legal defense was initially kept from seeing her. She claims that they had hoped to forcibly drug her to "cure" her, that is, obliterate her memories and belief that she had ever been a CIA asset.

Through the perseverance of both her uncle, Ted Lindauer, a sharp lawyer for over forty years, as well as her partner who crusaded for her cause through blogs and alternative talk shows, she was eventually released five days before the inauguration of President Obama. The Justice Department formally dismissed all charges against her, claiming she was not mentally fit to stand trial. She claims that without the Patriot Act that stripped her of normal due process, the cover-ups of 9/11 and Iraq would have failed.[12]

Some of you at this point may be tempted to toss this book into the trash because it messes with your head. But remember that the worldview that we hold so dear regarding world events in history has been shaped through years of being drip-fed certain information from our school textbooks, classrooms and mainstream media. This has been one of the most recent as well as devastating paradigm shifts for me to go through and I'm not even American. But it also has brought me into a greater appreciation, awareness and urgency to the spiritual battle in which we are engaged.

These are indeed dangerous and perilous days that are quickly moving towards a final showdown between the Kingdom of light and the pseudo-kingdom of darkness. But you and I were born for such a time as this to partner with Christ in the power of the Holy Spirit. But this involves not only "being about our Father's business" and "occupying until He comes", but also being alert, discerning and prayerful watchmen on the wall who seek to warn others so that we all remain faithful to our Lord and not fall into deception.

I urge you to do further investigation on these serious issues of which I am merely skimming the surface. Below I will recommend some books, websites, and You-tube video clips to consider.

So stepping away from the emotionally charged topic of the 9/11 tragedy, which is but one event on a timeline of many game changing events, a small piece of a very large puzzle, we need to wrestle further with the issue of whether there really is a global elite who are behind such events whose ultimate objective is that of complete rule of the planet.

Could there really be an Anglo-American global elite with an agenda to take over the world with a New World Order?

Here are some **quotes** from very influential individuals that are but the tip of the iceberg:

In 1877, Cecil Rhode's Confessions of Faith states,

"At the present day I become a member of the Masonic order I see the wealth and power they possess the influence they hold and I think over their ceremonies and I wonder that a large body of men can devote themselves to what at times appear the most ridiculous and absurd rites without an object and without an end.

"The gleaming and dancing before one's eyes like a will-of-the-wisp at last frames itself into a plan. Why should we not form a secret society with but one object, the furtherance of the British Empire, for the bringing of the whole uncivilized world under British rule for the recovery of the United States, for the making the Anglo-Saxon race but one Empire. What a dream, but yet it is probable, it is possible...To forward such a scheme what a splendid help a secret society would be a society not openly acknowledged but who would work in secret for such an object."[13]

After decades of research, Dr. Stanley Monteith, a Christian and a retired medical doctor, has written a book called, Brotherhood of Darkness, in which he claims Cecil Rhodes and many other students had been radically impacted by and dedicated the rest of their lives to the vision articulated by the eloquent Oxford professor, John Ruskin. Along with his occult roots, Ruskin had caught the vision of a one world government under British rule from a famous poem, Locksley Hall, written by Lord Tennyson in 1842. Tennyson sought to convey his belief that Great Britain had a moral obligation to unite the world under British rule. Winston Churchill claimed the poem "the most wonderful of modern prophecies", and U.S. President Truman carried the poem in his wallet throughout his life. Here is the most important portion of Tennyson's poem, Locksley Hall:

> For I dipt into the future,
> far as human eye could see,
> Saw the Vision of the world,
> and all the wonder that would be;
> Heard the heavens fill with shouting
> and there rain'd a ghastly dew
> From the nations' airy navies
> grappling in the central blue;
>
> Till the war-drum throbb'd no longer,
> and the battle-flags were furl'd
> In the Parliament of man
> the Federation of the world.
> There the common sense of most
> shall hold a fretful realm in awe,
> And the kindly earth shall slumber,
> lapt in universal law.[14]

In 1913, prior to the passage of the Federal Reserve Act President Wilson's The New Freedom was published, in which he revealed:

"Since I entered politics, I have chiefly had men's views confided to me privately. Some of the biggest men in the U. S., in the field of commerce and manufacturing, are afraid of somebody, are afraid of something. They know that there is a power somewhere so organized, so subtle, so watchful, so interlocked, so complete, so pervasive, that they had better not speak above their breath when they speak in condemnation of it."[15]

H.G. Wells, in his 1939 book, The New World Order, claims, "Countless people will hate the New World Order and will die protesting against it."

James Warburg, son of Paul Warburg, on Feb. 17, 1950, gave testimony to the United States Senate Foreign Relations Committee declaring, "We shall have world government whether or not we like it. The question is only whether world government will be achieved by consent or conquest."[16]

Congressman Larry P. McDonald argued in 1976 that, "The drive of the Rockefellers and their allies is to create a one-world government combining supercapitalism and Communism under the same tent, all under their control... Do I mean conspiracy? Yes, I do. I am convinced there is such a plot, international in scope, generations old in planning, and incredibly evil in intent." The congressman was killed in the Korean Airlines 747 that was shot down by the Soviets in 1983.[17]

In 1987, the same year he launched perestroika, Mikhail Gorbachev boldly proclaimed, "In October 1917, we parted with the Old World, rejecting it once for all. We are moving toward a new world, the world of Communism. We shall never turn off that road."

In that same year he gave a speech before the Politburo declaring, "Gentlemen, comrades, do not be concerned about all you hear about glasnost and perestroika and democracy in the coming years. These are primarily for outward consumption. There will be no significant internal change within the Soviet Union, other than for cosmetic purposes. Our purpose is to disarm the Americans and let them fall asleep."

Ironically Gorbachev won the Nobel Peace Prize in 1990 for his work in dismantling Soviet communism and with his worldwide popularity, has gone on to establish the Gorbachev Foundation, which seeks to promote a socialistic/humanistic one world order, largely through the concerns of the environmental movement.[18]

Exactly ten years before 9/11, George H. W. Bush, in his UN speech Sept. 11, 1991, declared, "It is a big idea, a New World Order, where diverse nations are drawn together in common cause... When we are successful, and we will be, we have a real chance at this New World Order, an order in which a credible United Nations can use its peace-keeping role to fulfill the promise and vision of the UN's founders."

Walter Cronkite, in a speech at the World Federalist Association Meeting, October 19, 1999, said, "Pat Robertson has written in a book a few years ago that we should have a world government but only when the Messiah arrives (crowd laughs). He wrote: 'Any attempt to achieve world order before that time must be the work of the devil.' Well join me. I'm proud to sit here at the right hand of Satan."[19]

"By 2020, will be a one world government." So Ray Kurzweil, futurist and inventor, predicted in 1999. Kurzweil has had a thirty-year track record of fairly accurate projections. For instance he predicted the Internet for the 90s and 1998 to be the year that a computer would beat the world's best chess player. It happened a year earlier.[20]

David Rockefeller, in 2002, wrote in his Memoirs, "Some even believe we are part of a secret cabal working against the best interests of the United States...And of conspiring with others around the world to build a more integrated global political and economic structure - one world, if you will. If that's the charge, I stand guilty, and I am proud of it."[21]

Rockefeller has also claimed that, "We are on the verge of a global transformation. All we need is the right major crisis and the nations will accept the New World Order."

Henry Kissinger, in a January 5, 2009 interview stated, "I think his (Obama's) task will be to develop an overall strategy for America in this period when really a New World Order can be created. It's a great opportunity. It isn't just a crisis."[22]

Though not in chronological order with the previous quotes, let me give some excerpts from President John F. Kennedy's speech at the Waldorf-Astoria Hotel in New York before the American newspaper Publisher's Association, April 27, 1961:

"The very word "secrecy" is repugnant in a free and open society; and we are as a people inherently and historically opposed to secret societies, to secret oaths and to secret proceedings...Today no war has been declared — and however fierce the struggle may be, it may never be declared in the traditional fashion. Our way of life is under attack...We are opposed around the world by a monolithic and ruthless conspiracy that relies primarily on covert means for expanding its sphere of influence — on infiltration instead of invasion, on subversion instead of elections, on intimidation instead of free choice, on guerrillas by night instead of armies by day...It is a system which has conscripted vast human and material resources into the building of a tightly knit, highly efficient machine that combines military, diplomatic, intelligence, economic, scientific and political operations."[23]

Such a "shadow government" involves secret societies such as freemasonry and the Illuminati whose roots go back a number of centuries. Adam Weishaupt, a freemason and Jesuit, founded the Order of the Illuminati May 1, 1776 in Bavaria with the destruction of Christianity and governments and the forming of a world government as its purpose.

An argument can be made that these dark secret societies go back ultimately to the mystery religions and the arrogant and godless empire building of Nimrod of Babylon and the building of the tower of Babel. But with the dawning of the twentieth century, the plan for a New World Order within these secret organizations was further fortified with the establishment of a Round Table Group followed by its offshoots.

With the vast financial backing of the Rothschild family dynasty, British aristocrat and freemason, Cecil Rhodes, established a monopoly over the diamond and gold industry of South Africa and formed a Fabian socialistic secret society called the Round Table Group (other names given to this group will be mentioned shortly) in 1891, a secret society along the lines of the freemasonry and the Illuminati with inner and outer circles and a pyramid hierarchy with the dream of British rule extending throughout the world.[24]

Other branch secret societies or roundtable committees were formed as front organizations and think tanks throughout the twentieth century. In 1920-21, the Royal Institute of International Affairs in London and the Council on Foreign Relations in New York were established with global government agendas.

In 1945, after WW II, the United Nations was formed and the headquarters built in New York City thanks to the generosity of the Rockefeller family (who are key players in the global elite). Families such as the Rothschilds, Rockerfellers, Morgans, Carnegies, Harrimans, Schiffs and Warburgs have been involved in this NWO agenda for generations.

The American think tank, the Council of Foreign Relations, in a report found on their website, speaks of their goal of developing a similar union to Europe's with Mexico, U.S., and Canada, the North American Union and its one currency, possibly called the Amero.[25]

The Bilderberg group first met in 1954 at the Bilderberg hotel in Holland under the leadership of Prince Bernhard of the Netherlands. They (influential politicians, bankers and corporate business men and women) secretly meet once or twice a year in different locations. They were successful in bringing about the European Community. They and other round table groups seek to form a one world government through the means of incremental steps. The European Union is the first of five or possibly ten regions that they seek to establish on the road towards a one world order and global currency.

In 1968, the Club of Rome was organized. They have been instrumental in stressing the need for depopulation of the world and on the development of the European Union.

With the blessing of the Bilderbergers and the CFR, the Trilateral Commission was founded on July 1, 1973 through the initiatives of Zbigniew Brzezinski and David Rockefeller. Rockefeller, who became its first chairman, saw this new and more public organization as a means of deflecting public attention from the activities of the Council for Foreign Relations. The Trilateral Commission includes the United States, European Union, and Japan, the three largest economies of the world (at least at that time).[26]

Author Jim Marrs in his book, Rule by Secrecy, claims that these roundtable committees are modern secret societies that play an important role in national and international events. He suggests we take a look at recent past U.S. presidents and the people surrounding them.

Bill Clinton was connected to three of the most sinister roundtables: the Trilateral Commission, the Council on Foreign Relations and the Bilderbergers. President George H.W. Bush was a Trilateralist, a CFR member and a brother in the Order of Skull and Bones (his father, Prescott, and son, George W. Bush, have also been members of Skull and Bones). Ronald Reagan did not officially belong to these groups but his administrations were chock full of members. And Jimmy Carter's administration was so packed full of members of the Trilateral Commission that even mainstream media began to talk.[27]

It appears quite evident that the so-called "most powerful leader in the world", the president of the United States, turns out to be more like a pawn, a puppet in the hands of the socialist puppet master elite, whether he or she be Democrat or Republican.

John Coleman, former intelligence agent of British MI6 and prolific researcher and author, claims that behind this plethora of secretive round table branches is one all powerful and concealed head office called "the Committee of 300." This Fabian socialist elite and aristocratic group (with Cecil Rhodes and company) has been the ultimate controlling body that has run the world for at least the last one hundred years and has roots in such organizations as the Illuminati and the opium trade run British East India Company.[28]

This controlling executive body of three hundred members, which Coleman claims is also called the "Olympians" makes the decisions then gives them to the Royal Institute for International Affairs and are executed by such groups as: the Council on Foreign Relations, Bilderberg Group, Trilateral Commission, National Security Council, and Club of Rome.

Coleman lists various tax-exempt foundations such as Ford, Carnegie, and Rockefeller, research institutions such as MIT and Stanford, and many other organizations that are useful instruments to further the elite group's agenda of dismantling Christianity and the U.S. Constitution with an endgame of the establishment of a socialistic global government, global currency and one world religion.

Coleman also lists what he believes to be many past and present members in his book, The Conspirator's Hierarchy: The Committee of 300. Here is but a very small sample of that list: Cecil Rhodes, Lord Alfred Milner (who gave leadership to the Rhodes Trust and secret society after Rhode's death in 1902), Arthur Balfour, the Rothschild family, various European royal dynasties and black nobility families, Aldous Huxley, Sir Bertrand Russell, H.G. Wells, Winston Churchill, Lord Thompson, Henry Kissinger, David Rockefeller and George H. W. Bush.[29]

Dr. Stanley Monteith believes that this same elite roundtable formed in the late 1800s with freemasons, occultists, Fabian socialists and British ruling aristocracy called themselves "the Group" or "the Band". It was a "Brotherhood of Darkness" secret society. He too claims that Cecil Rhodes (of Rhodes scholarship fame) was key in the forming of this secret society. Monteith confirms that in later years famous British figures like George Bernard Shaw, Bertrand Russell and H.C. Wells have been party to this dream of an Anglo-Saxon led socialist world government and have promoted it through their writings.

During the 20th century, four thousand and six hundred young men have gone to Oxford under a Rhode's scholarship where they were educated in socialism and world government. They became part of a unique group committed to changing the world. Bill Clinton was one of them. Another Rhodes scholar was Dean Rusk who became a leader in the Rockefeller Foundation on more than one occasion as well as in the State Department, playing an instrumental role in seeing communism come to China as well as American soldiers into the Korean and Vietnamese Wars.[30]

Monteith draws substantially from a Professor Caroll Quigley of Georgetown University, who thoroughly researched this for some twenty years and published it in 1966 under the title, Tragedy and Hope, by McMillan publishers.[31]

This arrogant ruling elite group who believe they are those most qualified to lead earth's citizens, is deeply anti-Semitic, anti-Christian and anti-God. Satan and his demonic principalities and minions control and drive these individuals and this godless agenda of global dominion and feeds and empowers it through such means as: the ancient mystery religions, the illuminati, freemasonry, the new age movement, humanistic atheism, Skull and Bones, and Bohemian Grove.

I have mentioned the word "socialist" to describe this British/American global elite. At the risk of being overly simplistic, let me elaborate on this ideology of socialism and how it compares to communism. Although they are both based on The Communist Manifesto of 1848, written by Karl Marx (who some claim was a Satanist), their means of achieving the same goals differ. According to Lenin, communism is socialism in a hurry. It is a direct and violent means of revolution. Socialism on the other hand, takes its time towards the same goal. "It is a movement governed by stealth."[32]

For several decades Americans had been conditioned to be distracted with the cold war (until 1989). While everyone was focused on the communist threat from Moscow, socialism had been free to worm its way into the very fabric of Washington and the American educational system.

The Council on Foreign Relations, the American branch of the socialist global elite, has been able to advance its agenda quickly and with relative ease. During the 1920s and 30s it gained considerable control of the Democratic party and by the 1940s made considerable headway into the Republican party. For decades now, every administration has been stacked with CFR, Bilderberger, and Trilateral Commission members, regardless of what party is in power (and CIA and FBI and other intelligence agencies are under their control). Regarding the CFR, Gary Kah states, "Their hope was to get Americans to the point where entering a world government would seem as natural and American as baseball and apple pie."[33]

John Coleman, in his book, One World Order Socialist Dictatorship, quotes Richard Gardner, a leading American socialist, in Foreign Affairs, the journal of the Council on Foreign Relations, April 1974: "We will build the New World Order piece by piece right under their noses (the American people). The house of the New World Order will have to be built from the bottom up rather than from the top down. An end run around sovereignty, eroding it piece by piece, will accomplish much more than the old fashioned frontal attack."

Coleman goes on to say, "Socialism is inherently evil because it forces people to accept deliberately engineered changes they have neither requested nor desired. The power of Socialism is disguised in soothing terms and hides behind a mask of humanitarianism."[34]

If such a socialist elite group with a globalist agenda truly exists, it could be argued, then they would need to gain control of the influential sectors or mountains of any society: the world's money, energy, food and water, healthcare, governments, religion, the arts, education and media.

If someone would dare take the time and be willing to go down the rabbit hole and do due diligence, I believe that person could not help but find some very sobering and compelling evidence that points in this direction. We will find that the elite have already infiltrated and taken control of these areas, these mountains of influence to move things towards their end goal:

money: central banking system, Federal Reserve, IMF, World Bank, Bank of International Settlements, multinational corporations, tax-exempt foundations, Fabian socialist teaching influencing monetary policies through the London School of Economics

energy: oil, gas, coal, nuclear energy, (suppressing free energy)

food and water: agribusiness, world trade, water sources

politics: socialistically and globalistically groomed government leaders, United Nations, the think tanks of: the Council on Foreign Relations, Bilderbergers, Club of Rome and Trilateral Commission, the military-industrial complex, NATO, Bohemian Grove, Aspen Institute, most labour unions etc., taking incremental steps towards global government by seeking to establish five to ten regions of which the European Union is the first. (North American Union next?)

health: pharmaceutical industry, medical schools, research, (suppressing natural alternatives)

indoctrination: Rockefeller financed and John Dewey established a humanistic compulsory standardized education in America and American media- the major TV networks, newspapers, magazines and many book publishers are owned and controlled by a handful of mega corporations (largely Rockefeller connected), Tavistock Institute of Human Relations, censoring the internet is in process

control dissent: undermining of Judea-Christian moral, marriage, and family values, population control, the Patriot Act, presidential executive orders, surveillance, RFID chips[35]

religion: pantheistic new age movement, freemasonry (with its masonic temples throughout the land, its symbols permeating the U.S. dollar bill, Washington D.C. architecture and their gift of the Statue of Liberty at America's gateway), World Council of Churches (1948), inter-faith movement (including the Vatican), United Religions initiative (2000), environmental movement (such as the Gorbachev Foundation) with a one world humanistic religion and government in mind.[36]

We can't do justice to these various topics in just one chapter so I'll leave it to you to check things out further if you desire. But let's look briefly at just a couple of areas.

Follow the Money

In 1922, Henry Ford stated, "It is well enough that people of the nation do not understand our banking and monetary system, for if they did, I believe there would be a revolution before tomorrow morning."

"Give me control over a nation's currency and I care not who makes its laws," bragged Baron Mayor Amschel Rothschild.[37]

"(The banks) are still the most powerful lobby on Capitol Hill, and they, frankly, own the place," observed Senator Dick Durban, on WJJG Radio 1530 AM, April 2009.[38]

In 1913, the Federal Reserve System was established by trickery in Congress just before Christmas after many had gone home. This was the result of the planning that came out of a secret financial leaders' gathering in November 1910 on Jekyll Island. They devised a scheme to create money out of nothing, a financial slight of hand called fractional reserve banking system, which makes them a lot of money. In the process the people (and governments) become debt slaves to the elite. The Federal Reserve, which is controlled primarily by the Rothschild, Rockefeller and Morgan dynasties, determines the interest rates on loans. It is a privately owned central banking system cleverly disguised as a public government system. It is neither federal nor a reserve. It is unaccountable and unelected.

American Christian economist, Norm Franz, states that, "It was at that time that the U.S. Congress lost its constitutional control of America's monetary system, which began a new era of control and manipulation of the financial markets. In 1916, just three years after the Federal Reserve Act was passed, President Woodrow Wilson admitted that: "...the growth of the nation...and all our activities are in the hands of a few men...We have come to be one of the worst ruled; one of the most completely controlled and dominated governments in the civilized world...no longer a government by conviction and the free vote of the majority, but a government by opinion and duress of small groups of dominant men."[39]

On the back of a U.S. one dollar bill you will find a masonic symbol, which consists of an unfinished pyramid with the all-seeing eye of Osiris or Baal above it. The capstone represents the elite who will complete the picture. Underneath the pyramid is written "Novus Ordo Seclorum," which means "The New Order of the Ages" (or The New World Order) in Latin. This has been on the one dollar bill since 1935 and placed there during Franklin D. Roosevelt's administration. Roosevelt himself was either a 32nd or 33rd degree mason and a close associate of the Council for Foreign Relations.[40]

According to the documentary, Thrive, the wealth gap between the rich and the poor is growing. Globally the richest two percent own more than fifty percent of the world's assets but in the United States, the richest one percent own more than ninety percent of the assets.[41]

Interesting that Forbes list of billionaires has the richest people in the world as Carlos Slim of Mexico (net worth of sixty-nine billion), then Bill Gates (sixty-one billion) followed by Warren Buffett (forty-four billion), both of United States. No one dares draw attention to families like the Morgans or the Rockefellers whose assets may conservatively be several trillion dollars or the Rothschild dynasty in the tens if not hundreds of trillions. Regarding the Rockefellers, Wikipedia states, "The records of the family archives relating to both the family and individual members' net worth is closed to researchers."[42]

Much of the wealth of these families is conveniently sheltered from taxation through foundations that are often used to further their globalist objectives under humanitarian appearances. And IMF as well as government foreign aid given to impoverished third world countries often increases control over those nation's resources and keeps them enslaved particularly to the mega corporations. The ungodly Babylonian banking system continues to unleash injustices and inequalities around the world and increased wealth and power in the hands of the elite few. In the minds of the global elite, the end (a warless globalized utopia) justifies the means.

Population Control

The following are a few quotes by influential individuals:

"We don't want the word to get out that we want to exterminate the Negro population." Margaret Sanger, a theosophist and eugenicist, founder of Planned Parenthood, Dec. 19, 1939.[43]

"The undeniably feeble-minded should, indeed, not only be discouraged but prevented from propagating their kind." Margaret Sanger

"Eugenic sterilization is an urgent need...We must prevent multiplication of this bad stock." Margaret Sanger

"I do not pretend that birth control is the only way in which population can be kept from increasing. There are others, which, one must suppose, opponents of birth control would prefer. War, as I remarked a moment ago, has hitherto been disappointing in this respect, but perhaps bacteriological war may prove more effective. If a Black Death could be spread throughout the world once in every generation survivors could procreate freely without making the world too full. There would be nothing in this to offend the consciences of the devout or to restrain the ambitions of nationalists. The state of affairs might be somewhat unpleasant, but what of that? Really high-minded people are indifferent to happiness, especially other people's." Bertrand Russell (1872-1970), socialist and philosopher.[44]

"Maintain humanity under 500,000,000 in perpetual balance with nature,"

is one of ten statements on the anonymously commissioned Georgia Guidestones, considered by many as a NWO version of the Ten Commandments.[45]

After his visit to China in 1973, David Rockefeller wrote an article, titled, From a China Traveler, which appeared in the NY Times on August 10, 1973. This article, not only in its lack of condemnation, but of its applause of Chairman Mao's leadership, conveys something regarding Rockefeller's take on the expendability of human life for a cause. Chairman Mao had slaughtered some forty to sixty million Chinese people in the process of establishing his atheistic communist empire (comparable to Stalin in Russia). Rockefeller wrote:

"One is impressed immediately by the sense of national harmony... There is a very real and pervasive dedication to Chairman Mao and Maoist principles. Whatever the price of the Chinese Revolution, it has obviously succeeded...The enormous social advances of China have benefited greatly from the singleness of ideology and purpose... The social experiment in China under Chairman Mao's leadership is one of the most important and successful in history."[46]

Julian Huxley, brother to the more famous writer, Aldous Huxley of Brave New World fame, was an evolutionary biologist and eugenicist and prominent member of the British Eugenics Society, committed to population control. Their grandfather, Thomas Henry Huxley, was a friend and supporter of Charles Darwin and a proponent of evolution.

At the instigation of the Club of Rome, a UN sponsored Earth Summit was held in Rio de Janeiro, Brazil in 1992 (with several follow ups, the most recent being June 2012). It formed the UN Agenda 21, which calls for, among other things, a reduction of population (in layman's terms, a culling of the useless eaters) to protect the environment and Mother Earth. Of course we have all heard the rumblings of carbon taxation coming due to the so-called global climate change problem. Such a mechanism of generating income could very well assist in financing a new level of government, a New World Order, that will be presented as the global solution to this and other global problems.

Other forms of Control

The American government's powers continue to expand at the expense of personal freedoms. We see this in the Patriot Act, which changed fifteen different laws and that was rushed through very manipulatively and hastily just six weeks after 9/11, with just a handful getting a chance to read the three hundred and forty-two pages before voting. We see this in a string of Presidential Executive Orders signed by Presidents Bush and Obama during their respective terms in office. One of the most recent executive orders was the NDAA that was signed by President Obama on Dec. 31, 2011 when no one was looking that takes a further step towards a Police State.[47]

In the Agribusiness, Monsanto, founded in 1901 in St. Louis, Missouri, now has ninety percent of the Genetically Modified Organism (GMO) market. The crops are genetically modified to resist the application of their highly toxic weed killer called Round UP. Monsanto had also produced the deadly chemicals, Agent Orange and PCBs, which were banned in the early 1980s. Monsanto has also developed and in 1994 began to sell to farmers a bovine growth hormone, which is injected into cows for an increase in milk production by twenty percent. Questionable safety testing issues regarding GMOs and this growth hormone are rightly being raised.[48]

Through the Bill & Melinda Gates Foundation, Gates seeks to help in humanitarian ways in terms of global health care and food. This week he is in the news because of his challenge a year ago to universities to create a new and innovative toilet in an effort to improve worldwide sanitation. About 2.5 billion people do not have access to modern toilets. The winners were announced this week (August 2012). So we applaud Bill and Melinda's efforts to improve world health conditions. But some have seen their generous humanitarian efforts as bringing mixed and questionable results. Evidence points to connections with both Planned Parenthood through his father, Bill Sr., (issues of population reduction) as well as with Monsanto and its increasing control of GMO crops and seeds in Africa and throughout the world.[49]

Censorship appears to be on the rise. A CNN article, June 18, 2012, by John D. Sutter titled: "Google reports "alarming" rise in government censorship requests" states:

"Western governments, including the United States, appear to be stepping up efforts to censor Internet search results and YouTube videos, according to a "transparency report" released by Google. It's alarming not only because free expression is at risk, but because some of these requests come from countries you might not suspect - Western democracies not typically associated with censorship", Dorothy Chou, a senior policy analyst at Google, wrote in a blog post on Sunday night..."In the last half of 2011, U.S. agencies asked Google to remove 6,192 individual pieces of content from its search results, blog posts or archives of online videos, according to the report. That's up 718 percent compared with the 757 such items that U.S agencies asked Google to remove in the six months prior."[50]

With increasingly turbulent days ahead, national sovereignty and the U.S. Constitution being relinquished piece-by-piece to global governance and personal rights and freedoms eroding under our noses, it may all be a recipe for disaster - civil unrest and martial law. It is conservatively estimated that there are two hundred and seventy million guns in the hands of civilians, making Americans the most heavily armed people in the world per capita. The last global small arms survey showed there are eighty-eight guns for every one hundred Americans. Yemen is second at fifty-four for every one hundred.[51]

The Department of Homeland Security (DHS), according to some sources, is preparing for civil unrest in various ways, one of which is they have ordered four hundred and fifty million rounds of hollow point ammunition in the first half of 2012. Things could get really ugly and bloody on the streets of America in the very near future.[52]

A growing number of American citizens are fittingly expressing concern about Homeland Security and their watch list of potential terrorists supposedly getting longer to include such groups as anti-abortionists (which is better termed, Pro-lifers) and right-wing Christians fixated on end-time issues. And while the majority of Americans and Westerners blissfully sleep away, a few are waking up to the subtle advancements in surveillance technology (personal info access on the Internet and big brother cameras watching you, including drones) and government agencies' greater legal latitude to use them.

There are also rumblings of coming martial law (with the U.S. Constitution suspended at least temporarily) and possible FEMA camps being established throughout the United States. It is hard to sift fact from fiction in some of these matters but we should remain alert and vigilant without being controlled by fear and paranoia.

Another potential form of control is the issue of controlling the weather. The American program is called, HAARP, High-frequency Active Auroral Research Program. Managed by the U.S. Air Force and Navy, it is the world's largest radio broadcasting station, built in the early 1990s near Gakona, Alaska. It is comprised of one hundred and eighty antennas about seventy-two feet tall. As one steerable antenna, it can direct the energy of 3.6 million watts into the ionosphere. That is seventy-two thousand times more powerful than the largest legal commercial radio station (fifty thousand watts) in United States.[53]

According to Jerry E. Smith, in his book, Weather Warfare, the U.S. military claims they are just studying the physical and electrical properties for civilian and defense purposes but in actuality they are heating up the atmosphere and causing weather changes. It can indirectly change the jet streams causing floods in one area and droughts in another as well as steer hurricanes and initiate earthquakes. In other words, it has the potential for weather warfare with deniability to go with it.

HAARP is one of five located around the world. Three are in the United States: Gakona, Alaska, Fairbanks, Alaska and in Arecibo, Puerto Rico. The other two are in Russia and Norway. Working in tandem, they can change the weather anywhere in the world. Nicolas Tesla experimented with such technology a century ago and was able to manipulate the weather.

Because Extremely Low Frequency radio waves (ELF) happen to be the same frequency that the human brain functions at, another possible application of this technology is that of the ultimate global mind control device.[54]

According to Smith, the Russians began directing a microwave beam at the U.S. Embassy in Moscow in the 1960s. They spent the next forty years using the workers in the embassy as guinea pigs for their electromagnetic radiation experiments. Then starting in 1976, the Russians began using a Tesla Magnifying Transmitter, an early model of a HAARP device, to send a series of broadcasts aimed at America that became known around the world as the "Russian Woodpecker." The off and on signal was like a woodpecker tapping.

Some scientists give the conservative and official line that it is an "over-the-horizon" radar system. Some scientists claim it is used as a weather weapon. Some see it as a prototype for a Star Wars weapons and shield system while a few others claim it is for mind control. It has the potential for all these possible applications and so much more. This is just the tip of the iceberg. HAARP demonstrates that the Americans followed the Russians in seeking to capitalize upon Nicolas Tesla's work and this top secret work would explain why Tesla's name, research and experiments have virtually vanished from American history books.[55]

We would do well to take President Eisenhower's advice in his farewell address on January 17, 1961:

"...In the councils of government, we must guard against the acquisition of unwarranted influence, whether sought or unsought, by the military-industrial complex. The potential for the disastrous rise of misplaced power exists and will persist.

"We must never let the weight of this combination endanger our liberties or democratic processes. We should take nothing for granted. Only an alert and knowledgeable citizenry can compel the proper meshing of the huge industrial and military machinery of defense with our peaceful methods and goals, so that security and liberty may prosper together...The prospect of domination of the nation's scholars by Federal employment, project allocations, and the power of money is ever present – and is gravely to be regarded. Yet, in holding scientific research and discovery in respect, as we should, we must also be alert to the equal and opposite danger that public policy could itself become the captive of a scientific-technological elite."[56]

Even a brief look at this seemingly un-ending pile of information can be quite overwhelming and despairing. After studying this heavy subject matter quite extensively for over a year, I was getting fairly heavy hearted. But in 2010, the Lord directed me to Psalm 37 and spoke clearly to me while soaking in the presence of the Lord during one of our sessions at our church sponsored house of prayer.

I was struck with the fact that three times in Psalm 37 God commands us not to fret or be anxious regarding evil men and their schemes. Five times He promises to give the land to the meek and the righteous and thirteen times He promises obliteration of the wicked that plan and scheme to gain wealth and power at the expense of others. In fact, the Lord laughs at them for He knows their day is coming!

This revelation deeply impacted me at a time when I was getting quite impressed with what the enemy was capable of doing and causing fear and anxiety to grip my heart. This helped to get me centered once again so my heart could be overflowing with awe and wonder and joyful confidence in how glorious and sovereign our God is and how decisively victorious He will be at the climax of history.

The Lord also showed me that like driving a car, it is wisest to spend the majority of your time gazing out the front windshield and focusing on where you are going. But from time to time, it is paramount that you take a look in the rearview mirror and side mirrors to see what is going on around you. But if you focus too much and for too long at those rear and side views, you could put yourself and loved ones with you in harm's way because you are not giving sufficient attention to where you are going.

So regarding what the enemy, Satan, is doing all around us, we do not want to be naive or in denial. But neither do we want to be so fixated and fascinated by what the devil is up to that our faith and trust in our sovereign Lord and what He is doing be overshadowed. We don't want to be like the ten spies in the promised land who came back with a bad report and said we cannot take the land for there are giants in the land and we feel like grasshoppers in comparison. Like Joshua and Caleb we want to confidently declare that with God in the equation, the enemy will surely be defeated.

We are living in exceptionally exciting times when the Kingdom of light and the pseudo-kingdom of darkness are increasingly colliding with sparks flying. Satan knows his days are numbered and like an injured animal with its back against the wall, is both dangerous and desperate. He will lash out with great intensity but our victorious King Jesus will rise up and the glory of the Lord will increase over all the earth. We truly are living in dangerous days but they are drenched in God ordained destiny. The global elite has a plan. But God has a better plan!

So with joy and confidence in our hearts that Jesus ultimately wins over all the demonically inspired competition, in the next chapter we will address the pressing issue of the Islamic attempt to bring the earth's citizens under submission to the false god, Allah and shariah law.

Recommended Resources:

Books:

The New World Order, Pat Robertson, Word Publishing, 1991
En Route to Global Occupation, Gary H. Kah, Huntington House Pub., 1992

The New World Religion, Gary H. Kah, Hope Int'l Pub., 1999
Brotherhood of Darkness, Stanley Monteith, Radio Liberty, 2000
Are You Ready? Paul McGuire, M House Pub., L.A., 2005
The Conspirator's Hierarchy: The Committee of 300, John Coleman,
Global Review Pub., Inc.
Las Vegas, Nevada, 4th edition, 2006
One World Order Socialist Dictatorship, John Coleman, World in
Review, 1998/2008
The Rise of the Fourth Reich:The Secret Societies that Threaten to
take over America, Jim Marrs, WM, Harpercollins Pub., 2008
The Revolution, A Manifesto, Ron Paul, Grand Central Pub. 2008
The Day the Dollar Died, Paul McGuire, M House Pub., L.A., 2009
Money & Wealth in the New Millennium, Norm Franz, Whitestone
Press, 2001
American Conspiracies, Jesse Ventura, Skyhorse Pub., 2011
63 Documents the Government Doesn't Want You to Read, Jesse
Ventura, Skyhorse Pub., 2012
Exteme Prejudice, Susan Lindauer, Create Space, 2010
9/11 Ten Years Later, David Ray Griffin, Olive Branch Press, 2011
(and other books by this theologian author, such as: The New Pearl
Harbor, Pearl Harbor Revisited, Debunking 9/11 Debunking, The
Mysterious Collapse of World Trade Center 7)

Websites:

God TV, "God on Demand" section, Apocalypse and the End Times,
Series 1, Gary Kah part 1 & 2, Barry McGuire, part 1 & 2, http://
www.god.tv/node/185, and Barry McGuire in Series 2, part 1 & 2:
http://www.god.tv/node/202
the end of the American Dream, http://endoftheamericandream.
com/archives/12-pictures-that-demonstrate-how-the-new-world-
order-openly-mocks-us
Thrive movement, free energy technology and its suppression by
the global elite (banking, oil, corporation families) who control the
industries of energy, food, health, education, media and banking
http://www.thrivemovement.com/the_problem-gda

A Chronological History of the NWO, D.L. Cuddy, http://www.crossroad.to/Excerpts/chronologies/cuddy-nwo.htm
article by Susan Lindauer, Digital Journal, http://digitaljournal.com/blog/14311#ixzz1zgTR6hza
article: "Totalitarianism:The National Defense Authorization Act (NDAA), Latest Chapter in the Road towards "Police State USA", http://www.globalresearch.ca/index.php?context=va&aid=28611
9/11 truth website: www.911truth.org,
website: 911docs.net, Free 9/11 Documentaries & Videos, http://www.911docs.net/loose_change_final_cut.php
Architects and Engineers for 911 Truth, www.ae911truth.org
Trunews.com (Christian news network, alternative news)
WND.com (America's Independent News Network)

DVDs:

Shadow Government, How the Global Elite Plan to Destroy Democracy and Your Freedom, Grant R. Jeffrey, 2009
Global Government Unleashed, Gary Kah, Steeling the Mind Bible conference, Compass Int.
Thrive:What on Earth will it take? Documentary, narrated by Foster Gamble (non-Christian perspective but valuable insights)
Endgame: Blueprint for global Enslavement, Alex Jones, 2007
Invisible Empire:A NWO Defined, Jason Bermas, Infowars, 2010
Expelled: No Intelligence Allowed, documentary hosted by Ben Stein, 2008 (conspiracy by the science establishment & educational system to only promote atheistic evolution & marginalize academics who see evidence of intelligent design in nature)

You-tube videos:

9/11 Cognitive Dissonance: Why People Are Afraid of 9/11 Truth http://www.youtube.com/watch?v=iGGXae4c3hY&feature=related
David Ray Griffin: 9-11 and Nationalistic Faith, uploaded Sept. 26, 2011 (accessed May 7, 2012) http://www.youtube.com/watch?v=wLnKiLonODk

"9/11:Explosive Evidence - Experts Speak out",uploaded Feb.5,2012,(or www.911Expertsspeak.org) http://www.youtube.com/watch?v=nBCu_pvhnzQ Documentary by Leonard Ulrich, called NWO: Secret Societies and Biblical Prophecy Vol. 1 (Revised), uploaded Mar. 19, 2011, http://www.youtube.com/watch?v=kg8S40E-LQM Documentary, Thrive, What on Earth Will it Take? narrated by Foster Gamble, 2011, http://www.youtube.com/watch?v=lEV5AFFcZ-s 9/11 you-tube video: "CIA whistle blower exposes everything! "Extreme Prejudice" (her book), Former CIA Asset, Susan Lindauer, Sept. 23, 2011, http://www.youtube.com/watch?v=68LUHa_-OlA&feature=related (accessed May 7, 2012)
"The world according to Monsato, GMO food Documentary", May 18, 2011, http://www.youtube.com/watch?v=Rml_k005tsU
Christian prophet Terry Bennett, part 1 of 5, word for the next 20 years starting 2008, first 7 years with economic upheaval, next 7 years political upheaval, last 7 years religious upheaval http://www.youtube.com/watch?v=MBfKTeYevD4

Notes:

[1] Jim Marrs, The Rise of the Fourth Reich, HarperCollins, 2008, pp. 149 - 177, also cites Linda Hunt's 1991 book, Secret Agenda: The United States Government, Nazi Scientists, and Project Paperclip, 1945-1990.

[2] Stanley Monteith, Brotherhood of Darkness, Radio Liberty, 2000, pp. 19, 44-47, 53, 62, 66-72, 91.

[3] Norm Franz, Money & Wealth in the New Millennium, Whitestone Press, 2001, pp. 58-60.

[4] Ken Blue, Authority to Heal, I.V. Press, 1987, pp. 92-94.

[5] David Pytches, Come Holy Spirit, Hodder & Stoughton, 1985, pp. 19-20.

[6] BBC reports collapse of WTC 7 too early, http://www.youtube.com/watch?v=oE2XpLXqs_8 also "WTC 7 Foreknowledge", http://www.youtube.com/watch?v=N1LetB0z8_o

[7] Ian Henshall, 9/11 Revealed, The New Evidence, Carroll & Graf Pub., 2007, p. 174., also "Is There a Secret to the 9/11 Insurance

Battle? by Steve Watson, Mar. 14/07, Infowars.net http://infowars. net/articles/march2007/140307Silverstein.htm;

[8.] You-tube video of the actual collapse of WTC 7 at around 5:20 p.m., http://www.youtube.com/watch?v=Zv7BImVvEyk

[9.] The Open Chemical Physics Journal, 2009, 2, pp. 7-31, 'Active Thermitic Material Discovered in Dust from the 9/11 World Trade Center Catastrophe', p. 29, PDF, http://www.benthamscience.com/ open/tocpj/articles/V002/7TOCPJ.htm

[10.] Ibid., pp. 25, 26.

[11.] 9/11 Truth movement, wikipedia website: http://en.wikipedia.org/ wiki/9/11_Truth_movement

[12.] Susan Lindauer, Extreme Prejudice, Create Space, 2010 (her story as a CIA Asset, whistleblower regarding 9/11 and Iraq War) see also: http://digitaljournal.com/blog/14311#ixzz1zgTR6hza

[13.] Cecil Rhode's quote from Confessions of Faith, 1877, Stanley Monteith, p. 117 & website: "1877: Cecil Rhodes, "Confession of Faith" - University of Oregon, http://pages.uoregon.edu/kimball/ Rhodes-Confession.htm (accessed August 17/12).

[14.] Stanley Monteith, Brotherhood of Darkness, p. 13.

[15.] A Chronological History of the New World Order, D.L. Cuddy, http://www.crossroad.to/Excerpts/chronologies/cuddy-nwo.htm

[16.] http://en.wikipedia.org/wiki/James_Warburg

[17.] Seed of Truth, NWO quotes, http://seedoftruth.com/#/new-world-order/4539694829

[18.] Gary Kah, The New World Religion, Hope Int'l Pub., 1999, p. 135.

[19.] Walter Cronkite speech, You-tube documentary by Leonard Ulrich, called NWO: Secret Societies and Biblical Prophecy Vol. 1, revised, uploaded Mar. 19/11, at 10:30 min., (accessed June 5/12). http://www.youtube.com/watch?v=kg8S40E-LQM also: "World Federalist Association - Walter Cronkite, NWO, WTF", at 7 min., http://www.youtube.com/watch?v=inu9vKXsrFA

[20.] Wikipedia, Predictions made by Ray Kurzweil, http://en.wikipedia. org/wiki/Predictions_made_by_Ray_Kurzweil

[21.] David Rockefeller, Memoirs, Random House, 2002, p. 405.

22. Paul McGuire, The Day the Dollar Died, M House Pub., 2009, p. 8, Henry Kissinger, January 5/09 interview on the New York Stock Exchange with CNBC's Mark Raines.
23. John F. Kennedy speech, April 27/61, http://wakeup-world. com/2011/05/20/jfks-speech-on-secret-societies/
24. Jim Marrs, Rule By Secrecy, Harper-Collins Pub., 2000, p. 86.
25. "Building a North American Community", a 59 page report from the Council for Foreign Relations, 2005, http://www.cfr.org/canada/building-north-american-community/p8102
26. Jim Marrs, Rule by Secrecy, pp. 22, 23.
27. Ibid., pp. 21, 22.
28. John Coleman, The Conspirator's Hierarchy:The Committee of 300, 4th ed. Global Review Pub., 2006, pp. 9,10,34.
29. Ibid., pp. 445-451.
30. Stanley Monteith, pp. 106, 110, 22, 23, 53.
31. Ibid., pp. 106-107, also You-tube: "Brotherhood of Darkness Secret Society"1997, http://www.youtube.com/watch?v=2QhVtlZt Yok&feature=relmfu
32. John Coleman, One World Order Socialist Dictatorship, World in Review, 1998/2008, pp. 7-11.
33. Gary Kah, Enroute to Global Occupation, Huntingdon House Pub., 1992, p. 36.
34. John Coleman, One World Order Socialist Dictatorship, p. 7.
35. Documentary, Thrive: What On Earth Will it Take? Foster Gamble, follows the money, 2011, http://www.thrivemovement. com/the_movie
36. Gary H. Kah, The New World Religion, pp. 206-223.
37. Thrive documentary, at 1:08:09 minutes.
38. Ibid., at 1:05:13 min.
39. Norm Franz, Money & Wealth, pp. 66, 67.
40. Gary H. Kah, En Route to Global Occupation, p. 34.
41. Thrive: What On Earth Will it Take? 1:02 min.
42. Forbes List, http://www.forbes.com/billionaires/ ; Wikipedia, http://en.wikipedia.org/wiki/Rockefeller_family
43. Margaret Sanger, http://margaretsanger.blogspot.ca/2011/05/six-quotes-hint-why-planned-parenthood.html

44. http://www.infowars.com/eugenics-quotes-from-lofty-ideals-to-highly-centralized-population-control-run-by-psychopathic-maniacs/ see also: http://thesustainablehome.blogspot.ca/2009/07/alarming-number-of-population-reduction.html

45. http://en.wikipedia.org/wiki/Georgia_Guidestones

46. Stanley Monteith, pp. 45, 46, citing Dennis Cuddy, Now is the Dawning of the New Age New World Order, Hearthstone Pub., 1991, pp 117-18; see also newspaper article: http://www.scribd.com/doc/15932367/From-a-China-Traveler-By-David-Rockefeller-New-York-Times-August-10-1973

47. Global Research, Totalitarianism: The National Defense Authorization Act (NDAA), Latest Chapter In the Road towards "Police State USA", by Sherwood Ross, http://www.globalresearch.ca/index.php?context=va&aid=28611

48. The World According to Monsanto, uploaded March 18/12, http://www.youtube.com/watch?v=DhHbm_Z_pW8

49. Bill Gates Foundation, http://www.organicconsumers.org/articles/article_21606.cfm http://www.naturalnews.com/035105_Bill_Gates_Monsanto_eugenics.html#ixzz1sWFkBtm1

50. CNN article, "Google reports alarming rise in government censorship requests", John D. Sutter, June 19, 2012, http://edition.cnn.com/2012/06/18/tech/web/google-transparency-report/index.html?hpt=hp_t3

51. CNN article: Analysis: why gun controls are off the agenda in America, by Jonathan Mann, July 23, 2012 http://edition.cnn.com/2012/07/23/world/americas/analysis-colorado-shooting-mann/index.html?iid=article_sidebar

52. Susanne Posel, "DHS Preparing for Disaster: Buying Bullets, Food Supplies, Activating Detention Camps", Apr. 10/12, http://occupycorporatism.com/dhs-preparing-for-disaster-buying-bullets-food-supplies-activating-detention-camps/

53. Jerry E. Smith, Weather Warfare, Adventuresunlimitedpress.comp, 2006, p. 159.

54. Ibid., p 159.

55. Jerry E. Smith, HAARP:the Ultimate Weapon of Conspiracy, AUP, 1998, pp. 49, 50; also: You-tube, "HAARP"- Chilling Information You Really Need To See! 6:51 min., Dec. 1, 2010, http://www.

youtube.com/watch?v=3MUNVuMkHh8 ; HAARP WEATHER CONTROL, 10:58 min., uploaded Nov. 14/09, http://www.youtube. com/watch?v=2TdIkI1ory8

[56.] Pres. Eisenhower's farewell speech, Jan. 17/61, http://mcadams. posc.mu.edu/ike.htm (accessed Aug. 17/12).

Chapter 18

Towards a Counterfeit and Temporary New world Order

Part 2

An Islamic Agenda to Subject the World to Shariah law and a Global Islamic State

I n the chapter on revival we touched on the fact that Muslims around the world are turning to Christ in record numbers. In Iran alone, estimates vary between four and seven million who are now followers of Jesus! We rejoice in this news. God loves Muslims and we are called to love them (not their false religion) as well. Many of these conversions follow after a spiritual dream or vision of Christ. With coming waves of revival, we anticipate even greater numbers of precious Muslims finding faith and freedom in Jesus Christ. Let us pray and work to that end.

Islamization of Europe and the West

That said however, we cannot ignore the fact that the second largest religion in the world (1.5 billion) is, at the moment, growing faster than Christianity, especially in western countries. This is primarlly due to the extremely high birth rates among Muslims (and the decline of Christianity in the West up to this point).

The birth rate in western nations is somewhere between 1.1 (Spain) and 1.8 (France) children per adult woman. The European Union nations average 1.3. However, a society cannot be sustained beyond one generation once it drops below 2.1. The German government, as of 2008, has admitted, "The fall in the (German) population can no longer be stopped. Its downward spiral is no longer reversible...It will be a Muslim state by the year 2050."[1]

Among Muslim women, the fertility rate is astronomically higher. In France, the birth rate is 8.1. We are seeing the Islamization of Europe before our eyes. Ninety percent of all immigration into Europe since 1990 has been by Muslims. As of 2008, there are fifty-two million Muslims in Europe and the German government expects that to double by 2028. France, Germany, the Netherlands, England, and Belgium have substantial Muslim communities and some of these nations may be thirty to fifty percent Muslim within a couple of short decades. Southern France, traditionally one of the most populated church regions in the world, now has more mosques than churches.

Great Britain had eighty-two thousand Muslims thirty years ago but today has over 2.5 million, a thirty-fold increase. For more than a decade the most popular male name given to a newborn male Brit has the name "Muhammad" in it. "One of every two births in Belgium and the Netherlands today is a Muslim child; half of the students in French kindergartens are Muslim; in fifteen years, half of the population of the Netherlands will be Muslim."[2] Belgium is already nicknamed "Belgistan"by some!

The late Colonel Muammar al-Gaddafi, former leader of Libya, made reference to this demographic conquest, stating confidently:

"There are signs that Allah will grant Islam victory in Europe - without swords, without guns, without conquests...The fifty million Muslims in Europe will turn it into a Muslim continent within a few decades."[3]

And it's worth noting that one in five Russians are Muslim with projections that the Russian Army will be forty percent Islamic in just a few short years.[4]

An Islamic conference held in Chicago in 2005 claimed that by 2035 they would have fifty million Muslims living in the United States.

Joel Richardson bemoans the fact that "we as the Western church have completely missed the undeniable worldwide significance of Islam". Based on present global trends (and not taking into account the coming end time revival), he predicts that within fifteen years we will see Islam surpass Christianity in numbers as well as influence and that the church needs to wake up and face reality.[4]

Islamic Eschatology

It is therefore crucial that we gain an increased understanding of Islam and its beliefs, including and especially Islamic eschatology. The Quran speaks of five things that a Muslim must believe: the belief in Allah, the Last Day, angels, scripture, and the prophets. (Sura 2:177; Pickthall)[6]

While belief in the end-times plays a very significant role in both the Old and New Testaments as well as in the life of the early church, in modern times, belief in matters pertaining to the last days seems to be treated as optional for Christians and is largely ignored.

But this is not so with Islam. The hadith literature, which records the sayings and deeds of Muhammad, provide substantial and authoritative teaching on the end times which fuels true Muslims to strongly believe in the last day and the events that precede it. In particular, the most anticipated sign of the last days is the coming of a man known as "the Mahdi", which in Arabic, means "the Guided One". Although there are some variations of belief between the Sunni and Shi'a sects within Islam, most Muslims passionately await his arrival on the scene. The Mahdi is Islam's messiah or saviour.

1924 saw the end of the Islamic Caliph known as the Ottoman Empire. We do not fully appreciate the depth of emotion Muslims feel when they see lands, such as Israel, that are no longer under Islamic rule of Allah or that Islam is not yet the supreme world religion. Throughout the Islamic world today there is a longing for the restoration of the Islamic Caliphate (comparable to the pope), especially with the increased confidence that has come with prosperity from oil in recent decades. Their call for the restoration of the caliphate is ultimately a call for the Mahdi, the final caliph, to arrive and lead military campaigns (jihad) to establish a new Islamic world order under shariah law.

Similarities between the description of this Islamic messiah and the Biblical description of the coming dictator we call the Antichrist

The similarities between the Islamic messiah and the biblical Antichrist are quite stunning. I am indebted to Joel Richardson for his eye-opening book, The Islamic Antichrist, for these insights. Walid Shoebat, a former Palestinian terrorist, in his book, God's War on Terror and Perry Stone, in his book, Unleashing the Beast, address many of these similarities as well. Here are just the major parallels:

One: Both the coming biblical Antichrist and the Muslim Mahdi are believed to be a political, religious, and military leader who will lead a global revolution and seek to establish a new world order in which the world submits to their rule.

Two: The Bible teaches that the Antichrist and his armies will attack Israel and Jerusalem and will set up his throne in "God's Temple". (2 Thess. 2:4) Today, the Temple Mount is the location of two mosques and is the third holiest site of Islam. Jesus makes reference to the occupancy of the temple by the Antichrist as "the abomination that causes desolation". (Matt. 24) Likewise the Mahdi is expected to join Muslim warriors carrying black flags and lead the army in seeking to re-conquer Israel for Islam. The Temple Mount in Jerusalem, they believe, will become the Islamic headquarters for the Mahdi to rule the world.[7]

Three: Jews and Christians will be required to convert to the one supreme religion (Islam) or be oppressed and killed.

Daniel, the prophet states: "As I watched, this horn was waging war against the saints and defeating them until the Ancient of Days came and pronounced judgment in favor of the saints of the Most High...He will speak against the Most High and oppress his saints and try to change the set times and the laws. The saints will be handed over to him for a time, times and half a time". (Daniel 7:21, 25)

The apostle John records: "I saw under the altar the souls of those who had been slain because of the word of God and the testimony they had maintained..." (Rev. 6:9-11) And in Rev. 12:17, John says: "Then the dragon was enraged at the woman and went off to make war against the rest of her offspring - those who obey God's commandments and hold to the testimony of Jesus". In Rev.13:7 John claims this leader is "given power to make war against the saints and to conquer them".

Ayatollah Ibrahim Amini articulates this vision: "The Mahdi will offer the religion of Islam to the Jews and Christians; if they accept it they will be spared, otherwise they will be killed".[8]

Also, there is a famous saying in the hadith literature that says: "The last hour would not come unless the Muslims will fight against the Jews and the Muslims would kill them until the Jews would hide themselves behind a stone or a tree and a stone or a tree would say: Muslim, or the servant of Allah, there is a Jew behind me; come and kill him."[9]

Four: The Bible says that the primary means of martyrdom in the last days would be by beheading, "And I saw the souls of those who had been beheaded because of their testimony for Jesus and because of the word of God". (Rev. 20:4)

Beheading is a tradition throughout Islamic history. Muhammad and his successors set the example. They practiced beheading as the primary means of executing their enemies. Whatever Muhammad says or does (found in the hadith writings) is considered just as authoritative and inspired as the Qur'an itself. The famous "beheading" verse in the Qur'an states: "If you encounter (in war) those who disbelieve, you may strike the necks" (Sura 47:4; Khalifa); "When ye encounter the infidels, strike off their heads". (Sura 47:4; Rodwell) In some Muslim regions this practice continues even to this day (Saudi Arabia and the Indonesian island of Borneo and the high profile execution of the Jewish American journalist, Daniel Pearl in

2002). The death sentence is also prescribed for those who are not willing to agree or submit to the authority of the caliph. Jesus warns his followers in John 16:1-4, that a day is coming when those who kill you think they are offering a service to God because they do not know the Father or Jesus.[10]

Five: The Mahdi is believed to ride on a white horse as found in Revelation chapter 6;1, 2. The seals that follow this rider are: peace is taken from the earth followed by famine, plagues and death, persecution and martyrdom of God's people, a great earthquake, and the wrath of God. Some claim this is the reason Saddam Hussein painted several murals that were placed around Baghdad portraying himself as a Muslim hero going to battle against the infidels riding on a white horse. Perry Stone points out that many Islamic leaders own white stallions and that Saddam Hussein was often seen in military parades riding on a white stallion.[11]

Six: He will make a seven-year peace agreement with Israel, giving it a false sense of security (Daniel 9:27).

In Daniel 8:25, we are warned regarding the Antichrist that, "He will cause deceit to prosper, and he will consider himself superior. When they feel secure, he will destroy many..."

Walid Shoebat argues that the word "Hudna" needs to be understood by non-Muslims. Shoebat claims, "In the Muslim mind, Hudna is an Arabic term for a truce meant to produce a period of calm with an enemy in order to gain concessions, regroup, rearm, and re-attack at the appropriate time. This has been its purpose throughout Muslim history." He goes on to point out that the ten-year Treaty of Hudaibiyah that Mohammed made with the tribe of Qurayash outside Mecca when Mohammed's army was seriously outnumbered became a precedent and example to follow. Once Mohammed's army had consolidated its strength and grown in numbers, they broke the treaty and attacked. Shoebat states that, "Muslims today all clearly understand "Hudaibiyah" to be a code-word, which in brief means, 'kiss the hand of your enemy until you have the opportunity to cut it off'". He cites Yasser Arafat's diplomatic signing of the Oslo Peace Accord as a modern example.[12]

Seven: He will "try to change the laws and the times" (Daniel 7:25). Islamic agenda seeks a one world order, that of imposing shariah law upon inhabitants of the earth. As for the "times", Muslims highly desire to impose the Islamic calendar, which is based on the life and career of Muhammad, upon the world. It is compulsory for all Muslims to observe the Muslim calendar. Jewish and Hindu calendars are different than our Gregorian calendar but only Islam matches this description of seeking to change the laws and times on the world.

So, we see that a number of the distinguishing marks of the person, mission, and actions of the biblical Antichrist seem to match up quite compellingly with the descriptions of the coming Mahdi as found in Islamic traditions and Muslim expectations. Am I claiming that the Antichrist will definitely be Islamic? No. But it seems very possible if not probable. We need to keep an eye on such developments.

The President of Iran, Mahmoud Ahmadinejad, feels that he is like John the Baptist who prepares the way for the Mahdi. For those who are not aware who the Mahdi is, many Muslims believe he was the 12th Islamic Imam who disappeared as a child in the year 941. Muslims believe that when he returns he will reign for seven years and he will bring in the final judgment and the end of the world. In the Muslim's eyes he is a sort of Messiah and the Christian Antichrist all rolled up in one.

Mark of the Beast

If it is true that the Antichrist will be from the Muslim community (some believe he may come from the area of Turkey) seeking to usher in a one world Islamic government under shariah law, then we might expect to see some Islamic connection to the mark of the beast spoken about in Revelation 13:16-18.

The American Bible teachers, Chuck Missler and Perry Stone, the New Zealand teacher, Selwyn Stevens, and also the former Islamic terrorist, Walid Shoebat, encourage us to stand back and re-examine the text with fresh eyes (remember the old lady/young lady image in chapter one?). They ask that we give consideration to the possibility that the three Greek letters, Chi, Xi, and Sigma, which have the numerical values of 600 + 60 + 6 = 666, may actually point to an Islamic Antichrist.

The letters may have been Arabic letters and that the apostle John simply wrote down what he saw in his vision, even though it was five hundred years before Islam began. Is it possible a scribe could have seen a scribble that was not Greek, but looks like the Greek numbers/letters for 666, and changed it accordingly? Just an interesting thought to entertain.

Nations east of Jerusalem have their language written and read from right to left and those west of Jerusalem (Greek and Latin) go from left to right. If these three characters are in fact Arabic, then they are read from right to left and the first two characters, though written on an angle (which is how it is displayed on the flag of Iraq), resemble the Arabic character called "Bismillah", which means, "In the Name of Allah". These two characters are on the headbands of many Muslims, which are worn on their forehead or on their arm. The third character, which resembles an "X" may be two crossed swords, which is an emblem of Islam and found on the Muslim Brotherhood logo.[13]

Further Biblical Evidence Pointing Towards a Possible Islamic Antichrist

A vast wealth of biblical evidence pointing towards an Islamic Antichrist has been compiled by Joel Richardson and placed in his 2012 "must read" book, MidEast Beast. I thought his first book, The Islamic Antichrist, which looks at both Christian and Islamic sacred writings pointing to a striking resemblance between the biblical Antichrist with the Islamic expectation of their coming Madhi messiah, was paradigm jarring for many of us. This sequel, which focuses solely on biblical prophecies and texts, further reinforces this unconventional concept of an Islamic leader and New World Order in a very credible, articulate and compelling manner.

In his introduction to his new book, Richardson writes, "Islam's end-times narrative, in so many ways, is simply the biblical end-time story flipped on its head...Our Messiah is their antichrist and our Antichrist is their messiah."[14]

In his gracious but unapologetic manner, Joel Richardson gives us western Christians a very much-deserved rebuke by pointing out that we tend to read the Bible from a western-centric perspective when in fact, the Scriptures are very Middle Eastern and Jerusalem centered. He insists that we must not continue reading into the text and imposing our western bias upon it which has caused us to automatically assume that an Antichrist empire of the last days would be based in Europe.

In my estimation, Joel Richardson walks through the relevant biblical prophecies in a very careful and responsible manner, acknowledging that they have had a measure of fulfillment throughout history yet insisting they will have their ultimate fulfillment in the Day of the Lord at the end of the age when Jesus the Messiah comes and executes vengeance on Israel's and God's enemies. Some of these prophetic words describe this execution of judgment in terms of crushing the head of the enemy. These enemy nations are consistently identified as Israel's neighbours, those nations surrounding Israel, which have been historically anti-semitic and are primarily Islamic.

A summary of a few biblical prophetic words that speak of the Messiah executing judgment on Israel's enemies, which are Muslim nations

Genesis 3:15, gives a synopsis of the redemptive story - that the Messiah will crush the head of the serpent.

Numbers 24:14,17-20, the prophet Balaam is hired by King Balak of Moab to curse the Hebrew people. Not able to help himself, three times he prophesies blessing to the Israelites, including a prophecy that in the last days a star would arise and crush the forehead of Moab, Edom and other anti-Semitic desert people groups east of Israel.

Isaiah 25:8-10, the Lord promises He will crush Moab facedown into a pile of manure.

Isaiah 63:1-6, we see Jesus coming out of Edom with his garments stained with blood.

Ezekiel 25.12-17, gives another prophecy that will only find ultimate fulfillment on the Day of the Lord when Jesus comes and brings divine judgment against Edom, including the ancient city of Deden, located in what is now Saudi Arabia.

Ezekiel 30:1-5, conveys a prophecy regarding the Day of the Lord when God brings judgment against Israel's enemies in Egypt, Sudan, Libya, Arabia, Turkey, and North Africa - all these countries that are marked for judgment are Islamic countries today.

Zephaniah 2:3-5, 12,13, we are told again that the Day of the Lord will bring God's judgment to Israel's neighbours, which are all Muslim majority nations.

In the midst of the Lord's judgment against the enemies of Israel, He will return to deliver those who have been taken captive by the neighbouring nations. In Luke 21:20-24 Jesus warns them to flee to the mountains lest they be taken captive.

Isaiah 34:5-9, declares that the sword of the Lord executes judgment against Edom to uphold the cause of Zion.

Richardson points out that everyone is familiar with the famous passage in Revelation 19, which depicts Jesus bursting on the scene riding upon a white horse with his robes soaked in blood. He will come and tread the winepress of the fury of God's wrath. But he appropriately asks the relevant question, "Whose blood is this"? He then proceeds to inform us that the answer is found in Isaiah 63, from which Revelation 19 is taken.

In Isaiah 63:1-4, we see Jesus marching victoriously toward Jerusalem after executing judgment upon the people of Edom, with blood stained on his apparel. The context is clearly the Day of the Lord when the Messiah comes and unleashes God's wrath. In Edom, He crushes His enemies like grapes.[15]

While these prophecies have seen partial fulfillment in history, the ultimate fulfillment of these passages will be when the Messiah returns on the Day of the Lord. Consistently they refer to Middle Eastern and North African nations surrounding Israel that have been enemies of Israel and made up of Muslim majorities. There is no mention specifically to European nations. Does that mean other nations will not be judged? Richardson makes it clear that other nations will be dealt with but that we don't have them mentioned in Scripture by name as we do the Arab nations surrounding Israel. Jesus will unleash vengeance on all His wicked enemies.[16]

Another new and important point that Joel Richardson makes in his book, Mideast Beast, is that the Scriptures seem to convey that **the Antichrist's empire, though powerful and ruthless, will be limited.** Most of us have been taught that his New World Order will be an absolute and all pervasive global empire. Eight times in the books of Daniel and Revelation it mentions that ten nations will be willing supporters of the Antichrist. He will expand his rule by conquering many nations but he will never conquer and control every last nation on the planet. Twice in Daniel 11 (verses 40, 42) we see that he will "invade many countries" (including Israel, the "Beautiful Land"). But right up to the end, the Antichrist will be at war with "many nations". (Daniel 11:44; 9:26) If the Antichrist had absolute and total control of the world, he would not be at war. There will be nations and pockets that resist his tyrannical rule. Though the Antichrist will seek global conquest, he will never fully attain it.

Only one person will ever rule the entire world and that is Jesus. In Revelation 11:15, loud voices in heaven are declaring, "The kingdom of the world has become the kingdom of our Lord and of his Christ, and he will reign for ever and ever.

The Greek word kosmos, which is never used in reference to the Antichrist's reign, is used here in reference to Jesus. Kosmos, meaning "the world, universe, or circle of the earth", removes all doubt that Jesus will be the only one to have absolute and total authority and dominion over the planet, and that forever.[17]

Four Scriptural texts that give further evidence of an Islamic Antichrist-led empire
(Daniel 2, Daniel 7, Daniel 9:26 and Revelation 17)

One: Daniel 2: Nebuchadnezzar's dream of a statue consists of:

Head of gold (Babylonian Empire),
Chest and arms of silver (Medo-Persian Empire),
Belly and thighs of bronze (Greek Empire),

Legs of iron (traditionally considered the Roman Empire but can alternatively be an Islamic empire)

Feet of mixed iron and clay (traditionally thought to be a revived Roman Empire but could possibly be a restored Islamic Caliphate).

In Daniel 2:40 we see that **this fourth kingdom "will crush and break all the others"**. According to Selwyn Stevens and Richardson, the Roman Empire only conquered about one third of the land controlled by the previous three empires. Rome's rule was predominantly farther west and does not come close to matching up with the geography of the Babylonian-Persian-Greek empires. On the other hand, the historical Islamic Empire or Caliphate, which began in 632 AD and ended in 1923 with the end of the Ottoman Empire, fulfills this prophecy to a tee. It totally conquered all the lands of the previous three kingdoms or superpowers.[18]

It is also worth noting that this fourth kingdom would be known for "crushing and breaking all the others" (Daniel 2:40) as well as "trampling it down and crushing it". (Daniel 7:23) Rather than obliterating Greek culture, religion and language whenever Rome conquered a people, it generally tolerated these things. Throughout the Middle East the Greek language was the common language of the day and Roman culture adopted much of the pagan Greek pantheon of gods and just changed the names. In Israel, the Jerusalem temple and Jewish religion were not only tolerated but even protected by Roman law. With the exception of dealing with insurrection and rebellion among the conquered people, Rome does not match up very well with this description of the fourth kingdom being known for its trampling down and crushing those under its rule.

The Islamic Caliphate on the other hand, from day one, was ruthlessly crushing and wiping out the religions and cultures of the peoples it conquered. Even the name Islam means "submission" to the prophet Muhammad and their god, Allah. This Arab-Islamic-supremacist force imposed the Arabic language onto the majority of those conquered. The Persians and the Turks were able to keep their languages but their alphabets were both Arabized (much later the Turk's alphabet was Anglicized). Like using a bulldozer, the all encompassing ideology and culture of Islam was spread and imposed upon all who were conquered and the symbols and evidences of the previous culture buried.

Regarding **the feet of this statue**, Daniel tells us it will be a mixture of clay and iron, indicating that the fourth kingdom of iron will be revived or come into a second phase but it will be characterized by division and mixture. The Roman Empire did experience a division between East and West. However Richardson argues that this division was only for about one hundred and forty years out of the Roman Empire's fifteen hundred year span and thus does not match this description as well as the Islamic Caliphate. The Islamic Empire went through a bitter division shortly after its founder and prophet, Muhammad, died in 632 AD. This deep division between the Shi'a and the Sunnis has lasted to this day, almost fourteen hundred years - ten times longer than the Roman Empire division. Their mutual hatred of the Jews and determination to destroy the nation of Israel is one aspect on which they are unified.

Furthermore, the feet are described as a "mixture" of clay and iron. The Aramaic word used four times in the biblical text is "arab". The descendants of Ishmael and Esau intermarried among the many desert tribes and were considered the Arabs, the mixed people who lived mostly to the east of the land of Israel.[19]

Perry Stone, though he comes to the same conclusion of the Antichrist and his empire being Islamic, sees the legs of iron of the Daniel 2 statue, as representing Rome. The two iron legs predict the split of Rome into two parts, east and west. These legs of iron eventually turned into two feet of iron and clay, representing Rome and Turkey and the final East-West division.

Stone would say that in the twentieth century we saw the iron and the clay visible through communism and democracy. Communism ruled its people with an iron fist. Their national symbol was the iron hammer and sickle and they were behind the iron curtain. With the decline of Russia, we now see the iron of Islam clashing with the clay of democracy of the West. For seventy years communism clashed with the clay of democracy but now the iron kingdom is the Middle East with a common vision of defeating Israel and the West.

The clay of western democracy is not mixing well with the warring iron of Islam.[20]

Two: In Daniel 7, the prophet Daniel had a vision of four beasts

Daniel's vision of four beasts corresponds to Nebuchadnezzar's dream of a statue in Daniel 2. The fourth beast has iron teeth while the fourth kingdom of the king's dream has iron legs, both with crushing and devouring power. Again, according to Richardson, the Roman Empire does not match this as closely as the Islamic Empire does. Rome would conquer then bring infrastructure, order and law while Islam was a very destructive force to those it conquered. Islam decimated Christian churches or converted them to mosques while Rome ended up being Christianized.

Three: In Daniel 9:26, it speaks of "The people of the ruler who will come will destroy the city and the sanctuary."

Many see this as an argument against an Islamic Antichrist and a support for the Roman Antichrist theory, pointing out that the people who destroyed Jerusalem and the temple in 70 AD were Roman soldiers and citizens.

Joel Richardson argues however, that the historical testimony and modern scholarship paints a very different picture than what is popularly taught and believed. As the Roman Empire expanded its borders, it became impossible to have ample numbers of Italian soldiers. So in AD 15 Emperor Augustus made changes to the ethnic make-up of the armies of Rome. As time went on, the army in the outlying regions of the Roman Empire, particularly in the Eastern regions, consisted more and more of non-Italians. Credible historians such as Publius Cornelius Tacitus and Titus Flavius Josephus confirm that the Roman legions used to attack Jerusalem in AD 70 were stationed in the Syria area and that the majority of these soldiers had been recruited from the eastern provinces of the Empire - ancestors of the modern-day inhabitants of the Middle East.

The historian Josephus, in his Wars of the Jews, gives the context for the Jewish temple being set on fire and destroyed as one not ordered by the Roman commanders but rather due to the undisciplined and vehement hatred of the eastern soldiers towards the Jews. Josephus writes, "And now a certain person came running to Titus, and told him of this fire...whereupon he rose up in great haste, and, as he was, ran to the holy house, in order to have a stop put to the fire...Titus supposing what the fact was, that the house itself might yet be saved, he came in haste and endeavored to persuade the soldiers to quench the fire...yet were their passions too hard for the regards they had for Caesar, and the dread they had of him who forbade them, as was their hatred of the Jews, and a certain vehement inclination to fight them, too hard for them also...And thus was the holy house burnt down, without Caesar's approbation."[21]

Four: in Revelation 17, we see a seven-headed beast which is the personification of Satan's activity of coming against God, His people and His purposes on the planet. These seven heads represent a series of ungodly imperialistic empires or superpowers throughout history. Verse 10 speaks of seven kings, stating that, "Five have fallen, one is, the other has not yet come; but when he does come, he must remain for a little while. The beast who once was, and now is not, is an eighth King. He belongs to the seven and is going to his destruction."

At the time the apostle John wrote his letter, five of the kingdoms were past ("five have fallen") but the sixth empire was presently ruling ("one is"), that of the Roman Empire. These superpowers were:

1. Egypt
2. Assyria
3. Babylon
4. Medo-Persia
5. Greece
6. Rome

After the Roman Empire gradually declined, another demonically inspired superpower burst on the scene and dominated the entire region. Eventually this militant Islamic force dismantled the eastern portion of the Roman Empire (Byzantine) in 1453, when it conquered Constantinople for Islam and renamed it Istanbul. So according to Richardson, the seventh empire after Rome appears to be the Islamic Caliphate.

According to Revelation 13:3 and Revelation 17:8, the final beast empire appears to suffer a fatal head wound but will astonish everyone when they witness a resurrection of the eighth and final beast empire. The Ottoman Empire ended in November 1, 1922 with the Ottoman Caliphate officially abolished on March 3, 1924. But in recent years we have witnessed a major resurgence within the Islamic world of wealth, confidence, population growth and determination to expand their influence. Could this be what the apostle John was referring to in his book of Revelation? It seems quite possible. So Richardson would see the last two kingdoms as:

7. The Islamic Caliphate
8. A revived Islamic Caliphate [22]

Perry Stone, however, believes that the seventh empire in Rev. 17 is actually the European Union, not the Islamic Caliphate. Verse 10 speaks of this king "must remain for a little while" and he doesn't see the Ottoman Empire (Islamic caliphate) lining up with that since it lasted over six hundred years (1299 to 1923). The European Union, developed since the 1950s, will be overrun by forces from the East (Islamic), consisting of a coalition of ten kings under the Antichrist. The European Union will not be the eighth and final empire but rather an Islamic Antichrist empire in the Middle East.

Regarding one of the heads of the beast appearing to have a fatal head wound, Stone sees the most plausible meaning to be referring to one of the previous kingdoms being mortally wounded. Of the previous seven empires, only Babylon no longer exists. He sees that ancient Babylon will be resurrected as the eighth and final empire. Ancient Babylon was situated in present day Iraq. He sees the Islamic Antichrist will build his headquarters in that region of the plains of Shinar, a section of flat land near Baghdad. In the last

3 1/2 years of the Great Tribulation, the Antichrist will establish his headquarters in Jerusalem. So for Stone, the last two kingdoms are:

7. European Union
8. A Middle Eastern Islamic Caliphate headquartered first in ancient Babylon (modern Iraq) followed by Jerusalem[23]

Many traditional prophetic teachers who see a revived Roman Empire that is of western/European orientation would claim that a Russian-Islamic alliance will be reduced to ashes at the war of Gog and Magog of Ezekiel 38. Russia and Islam as a joint military power and Islam as a major world religion, will no longer be a serious threat. Therefore an Islamic Antichrist is highly unlikely.

Both Walid Shoebat and Joel Richardson however, would argue that the war of Gog and Magog is the same as the Battle of Armageddon at the end of the Great Tribulation when Christ defeats the Antichrist and his armies. In fact the evidence Richardson compiles to demonstrate this point takes up three chapters of his book. Although Perry Stone sees the Ezekiel 38 war as separate from the last battle of Armageddon, he claims that it will not result in a virtual wipe out of Islamic might. Of the roughly fifty nations that are predominantly Muslim, only about five Muslim nations will be involved in this earlier war in which their armies are 5/6th destroyed.[24]

One further piece of biblical evidence that Richardson provides of a probable Islamic Antichrist is the passages that speak of "the Assyrian." The texts are primarily found in the book of Isaiah and Micah and follow the theme of the final conflict between Jesus the Messiah and the Antichrist who is referred to again and again as "the Assyrian."

Richardson states that the context of some of the most famous Messianic prophecies in Isaiah ("Immanuel, God with us" passage found in Isaiah 7 and "the Prince of Peace" passage in Isaiah 9) has the coming of the Messiah to conquer the Assyrian. The clearest picture is found in Micah 5. In verse 2 we are informed that the Messiah will be born in Bethlehem. But again, the bigger picture in the chapter is of the Messiah coming and defeating the Assyrian who has invaded the land. The Messiah will be their peace.[25]

After looking at the Scriptures to try to get a handle on the nature of the coming New World Order, I would like to now turn to the contemporary scene and look at the evidence of an encroaching Islamic threat to the West.

"Stealth Jihad" in Modern Times

I was shocked to discover that Islamists' primary means of accomplishing their objective is not through the use of violent jihad, that is, terrorist attacks that get such high profile media attention, which we are all familiar with and actually distracted by. Until they reach sufficient strength in numbers and influence in non-Muslim lands, their primary strategy actually entails a subversive pre-violent means of jihad, what they call "civilization jihad" or what Robert Spencer has coined, "stealth jihad".

This Trojan horse game plan to infiltrate within western perimeters has been going on for decades but is now advancing at an alarming rate while average citizens as well as our political leaders are fast asleep to this very clear and present danger. This internal threat has masked itself as a religion of peace and uses our western tolerance, political correctness and freedom of religion to exercise its seditious activities.

Islam means submission and the bottom line objective is that all of earth's citizens submit to shariah law under Allah. Since the terrorist attacks of 9/11, many believe public enemy # 1 in "the war on terror" is the fanatical organization called al Qaeda. They and other groups such as Hezbollah are definitely a real threat, particularly if they acquire nuclear capabilities (which they may have already). But, for the moment, the blatant attacks they inflict, though serious and deadly, are actually distracting government leaders and the general public from the very sinister Islamic tactic of a pre-violent, under the radar jihad. This subtle approach, led predominantly by the Muslim Brotherhood, is quietly building strength and momentum within the very fabric of western society.

This stealth jihad involves conquest by demographics, mentioned earlier. This involves large scale Muslim immigration into the West as well as encouraging Muslims to have large families.

It also involves Islamists subversively infiltrating and influencing the various sectors or mountains of western society (education, legal systems, federal, state, and local governments, military, prisons, etc.) with the aim of dismantling our democratic and free way of life and imposing shariah law and an Islamic state, the caliphate, in the West and throughout the world. It has been only the last decade or so that Christians have been giving greater attention to the seven mountain teaching of seeking to penetrate these public arenas for the Kingdom of God. Muslims began to establish their associations in these seven mountains in America back in the early 1960s.

Let me walk you through just a small portion of the evidence that is now freely available. Please hear me. This is not intended to be an attack on Muslim people, of which there are close to 1.5 billion in the world. Many Muslims are actually peace loving and simply seeking to carve out a descent life for themselves and their families. God loves them and we are called to love them as well. I am overjoyed to hear that in recent years millions of Muslims have been turning to Christ, largely through supernatural encounters. I believe and pray this amazing trend will only continue.

I agree with my friend, Loren Sandford, who in his book, Visions of the Coming Days, urges us not to live in fear that Muslims are migrating to our western countries but see it as a strategic opportunity from God to share the good news of Jesus and the Father's love with them.

I regrettably cannot concur with Loren, however, that Islam is not a danger or a threat to the West (though he rightly warns of the growing deception called "Chrislam", in which more and more Christian pastors and churches are partnering with Muslim groups such as sharing their pulpits, worship services and buildings, not realizing that Allah is not the same God, but rather a demon) or that Arab Spring is merely a sign of Islam beginning to crack and crumble. Below I will address the threat that appears to be growing in America.[26]

Regarding the issue of the Arab Spring uprisings that started December 18, 2010 in Tunisia, and have spread throughout the Middle East, I am inclined to agree with John Paul Jackson who believes they are a deliberate and cunning strategy by the Muslim

Brotherhood and others to remove nominal and self-seeking Muslim dictators by promising the youth a new life of freedom, prosperity and democracy if they revolt. Once government leaders are toppled, the leadership vacuum will inevitably be filled by Islamists who have the infrastructural capabilities and whose ultimate objective is to impose shariah law in that country and beyond. We have seen this disconcerting pattern begin to unfold in the elections in Egypt with the Muslim Brotherhood gaining power.[27]

So we need to be vigilant to not succumb to fear that would cause us to be unloving towards Muslim people and miss out on a divine mission opportunity, while at the same time seek to be as wise as serpents. We are called to love Muslims, not Islam, which is a demonically inspired idolatrous religion and ideology that seeks to compete with and replace the one true God, Yahweh. We must not be naive about the threat of the Islamic agenda in the West, in the Middle East and around the world. My intention is for us to look at the evidence and prayerfully come to terms with how the Lord would have us respond and move forward.

Islamic threat to America

In 2010, a groundbreaking report sponsored and published by the Center for Security Policy in Washington DC, came out entitled, "Shariah the Threat to America: An Exercise in Competitive Analysis, Report of Team B II".

After some six months of study, analysis, and discussion by a group of top security policy experts and specialists in shariah law, they drafted a report that claims the preeminent totalitarian threat of our time is the Islamic socio-political doctrine of shariah law. Shariah, which means "path" or "way", is a comprehensive economic, legal and political framework, not merely religious, that seeks to dictate and monitor all manner of behaviour, both public and private. It is an insidious ideology that threatens a nation's sovereignty and national security.

This Team B II follows its predecessors of Team B I that analyzed intelligence regarding American policies with the Soviet Union in the 1970s and presented an informed "second opinion", which challenged the prevailing government policy. President Reagan used it in his strategy in effectively dealing with the Kremlin and its ideology. Unlike its predecessors, this present Team B II report is entirely based on unclassified, readily available sources. But similar to the original Team B analysis, their informed second opinion also challenges the foundational assumptions behind the official line regarding today's totalitarian threat and calls for a long-overdue course-correction.[28]

I'll seek to give a short summary of some of the data found in this three hundred and fifty page report as well as refer to some other materials.

The official government line describes the threat strictly as "violent extremism." They have drawn the line between the few fringe violent jihadists on the one hand and the vast majority of peace loving Muslim citizens on the other.

However, according to this report, the issue of shariah is the critical dividing line. On the one side of the divide are Muslim reformers and moderates who see shariah as a reference point in a Muslim's personal life and conduct.

On the other side, are the Muslim Islamists or supremacists, some of whom are terrorists, but the majority is utilizing a stealthier means to reach the same objectives of imposing a totalitarian shariah system and establishing an Islamic state worldwide. On this side of the divide, "shariah is an immutable, compulsory system that Muslims are obliged to install and the world required to adopt, the failure to do so being deemed a damnable offense against Allah. For these ideologues, shariah is not a private matter. Adherents see the West as an obstacle to be overcome, not a culture and a civilization to be embraced...It is impossible, they maintain, for alternative legal systems and forms of governments peacefully to coexist with the end-state they seek."[29]

This ever increasing supremacist camp (whether of the violent variety such as: al Qaeda, Hezbollah, and Hamas or of the "stealth jihad" kind) has been, for many decades, financed and promoted by Islamic regimes such as Saudi Arabia and Iran and by organizations such as the Muslim Brotherhood and the Organization of the Islamic Conference.[30]

The Muslim Brotherhood was formed in Egypt in 1928. In 1938, Hitler had helped establish them globally by giving them millions of dollars. They may have up to two hundred thousand members worldwide today.

Groups like the Muslim Brotherhood share the same objectives as the violent jihadists but for the moment at least, believe the stealthier "pre-violent" means of jihad are likely to prove more effective in attaining their goals. The U.S. government, under both political parties, has failed to grasp the true nature of the enemy. Leaders commit troops and treasure to foreign battlefields to deal with Islamist suicide bombers and insurgents while on the home front stealth jihadists are quietly dismantling the laws and freedoms guaranteed by the U.S. Constitution. They have already deeply penetrated every fabric of American society as well as other western allies and are extremely skilled at using civil freedoms against us. Those promoting shariah law in America must be seen as treasonous. It is diametrically opposed to the U.S. Constitution. This is a high-risk war and the bottom line is that we must keep America shariah free. Former House Speaker Newt Gingrich has issued several warnings to this effect.[31]

This Center for Security Policy 2010 report speaks of a document titled "An Explanatory Memorandum: On the general Strategic Goal for the Group", which is one of the sources in which the concept of civilization jihad is found. It makes it clear that the Islamic movement, which is a "settlement process," is a Muslim Brotherhood effort and led by them in the United States. Specifically, the document explains that the process involves a "grand jihad in eliminating and destroying the western civilization from within and 'sabotaging' its miserable house by their hands and the hands of the believers so that it is eliminated."

In 2004, this critical document was stumbled upon in an FBI raid in Annandale, Virginia. This document, which demonstrates that many of the most prominent Muslim organizations in America are front groups for the Muslim Brotherhood, was entered as significant evidence in the 2008 United States vs. Holy Land Foundation terrorist finance trial in Dallas, Texas. It was written in 1991 by Mohamed Akram, a senior Hamas leader in the U.S. and a member of the Board of Directors for the Muslim Brotherhood in North America, also known as the Ikhwan. This full document has been reproduced as Appendix II in this report.[32]

So with a high value in western society to multiculturalism, political correctness and tolerance combined with sheer ignorance, the stealth jihadists have much to exploit. Our political leaders are afraid of calling a spade a spade and challenging the Muslim Brotherhoods' operations and propaganda. Who wants allegations of racism and bigotry brought against them? For example, President George W. Bush on September 20, 2001 declared that, "terrorists are traitors to their own faith" that "hijacked their own religion." And President Obama stated on January 7, 2010, that, "We are at war; we are at war with al Qaeda." The American political leadership has failed to define and explain the true nature of the enemy and its threat, the demand to submit to shariah law.[33]

Someone may ask, "What is so terrible about shariah law?"

Shariah means "the way, the path," a way of life and insists that all laws stem from Allah and are based on the Quran, hadiths and agreed interpretations. Therefore, legislating laws through the democratic process is totally impermissible. Shariah is all about power, that of enforcing a body of law on all aspects of society and life. Shariah commands Muslims to carry out jihad (holy war) indefinitely until shariah is fully enforced everywhere. Shariah also dictates that non-Muslims be given three choices: convert to Islam and submit to shariah, submit as second-class citizens (dhimmis), or be executed. Not everyone is given the second option.[34]

A sampling of further tenets of shariah include:

- The violent verses that come later chronologically in the Quran supersede the earlier more moderate verses but instruction given to westerners is limited to understanding Islam in its early peaceful stages (which reminds me of similar dynamics within freemasonry in which most participants are kept in the three lowest levels or degrees where considerable misinformation is dispensed).
- Adultery is punishable by lashing and stoning to death.

- Female genital mutilation - both men and women are to be circumcised.
- Women are inferior in status to men.
- Honour killing has no legal penalty.
- Islam is considered superior to all other religions, cultures and societies.
- Islam is deeply anti-Semitic.
- Anything that might offend a Muslim, even if true, is slander, blasphemy.
- It permits the marriage of young girls as young as age eight or nine.
- The law of Taqiyya permits Muslims to lie, especially to non-Muslims.[35]

Let me comment on the last tenet mentioned. The law of Taqiyya, of lying, particularly to further the cause of Islam gives much latitude for Muslims to be deceptive and misleading in their interactions with non-Muslims. Trust is foundational to relationships. We want to believe the best of others and give them the benefit of the doubt but we do need to exercise wisdom and discernment in the process.

The Muslim Brotherhood fully intends for America (and other western nations) to submit to shariah law. The founder of the MB, Hassan al-Banna, stated, "It is the nature of Islam to dominate, not to be dominated, to impose its law on all nations and to extend its power to the entire planet."[36]

In 1996, Abdurahman Alamoudi, who was one of the top leaders of the MB at that time and who enjoyed access to the Clinton White House, clearly stated this ambition by declaring at an Illinois convention, "I have no doubt in my mind, Muslims sooner or later will be the moral leadership of America. It depends on me and you, either we do it now or we do it after a hundred years, but this country will become a Muslim country." He is presently serving a twenty-three year federal prison term on charges related to terrorism.[37]

According to the Center for Security Policy 2010 report, this internal threat and the gravity of the situation is not even being taught at a basic level to FBI counterterrorism analysts and agents. Neither is it being communicated at the Justice Department, Department of

Homeland Security, Department of State, Department of Defense or the CIA. The conclusion of the team of analysts who compiled this report is that if "such ignorance is allowed to persist, the Muslim Brotherhood will continue infiltrating American society at every level and executing a very deliberate plan to manipulate the nation into piecemeal submission to shariah."[38]

I confess that this is pretty heavy stuff. But I believe such evidence of a very near and present danger needs to be brought out into the light for people, including Christians, to be aware of, pray about and wrestle with.

Recently my family and I attended an excellent conference at Morningstar Ministries in South Carolina. During one of the breaks, I got in the book signing line for two books I was buying. The author, a retired three star U.S. general, Wm. G. Boykin, had just given an insightful message on the Islamic threat to America. I asked him if he thought that there was also a real threat from a so-called global elite towards a one world government. His response to me was a resounding yes that such a threat exists. I asked him which of the two threats he thought might succeed. He reluctantly gave his opinion but it was given off the record so I don't feel free to say.

At the moment I vacillate between the two, depending on which track I am researching. I am sobered by the seemingly omnipresence and omnipotence of a European/American global elite to influence nations and events yet I see substantial evidence in both current events and Scripture that seem to point towards a final showdown coming out of the historical sibling rivalry of Isaac and Ishmael - with the coming Messiah, Jesus, decisively defeating a satanically inspired Islamic Anti-messiah. Who says it has to be either/or? Maybe it will be a combination of the two or more.

Rick Joyner writes in his book, A Prophetic History, "I can feel the encroachment of this same spirit (communism) into the fabric of America...the same evil is trying to take root in America...It will not come as a Nazi again, but it will somehow be a combination of Nazism, communism and Islamic extremism. I know it can be stopped from taking America, but only if the church in America awakens, and at this writing she is still sleeping pretty soundly...

Since I was first shown what would seek to take over America, and indeed the world, I have felt a calling to sound an alarm."[39]

Time will tell whether it is one or the other or a combination of all of the above. We need to remain vigilant. Jesus warned us on more than one occasion to be watchful, alert and prayerful so that we are not deceived. That does not give us license however, to become passive armchair theologians who merely speculate and debate on the details of developments that are unfolding with a one up-manship mindset. We are clearly instructed to watch and pray while we also "be about our Father's business" of obeying the Great Commission until He comes.

It is worth noting that Iran's President Mahmoud Ahmadinejad, who was elected in August 2005 and won re-election (though seriously controversial with many protests), can only have two terms in office. So he is finished as president August 3, 2013 (unless the policy is changed). He has stated that Allah has raised him up as leader to usher in their messiah, which requires wiping Israel off the map and creating chaos on the earth. We may soon see a pre-emptive strike by Israel against Iran's military facilities due to the likelihood that Iran is about to join the elite nuclear weapons club.

In late August of 2012, at the 16th Summit Conference of the Non-Aligned Movement (NAM), where the leaders of one hundred and twenty countries gathered, the spiritual leader, Ayatollah Ali Khamenei addressed the convention with a scathing rebuke against the West and a warm welcome to Egypt's new President Mohammed Morsi to Tehran. Khamenei stated, "Iran is in transition towards a new international order and the Non-Aligned Movement can and should play a new role." President Ahmadinejad also spoke at the summit arguing that, "Global management must change and we all must stand up for that...If we wait for years then our time will also come to an end without being able to make a change in the right direction...If we tap into this great global movement and use it the right way we will be able to usher in a beautiful new era for humanity, a New World Order."[40]

Of course our focus and foundation must be on what the Bible says about an issue. But I believe there is a place to also be attentive to current world events as well as what credible Christian prophetic voices are saying. In June of 1988, the Christian prophet, Paul Cain, gave a dramatic prophecy to Mike Bickle. I will summarize this word, which came in three parts:

1. George Bush would have Dan Quail as his running mate in the coming election.
2. God would take the wind out of the spirit of communism in eighteen months (by December 1989) and the fulfillment of these two would give more weight to the third part of the word.
3. The spirit of communism would rise up again and partner with the spirit of Islam, bringing pressure on Europe and other nations and release horrendous evil.[41]

Could the famous Prophecy of the Popes which is attributed to St. Malichy in 1139 AD be worth watching closely? In this supposed vision, the next 112 popes are briefly described. The present pope, Pope Benedict XVI, is 111th pope and the prophecy claims that during the rule of the 112th, named Petrus Romanus, he "will feed his flock amid tribulations; after which the seven-hilled city will be destroyed and the dreadful Judge will judge the people. The End."[42]

Could it be that a partnership between the spirit of communism and the spirit of Islam will rise up and destroy Rome and other portions of the West (New York, America, and/or Europe)? Could this possibly be the beast rising up and destroying the religious and political Babylon harlot described in Revelation 17 and 18? Some believe that ancient Babylon (modern Iraq) will be the headquarters of mystery Babylon. Walid Shoebat claims the Babylon harlot is actually Mecca, Saudi Arabia and that the sea captains will watch it burn from the Red Sea (Jeremiah 49:21, Rev. 18:17-20) I don't have any clear answers but again I recommend we remain vigilant and watchful yet not fearful and paranoid. God is certainly not breaking out in a sweat! He really is in charge.

Another contemporary Christian prophet, Terry Bennett, in a prophetic encounter with the Lord, saw the devil and the Lord in a card game. The devil had many supposedly winning hands but the Lord had a card that trumped all of them! So Satan can have several hands (Islamists, social-Marxists, Nazi and New Age global elites all pursuing global conquest) but God ultimately trumps them all with His hand.[43]

Jesus will inevitably have his own New World Order in which He rules the world with truth, justice and righteousness in the age to come. His Kingdom will have no end: "The kingdom of the world has become the kingdom of our Lord and of his Christ, and he will reign for ever and ever". (Rev. 11:15)

Recommendations:

Books:

Shariah The Threat To America, an Exercise in Competitive Analysis Report of Team B II, Center for Security Policy, Wash. DC, 2010
Islam Vs. the United States, Nicholas F. Papanicolaou, Oak Leaves Pub., Fort Mill S.C., 2010
Stealth jihad, Robert Spencer, Regnery Pub., 2008
The Islamic Antichrist, Joel Richardson, WND Books, 2009
Mideast Beast: A Scriptural Case for an Islamic Antichrist, Joel Richardson, WND Books, 2012
God's War on Terror, Walid shoebat & Joel Richardson, Top Executive Media, 2nd edition, 2008
Unleashing the Beast, Perry Stone, Front Line, 2009, 2011
Inside the Revolution, Joel C. Rosenberg, Tyndale, 2009, 2011 (a wealth of info but author only sees the extreme fanatical minority as a threat with most Muslims being moderate and harmless)
Apocalypse Soon:End Times Explained, Selwyn Stevens, Jubilee Resources, New Zealand, 2012
The End of America, John Price, Christian House Publishers Inc., 2009, 2011(builds a case, though I'm not convinced, for America being the end time Mystery Babylon that is destined for destruction, probably by Islamists who will then set up an Islamic Antichrist dictator in Europe)

Websites:

www.shariahthethreat.com
Joel Richardson's website: http://archives.joelstrumpet.com/
trunews.com (Christian news network, alternative news)
WND.com (Christian news and commentary, publishing co.)

You-tube clips:

"Islam in Bible Prophecy - Sid Roth with Joel Richardson (1/3)",
http://www.youtube.com/watch?v=M2HSZHTs4Nw Sid Roth with
Walid Shoebat 7-16-2012, http://www.youtube.com/watch?v=u8b9
QFsgHfo&feature=related (uploaded July 18, 2012)
Terry Bennett, Trump card word of encouragement, youtube:
http://www.youtube.com/watch?v=IBRM7G8-rds&feature=related

Notes:

[1] You-tube, Wake up Europe (Islam in Europe), May 3/12, http://
www.youtube.com/watch?v=IdfpbwnjgaE
[2] John Price, The End of America, Christian House Pub. 2nd ed.,
2011, p. 220.
[3] Ibid., p. 220.
[4] "Wake up Europe Islam in Europe), 4:09 min.
[5] Joel Richardson, The Islamic Antichrist, WND, 2009 pp.10,11
[6] Ibid., p. 18.
[7] Ibid., p. 45, citing Izzat & Arif, Al Mahdi & the End of Time, p.
40.
[8] Ibid., p. 42, citing Amini, Al-Imam Al-Mahdi.
[9] Ibid., p. 42, citing Sahih Muslim, Book 041, Number 6985.
[10] Ibid., p. 136; also Walid Shoebat, God's War on Terror, Top
Executive Media, 2008, pp. 162-166; also Perry Stone, Unleashing
the Beast, Frontline Charisma Media/Charisma House, 2009, 2011,
pp. 84, 137-138.

[11] Perry Stone, pp. 134, 135; Joel Richardson, pp. 29-30; Walid Shoebat, p. 84.

[12] Walid Shoebat, pp. 117-121; Joel Richardson, p. 47, citing Tabarani as quoted by Mufti A.H. Elias and Muhammad Ali ibn Zubair Ali, Imam Mahdi, article: http://fisher.osu.edu/-muhanna_1/hijri-intro.html.

[13] Selwyn Stevens, Apocalypse Soon: End Times Explained, Jubilee, 2012, pp. 62, 63; Walid Shoebat, pp. 363 – 379; "Sid Roth with Walid Shoebat 7-16-2012", http://www.youtube.com/watch?v=u8b9QFs gHfo&feature=related ; "Chuck Missler on the Mark of the Beast 666", July 6/09, http://www.youtube.com/watch?v=ka5v0REv8Us; Perry Stone, pp. 171-180.

[14] Joel Richardson, Mideast Beast: A Scriptural Case for an Islamic Antichrist, WND Books, 2012, Preface, p. IV.

[15] Ibid., pp. 31-32; see also Walid Shoebat, pp. 187, 188.

[16] Ibid., pp. 15-33.

[17] Ibid., pp. 47, 48.

[18] Selwyn Stevens, End Times Explained, pp. 49- 53; also Joel Richardson, Mideast Beast, pp. 58-63, 74-78.

[19] Joel Richardson, Mideast Beast, pp. 89-93.

[20] Perry Stone, Unleashing the Beast, pp. 52 - 55.

[21] Joel Richardson, pp. 100-101, citing Josephus, Wars of the Jews, bk. 6, ch. 4.

[22] Ibid., pp. 150-158.

[23] Perry Stone, pp. 27, 65-68.

[24] Walid Shoebat, pp. 267-274; also Joel Richardson, pp. 159 -197; also Perry Stone, p. 35.

[25] Joel Richardson, pp. 235 - 245.

[26] R. Loren Sandford, Visions of the Coming Days, Chosen, 2012, pp. 207-210.

[27] John Paul Jackson, Dare To Dream God's Dream II conference, Jubilee Celebration Center, Orillia, ON, Can. Aug. 12, 2011.

[28] Shariah the Threat to America: An Exercise in Competitive Analysis Report of Team B II, Center for Security Policy, 2010 ed., Team Leaders: Lieut. Gen. Wm. G. Boykin, US Army (Ret.), former Deputy Undersecretary of Defense for Intelligence & Lieut. Gen.

Harry Edward Soyster, US Army (Ret.) former Director, Defense Intelligence Agency, pp. 1, 2.

[29.] Ibid., p. 3.

[30.] Ibid., p. 4.

[31.] Ibid., pp. 10-12.

[32.] Ibid., pp. 7, 16-18.

[33.] Ibid., pp. 19-22.

[34.] Ibid., p. 37.

[35.] Ibid., pp. 41-53.

[36.] Ibid., p. 47

[37.] Ibid., p. 26.

[38.] Ibid., p. 29.

[39.] Rick Joyner, A Prophetic History, Morningstar, /09, pp.135-142

[40.] Jan Douglas Bish, Columnist & Middle East Analyst, article, "Khamenei - Time for New World Order", Aug. 31/12, http://jim bakkershow.com/blog/2012/08/31/khamenei-time-for-new-world-order/

[41.] Mike Bickle, session #1 Prophetic History, CD, Oct. 2002.

[42.] Bible Probe, Malachy's Prophecies, the Last 10 Popes, http://www.bibleprobe.com/last10popes.htm (accessed Aug.24/12)

[43.] Terry Bennett, "Trump Card" encouragement,Sept. 24/11, http://www.youtube.com/watch?v=IBRM7G8-rds&feature=relmfu

The End Times and the Return of Jesus, the True Heavy Weight Champion of the World
Part 1

"If we aren't acquainted with the end of the script, we can grow fearful or complacent in the play."
Max Lucado

"The more the church finds out who she is, the less she wants to be rescued."
Bill Johnson

*B*ack in the days of the Jesus movement in the early 1970s, the best-selling book, The Late Great Planet Earth, by Hal Lindsay, largely shaped my perspective on the end times and the return of Christ. It was the "talk of the town" in the Christian circles I was associated with. It not only stirred up excitement among Christians but it led many to a personal relationship with Christ (though some of course were simply looking for fire insurance).

Wearing my long hair, beard and bell bottom jeans, I would often pick up hitch hikers in my Volkswagen Beetle that was splattered with flower decals and a "Honk if you love Jesus" sticker on the bumper. I looked forward to having a captive audience to tell them about the soon return of Jesus, probably by 1980 or so. Jesus would break through the skies to rapture all those who loved Him so they wouldn't have to go through all the hellish and cataclysmic stuff that would then hit the earth. So they better get born again quickly.

I even questioned whether it was worth the bother of going to college since Christ would soon be coming but after working a couple of years after high school at minimum wage, I decided I enjoyed school more. I eventually went to ten more years of formal schooling. Maybe I'm just a slow learner.

I have gone through a series of paradigm shifts related to eschatology, the study of end things, over the last forty years, including a season of disillusionment in which I simply put the subject on ice. I saw it as too complex and confusing an issue. Maybe some of you can relate. But in recent years I have again gained a hunger to study this subject, seeing it as increasingly pertinent to our lives. But it is one of those topics that I think we will need to keep our views and conclusions quite fluid. The Lord probably has even more changes for us in our understanding, as we get closer to the Day of the Lord. There are probably many twists and turns in the redemptive drama at the end of the age which will be unfolding before our very eyes.

But over the last decade or two, whenever I have been asked, "Jerry, before Jesus comes back, are we going to see things get better and better or worse and worse?" My answer has usually been "yes". I usually get a baffled look in response because most of us tend to think in terms of either/or. But Scripture appears to speak in stereo on this question. While the light of the glory of Christ shines brighter upon His bride, the earth will increasingly experience darkness, chaos and great trouble. (Isa 60:1-3) We'll elaborate on this.

The topics of the end times and the second coming of Christ have spawned such a variety of emotions as well as much division in the body of Christ throughout the centuries. Many have run to extremes on these subjects, some so preoccupied and dogmatic regarding the finer details, others totally ignoring them.

And yet the second coming of Jesus is a vital doctrine of the Christian faith that is found throughout the Bible, in all the historical church creeds, and even in five thousand of Charles Wesley's seven thousand hymns. The New Testament calls this great truth of the second coming of Christ the "Blessed Hope" of the believer. (Titus 2:13) Thankfully, most Christians are in hearty agreement on the belief that at the end of the age the King of kings will return a second time in great glory and splendour.

Here are some interesting facts that point to **the certainty of Christ's return**:

- One out of every thirty verses in the Bible mentions the subject of the end of time or the return of the Messiah.
- There are three hundred references in the New Testament to His second coming.
- For every prophecy of His first coming, there are about seven of His second coming.[1]
- Only four books of the New Testament fail to mention Christ's return.
- One-twentieth of the New Testament is devoted to the topic of the return of Jesus.[2]
- Some New Testament passages either quote Jesus directly stating the fact, "I *will* come back" (John 14:1-3) or "Behold, I *am* coming soon" (3 times in Rev. 22) or stated by other authors that "this same Jesus...*will* come back", "*when* he comes" or "*when* Christ comes back" (Acts 1:11, Acts 3:20, 1 Cor. 15:23, 1 Thess. 2:19, 3:13, 4:16, 2 Thess. 1:7, Heb. 9:28, 1 John 2:28, 3:2; italics mine).

Jesus himself, let alone the authors of the New Testament, speaks with utter conviction and certainty. He IS coming back. He WILL keep His promise! As lovers and followers of Jesus Christ, we all revel in this wonderful truth.

Below is a chart showing linear human history. It begins with God creating the world, followed by man's fall, the first coming to earth of Jesus who died and rose again (providing a solution to sin and a new covenant) and then His ascension back to the Father in heaven. We live in this present evil age and though we have the Holy Spirit with us, we long for Jesus to return a second time in the same manner that He left and defeat evil and consummate His Messianic kingdom on earth. Paradise lost will become Paradise restored.

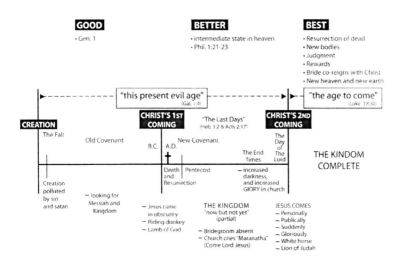

In regards to the details of Christ's second coming, unfortunately believers historically as well as presently argue and debate. Matters of when He will come, whether or not the bulk of biblical prophecies have already been fulfilled, if still in the future, what order of sequence will things take place (pre-tribulation, mid-tribulation or post-tribulation), and the nature of the one thousand year or millennial Kingdom (pre-mill, post-mill, or a-mill) have all been and still are very controversial issues that divide.

It is a sad commentary on our inability to be gracious and enjoy each other's fellowship while having stimulating conversations on these matters in an attempt to gain greater understanding together. Maybe the Lord deliberately left the finer details on this issue (and other issues) less clear in Scripture so that we would not only have to have a deeper hunger for truth and a greater dependence upon Him, but that we would have to learn to get along, stay flexible and extend grace and honour to each other.

But if we are possibly the generation (or our children are) that go through the last days and see the return of the Lord, it is imperative for us to grapple with these issues and seek greater understanding and be more prepared for the battles and challenges ahead.

Some may argue that giving attention to the end times and the return of Christ is a waste of time because it will distract us from being involved and making a difference in this world. That may be true of some. However, in 2 Timothy 4:7-8, the apostle Paul tells us that the Lord is pleased with and even rewards those who are watchful and on tip-toe with longing for His return as well as for having fought the good fight, finishing the race and having kept the faith. C. S. Lewis agrees with this when he writes:

"Hope is one of the theological virtues. This means that a continual looking forward to the eternal world is not (as some modern people think) a form of escapism or wishful thinking, but one of the things a Christian is meant to do. It does not mean that we are to leave the present world as it is. If you read history, you will find that the Christians who did most for the present world were just those who thought most of the next...It is since Christians have largely ceased to think of the other world that they have become so ineffective in this. Aim at heaven and you will get earth "thrown in": aim at earth and you will get neither."[3]

In this chapter we will seek to address, albeit briefly, the first five questions listed below to assist us in further preparation. In the following chapter, we will seek to respond to the last three questions.

1. Why bother to study the end times?
2. Why does one's view of the end times even matter?
3. What are the different views on the millennial kingdom?
4. What are the different views of Pre-millennialism?
5. What about the controversial issue of a separate secret rapture of the church before the tribulation and the public coming of Christ?
6. Why would God allow His bride to go through tribulation and suffering?
7. What should be our attitude towards the book of Revelation?
8. What might the end times drama and time frames look like?

So grab a coffee (or a healthy drink), relax and let us jump in to grappling with these questions.

1. Why Bother Studying the End Times?

- We may very well be the generation that experiences the end time revival, the turbulent tribulation as well as see the return of Christ.
- The end times generation is the most written about generation in the Bible.
- Many passages in Scripture sound the alarm, urging us to get ready for the intense and troubling events that will take place prior to the return of Christ. Studying the Scriptures regarding the end of the age helps to prepare the hearts and minds of God's people so they will be faithful and victorious during the most turbulent and challenging time in history.
- It prepares the church to partner with God in the coming revival rather than resist or fight it.
- It prepares the church to rightly discern and understand the crisis instead of being confused and offended at God. Jesus rebuked Israel for being able to predict the weather but not able to read the signs at His first coming. (Matt. 16:3) How much more could we be candidates for Christ's rebuke when we can predict the weather with greater precision today yet not able to read the many more (seven times more) signs of His second coming?
- It awakens the church to the urgency of intimacy and trust in Jesus and His brilliant leadership as well as the need to partner with God in prayer and intercession for advancing His Kingdom purposes.
- It strengthens our confidence in God's sovereignty by knowing He is in charge, nothing catches Him by surprise.[4]

I have come to realize that this subject of the end times is not just for the curious and eccentric, but that it has substantial relevance to all believers in this hour that we live in. I am grateful for the ministry and teaching of Kansas City leader, Mike Bickle, who has helped remove the intimidation I have felt for years in relation to the book of Revelation as well as the end times in general. Eschatology, the study of the end times, is not meant to be just for the elite scholar. Understanding of end time prophecies should be accessible to all God's people who truly desire truth.

Mike Bickle begins with the assumption that these end time prophecies should be taken literally, that is, in their natural and obvious sense, unless the text specifically tells you it is symbolic. "It says what it means and means what it says." He also urges us all to be like the Bereans (Acts 17:11) and search the Scriptures for ourselves to see if what anyone is teaching lines up with the whole counsel of God.

2. Why Does One's View of the End Times Even Matter?

Ideas have consequences. Our view will affect our ministry focus, prayer life and our daily walk. Mike Bickle, in his book, Omega, spells out three extremes to avoid:

- Too negative: thinking nothing will change for the good, leading people to be passive and not seek to extend the Kingdom of God in people's lives or make a difference in society.
- Too positive: thinking that most of society will be transformed before Jesus returns. Hope-filled desire is important but it must be tempered by Scripture and not humanistic optimism, which can underestimate coming trouble.
- Too vague: assuming that it is impossible to know and therefore, ignore the subject, carry on as usual and not prepare for the future.[5]

3. What are the Different Views of the Millennial Kingdom?

1. **Pre-millennialism**: Jesus returns before His literal 1000 year Messianic reign on the earth.

2. **A-millennialism**: not a literal thousand-year reign but rather a spiritual victory over sin in the hearts of men. This church age is the millennial period.
3. **Post-millennialism**: Jesus will come back after the millennium. The church establishes the Kingdom by fully Christianizing the whole world before Jesus returns.

Some Christians claim they are Pan-millennialists. They simply shrug their shoulders and say jokingly, "It will all just pan out in the end." That way they don't have to wrestle with the issue. I took this stance for years. But Jesus warns us of the perils of being unprepared.

Most A-mill and Post-millennialists hold a "partial-preterist" view of the end times. That is, they see most of the end time prophecies of Matthew 24, Luke 21, and the book of Revelation as being mostly fulfilled in the past, when Israel was at war with Rome (66-70 AD) and Jerusalem and the temple were destroyed. Many of them would also see these prophecies as partly symbolic, as a picture of spiritual conflict throughout church history.

Most pre-millennialists however, would claim that the events of 70 AD were only a partial fulfillment of these prophecies - a prophetic foreshadowing of end time events.

Pre-millennialism appears to be the earliest held belief of Christians. The timing of the rapture of the church was never an issue (until 1830, which we will soon discuss). It was assumed that persecution and tribulation would always be the lot of believers in this present evil age including the end of the age. Church Fathers such as Irenaeus and Justin Martyr embraced this perspective. A sample of modern supporters of this historic view would be: George E. Ladd, Robert Gundry, Derek Prince, David Pawson and Mike Bickle.

The A-millennial teaching, which interprets the one thousand years figuratively, became popular in the fifth century primarily through St. Augustine. This belief claims there is no literal one thousand year reign by Jesus on earth. The millennium represents Christ's rule in the lives of His people between His first coming and His second. When Christ returns, He will promptly defeat evil, resurrect believers and unbelievers, judge them and send them to their eternal destinations. Well known supporters of this A-millennial view include: Martin Luther, John Calvin, Abraham Kuyper, J. I. Packer as well as much of the Roman Catholic Church and Reformed Church denominations.

Post-millennialism is the belief that the second coming of Jesus will occur after the millennium is established. This very confident and optimistic view claims that through the preaching of the Gospel, much of the world will choose to submit to the Lordship of Jesus Christ and come into the Kingdom of God. They take the dominion mandate in Genesis 1:28 and Matthew 28:19-20 very seriously. In Romans 16:20, Paul claims that, "The God of peace will soon crush Satan under your feet." and Psalm 110:1 states:

"Sit at My right hand until I make Your enemies a footstool for Your feet." It appears that the Father is speaking to His enthroned Son, Jesus and hints that Jesus will not return to the earth until His enemies are defeated. Once Christ's enemies are made His footstool then Christ will return for His Bride.

During the 18th and 19th centuries, post-millennialism became popular as the Great Awakening and the Puritan and modern missionary movements were in full swing. Jonathan Edwards held the optimistic post-millennial belief in the 18th century. B.B. Warfield, A. H. Strong, and Charles Hodge held this view in the 19th century as did R.C. Sproul and Dennis Peacock in the 20th century.

During the early and mid 20th century, a Great Depression sandwiched between two world wars caused a shift from the optimistic mood of society improving to a more pessimistic mood of things getting worse and worse.

Let me conclude with the thought that while a person may hold to one view in particular, there are strengths or gems of truth in the other millennial views, which would be wise for us to embrace.

4. What are the Different Views of Pre-millennialism?

First let me say that there are some pre-millennialists (as well as a-millenialists and post-millennialists) who are "partial preterists". They believe that the vast majority of end-time Bible prophecies, particularly those found in Daniel, Matthew 24 and the book of Revelation, have been fulfilled in the past with the destruction of Jerusalem and the temple in AD 70.

The best book I am aware of that represents the partial- preterist view is Victorious Eschatology, by Harold Eberle and Martin Trench. I have read this fascinating book several times and have tried hard to embrace this perspective but I remain unconvinced of most of their main arguments. At first glance it appears quite impressive but on further investigation of Scripture, church history and current world developments, these arguments seem weak and selective.

Their evidence for an early date of the book of Revelation (before AD 70), which is critical for their case, does not match the evidence for a later date towards the end of the first century. As well, they don't seem to appreciate the fact that prophecies often have more than one layer of fulfillment - often in the day of the biblical writer as well as a further and more complete fulfillment in the future.

The authors also give the impression that virtually all "futurists" (those who believe the majority of end time Bible prophecies are yet to be fulfilled in the future) are pessimistic and focused on escaping the tribulation via a secret rapture. In other words, they lump all futurists (of which there at least five different views or camps) together in the most popular view called the dispensational pre-tribulation rapture theory. Eberle and Trench give the impression that their partial preterist view is the only option available if we wish to embrace a high expectation of the Lord raising up a victorious end-time church in revival and with a great harvest before the return of Christ.[6]

I don't know if Eberle and Trench are aware of the fifth view (described below), called the apostolic post-tribulation rapture view, but it too embraces a high expectation of what God will do in and through a victorious church before the second coming of Christ. But this fifth view also claims there is great trouble and tribulation yet ahead. It is not either/or but both/and. This more accurately and realistically represents the full breadth of Scriptural prophecies, church history, contemporary Christian prophecies and current world events.

My concern with the partial preterist view as well as the dispensational pre-tribulation rapture view is that people who hold to them could be totally unprepared to face future hardship, tribulation and persecution. The first group believes that is all in the past and the pre-tribulation group believes they will escape it just before it is fully realized in the future.

Now let's take a look at five futurist views of pre-millennialism:

1. Dispensational or Pre-Tribulation Rapture, which is the most popular view in North America.
2. Mid-Tribulation Rapture (also called mid-week/pre-wrath rapture).
3. Partial Pre-Tribulation or Mid-Tribulation Rapture, with some believers who are living holy lives, the wise virgins whose oil is full, being raptured prior to the Great Tribulation, other believers having to be refined and endure the tribulation.
4. Historic (Classic) Post-Tribulation Rapture, claims that believers will not escape the tribulation but rather will go through it by the grace of God.
5. Apostolic Post-Tribulation Rapture: term used by Mike Bickle to describe the historic post-tribulation view that also takes into account the biblical emphases of global revival, restoration of apostolic power, and a global harvest of souls before the return of Christ.

The following chart hopefully gives a helpful visual of the various views:

Various Christian Views of the End of the Age and the Second Coming

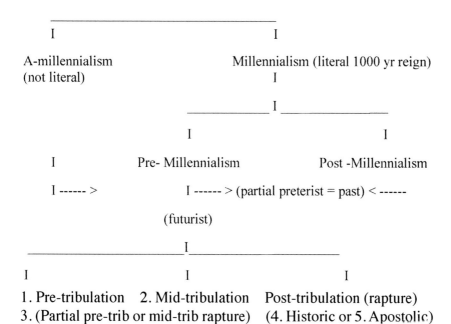

I	I
A-millennialism (not literal)	Millennialism (literal 1000 yr reign) I

                          I

            I   I

I   Pre- Millennialism   Post -Millennialism

I ------ >   I ------ > (partial preterist = past) < ------

           (futurist)

            I

I   I   I

1. Pre-tribulation   2. Mid-tribulation   Post-tribulation (rapture)
3. (Partial pre-trib or mid-trib rapture)   (4. Historic or 5. Apostolic)

ONE: Dispensational Pre-Tribulation Rapture teaching began in the 1830s with John N. Darby of Great Britain. This teaching divides up history into various dispensations, makes a clear distinction between the church and Israel and promotes a two-stage end time coming of Christ. The first stage is when Jesus comes secretly to rapture the church before the tribulation. The second stage is Christ's public coming after tribulation. He first comes for His saints then later He comes with His saints.

A sample of the many modern supporters of this extremely popular view would be Hal Lindsey, John MacArthur, John Walvoord, Charles Ryrie, Paul D. Feinberg, the late Grant Jeffreys, Charles Stanley, Chuck Smith, Chuck Swindoll, Chuck Missler, Tim LaHaye (of best selling Left Behind series fame) as well as Moody Bible

Institute and Dallas Theological Seminary. Because this appealing viewpoint has gained such a following in the last one hundred years or so and is potentially very harmful if not true, we will address this theory further in this chapter.

TWO: The Mid-Tribulation or Mid Week Rapture teaching sees Jesus coming for His bride after the Antichrist has been revealed and has broken the treaty with Israel half way through the seven-year period. These last 3 1/2 years are when the Antichrist's persecution kicks in and God's judgments will be poured out. After these last 3 1/2 years Christ will return publicly to establish His Messianic millennial Kingdom. Some call this view the pre-wrath rapture of the church. In 1941, Norman B. Harrison published his book, The End: Rethinking the Revelation, which presented this viewpoint. Gleason L. Archer Jr., presents a case for this perspective in a more recent book, Three Views on The Rapture.[7]

THREE: The Partial Rapture teaching (whether pre-trib or mid-trib) claims that only the devout Christians who are watching and waiting and filled with the Spirit will be raptured ahead of the coming tribulation. The rest of the believers, along with nonbelievers must go through the purging fire of tribulation. The parable of the ten virgins in Matthew 25 is one biblical passage used in support of this view.

Opponents would argue that the Christian life is based on the principle of grace, not works and that to make the rapture a reward for godly living goes contrary to this biblical principle. Some would also argue that it divides the unity of the body of Christ as well as ignores clear teaching of Scripture regarding the translation of all true believers. In 1 Corinthians 15:51, for instance, Paul claims "we will all be changed - in a flash..."

From her own reading as well as a prophetic revelation received in 1830, Margaret Macdonald, a young Scottish woman from just outside of Glasgow, appears to be the first to promote this view. Some however, claim the partial rapture theory originated with Robert Govett, who in 1853 presented it in his book, Entrance into the Kingdom: The Apocalypse Expounded by Scripture. G. H. Lang may have been the most prominent expounder in the 20th century.

Though this theory is not widely held, it is gaining some momentum, particularly among some charismatic groups. Certainly one strength to this teaching is that it urges believers to be watchful, faithful, walking in intimacy with Jesus, our Bridegroom, and continually keeping one's lamp full of the oil of the Holy Spirit.

FOUR: The Historic (Classic) Post-Tribulation Rapture doctrine holds to the belief that Christians will be raptured at Jesus' glorious second coming at the end of the great tribulation. His coming is seen as a single event rather than in two stages. The strength of the historic pre-mill view is that it has a literal interpretation of prophecy and it prepares for persecution and our responsibility to provoke Israel to jealousy. The weakness however, is its lack of confidence in a victorious church walking in her bridal identity, a global harvest, and the cultural mandate to transform society.

This perspective is the oldest taught position but had been outstripped by dispensational pre-tribulation teaching by the 1920s. A sample of modern theologians and Bible teachers who teach this post-trib perspective are Robert H. Gundry, Douglas J. Moo, David Pawson and John Piper.

Timothy Weber, in his book, The Future Explored, writes, "The Christian life is no joy ride to glory. There are dangers along the way. In what must rank as a classic understatement, the apostle Paul, after being in constant danger on his first missionary journey, observed, "We must go through many hardships to enter the kingdom of God". (Acts 14:22) But along with the inevitable challenges of the Christian life come the promises of victory in the end. Our Lord said, "I have told you these things so that in Me you may have peace. In this world you will have trouble. But take heart! I have overcome the world". (John 16:33) God has not left us to fight our battles alone. He has outfitted us with His own armor so that there will be no question of our ultimate victory." (Eph. 6:10-18)[8]

FIVE: The Apostolic Post-Tribulation Rapture teaching is an upgraded and higher octane version of the classic post-tribulation teaching just referred to. This version acknowledges that indeed God's people will be on earth and must go through the unprecedented pressures and trials at the end of the age. It will not be a walk in the park. But the good news is that we are not pulled out from being on the front lines of the action that is about to take place. In the midst of the chaos, turmoil, harassment and suffering, we don't have to miss out on the greatest and most powerful move of God and global ingathering of people into the Kingdom ever to take place in history.

The persecuted but victorious church will walk in apostolic power of signs and wonders as she partners with the Lord in doing great Kingdom exploits. Jesus' prophetic word found in John 14:12, "He will do even greater things than these" will finally be fulfilled. Not only will this prophetic, praying and fasting church walk in apostolic power and authority but also unity, intimacy and maturity as it is equipped by the fivefold ministry. (Eph. 4:11-14)

Apostolic Christianity will emerge in the end times which involves a release of the glory realm as well as the Spirit's gifts, fruit, and wisdom, that lead to impacting lives and transforming geographic areas. Passionate worship, intercession and fasting, the gathering of solemn assemblies of prayer, repentance and revival (Joel 2:12-17) as well as the establishing of cities of refuge and mercy that will have divine provision and protection are all part of what God will have His church participating in. Part of the church will fall away while others rise up to walk in apostolic Christianity – no in between.

Jesus will be returning for a unified, passionate, youthful yet mature bride. (Eph. 5:25-27) This bride will joyfully embrace the cross (persecution) as well as engage in God's purposes for Israel. Israel will be provoked to jealousy by the church standing in solidarity with them during persecution and by the church walking in apostolic power and glory.

Bible teacher, Derek Prince, Messianic leader, Dan Juster and Kansas City house of prayer leader, Mike Bickle are representatives of this faith-filled perspective and have written and taught extensively on it. I am indebted particularly to Mike Bickle and his teaching materials in this chapter. I have also heard prophetic voices such as John Paul Jackson, Bob Jones, Larry Randolph, Terry Bennett and Rick Joyner speak of the church's destiny of walking in both apostolic power and hardships at the end of the age.

Just in case it isn't obvious, this apostolic post-tribulation teaching is the paradigm that I have found to best represent the biblical data, church history, contemporary Christian prophecies and current world events.

5. What About the Controversial Issue of a Separate Secret Rapture of the Church Before the Tribulation and the Public Coming of Christ?

Although the pre-trib/mid-trib secret rapture theory is the most popular of all the pre-millennial views and the emphasis on being ready because Jesus could come at any time has resulted in some evangelistic fruit for which we rejoice, *I see the following weaknesses to this teaching:*

One: It does not seem to take seriously the biblical warnings to believers that tribulation would be the norm in this present evil age.

While many followers of Christ around the world are presently under intense pressures and persecution for their faith (100,000 to 200,000 are martyred every year), Christians in the West are living lives of exceptional ease, materialism and comfort. We are thankful for the relative peace and freedom of religion that we enjoy in the West, the fruit of Christianity's influence over the centuries, but we must not assume that it will always remain that way simply because that is all we have known. Neither should we embrace a theological view because it makes us feel good and comfortable. We must submit to the authority of Scripture, even if it doesn't line up with our personal preferences. The New Testament continuously warns us that followers of Jesus will experience trials and tribulation in this life. Embracing a theology of the cross, of suffering and of refining is not optional.

I encourage you to take the time to prayerfully read through the Scripture passages that pertain to tribulation for those who are loyal to Jesus and allow the Word, not our western comfort-seeking culture, dictate what and how we believe.

Two: It is a high risk belief system, leaving believers with a false sense of security and ill-prepared for hardship & persecution

Regarding signs of the end of the age, Christ warned his followers, "Watch out that no one deceives you...All these are the beginning of birth pains. Then you will be handed over to be persecuted and put to death, and you will be hated by all nations because of me. At that time many will turn away from the faith and will betray and hate each other...but he who stands firm to the end will be saved". (Matt. 24:4, 8, 9, 10, 13) Jesus spoke of a significant apostasy, a falling away from the faith, (which literally refers to "taking offence") at the end of the age. I am concerned that the popularity of this pre-tribulation rapture theory may become a major contributing factor to this taking offence and falling away

Chinese house church leaders have stated that they were extremely thankful to the Lord for the western missionaries who made great sacrifices in bringing them the gospel many years ago. But they also brought another teaching. They were told not to worry about trials and tribulations because Jesus would come and they would be raptured before that would ever happen. Of course, in 1949/50, communism came into power in China and the foreign missionaries had to flee for their lives (including my wife's parents), national pastors were imprisoned, and great persecution came to the struggling Christian church of one to two million believers. Many new believers gave up their faith, claiming Jesus had lied to them and let them down.

Corrie Ten Boom heard a Chinese bishop say, sadly, "We have failed. We should have made the people strong for persecution rather than telling them Jesus would come first." Turning to Corrie Ten Boom he said, "You will have time. Tell the people how to be strong in times of persecution, how to stand when the tribulation comes - to stand and not faint."[9]

In a 1974 letter written by Corrie Ten Boom (author of the book, The Hiding Place, and whose family helped hide many Jews from the Nazis in WW II), she states that:

"There are some among us teaching there will be no tribulation, that the Christians will be able to escape all this...Most of them have little knowledge of what is already going on across the world...I feel I have a divine mandate to go and tell the people of this world that it is possible to be strong in the Lord Jesus Christ. We are in training for the tribulation, but more than sixty percent of the Body of Christ across the world has already entered into the tribulation. There is no way to escape it. We are next. Since I have already gone through prison for Jesus' sake, and since I met the bishop in China, now every time I read a good Bible text I think, "Hey, I can use that in the time of tribulation." Then I write it down and learn it by heart."[10]

I believe it is much wiser to plan and prepare to go through tough times, including the Great Tribulation if it is in our lifetime, and be pleasantly surprised if we don't rather than believe in a secret rapture before a tribulation and be totally caught off guard if we do. If we are totally ill equipped for tribulation and feel God misled us, some, if not many, will inevitably get offended at God and renounce their faith, especially when push comes to shove.

Three: It downplays our cultural mandate to be salt and light and to seek transformation of society

The common response of this pessimistic view is escapism (why bother if we will soon be raptured) as well as defeatism (society cannot be effectively changed). It sees the church's mandate like a life raft seeking to rescue a few drowning people and leads to a passive disengagement and complacency instead of releasing an urgency of prayer and seeking Kingdom breakthroughs in partnership with a big God who desires that no one perish.

Four: It rules out the church participating in the great end time harvest

Scripture and contemporary prophetic words speak of great waves of revival and an end-time harvest of salvations (see chapters on revival). God is very capable of gathering in the harvest on His own but He generally chooses to use human vessels, His people in the process. To take them out of the equation at the apex of world revival and harvest doesn't make sense. That is to be their finest hour.

Matthew 13:39 has been used by some to argue that Christians won't be needed on earth for the end of the age harvest because the angels (and maybe some Jewish evangelists) will do the job of evangelizing and bringing in the harvest of souls for salvation.

However the Matthew text states that the harvest at the end of the age is in reference to both the matured good seed and matured weeds or tares. The job of the angels is not to evangelize but rather to separate the two - to pull up weeds and burn them in the fire.

Verse 41 states that the angels "will weed out of his kingdom everything that causes sin and all who do evil. They will throw them into the fiery furnace, where there will be weeping and gnashing of teeth. Then the righteous will shine like the sun in the kingdom of their Father."

Biblical evidence indicates that it will be the overcoming, mature, and passionate church that will partner with God in bringing in this mighty end time harvest of souls as well as partner with God in releasing the temporal judgments of the Lord upon the end time Pharaoh (the Antichrist) at the very end of the tribulation. This will be similar to Moses releasing the ten plagues on Pharaoh and the Egyptian people, while the Hebrew people were divinely protected from God's judgments in Goshen.

Five: It doesn't line up with various Scripture passages

a) Matthew 24:27-31, states that immediately after the tribulation of those days Jesus will appear in the heavens, He will send

His angels with a great sound of a trumpet and they will gather together His elect.

In 1 Thess. 4:14-17, Paul tells us that the Lord will descend from heaven with a shout, with the angels and with trumpets blowing, the dead in Christ rising first, then those still alive will be caught up with them to meet the Lord in the air.

In 1 Cor. 15:51-52, Paul proclaims that we shall be changed in a twinkling of an eye, at the last trumpet. For the trumpet will sound and the dead will be raised incorruptible and we shall be changed.

These three biblical passages are describing the same event, Jesus returning to earth with trumpets blasting, dead rising and those alive being gathered up to Him. It takes a little more fancy footwork to somehow make it into two comings, one secret and one public. Notice that the Corinthian passage states that the dead will be raised and others will be changed, all at the last trumpet call. "Last" means there will not be another one to follow it. The most straightforward way to take these passages is a simple one-time return of Christ. There is no hint of a two-stage theory here. You have to impose that into the text.

b) Let's look further at the passage of 1 Thessalonians 4:17, "After that, we who are still alive and are left will be caught up with them in the clouds **to meet** the Lord in the air."

The word, "meet," **"apentesis"**, is used four times in the Bible: Matthew 25:1, 6; Acts 28:15, and 1 Thess. 4:17. In Matthew it refers to bringing the bridegroom to the feast. In Acts it refers to bringing Paul to Rome and in Thessalonians to bringing Jesus to earth.

New Testament scholar, F. F. Bruce wrote, "When a dignitary paid an official visit or parousia to a city in Hellenistic times, the action of the leading citizens in going out to meet him and escorting him on the final stage of his journey was called the apantesis; it is similarly used in Mt. 25:6; Acts 28:15. So the Lord is pictured as escorted to the earth by His people - those newly raised from death and those who have remained alive."[11]

Oswald I Smith stated, "I learned, too, that the word for "meet" in 1 Thessalonians 4...meant "returning with" and not "remaining at" the place of meeting. When the brethren from Rome met Paul, they immediately returned to the city with him. When the virgins met the bridegroom they accompanied him back to the wedding. When the saints meet Christ in the air...they will return with Him...there is no secret Rapture. That theory must be deliberately read into the passage."[12]

c) The most debated verse on this subject of the rapture and its timing relative to the Great Tribulation is **Rev. 3:10,**

"Since you have kept my command to endure patiently, I will also keep you from the hour of trial that is going to come upon the whole world to test those who live on the earth".

The Lord reassures His own, promising that He will keep them from the great trials that are coming. Two possible interpretations come to mind:

1. He will remove or rapture us from the danger of the hour of trial or
2. He will protect us, guard us during the hour of trial.

The Greek word for "keep" is "tereo" and found seventy times in the NT. When in reference to people, it is to keep or obey God's commands. In reference to God keeping us, it's in reference to protecting us in the midst of danger.[13]

Robert Gundry, in his book, The Church and the Tribulation, writes,

"Where a situation of danger is in view, "tereo" means "to guard". The presence of danger is implicit in the idea of guarding. But if the church will be in heaven during the hour of testing, where will be the danger which would require God's protecting hand upon her? Throughout the LXX (Greek translation of the Old Testament) and the New Testament "tereo" always occurs for protection within the sphere of danger. In our Lord's priestly prayer for His own we find a striking confirmation that keeping necessarily implies the presence of danger:

"I am no more in the world; yet they themselves are in the world... keep them" (John 17:11, 12)...The keeping is required by their presence in the sphere of danger."[14]

The New International Version translates it, "protect" them.
Gundry goes on to state, "There is only one other place in biblical Greek where "tereo" and "ek" (from) occur together, John 17:15:

"I do not ask Thee to take them out of the world, but to keep them from the evil one."

The parallels between John 17:15 & Rev. 3:10 are very impressive. Both verses appear in Johannine literature. Both come from the lips of Jesus. A probability arises, therefore, of similar usage and meaning. In John 17:15 the words "take out of" (ares...ek) mean "to lift or raise up and remove". The expression gives an exact description of what the rapture will be, a lifting up and removal. Yet it is this expression against which Jesus throws "tereo ek" in full contrast and opposition. How then can tereo ek refer to the rapture...when in its only other occurrence the phrase opposes an expression which would perfectly describe the rapture?"[15]

Six: It is a new and novel doctrine apparently based on a prophetic revelation, not on clear and explicit Scripture

Prior to 1830, no such pre-tribulation secret rapture doctrine existed. It appears that Edward Irving followed by John Nelson Darby were the first leaders to promote this teaching. Modern teachers of dispensationalism claim the secret rapture doctrine originated from the Plymouth Brethren leader, John Darby, the "father of modern dispensationalism." However, Dave MacPherson, in his meticulously researched book, The Rapture Plot, claims this theory came from the Irvingite group called the Catholic Apostolic Church, particularly from one of its members, a young Scottish lassie and prophetess named Margaret Macdonald.[16]

Margaret Macdonald's "prophetic revelation" that created quite a stir, entailed a partial rapture, that is, she believed the more worthy Christians who were filled with the Spirit would be taken up to heaven before the tribulation. J.N. Darby drew from her teachings as well as others in the Irvingite group and changed it. Rather than making a distinction between believers who were living a more holy and Spirit filled life and those who were not to determine who is raptured, Darby made a distinction between Christians and Jews and claimed all Christians would be secretly raptured.[17]

As I have stated in an earlier chapter, God does speak prophetically to His children outside of the Scriptures but it must not be contrary to Scripture. Charismatic Christians virtually all agree that it is dangerous to ever establish a new doctrine based on a prophetic utterance. Prophecy can confirm biblical doctrine but not be the source for creating a new doctrine.

Though no clear and explicit Scriptural passages could be found that speak of a separate and secret rapture prior to the public return of Christ, several passages in the book of Revelation were conscripted by means of symbolic interpretation to build a case.

The two witnesses in Revelation 11:12 were told to "come up here" and so they went up to heaven in a cloud. Over the years, some believed these two witnesses were Enoch and Elijah while some claimed they represented the Old and New Testaments. In this case, the two witnesses were seen as symbols of the church. This is the view Margaret Macdonald took.

Another passage utilized by others to support this novel teaching was in Revelation 12, in which the male child was snatched up to God. While it has been traditionally viewed as referring to Christ and his ascension to heaven, some claimed it referred to the church being raptured.

Eventually Revelation 3 and the Philadelphia church as well as Revelation 4 and the instruction given to the apostle John to "come up here" were also passages symbolically interpreted as biblical support of this teaching.[18]

The dispensational theology that J.N. Darby developed places a rigid separation between Israel and the church. Darby had come to the conclusion that all Christendom, in its organized expression, was apostate. The true church was a heavenly people while Israel was God's earthly people, and that which is heavenly must be raptured out of the earthly tribulation.[19]

Thanks to C. I. Scofield and his 1909 Scofield Bible, the Bible conferences and Bible school movement, particularly Moody Bible Institute and Moody Press, dispensational theology, with its pre-tribulation secret rapture, has become extremely popular among Christian fundamentalists, most Pentecostals as well as many Charismatics and Evangelicals in North America. In fact, in some circles, this doctrine of eschatology has become a litmus test of one's orthodoxy.

It's worth noting however, that two great leaders whose roots were from the Brethren movement, rejected dispensational and pre-tribulation theology - George Mueller (of 19th century orphanage fame) and the late F. F. Bruce, considered one of the great New Testament scholars of modern Evangelicalism.

So, if a pre-tribulation secret rapture is not likely in God's game plan at the end of the age, that means that if we haven't died, we will be here for the turbulent and action-packed days of tribulation. In the next chapter we will tackle the questions:

6. Why would God allow His bride to go through tribulation and suffering?
7. What should be our attitude towards the book of Revelation?
8. What might the end times drama and time frames look like?

Note: Recommended Resources will be listed at the end of the next chapter

Notes:

---

[1] Winkie Pratney with Barry Chant, The Return, Sovereign World, 2nd ed. 1991, pp. 99-100.

[2] Charles Swindoll, Growing Deep, Zondervan, 1995, p. 268.

[3] C. S. Lewis, Mere Christianity, C.S. Lewis Pte. Ltd., 1952, renewed 1980, p. 104.

[4] Mike Bickle, Omega, End Times Teaching by Mike Bickle, Leader's Guide, Forerunner Books, pp. 13-16.

[5] Ibid., pp. 81, 82.

[6] Harold R. Eberle & Martin Trench, Victorious Eschatology: A Partial Preterist View, Worldcast Pub., 2nd ed., 2009, p. 293.

[7] Archer Jr., Feinberg, Moo, Reiter, Three Views on The Rapture, Pre-, Mid-, Post-Tribulation, Zondervan, 1984, 1996.z

[8] Timothy P. Weber, The Future Explored, Victor, 1978, p. 109.

[9] Nate Krupp, The Church Triumphant at the End of the Age, Destiny Image, 1984, 1988, p. 215, citing Jim McKeever, Christians will go Through the Tribulation, Omega Pub., 1978 p. 5, see also: Vernon Kuenzi, Restoring the Vision of the End-Time Church, Preparing the Way Pub., 2000, p. 70.

[10] Corrie Ten Boom letter written in 1974, liberty to the captives, http://libertytothecaptives.net/ten_boom.html

[11] F. F. Bruce, New Bible Commentary, Eerdmanns, 1970, article on 1 Thessalonians, p. 1159.

[12] Oswald J. Smith, Tribulation or Rapture -Which? pamphlet, p. 9; also Harold R. Eberle & Martin Trench, pp. 289-291.

[13] Collin Brown, editor, Dictionary of NT Theology, Vol. 2, Zondervan, 1976, pp. 132, 133.

[14] Robert Gundry, The Church and the Tribulation, Zondervan, 1973, p. 58.

[15] Ibid., pp. 58, 59.

[16] Dave MacPherson, The Rapture Plot, Artisan Pub., 2009.

[17] Ibid., pp. 28, 29.

[18] Ibid., p. 232.

[19] Ian Rennie, Dreams, Visions & Oracles, The Layman's Guide to Biblical Prophecy, edited by Carl E. Armerding & W. Ward Gasque, Baker Bookhouse, 1977, pp. 50-52.

Chapter 20

The End Times and the Return of Jesus, the True Heavy Weight Champion of the World

Part 2

"A diamond is just a piece of charcoal that handled stress exceptionally well."

"When a train goes through a tunnel and it gets dark, you don't throw away the ticket and jump off. You sit still and trust the engineer." Corric Ten Boom

"...the lawless one will be revealed, whom the Lord Jesus will overthrow with the breath of his mouth and destroy by the splendour of his coming." 2 Thess. 2:8

Question 6: Why Would God Allow His Bride to Go Through Tribulation and Suffering?

Scripture clearly testifies to the fact that we will face tribulation.

*D*ietrich Bonhoeffer, the German theologian who was executed weeks before the end of World War II, is famous for these words, "When Christ calls a man, he bids him come and die."[1]

This is merely a paraphrase of Mark 8:34 when Jesus said, "If any man would come after me, let him deny himself and take up his cross and follow me."

John Piper, in his book, Let the Nations Be Glad, writes, "The cross is not a burden to bear, it is an instrument of pain and execution. It would be like saying, "Pick up your electric chair and follow me to the execution room."[2]

Jesus frequently warned His disciples that they too would have to suffer persecution and possible martyrdom. He made it clear that "No servant is greater than his master. If they persecuted me, they will persecute you also". (John 15:20)

The apostle Paul bluntly states, "In fact, everyone who wants to live a godly life in Christ Jesus will be persecuted." (2 Timothy 3:12)

We are quick to point out that the apostle Paul emphatically stated, "For God did not appoint us to suffer wrath but to receive salvation through our Lord Jesus Christ". (1 Thess. 5:9) We are right to get excited about this promise. But don't forget that earlier in the same letter, Paul tells the new believers in Thessalonica that:

"We sent Timothy...to strengthen and encourage you in your faith, so that no one would be unsettled by these trials. You know quite well that we were destined for them. In fact, when we were with you, we kept telling you that we would be persecuted". (1 Thess. 3:2-4)

It comes with the territory of being in solidarity with Christ. It is part of our calling, our vocation. So if Christians are not appointed unto wrath but are appointed or destined for trials and persecution, what is the difference?

Tribulation versus Wrath of God

There are two Greek words most often used to describe tribulation. The first word is "diogmos" which occurs ten times in the New Testament and is translated "persecution". In every instance this word consistently refers to the persecution of Christians by non-Christians.

The second word is "thlipsis", which occurs forty-five times in the New Testament and is translated "tribulation(s)," "affliction(s)," "distress," "persecution," or "trouble." In forty-two of these forty-five occurrences, the word refers to the suffering believers received at the hands of non-believers because of their solidarity with Christ. One time the word is used of Joseph at the hands of his brothers (Acts 7:9-10), another instance of thlipsis is in reference to the famine in Joseph's day. (Acts 7:11) Only once does the term refer to the suffering of those who commit evil. (Romans 2:9) Rich Dean makes a very good point when he says, "On this basis alone one would seem to be on shaky ground in assuming that the tribulation is reserved only for non-believers (since it only refers to non-believers in only two percent of all verses)".[3]

In contrast, two Greek words are used to describe wrath or anger. The first word is "thumos" found eighteen times in the New Testament. About half the time it refers to God's wrath towards the unrighteous. It is found ten times in the book of Revelation and almost every time it refers to God's wrath.

The other word, "orgay", is found thirty-six times in the New Testament. The majority of the time it refers to God's wrath against the unrighteous. The book of Revelation speaks of the battle between angers. The anger of the nations (Rev. 11:18) and the anger of the dragon (Rev. 12:17) oppose the anger or wrath of God. God's wrath and judgments are described as the rod of iron, the winepress of the fury of God's wrath and the cup of His wrath that the wicked must drink.[4] Mankind has been warned, "Woe to those who call evil good and good evil". (Isaiah 5:20)

We can conclude that tribulation almost always refers to the persecution and suffering of Christians and wrath almost always refers to God's righteous anger towards unrepentant sinners and nations that will result in the execution of divine judgment and punishment.

New Testament scholar, Gordon Fee, in his book, Reading the Bible for All its Worth, confirms this:

"It should be noted here that one of the keys for interpreting the Revelation is the distinction John makes between two crucial words or ideas - tribulation and wrath. To confuse these and make them refer to the same thing will cause one to become hopelessly muddled as to what is being said. Tribulation (suffering and death) is clearly a part of what the church was enduring and was yet to endure. God's wrath, on the other hand, is His judgment that is to be poured upon those who have afflicted God's people. It is clear from every kind of context in the Revelation that God's people will not have to endure God's awful wrath when it is poured out upon their enemies, but it is equally clear that they will indeed suffer from the hands of their enemies. This distinction, it should be noted, is precisely in keeping with the rest of the New Testament."[5]

The author of the book of Hebrews tells us that Jesus suffered outside the city gate to make people holy through the shedding of His blood but then exhorts us to go to Him outside the camp and bear the disgrace and abuse He had to put up with. Outside the camp involves being outside the borders of safety, comfort and reputation. (Heb. 13:12-14)

The apostle Peter exhorts us that, "since Christ suffered in his body, arm your selves also with the same attitude..." (1 Peter 4:1) Peter goes on to instruct us to "not be surprised at the painful trial you are suffering as though something strange were happening to you. But rejoice that you participate in the sufferings of Christ, so that you may be overjoyed when his glory is revealed. If you are insulted because of the name of Christ, you are blessed, for the Spirit of glory and of God rests on you". (1 Peter 4:12-14)

In Revelation we are told that at the fifth seal, John saw the souls of the martyrs under the altar and heard them call out, "How long, sovereign Lord, holy and true, until you judge the inhabitants of the earth and avenge our blood?" Then each of them was given a white robe and they were told to wait a little longer, until the number of their fellow servants and brothers who were to be killed as they had been was completed". (Rev. 6:9-11) We can be offended at God, at our own peril, but we do not have the liberty to water down what the Bible tells us. The all-wise God has a certain quota of martyrs in mind before He will dispense vengeance and justice on His evil enemies.

We could go on and on with Scripture after Scripture stating the fact that God not only allows Christians to suffer opposition for their faith but also exhorts us to anticipate it as part of our calling, prepare for it in our heart and head and even rejoice in it.

So let's go back to the burning question, "Why would God allow and even ordain His bride to suffer in this present evil age and even more so at the end of the age?"

Or let me put it more graphically, "Why would any bridegroom let his bride be beaten up before their marriage?"

I admit there is a mystery to it all and with our natural wisdom it seems ludicrous if not twisted. But God has told us that His thoughts and ways are higher than our thoughts and ways. (Isaiah 55:8, 9) We need to trust where we don't have understanding. Our faith is precious to the Lord and without it, it is impossible to please Him. (Heb. 11:6) Our faith is like gold that needs to be purified by fire. Like Job, we need to say, "Though He slay me, yet will I trust Him."

Rick Warren, in his book, The Purpose Driven Life, writes:

"God continually tests people's character, faith, obedience, love, integrity, and loyalty. Words like trials, temptations, refining, and testing occur more than 200 times in the Bible. God tested Abraham... Jacob...Joseph, Ruth, Esther, and Daniel. Character is both developed and revealed by tests, and all of life is a test. You are always being tested...When you realize that life is a test, you realize that nothing is insignificant in your life. Even the smallest incident has significance for your character development. Every day is an important day, and every second is a growth opportunity to deepen your character, to demonstrate love, or to depend on God. Some tests seem overwhelming, while others you don't even notice. But all of them have eternal implications."[6]

Benefits that the Bible promises will be ours if we patiently endure tribulation and suffering

• Trials separate the men from the boys. It sifts out the false from the true follower. (Matt. 13:21; 1 Thess. 1:6)

447

- The light and momentary tribulations are actually working in our favour in terms of releasing a far more and exceeding weight of glory. (2 Cor. 4:17; 1 Peter 4:12-16) John Piper points out that, "There seems to be a connection between the suffering endured and the degree of glory enjoyed."[7]

  But Paul doesn't think the present sufferings are even "worth comparing with the glory that is to be revealed in us". (Rom.8:18)
- We are sharing in the fellowship of the sufferings of Christ so that we can also share in the fellowship of His resurrection. (Phil. 3:10)
- We are becoming like Christ in His death. (Phil. 3:11)
- Through tribulation we enter more fully into things of the Kingdom of God. (Acts 14:22)
- We are to rejoice in our persecutions because our reward is great in heaven. (Matt. 5:11-12)
- Our confidence and perseverance will be richly rewarded. (Heb. 10:32-39)
- For a little while we may need to suffer various trials so that our faith would be refined by fire and proved genuine, resulting in praise, glory and honour when Jesus is revealed (1 Peter 1:6,7)
- The person who has suffered in his body is done with sin and now lives for the will of God rather than his own selfish desires. (1 Peter 4:1-3)
- We are to consider the trials we face as pure joy because the testing of our faith develops perseverance, which moves us to maturity and completeness, lacking nothing. (James 1:2-4) Jesus is coming back for a pure, spotless and mature bride that will be equally yoked with Him.

The story of Esther is a prophetic picture of the beauty preparations that the church, the bride of Christ, will experience before seeing the King. Esther experienced six months of treatment of oil of myrrh, the burial spice, which represents death, as well as a six-month treatment of fragrant perfumes. When presented to the king, a crown was set upon her head and she was given much favour and grace. In the Great Tribulation the bride of Christ will experience the manifestations of the oil of myrrh of martyrdom and fragrant perfumes of God's unprecedented power and glory.[8]

- The pressures and hardships Paul and his companions suffered in the province of Asia felt like "the sentence of death." But Paul concludes, "this happened that we might not rely on ourselves but on God, who raises the dead". (2 Cor. 1:8-10) In our western culture that is characterized by rugged individualism and independence, even in the church, God desires to wean us from self-reliance and deepen our child-like trust and dependence upon Him through the crucible of affliction. It then becomes an opportunity to spotlight God's power and grace and make it sparkle for His glory.

- We are to endure hardship as discipline. God is treating us as sons, not as illegitimate children, "for our own good, that we may share in his holiness. No discipline seems pleasant at the time, but painful. Later on, however, it produces a harvest of righteousness and peace for those who have been trained by it". (Heb.12:7-11)

- It appears God uses the suffering of His servants and missionaries to wake other believers up out of their slumber of complacency and to stir them to bold risk taking ventures as well. Regarding the stoning of Stephen, we would think he was more valuable to the Kingdom alive than dead. But with his martyrdom, a young guy later named Paul was impacted as well as persecution broke out in Jerusalem forcing disciples of Jesus to flee Jerusalem and scatter like salt out of a salt shaker, gossiping the gospel wherever they went.

We see this dynamic when five missionaries were speared to death in 1956 in Ecuador while attempting to reach the Auca tribe. Their wives went back to that very tribe and led their husband's murderers to Jesus. Some may see this tragedy as such a waste. But the impact these martyrs and their wives have made, inspiring a future generation of missionaries, cannot be measured. A 2005 movie called "End of the Spear" was produced to tell this dramatic story for years to come.

The missionary pilot, Jim Elliot, made this famous statement that has further inspired an untold number of believers, "He is no fool who gives what he cannot keep to gain what he cannot lose." In John 12:24, we are told the principle that, "Unless a kernel of wheat falls to the ground and dies, it remains only a single seed. But if it dies, it produces many seeds." Tertullian stated it this way, "The blood of the martyrs is seed of the church".

John Piper challenges the massive number of baby boomers of today who have been conditioned with the American dream mindset of looking forward to a leisurely time of retirement to choose instead to make a difference for eternity in terms of sacrificially reaching the unreached millions who don't know Christ.

Piper tells the humorous story of an aging Christian who objected to John G. Paton's plan to go to the South Sea Islands as a missionary by saying, "You'll be eaten by cannibals!" Paton replied with, "Mr. Dickson, you are advanced in years now, and your own prospect is soon to be laid in the grave, there to be eaten by worms; I confess to you, that if I can but live and die serving and honoring the Lord Jesus, it will make no difference to me whether I am eaten by Cannibals or worms; and in the Great Day my resurrection body will arise as fair as yours in the likeness of our risen Redeemer."[9]

Question 7: What Should Be Our Attitude Towards The Book of Revelation?

I am indebted to David Pawson and his extremely scholarly yet devotional book, Unlocking the Bible, for a number of the insights that I will share regarding the book of Revelation. I highly recommend this Bible reference tool to every serious Bible student to consider having in his or her library. Mike Bickle's Book of Revelation Study Guide is also extremely helpful.

The assumption of many unbelievers about the book of Revelation is that it is the result of "indigestion at best or insanity at worst". The reaction of unbelievers is understandable, since the book is not intended for them.

Yet, surprisingly, even among Christians we see attitudes that range from the fearful who avoid the book like the plague to the fanatical that can't get out of it!

Most Protestant reformers had an extremely low view of this book. Martin Luther stated it as "neither apostolic nor prophetic" and "there are many nobler books to be retained". John Calvin left the book of Revelation out of his New Testament commentary altogether. And Zwingli didn't take it seriously. He claimed, "It is not a book of the Bible." This attitude obviously has influenced the Reformational denominations.[10]

The book of Revelation is unique in that it is a blended combination of three distinct literary types: apocalypse, prophecy and letter. The book is primarily apocalyptic which is characterized by roots in Old Testament prophetic literature, especially Isaiah, Ezekiel, Daniel and Zechariah and filled with pictorial and cryptic language of dreams and visions. Apocalypse was a literary work born in a time of oppression and persecution whose author was concerned to reassure the reader that in spite of appearances, God was very much in control of history. He looked forward to a time when God would break in and bring a violent and radical end to history, with the triumph of righteousness and justice and the judgment of evil.[11]

The Date of the book of Revelation

Those that take the partial preterist view that most events found in biblical prophecy were fulfilled in the first century would say that the apostle John received and wrote down the book of Revelation at an earlier date than traditionally held. This date would have to be before, during or just after the days of the Roman emperor, Nero, who would be considered the beast of Revelation. The harlot would be unfaithful Israel who experienced Rome's destructive wrath in AD 70. The events described in Revelation are thus fulfilled in the first century and not to be repeated in the future.

Yes, Nero persecuted Christians (and can be considered one of many Antichrists), but it was confined to Rome and it was not over Caesar worship but because he had to find scapegoats for the great fire of Rome in AD 64. The more accepted date for the writing of Revelation is somewhere around AD 90 or 95 during the terrifying reign of Domitian who demanded worship and ruthlessly persecuted Christians for not doing so. This persecution was more systematic and widespread. Such universal persecution is what the book of Revelation envisions.

The spiritual decline of the churches in Ephesus, Sardis and Laodicea and the existence of a distinct and well-known heretical group called the Nicolaitans (which are never mentioned in apostolic epistles), all would require some distance in time and would be further evidence pointing to a later date. Proponents of an early date prior to AD 70 often argue that the instructions given to John in Revelation 11:1-2 to measure the temple could only be because the literal temple in Jerusalem was still standing. The reference could be symbolic however. Remember John was on the island of Patmos, not in Jerusalem. Furthermore, in 11:8 John refers to Jerusalem as "Sodom", possibly indicating that the city had already fallen. Many more points could be made for either an early date or later date. Though a later date appears to have more evidence in its favour, we are not able to come to a conclusion with complete certainty.[12]

The Importance of the book of Revelation

David Pawson points out that Satan hates the whole Bible but perhaps even more the first few pages of Genesis that reveal how he gained control of our planet and the last few pages of Revelation, which reveal how he will lose control of it. If he can convince people that Genesis speaks of ridiculous myths and Revelation of bizarre and unintelligible symbolic mysteries, he is quite content. Pawson brilliantly states, "The book calls his bluff. He is only prince and ruler of this world by God's permission. And that has only been given temporarily."[13]

We see God's high opinion of the book of Revelation by the fact that it is the only book in the Bible that has promises of reward and punishment attached to it. A special blessing awaits those who read it aloud (1:3) and who "keep the words", by meditation and application (22:7). On the other hand, a special curse awaits those who tamper with the text. This shows how seriously God takes the truth being revealed in this book.

Since the book completes the story that is told throughout the Bible, it is so fitting that it be positioned last. That story is of a heavenly Father seeking an earthly bride for His Son. Like every good romance, they "get married and live happily ever after." But we wouldn't know the end of the story without the book of Revelation.

Even though many Christians don't use the book much nor are very well acquainted with it, most are glad that the book of Revelation is there, even if just for the fact that it lets us know how it all ends. They can usually handle the first few chapters and the last few, but the large portion in the middle they have no idea what to make of. It is so foreign and different to them. I have to admit that for years I had been quite perplexed and even intimidated by this portion of the book as well and have therefore stayed pretty much clear of it.

Yet, ironically, the book is called the book of "Revelation", the Greek word being "apokalypsis", meaning "unveiling". It is the pulling back of a curtain to reveal what has been hidden. In this case, it reveals what is happening in heaven and what will happen in the future. And of course, it is the revelation of Jesus Christ as the sovereign Lord of history and the champion of the world. God is working out His plans and purposes within time and this book gives us the big picture of world events from God's eternal perspective. Although life seems very unjust with the righteous suffering and the wicked prospering and many questions raised about how God can allow such things to go on, a long term view takes the ultimate outcome into account. This long-term view is clear that God is a good God and He is very much in charge. Wrong will ultimately be made right. There will be rewards for the righteous and punishment of the wicked. God is a God of righteousness and justice.

One other characteristic of apocalyptic writing is that it has its share of symbolism. How can it not since it seeks to communicate truth that is unfamiliar to the reader. The unknown has to somehow be related to the known, usually by analogy ("it's like..."). If they can use their imagination and picture it in their mind, it will be much easier to grasp. The book of Revelation is full of pictorial language that is intended to help our comprehension and understanding, not hinder it.

Pawson categorizes the symbols into four categories:

1. Some are obvious in their meaning. The "dragon" or "serpent" is the devil.
2. Some are explained in the context. The "stars" are angels. The "lamp stands" are churches. The "seals", "trumpets" and "bowls" are disasters.
3. Some are paralleled elsewhere in Scripture. We find the tree of life, the rainbow, the morning star, brutal regimes pictured as wild "beasts" in the Old Testament.
4. Some are obscure, but very few. One example is the "white stone".

The fact that so much symbolism in Revelation is actually in the first three categories and quite clear that there is no excuse for us to dismiss this book. We should be able to handle a few obscurities, trusting that the Lord will make them clearer some day as necessary. About half of all the predictions of future events in Revelation are in clear and straightforward language. The other half is in pictorial language.[14]

The practical reason for the book of Revelation was to help prepare God's people for what was coming. In Revelation 1:9-10 we see the author, the apostle John, already suffering for his faith as a prisoner on the island of Patmos. His exclusive devotion to Jesus as Lord was considered treason by the Roman authorities. Roman citizens were expected to believe in many gods and the emperor was considered to be one. In the last decade of the first century (the time frame most accepted as the date for the writing of Revelation), Domitian was coming on the scene ushering in intense and more widespread persecution of Christians that would continue off and on for roughly two hundred years. The Christian church was about to face its fiercest test so far. Tough times lay ahead. The apostle John was the only one of the twelve disciples left. All the others had been martyred.

David Pawson describes the book of Revelation as a **"manual for martyrdom"**. Its purpose is to prepare believers to face persecution and even martyrdom. The saints are encouraged to "be faithful, even to the point of death". (2:10) **Two key words** of exhortation are frequently found in the book. The first is urging believers to "**endure**". "This calls for patient endurance on the part of the saints who obey God's commandments and remain faithful to Jesus." (14:12) The second exhortation is found even more frequently and is a more active stance towards any suffering for the sake of Jesus and that word is to "**overcome**". Some would say that this is the key word in the whole book.

Each letter to the seven churches describes various internal and external pressures and temptations and ends with a challenge for each believer to be an "overcomer".[15]

Because the churches in the West live quite comfortably with minimal hassle and virtually no persecution, we fail to find this book very relevant. But for believers under considerable pressure Revelation becomes extremely practical and meaningful. It provides a heavenly and an eternal perspective to it all, giving encouragement and hope. Any momentary suffering will be worth it all in light of the fact that Jesus will return to put things right and to establish His glorious Kingdom that will have no end. The sovereign King will come on His white horse to defeat the unholy trinity and their armies and He and His overcoming bride will reign for all eternity.

According to Mike Bickle, the purpose of the book is not only to strengthen and encourage believers to endure and overcome intense trouble, but also to serve as a "**canonized prayer manual**" for the saints as they partner with God through prayer to release signs and wonders as well as God's temporal judgments that seek to remove whatever hinders love. Bickle sees Revelation focusing primarily on God's judgments against the Antichrist and his wicked followers and only secondarily on the persecution of the saints by the Antichrist. Because of this, Bickle further describes Revelation as "the end-time book of Acts." **As the book of Acts describes the power of the Holy Spirit that was unleashed through the early church so the book of Revelation describes the power of the Holy Spirit that will be unleashed through the end-time church.**[16]

Mike Bickle provides a simple yet very helpful breakdown of the **structure of the book of Revelation into four parts:**

Part 1 is the apostle John's calling by the risen Christ to prophesy about the end-times. Chapter one also provides valuable revelation of the greatness and majesty of Jesus Christ that can help carry His followers through the coming events.

Part 2 is Jesus' seven letters to the seven churches in chapters 2 and 3 in which Jesus challenges them (and us) to repent of specific sins so that they may overcome the enemy.

Part 3 is where Jesus takes the scroll, which contains the title deed to earth as well as God's battle strategy to cleanse the earth of evil. (Rev. chapters 4 & 5)

Part 4 covers chapters 6 through 22 and spells out the complete battle plan of Jesus, which includes the tribulation judgments of seven seals, seven trumpets and seven, bowls against the Antichrist and his followers. These judgments appear to intensify in severity and in the speed in which they come. By the time the bowls are released, they may be a matter of days apart.

God's plan fits into five chronological sections with five angelic explanations that function as a parenthesis to give clarity and reassurance to John:

Rev. 6 Chronological Section # 1:Seal Judgments
Rev. 7 Angelic Explanation # 1:Protection from Judgments
Rev. 8-9 Section # 2: Trumpet Judgments
Rev. 10-11 Explanation # 2: Direction from prophetic
Rev. 11:15-19 Section # 3: 2nd coming, rapture, 7th trumpet
Rev. 12-14 Explanation # 3: Antichrist's assault of saints
Rev. 15-16 Section # 4: Bowl Judgments of evil structures
Rev. 17-18 Explanation # 4: Babylon's lust must be destroyed
Rev. 19-20 Section # 5: Jesus' grand entry into Jerusalem
Rev. 21-22 Explanation # 5: the restoration of all things[17]

The book of Revelation is not a book to despise but rather an invaluable manual to prize, all the more as we step into the very events described within it.

Question 8: What Might the End Times Drama and Time Frames Look Like?

From an apostolic post-tribulation and pre-millennial perspective (sorry for all the big words), let me attempt to paint, in broad strokes, how this transition from our present evil age into the new age of Christ's one thousand year earthly reign and beyond might look like. And let me again state that we must humbly hold to details lightly as well be gracious to one another in our differences, knowing that we only see in part and that further revelation and insight will be given to the church as needed by the Lord.

Three Distinct Time Frames in God's End Time Plan

In his very practical manual called, Omega: End Times Teaching by Mike Bickle Leader's Guide, Bickle provides great clarity and insight regarding the end time events and time periods and I draw heavily on this work in this section.

Three specific periods or time frames can be seen when comparing Matthew 24 with 1 Thessalonians 5:2-3 and Daniel 9:27. The end times are described in Scripture like labour pangs that a woman endures just before giving birth to her child. This is a prophetic picture of the trauma that the earth will endure just before the birthing of the age to come and the millennial reign of Christ.

In Daniel 9:24-27, the angel Gabriel spoke of seven years as a week. This final seven-year period just before Jesus' return is referred to as "Daniel's prophetic week".

Just prior to this seven-year period, we have the first stage of this end time drama. It is called **"the beginning of birth pains"** in Matthew 24:8. During this time there will be wars and ethnic cleansings as well as other "signs" such as natural disasters and they will all increase in frequency and intensity. Bickle believes that this first stage of the end times began either at the birthing of Israel as a nation in 1948 or when it captured Jerusalem in 1967. The prophetic clock is now ticking and getting louder.

The **second stage** in the end times time frame is **the period of "counterfeit peace and safety", which involves the first 3 ½** years of the seven year week. The brilliant and diplomatic world leader, the Antichrist, will form a peace treaty with Israel and other Middle East nations and bring global solutions to global problems. This will be a season with no wars or economic problems, a time of peace, but discerning Christians will see that this is not genuine. The time of trouble for the church will begin as discerning Bible believing followers of Jesus are seen as extreme and dangerous and not aligning themselves with political correctness and the world religion of tolerance.

The **third phase** of the end times will begin when the false peace will suddenly end and the **Great Tribulation starts (hard labour pangs) and it too lasts 3 ½ years.** (Daniel 12:7; Rev. 11:2; 12:7; 13:5) The Antichrist will suddenly break the treaty, defile the temple (Daniel 9:27), take off his mask of diplomacy and kindness and show his evil colours. He will demand to be worshipped and will insist on people taking on the "mark of the beast", which represents utter allegiance to him, if they wish to do normal business transactions. He will aggressively persecute Jews and Christians, killing many. God will use the praying church to unleash His wrath and judgments on the Antichrist and his armies and it will all come to a crescendo with the stunning return of the Lord of Lords in the sky. The sun, moon, and stars will be dimmed as Jesus the light of the world takes center stage. Those celestial objects worshipped by man for centuries will pale in comparison to the glory and splendour of our Warrior King who comes in royal procession with every eye beholding Him.[18]

The phrase, "**the Day of the Lord**", which is found about one hundred times, is often referred to as "the great and very terrible (or dreadful) day of the Lord". (Joel 2:11; Malachi 4:5) **It not only refers to the actual day Jesus returns, but to the final 3 ½ years** before Jesus returns. This day is a unique time frame in which Jesus acts in the earthly arena in great power for His people and for the harvest as well as against His enemies- great blessing for those who call on Jesus and terrible judgment for those who refuse Him. No wonder it is called "the great and dreadful day of the Lord."

There will be the greatest outpouring of the Spirit in history with the **miracles seen in the book of Acts and Exodus combined** bringing in a great global harvest of Gentile and Jewish souls. **The bride of Christ will walk in victory and authority with supernatural provision, protection, and prophetic direction.**

In the Great Tribulation, intense pressure and calamity will come from four sources:

1. God's judgments upon the rebellious
2. The rage of Satan – will persecute and even martyr some of the saints through the reign of terror of the Antichrist
3. Sinful actions of evil people against one another
4. By convulsions in creation (earthquakes etc.)[19]

These pressures, like labour pains, will increase in frequency and intensity leading up to the grand finale of Jesus' second coming. This present evil age will transition into the age to come, but through the birthing process that is painful, bloody, and stressful. The judgments of God as described in the book of Revelation as seven seals, seven trumpets, and seven bowls will be increasingly severe and increasingly rapid fire. With a great shout and the blowing of the seventh trumpet, Christ will split the sky open as He descends from heaven with His army and flaming fire, believers will be raptured, given resurrected bodies and meet Him in the air then travel with Him to the Middle East.

Israel has always been center stage in God's heart and covenant plans and Satan has always been out to destroy them. A thoroughly researched book by Dalton Lifsey called The Controversy of Zion and the Time of Jacob's Trouble, strongly argues this, including the biblical legitimacy of the Jews back in the land, the critical need for Christians to stand with them and a coming final national purging and war at the end of the age (Zechariah 13:8-9 speaks of two thirds perishing and the remaining third refined in the fire and ultimately calling on the Lord).[20] Though they have been blind to the identity of Jesus as their Messiah, Jesus prophesied that He would come again when they cry out, "Blessed is he who comes in the name of the Lord". (Matt. 23:39) He will return to earth and rescue them from captivity and from defeat at the hands of the Antichrist and his warring armies.

Jesus will return just in time. In Matthew 24:22, Jesus tells us that, "If those days had not been cut short, no one would survive, but for the sake of the elect those days will be shortened." Far from promoting a replacement theology (Israel blew it so they are now replaced by the church), the apostle Paul insists that Gentile Christians not be ignorant or conceited. "Israel has experienced a hardening in part until the full number of the Gentiles has come in. And so all Israel will be saved...for God's gifts and his call are irrevocable." (Romans 11:25, 26, 29) Those who survive the coming invasion will repent and embrace Jesus as their Messiah.

Mike Bickle suspects that Christ will first land at Mount Sinai in Egypt (Isa. 19:1), the Mountain of God (not the Mount of Olives), then collect Jewish captives from their prison camps (Micah 2:12-13) throughout Egypt. Jesus will lead the procession from Egypt, through the Sinai wilderness, through Jordan (Edom, Bozrah, Teman) in His journey to Jerusalem. (Hab. 3:3-13) In setting the Jewish prisoners free and defeating His enemies in these places while on His way to Jerusalem, the blood of His enemies will be splattered on His robes. (Isaiah 63:14) During a 30 day window (Daniel 12:11), Jesus, the new and greater Moses, will be releasing on His enemies the seven bowls that will be similar to the plagues Moses released upon Pharoah and Egypt. The seventh bowl, which involves a massive earthquake and one hundred pound hailstones, will be released by Jesus from the Mount of Olives. **Jesus will then march into Jerusalem at the Battle of Jerusalem, defeating the Antichrist and his armies and ending the 3 ½ year Armageddon campaign.**[21]

Jesus the great Warrior King is coming to overthrow the governments of the world and establish His Kingdom permanently on earth. He will destroy the Antichrist and the false prophet with the breath of His mouth (2 Thess. 2:8), throw Satan into prison for one thousand years (Rev. 20:2,3) and **set up His Messianic millennial reign on the earth (Rev. 20:4-6), headquartered in Jerusalem. This will be a one thousand year period of worldwide peace, righteousness, prosperity,** and unprecedented blessing as the earth is progressively restored to the conditions seen in the garden of Eden (with the Tree of Life and River of Life restored, Rev. 22:1,2).

Our life on earth in this present evil age can be likened to a seventy or eighty year internship that prepares us for our life on earth in the age to come. The choices we make in this period determine where and how we will serve in our millennial assignment. Christians will be judged and given rewards at the judgment seat of Christ. (2 Cor. 5:10)

Three types of people are on the earth when Jesus appears:

1. Redeemed who are given glorified bodies when Jesus returns
2. Reprobate who take the mark of the beast and will be judged and killed
3. Resistors, the unsaved survivors of the tribulation who refused to worship the Antichrist. Scripture refers to them as "those who are left or remain" and will have opportunity to be converted when Jesus returns and will populate the millennial earth. (Isaiah 4:3; 10:20; 11:11; 49:6; 65:8; 66:19; Jeremiah 31:2; Exekiel 20:38-42; 36:36; Daniel 12:1; Amos 9:9-10; Joel 2:32; Zechariah 12:14; 13:8; 14:16)[22]

God's purpose is to have Jesus rule the earth with His bride by His side and bring the heavenly realm and earthly realm together. Paradise lost will become Paradise restored. The heavenly Jerusalem and earthly Jerusalem will be brought together creating a vast governmental complex as the center of the government of heaven, earth, and the universe.

At the end of this millennial reign, Satan will be released from prison and allowed one final rebellious uprising against God before he is thrown into the lake of fire. History then concludes with a day of judgment. **The final judgment at the Great White Throne** will take place whereby sinners without Christ will be justly judged.

Hell is a very real place that Jesus urged people to avoid at all costs. (Mt. 5:29, 30) Of the twelve times the word, Gehenna, the most intense word for hell, occurs in the Bible, eleven times they are found on the lips of Jesus. The wages of sin is death - eternal punishment in hell (but the good news is, "...the gift of God is eternal life in Christ Jesus our Lord," Romans 6:23). This final Hell is called by different names, the pit (Rev. 9:1); the abyss (Rev. 20:1); Lake of fire (Rev. 20:10) and Gehenna (Matt. 5:29). This is the final abode of Satan, fallen angels, the Antichrist, the false prophet and all unrepentant sinners whose names were not in the book of life. (Mt. 25:41; Rev. 20:10-15)

The concept of hell is offensive to our intellects. A frequently asked question is: "How could a loving God possibly send people to hell?"

First, God does not "send" people to hell. He merely honours their choice. G.K. Chesterton declared, "Hell is God's great compliment to the reality of human freedom and the dignity of human personality." God is saying that we are significant. He takes us seriously. If we choose to reject Him and choose hell, which is a place of separation from Him, He will let us go (although He is patient and not wanting anyone to perish but all to come to repentance, 2 Peter 3:9).

Furthermore, "people" do not go to hell. Sinners do. The word "people" is neutral, implying innocence. Scripture declares that we have lost our innocence, "all have sinned and come short of the glory of God." God is simply honouring the choice of sinners. C. S. Lewis argued, "There are only two kinds of people in the end: those who say to God, "Thy will be done" and those to whom God says, in the end, "Thy will be done". All that are in hell choose it."[23]

Those who have been redeemed by the blood of the Lamb, Jesus, will dwell for all eternity with the Father, the Son, and the Spirit in the fullness of beauty, intimacy and adventure. It really will be "heaven on earth!" And this new heaven and new earth combo will be mind blowing. The apostle Paul declared, "No eye has seen, no ear has heard, no mind has conceived what God has prepared for those who love him". (1 Cor. 2:9)

Whether we have five more years or five more decades before these climactic end time events of history fully kick in, followed by our Lord's return and violent takeover of evil governments of the world, we, the end time generation have been called to an astounding season and destiny. We are "training for reigning." The best days and the worst days are just ahead as we are about to transition from this present evil age into the glorious age to come when "the kingdoms of this world become the Kingdoms of our Lord of His Christ". What a time to be alive!

May we go through the preparation process of being stripped of ambition for glory and fame, unimpressed with ourselves and filled with wonder at who the Lord of glory is. May our hunger for a simple and uncomplicated life of intimacy with Jesus intensify and may Christ-like character grow and deepen within us to bear the weight of the power and glory of the Lord that will soon rest upon us to touch precious lives all around us in the coming storms.[24]

Scripture is very clear that we must avoid setting dates for Christ's return (though history has plenty of examples of fools who did). No one knows the precise day or the hour, but the Father. But we are to be alert and watchful to know and discern the times and the seasons.

I've noticed however, that some of us, based on our age in life, may subconsciously "discern" that Christ is coming back within a certain time frame that just happens to coincide with our probable lifetime. If we are in our 80s, we may think Jesus is coming back within the next five years. If we are in our 60s or 70s, we may project a five to fifteen year time frame. If considerably younger, we may be hoping for a twenty to fifty year window before Jesus returns, so that we can get married and raise a family. So it is interesting to see how our emotional preferences can play into our eschatology. Not only do many of us have a desire that He return before we must face physical death in old age, but we would love for Him to come rescue us before things get really nasty in any kind of tribulation.

But bottom line, as much as I want a pain-free future like anyone else (maybe even more so), I cannot let my preferences shape and determine my theology.

We are called to submit to the Word, embrace the Cross and keep in step with the Spirit.

That doesn't sound like a pain-free, hassle-free lifestyle. A secret pre-tribulation rapture is a very attractive teaching that is understandably popular among Christians in the West whose lives have been lived out in a bubble of exceptional comfort, ease and safety compared to the rest of the world and the rest of human history. But why should we be a privileged generation and civilization, an exception to the biblical and church historical pattern? As much as we have a preference for the pre-tribulation rapture theory, I believe it leaves us vulnerable.

Let me quote Oswald J. Smith, the Canadian pastor, author and missions advocate, again on this matter, "I am sure that with the true child of God it is not a question of preference but of truth. Does God's Word say so? Why then rebel? Is not His plan best? Besides, what difference does it make so long as we are ready? 'Spiritual Preparedness' is the only important factor after all.

"I wonder if we have been lulling the Church into a false security? Can it be that we have been preaching an easy escape? Ought we to prepare the Church for the greatest of all ordeals? Should not our teaching harden her for the fires of the Tribulation? What kind of soldiers are we training? I am afraid that we have been very guilty and that God will certainly hold us responsible for the type of Christian our preaching is producing. We need men and women today of the martyr spirit. The test of the Inquisition is coming again and woe betide the pre-millennialists who are not ready. The Church must be purified in the fires of persecution."[25]

While writing this book over the past year, I often listened to and was inspired by a powerful song called "Tree", by Justin Rizzo, on the "Unceasing" album. Justin is a worship leader at International House of Prayer (IHOP) in Kansas City. You can hear the song on You-tube or of course purchase it on-line. With his permission, here are the lyrics:

"I wanna be unmovable and unshakable so that my roots go down deep
Unmovable and unshakeable in You (4x)
And I, I wanna be like a tree planted by the streams of Living Water (4x)
This will be my song God, this will be my prayer - til the end, til the end (2x)

In the midst of the coming storm
In the midst of the coming blessing
That my life would be built upon the rock that I would not be moved, would not be shaken."[26]

May this be our mindset and heart's desire. May our roots go down deep in Christ Jesus so that we do become unmovable and unshakable in the coming storm and coming blessing. I encourage you to prepare for some pretty intense turbulence (which in light of eternity is but a tiny blip on the radar screen or an insignificant speed bump on the road of life), to be a man or woman of resolve to stay true to the Lord no matter what comes our way and learn to fully trust Him and instantly obey Him in whatever He asks of us. If we do, we will have the honour and privilege of being junior partners with Him in seeing great and stunning exploits accomplished for the Kingdom, May our prayer be, "Lord, let me be change in your pocket. You can spend me any way You like."

Like the Islamic terrorists who are so dangerous to their enemy because of their willingness to sacrifice their lives for their cause, so Christians will be dangerous to the enemy as they too are willing to do the same. In Revelation 12:11, we are reminded that, "They overcame him by the blood of the Lamb and by the word of their testimony; they did not love their lives so much as to shrink from death. Therefore rejoice you heavens and you who dwell in them!"

The saints who have gone on ahead of us are rejoicing and cheering us on in our race of faith. Though we look forward to meeting them, they are looking forward to meeting us at the end of the battle because of our unique end-time role in the grand finale. But right now, they are urging us to "throw off everything that hinders and the sin that so easily entangles, and to run with perseverance the race marked out for us...fix(ing) our eyes on Jesus, the author and perfecter of our faith, who for the joy set before him endured the cross, scorning its shame, and sat down at the right hand of the throne of God. Consider him who endured such opposition from sinful men, so that you will not grow weary and lose heart". (Hebrews 12:1b-3)

And in the midst of the turmoil, persecution and in some cases, martyrdom, we will have a date with destiny and the adventure of a lifetime, seeing God move in impressive and miraculous ways to redeem lives and to deal decisively with evil. God will not be mocked. Like the Hebrew people of Goshen in Egypt when God unleashed His plagues on Egypt through Moses, God is quite capable of protecting His own during the season He releases His temporal judgments on the end-time Pharoah, the Antichrist, and the wicked who are aligned with him, without having to extract us from the battlefield. He promised us that we would not have to face His wrath. (1 Thess. 5:9)

But some of us may have the privilege of laying down our lives for our faith and loyalty to our Master, not due to God's wrath, but the Antichrist's venomous hatred and harassment. If so, we must trust our Lord to give us the grace we need at that moment. Like Job, may we have the child-like trust and resolve to declare, "Though he slay me, yet will I trust him'. (Job 13:15)

And may we have the faith and attitude of the three Hebrew boys in Daniel 3:16, 17, who fearlessly declared:

"O Nebuchadnezzar, we do not need to defend ourselves before you in this matter. If we are thrown into the blazing furnace, the God we serve is able to save us from it, and he will rescue us from your hand, O king. But even if he does not, we want you to know, O king, that we will not serve your gods."

I've often thought that if martyrdom was on the list of spiritual gifts in the Bible, I guess it would be the one grace gift that we only get to exercise once!

I suspect that part of God's grace in the moment would be not only sensing His empowering presence, but a strong knowing in our hearts that our death will not be in vain - that there is purpose and victory even in death. And that victory in death includes the unleashing of further spiritual power for Kingdom and harvest purposes. It's like throwing gas on a fire. Through the victorious stoning death of Stephen, hardened characters like the apostle Paul were impacted for Christ, creating a rippling effect around the world for God's unshakable Kingdom.

In Psalm 116:15, we are told that, "Precious in the sight of the LORD is the death of his saints." And Paul assures us that nothing can separate us from the love of Christ not trouble or hardship or persecution or famine or nakedness or danger or sword..."No, in all these things we are more than conquerors through him who loved us. For I am convinced that neither death nor life, neither angels nor demons...will be able to separate us from the love of God that is in Christ Jesus our Lord". (Rom. 8:35-39)

Read Fox's book of Martyrs and see how God enabled many of them to die a glorious death, some singing hymns of praise with such joyful countenance that would have given their executioners night-mares at night. Some were spared supernaturally from death, such as in the revival in France in the late 1600s and early 1700s where one of the manifestations of the Spirit was that some believers just wouldn't die when struck repeatedly with sword, knife or sledge hammer!

We need to come to the place where we have such a Kingdom mindset, such an eternal perspective and such a deep trust and passion for Jesus that these details become incidental rather than our anxious fixation. Our life is not our own, we have been bought with a price, the precious blood of Jesus. I encourage you to do a prayerful read through of Scripture verses that relate to tribulation and persecution of the saints and how that just comes with the territory. It is the norm, not the exception. We really are in a war and they are not rubber bullets coming at us. We need to hear again and again the Apostle Peter's exhortation:

"Dear friends, do not be surprised at the painful trial you are suffering, as though something strange were happening to you. But rejoice that you participate in the sufferings of Christ, so that you may be overjoyed when his glory is revealed". (1 Peter 4:12, 13)

From time to time when speaking to a church group, I'll ask them, "Who wants to be a great champion for God?" Virtually all the hands shoot up. I'll reply with, "Then we need great battles". I'll continue with, "Who wants to be an overcomer?" Again, most hands bolt up. I'll answer with, "then we need obstacles in our lives to overcome." (see You-tube video, "Are you going to finish STRONG?" with Nick Vujicic) Hearing of coming trouble should get us excited once we have come to realize that with every trial there is a doorway, a gateway to the Kingdom of God. The apostle Paul wasn't kidding when he declared, "we must go through many hardships to enter the Kingdom of God." (Acts 14:22)

And at the end of the day, if the Lord throws in a surprise and gathers us up to Himself before we thought, that is fine with me. I'd be happy to be wrong on the timing of the rapture or any other detail. I just want to be where Jesus wants me at any given moment - if with Him before He returns because I died of old age, got hit by a Mac truck, martyred for my faith or get to be zapped up to meet Him in the air before, during or after a tribulation, it's a win/win!

This is not about one-up-manship and being able to say, "See, I was right and you were wrong." We are all in this thing together and none of us have it all sorted out yet. Let's stay humble, teachable and function in teamwork, regardless of our theological differences, because one can only chase a thousand but two working together can put ten thousand to flight. (Deut. 32:30) Benjamin Franklin's observation is worth noting as well, "We better hang together because if we don't, they'll hang us separately."

The fact that the Lord told Daniel to seal the scrolls up until the end and that Paul tells us in his first letter to the Corinthians that we only see in part, we must humbly acknowledge that we don't have it all figured out. God uses the most unlikely people to accomplish His sovereign purpose and He alone is capable of turning the tables in unexpected ways. We will see twists and turns as things unfold. None of us will be able to say, "I told you so" by the time this thing finishes up. Peter tells us that we can hasten the day of the Lord by living holy and godly lives. (2 Peter 3:11, 12) So there must be some latitude in God's end time game plan as we participate in this venture with Him.

As we cultivate intimacy with the Lord, soak in His sweet presence and remain interdependent on our brothers and sisters in Christ, we need not simply endure the days ahead. The ride is about to get very turbulent but exhilarating. We will have the privilege of overcoming, of thriving with unshakable hope and bringing our God of hope and His divine solutions to others living in a very shakable world. We can rest assured that our Lord really has things under control. As John Paul Jackson has said, "Don't make God too small; you can never make Him too big." We may not know the future in detail but thankfully we do know who holds the future, including every detail.

Rather than be tempted to join the rest of the world and be all stressed and perplexed at all the turmoil on land and sea, we will keep our focus on the Lord Jesus, the Prince of Peace and our heavenly Father who loves to provide for and protect His own. We will seek to live in the secret place of His presence and declare with the psalmist in Psalm 91, "He who dwells in the shelter of the Most High will rest in the shadow of the Almighty. I will say of the LORD, 'He is my refuge and my fortress, my God, in whom I trust.'"

Jesus instructed us "when these things begin to take place, stand up and lift up your heads, because your redemption is drawing near". (Luke 21:28)

Jim Bakker testifies that, "We are not merely preparing for the tough times of tribulation. We are getting ready for the Wedding! Soon, the Bridegroom, King Jesus, will be united with His bride, the church...I don't know about you, but I'm going to a wedding! The marriage of the Lamb, the Lord Jesus, to His bride, the church, is soon to take place! And, oh! What a celebration it is going to be! People from every nation, every tribe, and every tongue will be there, all gathered to give honor and praise to the King of kings and Lord of lords."[27]

The apostle John wrote of this stunning event: "Hallelujah! For our Lord God Almighty reigns. Let us rejoice and be glad and give him glory! For the wedding of the Lamb has come and his bride has made herself ready". (Rev. 19:6,7)

"Amen. Come, Lord Jesus."

Now some of you reading this may have never actually given your life to Jesus before. Some of you may not be sure if God even exists but you are a seeker of truth. I encourage you to simply talk to Him as if He does exist and ask Him to reveal Himself to you. If you are in a place in which you would like to come into a personal relationship with Jesus Christ and are ready to invite Him into your life, then I encourage you to stop right now and pray this simple prayer:

"God, I acknowledge that I have messed up in the past. I have sinned and fallen short. I know that I am a sinner. I believe that Jesus came to earth and died on the cross to pay the price for me and my sins. I ask that you forgive me of my sins and wash me clean. Jesus, come into my heart and life and be my Saviour and my Lord. Fill me with your Holy Spirit and enable me to live for You Jesus every day of my life. Thank You Jesus. Amen."

The Bible tells us that when a sinner repents and makes Jesus his or her Lord, the angels in heaven get excited and throw a party! It would be wise if you found at least a few other followers of Jesus to hang out with (it's called fellowship) and grow in your new faith in Christ as well as get a Bible, God's love letters to you, and read it frequently, learning to listen to His voice as well as talk to Him often. If I don't get to meet you in this life, I hope we might meet at the wedding party that Jesus will throw for us all when this age is all over.

Conclusion

Let me conclude with three inspiring statements, the first from the British revivalist, Arthur Wallis, followed by portions of a prophetic word given July 25, 1961 from Tommy Hicks, an American revivalist in Argentina, and then a portion of a recent prophetic word by Canadian Kayle Mumby:

"Distress for the nations and tribulation for the church is predicted by the Spirit for the time of the end. But growing darkness will only make the light shining from God's people seem all the brighter. God will conclude this age as He commenced it. Great power and glory in the church, great victories over Satan, but in the context of great persecution and opposition. But the difference will be that what was then confined to one small corner of the globe will in the end be worldwide. I believe that the greatest chapters of the church's long history have yet to be written, and that it will be said of the generation that brings back the King, 'This was their finest hour.'"[28]

"God is going to take the do-nothings, the nobodies, the unheard of, the no-accounts...and going to give to them this outpouring of the Spirit of God...the last days will have a double portion of the power of God...my people in the end times will go forth as a mighty army and shall sweep over the face of the earth...I watched these people as they were going to and fro over the face of the earth. Suddenly there was a man in Africa and in a moment he was transported by the Spirit of God, and perhaps he was in Russia, or China or America or some other place, and vice versa. All over the world these people went, and they came through fire, pestilence, famine, persecution, nothing seemed to stop them...God is going to give the world a demonstration in this last hour as the world has never known...as these people were going about the face of the earth, a great persecution seemed to come from every angle...suddenly from the heavens above, the Lord Jesus came, and said, "This is my beloved bride for whom I have waited. She will come forth even tried by fire. This is she that I have loved from the beginning of time"...."[29]

"...Everything is changing. It has just begun. Hold fast to the Changeless One. He is our only hope and security. He is our light, our purity, our hope. Let your heart be bathed in His presence, His excitement, His joy. Let it wash away the fear, the trepidation, the confusion.

"We can do this. Hold fast. Hold fast to the Truth that woke your soul so long ago. You know Who it is. You've touched it before. Now hold onto that Pillar with everything you have. He will be strong. He will be true. He will be real. He will be vibrant. He is moving like never before. Hold onto Him.

"It's the ride of our life that we've all been longing for. We forgot that it might be scary. But that fear will turn into a thrill when we see how big His hands are, until we see the strength of the eternal arms that are holding us.

"Everything is changing my friends. Hold fast. We can do it. I've seen the other side. It's so worth it. The reward is coming, and coming quickly. Risk it all again. You can do it. It's okay to be scared. It's okay to not know. Because we know the One who does. He's coming. He's our goal, our foundation, our security, our everything. Fix your eyes. Hold fast. Once you lock in, get ready for light speed... which means a lot of G-force... a lot of pressure... but the ride of a lifetime.

"Take another step closer, another step further on that path you know is laid out before you. It's been there for a very long time longing for you to walk down it. The destination...words do not describe... It's so worth it. Trust me...

"Come with me... baby steps, full tilt sprint, walking, flying, I don't care... fix your eyes, hold on, the ride is about to get wild. Everything is changing my friends. Everything."[30]

"May the God of hope fill you with all joy and peace as you trust in him, so that you may overflow with hope by the power of the Holy Spirit." (Romans 15:13)

Recommended Resources:

Books:

When Christ Comes, Max Lucado, Word Pub., Nashville, 1999
The Return, Winkie Pratney, Barry Chant, Sovereign World, 1988
Restoring the Vision of the End-Times Church, Vernon L. Kuenzi,
Preparing the Way Pub., 2000
End-Times Simplified: Preparing your Heart for the Coming Storm,
David Sliker, Forerunner Books, 2005
Omega Student Manual & Leader's Guide, Mike Bickle, Forerunner
Books
Book of Revelation Study Guide, Mike Bickle, Forerunner, 2009
When Jesus Returns, David Pawson, Hodder & Stoughton, 1995
Come with Me Through Revelation, David Pawson, Terra Nova
Pub., UK, 2008
Unlocking the Bible: A Unique Overview of the Whole Bible, David
Pawson, True Potential Pub., 2007
The Return, Gene Edwards, Tyndale House, 1996
Every Eye Shall See! The Rapture, The Tribulation & Christ's
Return, Selwyn Stevens, Jubilee Resources, 1999
Prophetic Guide to the End Times, Derek Prince, Chosen, 2008
Visions of the Coming Days, R. Loren Sandford, Chosen, 2012
Three Views on the Rapture: Pre-, Mid-, or Post-Tribulation, Gleason
L. Archer Jr., general editor, Zondervan, 1984, 1996
Four Views of the End Times, Timothy Paul Jones, RW Research,
Inc., Rose Pub., 2009
Victorious Eschatology, Harold R. Eberle & Martin Trench,
Worldcast Pub., 2006 (excellent presentation of the "partial pret-
erist" view but incorrectly lumps all those in the futurist view as
fixated on a pessimistic outcome and pre-trib rapture)
The Church & the Tribulation, Robert H. Gundry, Zondervan, 1973
Epic Battles of the Last Days, Rick Joyner, Morningstar Pub., 1995
Let the Nations Be Glad, Chapter 3, on suffering & missions, John
Piper, Baker, 1993
Desiring God, Chapter 10, Suffering, John Piper, Multnomah 1996

The Heavenly Man, the remarkable true story of Chinese Christian Brother Yun, Monarch Books, UK, 2002
Israel:
Israel, the Church and the Last Days, Dan Juster & Keith Intrater, Destiny Image, 1990
One New Man, Reuven Doron, Embrace, Cedar Rapids, 1993
The Race to Save the World, Sid Roth, Charisma House, 2004
Praying for Israel's Destiny, Jim W. Goll, Sovereign World, 2005
God's Promise & the Future of Israel, Don Finto, Regal, 2006
The Controversy of Zion and the Time of Jacob's Trouble, Dalton Lifsey, Maskilim Pub., 2011.

Websites:

Trunews.com http://www.trunews.com/about_us.htm
WND.com http://www.wnd.com/
Voice of the Martyrs http://www.persecution.com
International Christian Concern http://www.persecution.org
One Free World International, founder: Majed El Shafie, http://www.onefreeworldinternational.org/

You-tube video:

Justin Rizzo's song, Tree, http://www.youtube.com/watch?v=YPuzJFzXgU4
"Arthur Burk, Preparing for the Fire", Apr. 2/12, http://www.youtube.com/watch?v=TnmNxqjsjbU
Never Give Up, be inspired, Heather Dorniden's amazing race, http://www.youtube.com/watch?v=np-1Kui0g3E
Are you going to finish STRONG? Nick Vujicic, http://www.youtube.com/watch?v=c3Ffkvb7S3c
Terry Bennett prophecy for 2008 to 2028, http://www.youtube.com/watch?v=jUSYUi9Z2e8&feature=relmfu

Notes:

1. Dietrich Bonhoeffer, The Cost of Discipleship, Macmillan Co., 1963, p.99.
2. John Piper, Let the Nations Be Glad, Baker, 1993, pp. 74-75
3. Rich Dean, "Will Christians Go Through the Great Tribulation? http://www.godandscience.org/doctrine/tribulation.html#n05
4. Colin Brown, editor, Dictionary of New Testament Theology Vol. 1, Zondervan, 1975, pp. 105-112.
5. Gordon Fee, How to Read the Bible For All Its Worth,, Zondervan, 1982, p. 212.
6. Rick Warren, Purpose Driven Life, Zondervan, 2002, pp.42-44.
7. John Piper, p. 89.
8. David Sliker, End-Times Simplified, Forerunner, 2005, p. 55.
9. John Piper, p. 111, citing the book, John G. Paton: Missionary to the New Hebrides, An Autobiography, The Banner of Truth Trust, 1965, originally 1891, p. 56.
10. David Pawson, Unlocking the Bible, HarperCollins Pub. 2007, p.1038.
11. Gordon Fee, pp. 206-213.
12. Robert H. Mounce, The New International Commentary of the New Testament, Revelation, Eerdmans, 1977, pp. 31-35; also William Barclay, Daily Study Bible Series, The Revelation, Westminster Press, 1976, pp. 18, 19; also Leon Morris, Tyndale N.T. Commentary on Revelation, Eerdmans, 1969, pp. 34-40.
13. David Pawson, Unlocking the Bible, p. 1038.
14. Ibid., pp. 1045, 1046.
15. Ibid., p. 1059.
16. Mike Bickle, Book of Revelation with Notes, Study Guide, Forerunner Books, 2009, pp. 4, 5.
17. Ibid., pp. 6, 7.
18. Mike Bickle, Omega, Forerunners Books, pp. 97-113.
19. Ibid., p. 28.
20. Dalton Lifsey, The Controversy of Zion & the Time of Jacob's Trouble, Maskilim Pub. 2011.
21. Mike Bickle., pp. 63-73.

[22.] Ibld., pp 42, 43.

[23.] Max Lucado, When Christ Comes, Word, 1999, pp. 122-123, C.S. Lewis, The Great Divorce, Macmillan, 1946, pp. 66,67

[24.] R. Loren Sandford, Visons of the Coming Days, Chosen, 2012, pp. 31, 117, 119.

[25.] Oswald J. Smith, Tribulation or Rapture - Which? pamphlet, on the website: Liberty to the Captives, http://www.pbministries.org/Eschatology/miscellaneous/smith_01.htm

[26.] Justin Rizzo, song, "Tree", 2011, website, http://justinrizzo.band-camp.com/track/tree-extended-version

[27.] Jim Bakker (and Ken Abraham), The Refuge, Regency Pub., House, 2000, pp. 239-40.

[28.] Arthur Wallis, Rain From Heaven, Bethany, 1979, p.124.

[29.] Tommy Hicks, Revival End-Times Vision, www.revivalcentral.com/Prophecies.html

[30.] Kayle Mumby, Can. Prophetic Council, Sept. 2010, http://revivalnow.com/eyesandwings/glob_proph/Everything_is_changing.html

Final Thoughts of a Personal Nature
October 15, 2012

I have mentioned earlier in the book that my married and pregnant daughter, Joanna, is fighting a serious illness. I also expressed that I feel that what is going on in our family on the personal level has a parallel with the macro level of which I am writing about in this book.

Shortly after my wife and I received the exciting news that we were going to become grandparents for the very first time - one of the happiest times of our lives, we got the dreaded news that our daughter was diagnosed with cancer. The best of times and the worst of times all wrapped up together in one package.

Well, the update on our daughter is: she gave birth naturally to a beautiful bouncing baby boy June 19, 2012. He is thriving fabulously. His weight has more than doubled after 4 months. Joanna has her ups and downs but she is a trooper and by God's grace she is definitely winning the war against the cancer. Utilizing the army, the navy, and the air force in her battle, we can see victory in sight. (This is not her first time fighting a life-threatening scenario. When she was first born, she came down with spinal meningitis and there was little hope but the Lord miraculously healed her so she knows God has a plan and destiny for her that the enemy desires to undermine.)

We feel so encouraged, so loved and cared for by God and by so many friends from around the world who have been praying for her and us. We have seen God's provision in so many ways, including prophetic encouragement, meals brought to the door, donated mother's breast milk for the baby (from moms who have been blood tested) and the incredible house the four of us are renting together (for an exceptionally affordable price). We call the house a double blessing because this former bed and breakfast home has double everything an average house would have: two driveways, six bedrooms, four full bathrooms, and two kitchens! And recently our middle child, Michael, who travels a lot internationally doing wedding photography, has moved in with us. As well, our oldest son, Jonathan, who lives in Nashville, has come home to visit a number of times. So we have gone from being empty nesters to having a perpetual family reunion! And with everyone being musically gifted, the house is flooded with lots of praise and worship music. We feel so spoiled by the Lord even in the midst of personal crisis. And we are so grateful to Him. It truly energizes my faith for how God will come through for His children in very impressive ways in the coming days of great exploits and great trouble. Yeah God!

In the introduction of the book, I spoke of my childhood experience of being sent home from school in kindergarten and the embarrassment I experienced crawling under the classroom windows so I wouldn't have to face my fellow classmates as I was sent home for wetting my pants. I had made a vow that day that I would play life safe to avoid a repeat of the shame and humiliation of that moment at the class window.

Well, years later, after that vow has been renounced and broken and I have surrendered my life and future to the Lord where I am willing to be a "fool for Christ", the Lord brought a very precious healing experience to me. My wife, Pam, a prophetic friend of ours named Terry Lamb, and I went on a ministry trip together to the United Kingdom a number of years ago. Terry and I had the privilege one day of being guest speakers in a world religions class at a public high school. The teacher was from the church we were ministering in that week and he invited us to come share about what God was doing out of the Toronto outpouring.

The students were mildly interested in what we were saying but just before the bell rang to end the class, Terry got a word from the Lord for one of the students. He asked if someone had some kind of stomach problem. No one responded. The room was silent for a moment then all of a sudden Terry pointed to a girl and said, "Sarah, is that you?" She looked to the teacher and asked, "How did he know my name?" The teacher said, "God told him". The classroom became electric with excitement. At that very moment the class bell rang but none of the students wanted to rush out of the room. All eyes were on Sarah. The girl reluctantly admitted she had an ongoing stomach ailment and so we asked if we could pray for her. She agreed. Without laying hands on her (school policy) Terry and I prayed for God to heal her in the name of Jesus. She began to shake and her stomach got very hot. All the students were dumbfounded. But after a couple of minutes, the teacher insisted that all the students move on to their next class as students were waiting in the hall to come in for theirs.

The teacher invited Terry and me to join him an hour or so later for the weekly lunch hour Christian prayer meeting in his classroom. As it turned out, not only did a half a dozen faithful Christian students show up to eat and pray, but in came Sarah and three of her friends. After God called her by name and healed her, He now had her attention!

After the lunch prayer gathering was over and students were off to their afternoon classes, it was time for Terry and me to head back to the house where we were staying. As we stepped outside and were walking past the windows of several classrooms, we looked over and saw a number of students standing at the windows, staring at us. We could see that some were also pointing at us and beckoning their friends to come take a look at those Canadian visitors who created such a fuss that day.

We walked out of that school rejoicing that we had the privilege of representing Jesus to those young people and seeing Him demonstrate His love and power in a very tangible way. Jesus has promised in His Word that signs and wonders would accompany the preaching and sharing of the gospel. (Mark 16:17-20) We knew it wasn't about us. It was all about Him. Like the young donkey that carried Jesus into Jerusalem, we must not fool ourselves and think the crowds are cheering for us. It's just that we get to be carriers of the King of Glory.

In Isaiah 61:7, the Lord promises to exchange our shame and disgrace and give us a double portion of blessing and inheritance and that everlasting joy will be ours. The Lord had taken that childhood trauma which the enemy planned to use to keep me paralyzed for life and flipped it around to become a landmark or trophy of God's honour and victory. What the enemy meant for harm, the Lord meant for good. And regardless of the challenges you face, He wants to do that for you.

In declaring that we are about to enter into a time of turbulence and end-time revival equivalent to all the previous revivals combined, Rick Joyner claims, "A generation is arising that will see all of the things that every prophet and righteous man from the beginning longed to see. For those who love God, there has never been a greater day to be alive. The Lord has saved His best wine for last."[1]

---

[1] Rick Joyner, Shadows of Things to Come, Thomas Nelson Pub., 200, p. 222.

If you would like to contact me, you can email me at:

jerry@jerrysteingard.com
www.jerrysteingard.com

Shalom

CPSIA information can be obtained at www.ICGtesting.com
Printed in the USA
BVOW080018151212

308185BV00005B/13/P